Social History of Western Civilization

Volume II

THIRD EDITION

Social History of Western Civilization

Volume II

Readings from the Seventeenth Century to the Present

THIRD EDITION

RICHARD M. GOLDEN

University of North Texas

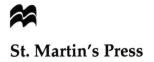

St. Martin's Press   **New York**

Manager, publishing services: Emily Berleth
Project management: Richard Steins
Production supervisor: Melissa Kaprelian
Cover design: Richard Emery Design, Inc.
Cover art: Auguste Renoir, *Pont Neuf, Paris,* 1872, Ailsa Mellon Bruce Collection
  © 1995 Board of Trustees, National Gallery of Art, Washington.

Library of Congress Catalog Card Number: 94-65213

0 9 8 7 6
f e d c b a

For information, write:
St. Martin's Press, Inc.
175 Fifth Avenue
New York, NY 10010

ISBN: 0-312-09646-1

Acknowledgments
It is a violation of the law to reproduce these selections by any means whatsoever without the written permission of the copyright holder.

"Private and Public: The Boundaries of Women's Lives in Early Stuart England." Retha Warnicke. From *Privileging Gender in Early Modern England.* The Sixteenth Century Journal Publishers, Inc. Copyright © 1993 by The Sixteenth Century Journal Publishers, Inc. Reprinted by permission.

"Popular Reading and the Supply of News in Seventeenth-Century Holland." A. T. Van Deursen. From *Plain Lives in a Golden Age.* Cambridge University Press (1991) pp. 134–143, 145–148, 150–152. Reprinted with the permission of Cambridge University Press.

"Guilds." Reprinted from Mack Walker: *German Home Towns: Community, State, and General Estate, 1648–1871.* Copyright © 1971 by Cornell University. Used by permission of the publisher, Cornell University Press.

"The Peasants." Blum, Jerome. *The End of the Old Order in Rural Europe.* Copyright © 1978 by Princeton University Press. Reprinted by permission of Princeton University Press.

Acknowledgments and copyrights are continued at the back of the book on pages 324–325, which constitute an extension of the copyright page.

Preface

Social History of Western Civilization, Third Edition, is a two-volume reader for Western Civilization courses. The essays in each volume deal with social history because I believe that the most original and significant work of the past two decades has been in this area and because Western Civilization textbooks tend to slight social history in favor of the more traditional political, intellectual, and cultural history, though this bias is slowly changing. In the twenty years that I have taught Western Civilization, I have used many books, texts, and readers designed specifically for introductory courses. I decided to compile this anthology because I perceived that other collections generally failed to retain student interest. My students found many of the essays in these other books boring, often because the selections assumed a degree of background knowledge that a typical student does not possess. To make this reader better suited to students, I have attempted to include essays that are both important and readable. This has not been an easy task, for many significant history articles, which have been written solely for specialists, are, unfortunately, simply too difficult for college undergraduates. I have gone through hundreds of articles searching for the few that are challenging, fascinating, important, and readable. To further enhance the readability of the selected articles, I have translated foreign words and identified individuals and terms that students might not recognize. All footnotes are therefore my own unless otherwise indicated. I, for one, do not understand why anthologies intended for college students do not routinely translate foreign expressions, phrases, and book titles and, moreover, seem to take for granted that students will be familiar with Tertullian, Gustavus Adolphus, or Pearl Buck, to mention some examples.

A Western Civilization reader cannot be all things to all instructors and students, but I have consciously tried to make these two volumes useful for as many Western Civilization courses as possible, despite the widely varying ways in which such courses are taught. The readings in these volumes cover many geographical areas and a broad range of topics in social history. Some historians argue that Western civilization began with the Greeks, but I have included in Volume One a section on the Ancient Near East for the courses that begin there. Both volumes contain material on the seventeenth century; indeed, Volume Two includes in its first selections some material that precedes the seventeenth century. This chronological overlap is intentional because Western Civilization courses break differently according to the policies of instructors and institutions.

To show how the articles in *Social History of Western Civilization* may be used in most Western Civilization courses, there is a correlation chart at the beginning of each volume that relates each essay to a relevant chapter in the major Western Civilization textbooks currently on the market. Though the textbooks do not always offer discrete discussions on all the subjects covered in the essays, they touch upon many of the subjects. As for the others, students will at least be able to place the articles in a historical context by reading the standard history of the period in the relevant textbook chapter, thereby gaining fresh insight into that historical period.

I have also provided introductions to the major periods in history for each volume as well as an introduction to each selection where I have asked pertinent questions in order to guide students through the essays and to encourage them to think about the problems and issues the authors of these essays raise. These introductions do not contain summaries and so may not be substituted for the reading of the selections.

The preparation of this reader was more time-consuming than I had originally thought possible. There always seemed to be somewhere a more attractive article on every topic. This has been true for both the first and second editions. In the third edition, I have changed approximately one-quarter of the essays, substitutions based on my own searching, conversations over the past three years with historians around the country who adopted *Social History of Western Civilization* for their classes, and on the results from two dozen anonymous readers' reports solicited by the publisher. Many people also suggested essays to me, critiqued what I wrote, and helped in other ways as well. I thank Ove Anderson, Jay Crawford, Fara Driver, Phillip Garland, Laurie Glover, Tully Hunter, and Laurie McDowell. Especially generous with their time and comments were Philip Adler, Kathryn Babayan, William Beik, Robert Bireley, Richard Bulliet, Caroline Walker Bynum, Elizabeth D. Carney, Edward Coomes, Suzanne A. Desan, Lawrence Estaville, Hilda Golden, Leonard Greenspoon, Alan Grubb, George Huppert, Thomas Kuehn, Charles Lippy, Donald McKale, Steven Marks, Victor Matthews, John A. Mears, William Murnane, David Nicholas, Thomas F. X. Noble, D. G. Paz, James Sack, Carol Thomas, and Roy Vice. The editorial staff at St. Martin's Press has been tolerant of my lapses, supportive throughout, and wonderfully professional.

I would also like to thank the following individuals who reviewed or responded to questionnaires for this edition for St. Martin's Press: Steven D. Cooley, University of Dayton; Charles T. Evans, Northern Virginia Community College; Anita Guerrini, University of California; Christopher E. Gutherie, Tarleton State University; Sarah Hanley, University of Iowa; Benjamin Hudson, Penn State University; Jonathan Katz, Oregon State University; Donna T. McCaffrey, Providence College; Maureen Melody, Oakton Community College; Kathryn E. Meyer, Washington State University; Lohr E. Miller, Auburn University; Gerald M. Schnabel, Bemidji State University; Paul Teverow, Missouri Southern State College; Sara W. Tucker, Washburn University of Topeka; and Lindsay Wilson, Colby College.

Contents

Topical Table of Contents

RELIGION

RURAL LIFE

SEXUALITY

URBAN LIFE

WAR, TERRORISM, VIOLENCE

WOMEN

WORK AND ECONOMIC LIFE

	Retha Warnicke, *Private and Public: The Boundaries of Women's Lives in Early Stuart England*	A. T. Van Deursen, *Popular Reading and the Supply of News in Seventeenth-Century Holland*	Mack Walker, *Guilds*	Jerome Blum, *The Peasants*	Neil McKendrick, *The Commercialization of Fashion*
Winks et al., *A History of Civilization*, 8/e (1992)	15	13	16	17	16
Willis, *Western Civilization: A Brief Introduction* (1987)	10	10	12	12	12
Willis, *Western Civilization*, 4/e (1985)	15	15	15	15	15
Wallbank et al., *Civilization Past and Present*, 7/e (1992)	17	17	19	19	19
Sullivan, Sherman, Harrison, *A Short History of Western Civilization*, 8/e (1994)	31	33	31	31	31
Stearns, *Life and Society in the West*, (1988)	2	2	4	3	4
Spielvogel, *Western Civilization*, 2/e (1994)	15	15, 16	19	19	19
Perry et al., *Western Civilization: Ideas, Politics & Society*, 4/e (1992)	16	16	18	16	18
Perry, *Western Civilization: A Brief History*, 2/e (1993)	9	9	9	9	10
Palmer & Colton, *A History of the Modern World*, 7/e (1992)	13,28	14,28	29	26,41	28
Noble et al., *Western Civilization: The Continuing Experiment* (1994)	17,18	18	20	20	20
McNeill, *History of Western Civilization*, 6/e (1986)	III, C-1	III, C-1	III, C-2	III, C-2	III, C-2
McKay, Hill, Buckler, *A History of Western Society*, 5/e (1995)	20	15,20	19	17,19	20
Lerner et al., *Western Civilizations*, 12/e (1993)	15	16	16	16	16
Kishlansky et al., *The Unfinished Legacy* (1993)	12, 15	13	15	15	15
Kishlansky et al., *Civilization in the West* (1991)	16	15	19	19	19
Kagan, Ozment, Turner, *The Western Heritage*, 5/e (1995)	11	12	16	16	16
Hunt et al., *The Challenge of the West* (1995)	16	16	19	19	18, 19
Greaves, Zaller, Roberts, *Civilizations of the West* (1992)	14	14	14	14	14
Greer, *A Brief History of the Western World*, 6/e (1992)	9	9	11	11	10
Goff et al., *A Survey of Western Civilization* (1987)	20, 21	21	24	22	24
Esler, *The Western World*, (1994)	14, 15	14, 15	18	18, 21	18
Chodorow, Knox, Schirokauer, Strayer, & Gatzke, *The Mainstream of Civilization*, 6/e (1994)	17,19	19	20	22	21
Chambers et al., *The Western Experience*, 6/e (1995)	15, 16	16	18	18	18
Blackburn, *Western Civilization* (1991)	11	11	12	12	12

	B. Robert Kreiser, *The Devils of Toulon: Demonic Possession and Religious Politics in Eighteenth-Century Provence*	John McManners, *Death's Arbitrary Empire*	Albert Soboul, *The Sans-Culottes*	Sidney Pollard, *Factory Discipline in the Industrial Revolution*	J. F. Bergier, *The Industrial Bourgeoisie*	Wolfgang Schivelbusch, *Lantern Smashing in Paris*	K. H. Connell, *The Potato in Ireland*
Winks et al., *A History of Civilization*, 8/e (1992)	15, 17	17	18	20	20	19	20
Willis, *Western Civilization: A Brief Introduction* (1987)	11	12	13	14	14	15	15
Willis, *Western Civilization*, 4/e (1985)	16	16	16, 17	19	19	19	20
Wallbank et al., *Civilization Past and Present*, 7/e (1992)	13,20	19	21	23	23	24	25
Sullivan, Sherman, Harrison, *A Short History of Western Civilization*, 8/e (1994)	36	36	38	40	40	42	43
Stearns, *Life and Society in the West*, (1988)	2, 4	4	4	5	5	5	5
Spielvogel, *Western Civilization*, 2/e (1994)	15, 18	19	20	21	21	22	21
Perry et al., *Western Civilization: Ideas, Politics & Society*, 4/e (1992)	17	18	19	21	21	23	23
Perry, *Western Civilization: A Brief History*, 2/e (1993)	10	10	11	12	12	14	12
Palmer & Colton, *A History of the Modern World*, 7/e (1992)	28,36	28	44	52	57	54,56	57
Noble et al., *Western Civilization: The Continuing Experiment* (1994)	18	20	21	23	23	22,23	23
McNeill, *History of Western Civilization*, 6/e (1986)	III, C-2	III, C-2	III, C-3	III, C-3	III, C-3	III, C-3	III, C-3
McKay, Hill, Buckler, *A History of Western Society*, 5/e (1995)	15,18	19,20	21	22	22	23,24	23
Lerner et al., *Western Civilizations*, 12/e (1993)	15, 18	16	19	20	20, 21	21, 22	21
Kishlansky et al., *The Unfinished Legacy* (1993)	12, 15	15	16	17	17	18	18
Kishlansky et al., *Civilization in the West* (1991)	19	19	20	21	21	22	22
Kagan, Ozment, Turner, *The Western Heritage*, 5/e (1995)	14,18	16	19	22	22	22	22
Hunt et al., *The Challenge of the West* (1995)	16, 18	18, 19	20	22	22	22	22
Greaves, Zaller, Roberts, *Civilizations of the West* (1992)	11,18	14	19	20	20	21	21
Greer, *A Brief History of the Western World*, 6/e (1992)	10	10	11	12	12	12	12
Goff et al., *A Survey of Western Civilization* (1987)	22, 24	24	27	29	29	29	29
Esler, *The Western World*, (1994)	15, 20	18	22	23	23	25	23
Chodorow, Knox, Schirokauer, Strayer, & Gatzke, *The Mainstream of Civilization*, 6/e (1994)	18,21	21	23	24,25	25	26	24
Chambers et al., *The Western Experience*, 6/e (1995)	16, 19	19	20	22	22, 23	23, 24	23
Blackburn, *Western Civilization* (1991)	12	15	15	15, 16	16	17	16

Reading	1	2	3	4	5	6	7	8	9	10	11	12	13	14	15	16	17	18	19	20	21	22	23	24	25
F. M. L. Thompson, *Victorian England: The Horse-Drawn Society*	16	25	24	23	29	12	23	24	24	22	17	21	24	III, C-3	23,25	72	12,16	21,26	24	6	40	25	20	17	20
Eugen Weber, *Is God French?*	16	24	28	27	33, 35	12	25	23	25	23	18	25	24	III, C-3	25	76	15	24	25	8	46	25	21	16	20
William L. Langer, *Infanticide: A Historical Survey*	16	25	28	26	35	12	23	24	24	24	18	21, 25	24	III, C-3	25	71	16	26	24	6	45	23,25	20	17	20
Cathy Frierson, *Crime and Punishment in the Russian Village: Rural Concepts of Criminality at the End of the Nineteenth Century*	17	24	28	26	34	12	23	24	24	23, 24	18, 19	26	24	III, C-3	24	67	16	26	24	6	48	24	22	16	21
Theresa M. McBride, *A Woman's World: Department Stores and the Evolution of Women's Employment, 1870–1920*	16	26	28	23	34	12	23	24, 25	24	24	19	26	24	III, C-3	25,26	73	16	26	24	6	45	25	21	17	20 21
Alistair Horne, *The Price of Glory: Verdun 1916*	19	27	30	29	38	13	26	26	26	26	20	27	27	III, C-4	27	86	18	30	26	7	51	30	22	18	23
Alex de Jonge, *Inflation in Weimar Germany*	20	27	31	30	42	13	27	26	27	27	21	28	28	III, C-4	28	98	20	32	27	7	53	31	24	19	24
Henry Friedlander, *The Nazi Camps*	20	29	33	31	43	14	28	27	29	28	22	29	29	III, C-4	30	107	21	34	28	7	55	34	24	19	26
Philippe Ariès, *Forbidden Death*	22	30	34	34	40	15	29	29	31	29	23	30	28,31	III, C-4	31,32	125	22	33	29	9	57	37	26	20	27
Juliet du Boulay, *Past and Present in a Greek Mountain Village*	22	30	34	33	44	29	15	29	31	29	23	30	30	III, C-4	31	110	22	35	29	9	57	35	26	21	28
Ellen Furlough, *Packaging Pleasures: Club Méditerranée and French Consumer Culture, 1950–1968*	22	30	34	33	39	15	29	29	31	29	23	30	30	III, C-4	31,32	110	22	35	29	9	57	35	26	21	28
Kristina Orfali, *The Rise and Fall of the Swedish Model*	22	30	34	33	39	15	29	30	31	30	23	30	30,31	III, C-4	31,32	125	22	35	29	9	57	35	26	21	28
Nikki R. Keddie, *Deciphering Middle Eastern Women's History*	22	30	35,36	35	39, 45	15	30	30	31	30	24	31	31	III, C-4	32	125	22	36	30	10	57	37	26	21	28

Introduction

This is a volume of selections in the social history of Western civilization from the seventeenth century to the present. Social history encompasses the study of groups of people, avoiding prominent individuals such as kings, prime ministers, intellectual giants, and military leaders. Over the last two decades, social historians have examined a host of topics, many of which are included here: the family, women, sex, disease, death, social groups (such as the peasantry and nobility), entertainment, work, leisure, popular religion and politics, criminality, sports, the experience of soldiers in war, economic conditions, and collective mentality (the attitudes, beliefs, and assumptions held by a population). Social history, then, sheds light both on previously neglected areas of human experience and on a forgotten and nameless people. Indeed, some recent historians, perhaps a bit too optimistically, have offered as a goal the writing of "total history," including all aspects of people's lives.

Unlike political, military, diplomatic, or biographical history, for example, social history rarely includes specific dates. The problem of periodization, always a thorny one, is especially difficult when covering topics that can often be understood only as long-term developments rather than as ephemeral events. Social historians tend to be interested in trends that unfold over a long duration rather than in daily episodes and yearly happenings. Thus, infanticide, though surely declining in frequency in the late nineteenth century, cannot be understood without looking back to antiquity and to the Middle Ages. Another example is human sexuality. Any discussion of sexual practices of the Victorian Age must be set against the durable sexual relations that, in significant ways, changed little in the course of millennia. In social history, then, what has not changed is often more important than what has changed. The political historian can conveniently end a chapter or a period of history in, say 1648, with the Peace of Westphalia, or in 1789, at the outbreak of the French Revolution. Even then, the periods of history are arbitrarily chosen, but the decision of where to divide, cut off, or end a subject is much easier for the political or diplomatic historian.

As a way out of this difficulty, social historians have come to favor a simple division between pre-modern (or traditional or pre-industrial) society and the modern (or industrial) world. This split has several advantages. One can present a cogent argument affirming that the Industrial Revolution constituted a watershed, affecting lifestyles and human relationships throughout society. The Industrial Revolution raised new problems and new questions involving workers' movements, nationalism, mass democracy, and women's emancipation, to name a few topics. In the industrial era, developments have occurred more rapidly than in pre-industrial society, where dietary habits, family relationships, and work patterns, for instance, inclined to change more slowly over time. Second, the terms "traditional" and "pre-modern," on the one hand, and "modern," on the other hand, are loose enough to permit historians to use the words while disagreeing about their meanings. What, exactly, does it mean to be "modern"? What is the process of modernization? Were people in the nineteenth century modern?

I am sympathetic to the division between pre-modern and modern, but, for the sake of convenience, I have grouped the selections in this volume into three parts. Part I, "The Old Régime," concerns traditional Europe. The essays focus on the seventeenth and eighteenth centuries—the final two of pre-modern Europe—but several necessarily go back to the sixteenth century or even farther. Part II, "The Nineteenth Century," begins with the Industrial Revolution. But, because the Industrial Revolution actually began in England in the late eighteenth century, a few of the articles start there. Some of the selections discuss much earlier material as they trace developments that reached fruition or ended in the nineteenth century. Part III, "The Twentieth Century," treats the Great War as a great divide. Here again, some essays go back in time to discuss the prior century and traditional Europe. In sum, historians impose periods on history that are always debatable and sometimes capricious but certainly essential in providing some order to the study of the past.

In any case, social history well researched and well written should convey excitement, for it brings vividly to us the daily lives, habits, and beliefs of our ancestors. In some ways, their patterns of behavior and thought will seem similar to ours, but in other ways our predecessors' actions and values appear quite different, if not barbaric or alien. Those living conditions and attitudes that have survived to the present are not by definition superior to those of the distant or recent past. Social history does not teach progress. Rather than drawing facile lessons from the daily lives of those who came before us, we might, as historians, attempt to immerse ourselves in their culture and understand why they lived and acted as they did.

Social History of Western Civilization

Volume II

THIRD EDITION

I

THE OLD RÉGIME

Politically, the Old Régime was the Age of Absolutism, the era before the French Revolution; intellectually, it encompassed the Scientific Revolution and the Enlightenment; artistically, the Baroque and Rococo styles set the tone. Socially, the seventeenth and eighteenth centuries saw the nobility preeminent over a rural order marked by the growth of towns. Most people were poor physical specimens who worked hard, suffered from vitamin deficiency and malnutrition, and lived short lives. Although it is often hard to read the minds of people who left little documentation to record their feelings, one can suppose that happiness and enjoyment seemed out of the reach of the majority of Europe's population, save for that happiness that accompanies survival or the brief interlude of an exceptional occasion, such as a religious feast, a wedding, or some small victory extracted from a harsh and severe world.

Although there were, to be sure, some outside the Christian fold—Jews, Muslims, and a sprinkling of atheists—nearly all Europeans in the Old Régime were Christians. After the Protestant Reformation had exploded a relatively united Christendom in the sixteenth century, most states maintained an established church and discriminated legally against Christians who belonged to other denominations. Christians venerated order and authority, though some found it in a church, some in the pope, and some in the Bible. The body politic likewise signified harmony and obedience, monarchy being the model, for that government mirrored God's supremacy over the cosmos. Few were the religious and political visionaries who dared affirm the possibility or desirability of an alternative to monarchial rule.

Deference and order permeated the social structure. Kings governed subjects, lords dominated peasants, men ruled women, and parents regulated their children's lives. Rank in the Old Régime was everything, and it certainly had its privileges. If men of commerce and industry rose in stature—in Great Britain and the United Provinces, for example—this in no way implied an assault on the belief that hierarchy provided the ideal basis for society. Throughout most of Europe, the aristocracy stood at the pinnacle of the social pyramid, and, in many places as far apart as France and Russia, the nobles experienced a resurgence of power and prestige. The aristocratic ethos offered a model of behavior, a set of values that others could only wish to emulate. Again, only a small number of individuals, primarily some intellectuals or those on the fringes of society, dreamed of a democratic revolution that would sweep the aristocracy and their privileges into the dustbin of history.

1

The Old Régime therefore possessed a certain unity in the midst of great diversity, a unity grounded in the respect, even veneration, of religious, political, and social order. Though changing, the Old Régime welcomed a stability that accompanied faith in respected institutions. The preferred form of change was individual change, a modest improvement in one's personal fortunes or those of one's family. Such alterations of stature, however, did little to dispel the terrible and brutal conditions of daily existence that faced the vast majority of Europe's population before the deluge of the Industrial and French Revolutions, which together helped create a new régime.

Private and Public: The Boundaries of Women's Lives in Early Stuart England

RETHA WARNICKE

Recently, historians have attempted to explore the private lives of individuals and groups in the past and to examine the origins of the idea of privacy. Here Retha Warnicke surveys the private lives of women in seventeenth-century England and the extent to which the public felt able to impose in women's private activities.

How did the English people understand the distinction between public and private? What did the word "private" mean as applied to women? In what ways and areas were women's lives private? What did women do with their private moments? How did patriarchal society affect the marital, educational, and religious lives of women, and, therefore, women's public and private lives? What endeavors were forbidden to them? How did Englishmen believe women should behave both in society and at home? What authority did women have in and outside of the household? Did widows possess more opportunities for privacy than married women?

Were these women's lives more restricted than those of women in earlier societies, in the ancient Near East or in classical Greece and Rome, for example? How do the concepts of public and private in seventeenth-century England differ from the understanding of those notions today?

In the seventeenth century, the Countess of Bridgewater[1] wrote that when a husband was

> fickle and various, not careing much to be with his wife at home, then thus may the wife make her owne happinesse, for then she may give her selfe up in prayer . . . and thus, in his absence, she is as much God's as a virgine.

Taking advantage of the opportunity that spiritual devotions offered for solitude had long been a tradition of early-modern English people, for ample evidence indicates that they did value time by themselves. In the account of John Fox's[2] life, which was written by his son and added posthumously to the *Book of Martyrs*, it was noted, for example, that while Foxe was a fellow at Magdalen College, Oxford, he had taken numerous solitary walks. Despite these and other examples, modern historians have continued to believe and to claim that early-modern people ignored the distinctions between private and public and blended them together in ways that are incomprehensible.

---

[1]Elizabeth, Countess of Bridgewater (1626–1663), wife of John Egerton, Second Earl of Bridgewater. She wrote, but did not publish, her prayers and meditations.

[2]English Protestant clergyman (1516–1587), famous for his *Book of Martyrs*, which praised Protestants martyred during the reign of the Catholic queen Mary (1553–1558).

Since the contemporaries of Bridgewater and Foxe used the words public and private frequently, it is unlikely that they had a blurred understanding of these two concepts. The evidence of prying individuals reporting their neighbors for sexual irregularities or disorderly conduct seems to be largely responsible for fueling modern speculations that no real value was attached to individual or family privacy. Even though it is true that ministers thundered from pulpits against spouses who, like "brute beasts," used the marriage bed for lustful behavior, in practice ... the church courts, which were relatively efficient during this period, made little effort to regulate marital sexual relations. These activities of the neighborhood spies, who were actually the equivalent of modern private detectives, did not ... "represent normal, spontaneous neighbourly behavior."

Sharp contrasts do, nevertheless, exist between the kinds of acts that resulted in arrest and trial then and now: minor sexual offenders and alleged disorderly wives, called shrews, no longer loom large in court rooms. Changes in the way governments support family integrity mean that local authorities are much more likely to thwart patriarchalism by arresting husbands for beating their wives or parents for abusing their children. Furthermore, modern medical and technological discoveries have neutralized the efforts of the religious establishment to impose or enforce the view that God punished sexual offenders by, as Amelia Lanyer[3] warned her readers, raining "fire and brimstone" on their communities. Usually, only illicit sexual acts committed in public places or for financial gain are now subject to state regulation. Despite the differences in the nature of the cases, it is unclear whether generally family life was any more infringed upon in that period than now .... [A]dvanced technology has given governments the power to intrude into households in a way that those English people would have considered "grossly tyrannical."

Another social custom that seems to have given rise to the notion that the public intruded into private affairs was the ritual surrounding the dying. Since the rites of passage were controlled by the established monopoly church, parish clergy participated in every step of the pilgrimage of life from birth to marriage to death. Christenings, confirmations, and weddings were expected to take place at Church in a public setting, but the ritual surrounding death, the last rite of passage, usually began at home, rather than in hospitals or in nursing homes as it does now with medical personnel monitoring the dying process.

Since the custom was for the dying to have the support of witnesses, including ministers, kindred, and neighbors, who could testify to how well they had responded to Satan's last temptation and to how well they had prepared for death in the spirit of the *ars moriendi*,[4] the community did penetrate into the private bedchamber, such as guests might enter the

---

[3]Poet (1569–1645).
[4]The art of dying.

modern home. These witnesses were expected and welcomed, and people with diseases such as smallpox who could not have their friends and family present at their deathbed, felt greatly deprived. The community did not otherwise normally intrude into privy chambers, except in the crudely built or very small structures of the lower classes whose poverty prevented them from building the withdrawing chambers present in more expensive homes.

Part of the scholarly confusion about these concepts may well have arisen from the various meanings the words can have. A review of these meanings, which in great part still prevail, although with different emphases, is important to an understanding of early-modern family and community life. Private and public deal with the following issues: 1) relationships, 2) business or trade, 3) spatial dimensions, and 4) secret matters. The family, a term that was used synonymously with household in this period, had a mean size of 4.7 members . . . and included the nuclear family plus servants. Households varied in size among the social orders, some of the poorest having no servants at all while a few of the wealthiest having one hundred or more; but all, regardless of the numbers, including even the king's court, were viewed as a private family. Then, as now, the domestic unit was far from static: children grew up; parents died; servants left to be married.

Today's greatest difference in terms of family membership is that a live-in servant is now a rare household figure. In contrast, whenever early-modern authors of household books defined family relationships, which they always referred to as "private," they inevitably included a discussion of masters and servants. In 1600, for example, William Vaughan[5] identified three private family relationships: they were the "communion and fellowship of life" between husbands and wives, parents and children, and between masters or mistresses and servants.

Except for a small percentage of elite families, cousins, aunts, uncles, grandparents, and in-laws did not live in the household, and the question of whether strong kinship relations with them even existed beyond the domestic unit has been debated extensively. Scholars agree that among elite families, especially those in which members of the older generation experienced great longevity, remote kinship relationships were kept up. In some villages . . . community relations may have prevailed over distant private kinship ties, although scholars . . . have recently been challenging this view with some success.

People differentiated sharply between public business that was accomplished on behalf of the community, and private economic enterprise that was undertaken, often in the household, for family gain. In 1630, for example, Richard Brathwait[6] described the vocation of a gentleman as: "Publike, when

---

[5]English poet and colonial pioneer (1577–1641), author of *The golden-grove, moralized in three bookes: necessary for all such as would know how to governe themselves, their houses, or their countrey* (1600).

[6]Poet, satirist, and essayist (1588–1673).

employed in affaires or state, either at home or abroad. . . . Private, when in domesticke businesse he is detained," as in the ordering of his household. This difference had been highlighted during the early sixteenth century. Erasmus[7] included the following dialogue in his colloquy, "The Poetic Feast." The first speaker inquired:

"Are you a private citizen or do you hold public office?" And the second responded:

> I have a public office. Bigger ones were available, but I chose one that would have sufficient dignity to assure respect and be the least troublesome . . . and what's more, I have means of assisting my friends occasionally.

The holding of public office brought prestige to individuals and was considered praiseworthy. James Cleland,[8] expressed his contemporaries' attitude in 1607 with the words, "a private person is bound to honour those who are publike and in office."

These distinctions still obtain but in slightly different ways. In modern society, references are made to the private business sector but with the difference that most business is now conducted outside the home, for the workshop has been separated from the household. In early Stuart England, private business, which was the family business, was accomplished in the household, which functioned as a unit of production as well as consumption. Rather than performing domestic occupations, many live-in servants were actually apprentices, journeymen, or other employees retained for the family's trade or business. Another variation is that publicly owned corporations now perform business that was formerly conducted in private. Joint-stock companies, primitive institutions that grew into lucrative corporations, such as the East India Company, played a negligible financial and economic role at this time. In their references to public officials, contemporaries explicitly named military, church, and civil office holders, such as magistrates, judges, mayors, soldiers, bishops, and clerics.

The spatial definitions have changed somewhat, for, in the modern period, some public areas, such as church buildings, are overseen by community groups unassociated with the government. In contrast to the public grounds, are the lands and quarters of a private household. Despite many early-seventeenth-century claims that male heads of families operated as "kings" in their public households, scholars have maintained that they and their contemporaries actually placed no great value on privacy, assuming thereby that the space of modern households is more immune to community interference than early-modern ones. Service people of all kinds, nevertheless, have the right to intrude into modern gardens to check a battery of meters, a spatial invasion that hardly existed before the twentieth century. . . .

[7]Desiderius Erasmus, Dutch humanist (c.1466–1536).
[8]Writer and chaplain, early seventeenth century.

In discussions of private and public, scholars also seem to have been concluding that formerly no personal or solitary time existed, that everyone acted out her life in the open with witnesses remarking on all that she did or said. A characteristic of early-modern homes that may have led to these assumptions about the lack of solitariness was the way in which chambers were arranged. Even in royal palaces and aristocratic houses rooms emptied one into another; without hallways to separate them, places for sleeping and toiletry were not secreted away as they are today, but screens and draperies did provide some escape from witnesses for those intimate occasions. Private moments, moreover, do not absolutely require being physically out of sight, for people can "internalize a set of barriers." The possession of moments without interruption, even if the individual merely withdraws into a corner of a room, can also be defined as solitariness. In addition, the homes of the elite had small private rooms, called closets because of their diminutive size, which were available for individuals desiring to be alone. In 1581, William Lowthe,[9] for example, translated for publication a work of Bartholomew Battus[10] into English with the title, *The Christian mans closet.* Clearly, at least for religious devotions, some people did seek a few solitary moments.

In admonishing their readers to say prayers every morning and evening, religious authors usually gave advice similar to that of John Brinsley:[11] "The meetest place is, where we may be most secret, and freest from distractions." Lewis Bayley[12] also told his readers:

> And thus having washed thy selfe, and adorned thy body with apparell . . . : shut thy chamber-doore, and kneele downe at thy bed-side, or some other convenient place, and in reverent manner lifting up thy heart together with thy hands and eyes, as in the presence of God. . . . offer . . . thy Prayer as a Morning Sacrifice.

A variety of words were used to refer to these secret moments, some people differentiating them from private family prayers by calling them personal or "more private." Emphasizing the common availability of secret times, furthermore, ministers warned their parishioners against being too open about their religious and charitable activities, advising them to perform them privately to avoid public commendations.

People must have regularly withdrawn from the company of others for moments alone, since writers frequently admonished them about their solitary behavior. Although ministers believed that secret times for prayer and meditation were essential for everyone's religious well-being, they suspected that individuals might be tempted to misuse or abuse these moments. In 1614, Robert Horne[13] warned his readers that when they were

---

[9]Sixteenth-century Englishman who published nothing except this translation.

[10]Latin name of the cleric, Bartholomeus Batty.

[11]Puritan divine, translator, and author of educational books.

[12]Puritan, bishop of Bangor (d. 1631). His book, *The practice of pietie* (1613) was extraordinarily popular.

[13]Oxford theologian (1565–1640).

in their "privatest" rooms such as privy chambers or bed chambers, they were "to do nothing that shall be uncomely" and to refrain from doing "privately that we should be ashamed should it be brought before the face of men." Three-quarters of a century earlier, the excessive number of John Foxe's solitary walks in the dead of night to wrestle with the question of his religious faith aroused the suspicions of the Catholic fellows at Magdalen, and, after inquiring into his beliefs, they expelled him from that college.

Within this early-modern framework, women's lives were expected to be and were much more private than those of their modern counterparts. In sermons and treatises ministers warned women, whether they were puritan or conformist, to remain in the household and to go into public areas only rarely: a housewife was not a "Field-wife" or "Street-wife," and only "gossipy busy bodies" went abroad. That so much attention was directed toward preventing them from straying from home probably means that this rule was not always well kept. A few foreigners even claimed that England was a paradise for women. It may have been the bustling activity of the wives and daughters of shopkeepers as well as that of tourists in London that made strangers think these customs prevailed universally. Quantitative analyses are not feasible, but evidence does indicate that some Englishwomen did live by the public and private standards set out for them in sermons and treatises. It will be useful to review that evidence, which mainly describes members of the elite, propertied social orders, and see how these concepts influenced women in their pilgrimages of life from youth to old age.

In a patriarchal society, such as Stuart England, in which family life was viewed as the kingdom writ small, householders expected their wives, children, and servants to obey them as though they were kings. Disorder in the family, it was feared, would give rise to disorders in the kingdom. A softening of this autocratic domestic rule did exist, men being admonished, for example, not to be abusive or to provoke their children to wrath, although daughters, it was thought, would more easily accept the governance of their future husbands if they had learned obedience in their youth. Masters were also to treat their servants with respect and to love their wives, whose private suggestions for improvement, especially in religious matters, should be heeded. Depending on the personality of the family members, room for much give and take existed within this arrangement. . . . "Married life was neither perpetual friendship nor constant dissonance, but rather a fluctuating compromise in which relations of power continually presented themselves."

The education of women was directed toward keeping them absorbed in the business of the private household and preventing them from becoming knowledgeable about public matters. Only a few women attended day schools outside the home and none went to the two universities or to the inns of court. Rarely did any of them learn Latin, the language of the scholar and the cleric, primarily because it was of little practical value for their employment opportunities, which centered in the household. Reading material for them was supposed to be pious and elegant rather than classical and solid, and some girls who showed an interest in classical languages, as did the goddaughter of Sir Ralph Verney[14] in 1652, were discouraged with the advice:

> Good sweet hart bee not soe covitous; beleeve me a Bible (with the Common prayer) and a good plaine cattichisme in our Mother Tongue being well read and practised is well worth all the rest and much more sutable to your sex.

No young gentlewoman was, moreover, permitted to go on a Grand Tour to the continent, an expensive practice indulged in by most young gentlemen, and in Elizabeth's reign,[15] when a proposal was made to establish an academy for her male wards, no comparable suggestions were put forth to benefit her maids of honor.

The education of girls was the responsibility of their mothers or their governesses. Under the general supervision of their husbands and of the clergy, who warned them against cockering or spoiling their children, women inculcated in the younger generation the negative view of their sex that prevailed in church and society. Men were advised, in fact, to choose virtuous wives so they could bring their children up in religious education and feminine virtue, which were the passive qualities . . . of chastity, obedience, piety, and silence; indeed, loquaciousness was considered a particular female vice. They were also to learn housewifery and needlework, since the private household was to frame their world.

Warnings about the need to remain chaste abounded: "Chastity," one mother remarked, "is the beautie of the soule and the puritie of life." Women, and especially young girls in their vulnerable youth, were thought to be susceptible to all kinds of wickedness. When Elizabeth Jocelin, whose grandfather, William Chaderton, Bishop of Chester and Lincoln, had provided her with a classical education, was obsessed by a premonition that she would die in childbirth, she wrote a book of advice as a "Legacy" to her unborn child. Advising against the sin of vanity, she said: "If a daughter, I confesse thy task is harder because thou art weaker, and thy temptation to this vice greater." Girls consequently had extensive supervision and less private time than adults. Juan Luis Vives,[16] whose guide for the instruction of young women was printed as late as 1592, even warned that for the sake of their chastity young girls should never be alone or in a crowd of people but should always be monitored by sober chaperons. Lady Grace Mildmay, who in 1619 wrote the first extant autobiography in English by a woman, recalled the attentiveness of her governess at her childhood home in Wiltshire in the 1560s:

---

[14]1613–1696, fought for the Parliament during the Puritan Revolution, exiled, and later returned, becoming a Member of Parliament.

[15]Queen Elizabeth I (reigned 1558–1603).

[16]Spanish humanist and philosopher (1492–1540).

And when I was not with her she would be sure to be with me at my heels to see where and with whom I was and what I did or spake.

Admitting that she was grateful to her parents for this strict education, Lady Mildmay also remembered that she and her sister had been forbidden to have close contact with their male servants, one of whom was whipped for unbecoming behavior toward them. Parents were expected even to oversee their children's personal correspondence. For example, after Sir Thomas Coningsby's daughter received and read a letter in 1605, upon her father's orders she had to relinquish it to him.

Despite fears that they might misuse their time, young women were encouraged to pray alone. As a child, Lettice, Viscountess Falkland,[17] who lived at Tooley Park, near Leicester, often read a book in her closet when it was thought that she had gone to bed. The minister, John Duncon, who wrote an account of her life, also noted that she has been "constant" in her private prayers as a youth, and if visitors occupied the chamber to which she commonly retired for her devotions, "she would ask the steward for the key of some other room for that purpose, at her hour of prayer."

With the center of their world in the household, these young Protestant females had their future mapped out for them in the words, "women to be married," for no other occupation was possible for them, the last of the English nunneries having been dissolved at the accession of Elizabeth. Although a certain number of women did remain single, since they were given some choice in the matter and could turn down parental candidates for their husbands, they were not permitted to live alone but had to reside in the households of their parents or married siblings. Whether children or servants of the family, unmarried females were expected to be watched closely and to be kept from frequent mingling in society. When they failed to marry, they doomed themselves to performing tasks that were described by their contemporaries as "servile," since they continued merely to work for someone else rather than to function as a mistress with authority over children and servants. The honorable future for them lay in marrying and assuming parental and spousal responsibilities.

Wives, especially, were instructed to wear the home as a snail or tortoise wears his shell, for private family activities were their major concern or, as Thomas Gataker[18] said, women were created for "domestical and houshold affaires." Besides attending holy services, family business might well take wives, with their husband's permission, into the public arena to sue for their family's estate, to purchase property, or to transact other private business. Even so, some authors were of the opinion that wives should venture abroad less often even than young girls.

Women, whose lives were "more private" than men, were prohibited from holding public office, either civil, military, or church, although as the

[17]1622–1647, wife of Lucius Cary, second viscount Falkland.
[18]Puritan divine (1574–1654).

wife, child, or other kin of an officeholder, they might indirectly influence public action through manipulation of the male relatives. When women were referred to as private people, then, the word private did not mean that they were confined to their households, although those areas were viewed as their special domains, but that they could not personally conduct public affairs. Even the queen consort of England, although technically a public figure, had merely a ceremonial role to play. An exception to this rule would be made only if she were appointed regent or if she were to inherit the crown.

In their households, wives were given considerable authority. They had control of the religious and domestic education of their young children, who should never, it was warned, be treated with too much indulgence. They also supervised the training and work of all females, their servants as well as their offspring. Husbands, who took charge of the male servants, could, but usually did not, interfere in their wives' housekeeping routine, although ultimately it was their duty to respond privately to the questions of their wives about religious matters and to see that the whole family attended household devotions and public services.

It will be useful to review how some wives conducted their lives within this framework. Information about Lady Mildmay's married life can also be found in her autobiography. In 1567, when at the age of fifteen she wed Anthony Mildmay, she continued the daily religious meditations she had begun as a child under her mother's guidance. Ultimately, she bequeathed to her daughter and grandchildren more than one thousand manuscript pages along with her autobiography in which she instructed them about the desirability of relying on private religious devotions for comfort and help in dealing with the struggle of life. When she is compared to the other members of the Elizabethan and Jacobean[19] Church of England, she must be judged extraordinarily religious. Christians regularly accounted privately for their daily sins and participated in religious devotions, but it was unusual for them to write down their meditations in such detailed fashion.

Lady Mildmay's marriage was a particularly unhappy one. Her husband Anthony, the son of Sir Walter, Queen Elizabeth's Chancellor of the Exchequer, often traveled to court on business or abroad on diplomatic journeys, leaving her behind at the family estate in Northamptonshire. Consequently, her days were spent in "solitariness." This isolation was partly the result of her own decisions, for she refused invitations from friends to attend court and to go to feasts, marriages, and plays, for fear that she would be unable to withstand worldly temptations. Authors and ministers did warn that women should be accompanied to social functions by their husbands, and Lady Mildmay contented herself with the answer that "God had placed me in this house, and if I found no comfort here, I would never seek it out of this house."

During Anthony's absences, she insisted that she held no resentment toward him, but she also admitted that when he was home, he sometimes

[19]During the reign of King James I (reigned 1603–1625).

mistreated her. Having lived the life of a patient and silent wife according to the precepts of St. Paul, she confessed at his death, while she was meditating over his body, that she had

> carryed alwaye that reverent respect towards him, in regard of my good conceipt which I ever had the good partes which I knewe to be in him, that could not fynde in my harte to challenge him for the worst worde or deed whichever he offered me in all his lyfe.

Lady Mildmay's life was especially isolated; others who attempted to follow the precepts set out by religious writers had less solitariness and were less homebound. One example is that of Lady Margaret Hoby, a Yorkshire resident, who between 1599 and 1605 kept the first known diary written in English by a woman. She may have begun it as part of her daily self-examination ritual, for she worried in 1599 that "the divell laboreth to hinder my profittable hearinge of the word." Earlier that same year she had characterized her headache and upset stomach as God's "Just punishment" for her sins. The diary is mainly, however, a recitation of her daily activities and shows "no real capacity for self-knowledge or ability in self-analysis."

Unlike Anthony Mildmay, who seems not to have been a particularly religious man, Lady Margaret's husband, a puritan, took care to perform the religious duties of a householder. He read the works of divines to her, prayed with her, educated her about theological issues, and maintained family prayers. In addition, she said personal prayers twice a day, read religious works with her maids, and attended church services. Her world was bound by this household routine, which was interspersed with public worship and occasional visits to friends and relatives. She also traveled to London at least three times in the company of her husband when his legal business drew him there. Her favorite public entertainment in the city was the hearing of sermons and the visiting of churches, although she attended court with her sister-in-law and bought a New Year's gift at the royal exchange. She refrained from going to fairs with her husband, however.

Some women even lived alone. Modern misconceptions about the size of Stuart families notwithstanding, the mean was, as stated above, only 4.7 members. While some households were very large, others had single dwellers, and most aged widows, especially the poorest ones, must have spent many hours alone since they tended to reside alone. Very few over the age of forty remarried or resided with their adult children. Even in London where widows of craftsmen and tradesmen often remarried, 40 percent remained single. In this, as in other social habits, London did not represent the provinces where the remarriage figures for women were lower. Despite these numbers, the "enduring stereotype of the early-modern widow as a woman who anxiously sought a husband at any cost" prevailed. This stereotype was an extension of the view that women were "biologically driven to intercourse" and the more lascivious of the sexes. Affirming this worldview, ministers admonished women to spend their widowhood in solitary religious exercises and in honoring their dead husbands, who in some sense could be viewed as cuckolded if they remarried. As late as the 1934 issue of Emily Post's *Etiquette,* in fact, elderly widows were advised about the different colors of clothing to wear for their required lifelong mourning; younger widows had to don mourning clothes for at least one full year.

To the clerical advice about widowhood, women of the wealthy classes in early Stuart England had myriad responses, which do not seem to reflect a particular attitude toward the Church of England and its ceremonies. Many such as Anne Clifford, countess of Pembroke, who married Philip, third earl of Pembroke and Montgomery, after the death of her first husband, the earl of Dorset, and then was widowed a second time, led busy, productive private lives, overseeing their family estates or businesses. The second Englishwoman to have kept a diary that is extant, but only in her youth from 1602 to 1619, Lady Pembroke wrote of her struggles to regain control of her father's Westmorland estates that had descended to her uncle and his son. When, after the death of these relatives, she finally inherited the property, she spent the remainder of her life restoring the buildings of her ancestors, including some almshouses for poor women, and repairing places of worship. As a widow she dressed more humbly than before, stayed away from court, and even ate with the almswomen. The custom of noble widows retiring from "worldy vanity and ostentation" and wearing plain apparel was practiced not only in England but also in other parts of Christendom, especially Catholic Spain. At Lady Pembroke's death in 1677, her minister, Edward Rainbow, bishop of Carlisle, pointed out that some who were devoted to the Church of England had promoted the foundation of Protestant nunneries but that her example proved that "to overcome the world is more generous than to fly from it."

Some women had more intriguing responses to widowhood. In 1623, Lucy, duchess of Bedford, wrote to her friend, Jane, Lady Cornwallis, about the reaction of Frances, duchess of Richmond and Lennox, to the expected death of her ailing husband Ludovic:

> Her haire, in discharge of a vowe she had formerly made, she cutte off close by the rootes that afternoone, and told us of som other vowes of retirednes she had made if she should be so miserable as to outlive him, which I hope she will as punctually performe. For my part, I confesse I encouradged her to itt, which, som say, hereafter she will love me nothing the better for; but itt is the counsell I should take to myselfe in her case, and therefore I cannot spare to give it.

Other examples of self-imposed retiredness can be found. When Lucius, Lady Falkland's royalist husband, died in battle in 1643, she feared that his death was a divine punishment for her sins. Afterwards, according to the Reverend John Duncon, who wrote an account of her life, she led "a more strict course of life" at her home in Oxfordshire, dispensing with "vanity of apparel" and "all worldly pomp." One of her most cherished projects, which never came to fruition, was to establish a place for the retirement of widows and the education of young gentlewomen so they could have a greater opportunity for worshiping God "without distraction." She, herself, sought lengthy private times for meditation. To prepare for Sunday services, she sequestered herself every Saturday and "seldom came out of her closet til towards evening." She did not always remain in her home, however, for it was noted, when she had cause to visit Oxford or London on business, her first inquiry was about attending church services there.

One of the most interesting and most unusual Stuart widows was Jane Ratcliffe, a citizen of Chester, who died in 1638 on a visit to London. John Ley, prebendary of the Cathedral Church of Chester, who knew her well but who had not been given the opportunity to preach her funeral sermon, published an account of her life in 1640. He complained that the preacher who had officiated at her funeral had not given her the "discourse" she deserved and that some people were accusing him of being "a Traducer and contemner of Women-kinde." Observing that it was unusual for householders, and especially women, to die so far from their homes, Ley noted that she had been visiting her daughter in London.

In her youth, he pointed out, she had liked dancing, stage plays, and other "publique vanities," but after her conversion:

> by the immediate hand of God, who having taken away her first child (which she took much to heart) made that an occasion to make her apparently his owne child.

Ley praised Ratcliffe's religious abilities, thereby ignoring the usual clerical convention of warning women against teaching others and of advising them to be instructed privately by their husbands and ministers. Praising her as a Priscilla and an Abigail,[20] he pointed out that she performed private religious services for her servants and "secret" female friends. About her women friends he said,

> they thought it some honour to themselves, that one of their owne sexe (so contemned by some both as weake and wicked) was graced by God with such an holy and excellent gift: and so in time . . . it became a graduate from privat praise to a common fame of the truth.

When she read the psalms, he recalled, he thought he had never heard David "with more effectuall feeling," and he had often but without success requested her to write down her "observations of the Bible." Shortly before

---

[20]That is, as a woman who uses her house as a church and who offers good advice to her husband. The references are to the Priscilla who, with her husband, opened their house to the first Christians in Rome, and to Abigail, who, according to Hebrew scripture, reconciled her husband with Kind David.

her last trip to London, she had promised him she would turn to that project when she returned home. Unlike the vain *"Pharisaicall Puritans,"* who practice their religion publicly to win applause, she had attempted to keep her skills in scripture reading and teaching a secret. Her example predates the more daring activities of the women who participated in various radical religious sects during the civil-war period.[21]

The Protestant writers of early Stuart England, regardless of whether they were opposed to or approved of the Church of England's rituals and ceremonies, seemed to have agreed that women should have solitary moments alone for prayer, reading, and meditation. The importance to them of the religious experience, which had "contradictions" in its impact on women's lives, cannot be overstated. Clerics did emphasize the inferior status of women and required them to be obedient to their fathers, masters, and husbands: "let him match with religious woman," Francis Dillingham[22] said, "for religion teacheth her subjection." And yet those same clerics also sought to convert women to sincere religious callings and to give them an important supervisory role in the family. Women's conversions, moreover, opened up to them a world of serious literature while at the same time affording them increased opportunities for teaching other females and for solitary moments for creative writing. Given the environment in which they functioned, it is no wonder that most of the works written and published by early-modern women were of a religious nature.

That their lives were private does not mean that women never entered the public arena or never pursued family business outside the home. It did mean that they could only affect public policy in indirect ways through the manipulation of their male relatives who actually held community or royal office. Private sometimes referred to the activities of the whole family but could well refer to the solitary times an individual had for reading or writing. Private and public matters were organized somewhat differently than now but with distinctions that were just as obvious and definitive. The application to early-modern women of these concepts of public and private clearly resulted in social roles that differed greatly from those of their modern counterparts.

---

[21]The English Civil War lasted from 1642 to 1649, when King Charles I was beheaded. However, the Civil War period extends to 1660, when Charles II ascended the throne.

[22]Rector, Protestant controversialist, court preacher, and one of the translators of the King James version of the Bible. Died 1625.

Popular Reading and the Supply of News in Seventeenth-Century Holland

A. T. VAN DEURSEN

The history of reading is an important part of social history. Historians are concerned to know who read, what they read, and what meanings they ascribed to their reading. Why indeed did people read at all? The Dutch historian A. T. Van Deursen here analyzes the reading of the populace in seventeenth-century Holland, the "Golden Age," when the Dutch dominated Europe commercially, offered a model of prosperity and tolerance, and created a culture markedly different from those in the court-dominated states of the Continent.

What types of books and subjects attracted Dutch readers? Did current events affect their reading interests? What problems does the historian of Dutch reading face in attempting to measure what and how much people read?

Both the state and the church paid great attention to Dutch reading habits. Why? How did the government transmit information quickly to the people? What current events interested readers? How did people who could not read receive information?

Pamphlets and books—and in Holland, rhetoric and drama companies— provided misinformation as well as information. What propaganda, stereotypes, and falsehoods did the people receive in their reading and in the news given to them?

How do Dutch reading materials and habits differ from those in the West today? Do people read for the same reasons? Was there a public opinion in the seventeenth century analogous to public opinion today?

There were people who could read, and probably a considerable number of them. But did they do it? Inventories of possessions recorded in the sixteenth and seventeenth centuries seldom include books. If they mention any at all, it is almost invariably the Bible or an edifying work. The cooper Thijmen at Medemblik in 1568 had nothing except 'one book with clasps, of the passion of our Lord, printed at Gouwe, anno 1519'. Cors Steffensz., a farmer of Naaldwijk, owned in 1569 one Dutch Bible, printed three years earlier by Plantijn at Antwerp. Mary Gijsbertsdr., widow of an Amsterdam wine-tax collector, left two books behind in 1578: 'the one of the Legends and the other of the Gospels'. The first-mentioned is probably the same book that we find among the possessions of the Leiden miller's widow Maria Dircksdr. around 1580: 'Jacobus de Voragine, *Historia lombardica quae a plerisque Aurea legenda sanctorum appelatur*',[1] in an edition published 1496. In that household there

---

[1] *The Lombard History that is Called by Many the Golden Legend of Saints.* Jacobus de Voragine was an Italian Dominican (c.1230–1298).

was also a New Testament, and a book by Henricus de Herph,[2] *Dits die groote ende nieuwe spieghel der volcomenheit* (The Great New Mirror of Perfection). In 1581 the Leiden barge-skipper Simon Willemsz. Wassenaer left only a New Testament to his heirs. For that matter, higher up the social ladder we do not always see any substantially greater selection. At the house of the Leiden draper Gerrit Jacobsz. we find a total of four books: one Bible, one chronicle of Holland, and two other unspecified works. The widow of *jonkheer*[3] Johan van der Bouchorst in 1591 did carry matters a bit further: a collection of six items, of which only the Bible, psalter and New Testament are specifically named.

If these were our only sources, then the conclusions would be obvious: Hollanders read little, and when they did read it was not for amusement but for edification. The first could also be true insofar as Hollanders were not much inclined to while away their evenings, the most suitable hours, in reading. When Brill received an English garrison in 1586, the magistrate raised the quartering costs for soldiers, 'since the English nation have a great need for fire and light'. Apparently these English soldiers spent their evenings by candlelight at the hearth, while the Hollanders did not. In the States' College at Leiden, where the young theologians were lodged, the use of the fire and light in the evenings was forbidden. Evidently there was a rule that after sunset students could not and must not open books. Albrecht Haller's eighteenth-century statement that Netherlanders of all classes did not make fires in the evening acquires some credibility. The directors of public buildings evidently took it as axiomatic that human beings should go to bed with the sun. Thus they could do without light and warmth in the evenings, in the Leiden hospices as well as in the Amsterdam house of correction, where no traces of heating facilities have been discovered in the inmates' cells.

Yet the overall impression is misleading, if it makes us think that the sleep-inducing reading (or rather spelling-out) lessons at school had caused the pupils to reject books once and for all. There can be no doubt whatsoever that a reading public existed, and not only among the upper classes. 'All the meetings, negotiations, and travels of common people, were they not enlivened with tales of histories, and made appealing?' Some part of the material for stories was certainly found in reading matter. People read in order to edify themselves, to relax, to stay informed about politics and current events, and to improve themselves. Edifying literature held an important position in this parcel of reasons.... Nor will self-improvement get much attention here. As a separate genre, popular works of self-improvement barely existed in the sixteenth and seventeenth centuries. Not until the nineteenth century, with its penny magazines and other education publications, were

---

[2]Dutch cleric and mystical writer (c.1405–1477).
[3]Lesser nobleman.

there conscious efforts to raise the level of knowledge of the unskilled and to broaden their interests. Seventeenth-century publications sought these goals only in limited areas—particularly in religion, and medical self-help—or accomplished them incidentally in travel accounts that were probably read primarily for adventure, yet on the way informed the reader about foreign lands and distant peoples.

Of the most important genres, two remain: the popular book for relaxation, and the pamphlet for information. Neither of them was unique to Holland, certainly not the first. The stream of pamphlets flowed more slowly in countries that had strict state supervision and careful, authoritative religious censorship. In Holland there was thus more liberty than in many a monarchy. But the popular book was international in its themes and distribution. Knights and giants found their admirers all over Western Europe. Thomas Overbury[4] in his character sketches had a chambermaid become so infatuated with the stories of Robert Greene[5] that she half thought about becoming a wandering noblewoman herself. She had a masculine pendant in Ralph, the grocer's boy, who actually fulfilled the role of knight errant in Beaumont's[6] *Knight of the Burning Pestle*. Dutch literature has not preserved such figures for us. Perhaps we lacked a Greene who could turn the heads of Dutch chambermaids with equal facility. The Netherlandish popular book was often a pitiful mass-product, in which typographical errors were preserved from one publication to the next, and even omissions that made the text incomprehensible were repeated from edition to edition. This had no ill effects on the demand for adventure tales. Many were glued to their books.

Of Amadis,[7] of Palmerijn,[8]
Of Orssen and of Valentijn,[9]
Of Malegijs,[10] and of Mandeville,[11]

[4]English courtier and poet (1581–1613).

[5]English dramatist (1558–1592).

[6]This was a burlesque by the English dramatist Francis Beaumont (1584?–1616).

[7]*Amadis of Gaul* was a medieval chivalric romance about the exploits of Amadis.

[8]The hero of sixteenth-century Spanish chivalric romances. Palmerin (Palmerijn) is a pilgrim to the Holy Land who returned with a palm branch as a token of his pilgrimage.

[9]Heroes in a French romance connected with the Carolingians, the dynasty that came to the throne in 751. Orson (Orssen) and Valentine (Valentijn) were twins. A bear abducted Orson, who became a wild man. Valentine's uncle, King Pepin, abducted him. Eventually Valentine and Orson reunited and had many adventures.

[10]Maugis (Malagigi, Maligijs) was an enchanter or magician in medieval stories about Charlemagne.

[11]Sir John Mandeville was an English knight whose fictitious travels to the Holy Land and Asia became one of the most popular books in the late Middle Ages.

Of Blancefleur[12] and of Virgil,[13]
Of Uilenspiegel's[14] roguish pranks

Or of Marcolphus[15] and his wife,
Of Fortunatus'[16] purse and hat,
All that tastes so wondersweet to these folk,
Everyone who would much rather hear
And read these works, than God's holy word.

The critical distance that appears in the last lines is expressed more explicitly by most contemporary commentators, especially when they evaluate these popular novels for their worth as reading matter for children. Master Valcoogh[17] almost certainly had these popular histories in mind when he pronounced his damning judgment on 'joky and useless books' which children sometimes brought to school: 'put them away at once, or God will take vengeance upon you!' Popular novels were censored and ridiculed by educators of all persuasions, as if ecumenical consciousness in the seventeenth century found expression only in an interconfessional rejection of all forms of recreational literature. The bishop of Antwerp in 1621 forbade an entire series of popular books, such as *Mariken of Nijmegen, Uilenspiegel*, and *Floris and Blancefleur*. Jacob Cats[18] did not want children's brains to be overexcited 'by anything that Faustus does, or Wagenaer tells'. But all these condemnations had so little effect that at the end of the century Balthasar Bekker[19] could still get irritated by the 'popish jokes and novels of Amadis of Gaul, of the knight Malegijs, of Valentijn and Ourson, of Fortunatus, and that kind of quacks'.

The catalogue of works in circulation was considerably larger. In 1837 L. Ph. C. van den Bergh's *Dutch Popular Novels* discussed twenty-eight different stories, and his list is by no means complete. From van den Bergh's work, however, it is possible to get an idea of the tastes that this literature had to satisfy. Novels about knights clearly stood at the top of the list.

[12]In a medieval poem, Blancefleur and her sister, Florence, discussed the merits of clergymen and knights as lovers.

[13]The greatest Roman poet (70–19 B.C.), known especially for his epic, *Aeneid*, that told the story of the founding of Rome by Aeneas, a son of the king of Troy. Because Virgil was wise, medieval fables came to represent him as a magician, often depicting him as outwitting the devil.

[14]Till Eulenspiegel (Uilenspiegel) was a German peasant celebrated as a clown and practical joker in numerous poems and stories.

[15]Marcolf (Marculf) was the hero of a medieval tale, "The Fool and the Philosopher" or "Marcolf and Solomon." In the dialogue, Marcolf outwits Solomon by cunning and trickery.

[16]Legendary medieval hero who possessed a bottomless purse or some other magical means to get rich or to accomplish fantastic things.

[17]Master Dirck Valcoogh, author of a pedagogical manual for Dutch schoolteachers.

[18]Dutch statesman and poet (1577–1660).

[19]Protestant pastor (1634–1698), famous for his book, *The World Bewitched*, that attacked the belief in witchcraft.

This genre produced the most titles and probably also the greatest number of copies, at least for the truly popular items. The *History of the Four Sons of Aymon* was apparently the most beloved and most-read popular book. *Floris and Blancefleur* and the adventures of the wizard Malegijs achieved a high rating. The holy legends probably lost some ground, although they were still reprinted sometimes in the Republic, for example *Mariken of Nijmegen*, published at Utrecht in 1609. Popular books of genuinely Protestant inspiration did not really take their place. Naturally there were the books of martyrs, but these came in folio format as bound volumes, not in the ephemeral pamphlet format of popular books. Some older stories such as *Til Uilenspiegel* did undergo Protestant rewriting.

Perhaps it is possible to find traces of indirect Calvinist influence here, since in the seventeenth century the popular novel sometimes received a moralistic introduction. The 1648 edition of the *Châtelaine of Vergi* warns all readers against the 'sin of adultery'. It may not matter that this flag of convenience covers a highly improper cargo, and that the medieval author intended instead to teach enterprising lovers how to conceal their amorous adventures from the public eye. Several editions of the *History of Amadis of Gaul* were likewise enriched with a religious-didactic introduction; the author could hardly have objected, since it was simply impossible to spice this light dish with moralistic herbs. The moral offered was often of the cheapest kind: the popular book became an instructive example of what not to do. The first Dutch edition of *Faust*[20] recommended itself thus on the title page: to 'all haughty, pompous, wicked and godless people, as a terrible example, and warning'.

Among the folk heroes, Faust was a new phenomenon of the sixteenth century. There were several others as well, who acquired a place in the pantheon alongside the traditional popular inheritance of the Middle Ages. The Spanish picaresque novels fall in this category, with *Lazarillo de Tormes*[21] at the head of the list. The new heroes include the giant Gilias, Ahasverus the wandering Jew, the fable of Jack and the Beanstalk, translated from English, and the pure Netherlandish product, the fortunes of the Zaankant pirate Claes Compaen. Whether new or old, all of them were influenced to some extent by the transformations of the changing times. The knightly novels of the seventeenth century related an almost extinct culture to a broad public that itself had never played any part in courtly culture. The image thus became coarser, cruder and simpler. Exactly how the knightly armour was supposed to look, or whether the countless battles correctly followed the rules of engagement, were questions about which the lower-class reading public did not bother much. Not only in the picaresque novel was the hero sometimes a young man of insignificant origin. In *Gilias*, the giant is not conquered by a nobleman or a prince, but by 'a blacksmith's apprentice

---

[20] Johann Faust was a sixteenth-century German doctor who, according to legend, had sold his soul to the devil. Many dramatists and poets have told his story.

[21] A 1554 Spanish picaresque novel that recounts the adventures of Lazarillo.

of incredible power and strength'. It is true that matters turned out badly after the marriage of the simple Sievreedt and the rescued princess Eulalis. 'Finally the twenty-four brothers, at the instigation of other courtiers, who would not allow a blacksmith's apprentice to be raised to such a state, killed Sievreedt with poison, and not long afterwards Eulalis died of a broken heart'.

The happy ending is missing in other popular novels, too. Did people read them less because of a need for identification than for a desire for suspense and adventure? Sensational adventure was certainly the chief attraction in many popular books, although there was ample room for amusement, as Uilenspiegel and the picaresque novels testify. Seldom was it amusement of the highest sort: popular humour was not so refined as to reject coarse jokes. Thus the story of Jack and the Beanstalk turns on the fulfillment of three wishes that an old wizard had granted to the eponymous hero. The comical point is hidden in the last wish, by which Jack hopes to teach his wicked stepmother a lesson:

I wish, that if she begins to stare at me,
She will have to let a fart
Heard everywhere, in all places.

When Jack came home he could immediately test the power of his wish:

She cast on Jack a harsh glare
And then let out such a great fart
That it resounded far and wide.

Every time she became angry with Jack, the woman felt the force of the magic:

She began to blast with her ass
And let out many a fart;
They all laughed far and wide;
Some said, 'Woman, control your bum!
Aren't you ashamed to uncork that cask?'

Contemporary readers and hearers found that funny. That they should have bought or borrowed or read such books is easy to understand. Yet at the same time a quick survey is enough to make us understand why no popular books are mentioned in the catalogues of private libraries or inventories of possessions taken at death. These books were disposable articles of no value, and for an evaluation of someone's property they were as insignificant as the loose issues of an illustrated weekly magazine or railway-novel would be today.

The same generally held true for pamphlets. In most cases they were also ephemeral products. Presumably that applied particularly to pamphlets that had no other purpose than reporting current events to a wider cir-cle. Once they had satisfied public curiosity, their worth declined to that of yesterday's newspaper. Longer popularity may have been achieved by the many pamphlets that were also or exclusively oriented toward forming public opinion: in these writings authors gave commentary, took positions, blamed, praised, and judged. No kind has been preserved in its entirety; but enough remains to permit some generalisations, though certainly no definitive judgment. Catalogues of the large collections are available, yet we lack an overview of pamphlets as a whole, which could inform the user about every extant pamphlet known to have been printed or sold in the Netherlands. We can however provide some preliminary impressions. As a starting point we can choose the most important collection, that of the Royal Library at The Hague, described in the catalogue by Knuttel.[22] First of all, we can examine carefully how many pamphlets per year are listed there, as appears in the table that follows. The first conclusion suggested by this table is the most significant, and at the same time limits the value of all others; we must treat these figures with great suspicion. This is, after all, only the catalogue of a single collection. A particular year may be shortchanged for all sorts of reasons, with the result that the figures do not present the reality of the offering available at that time. Even the view that more pamphlets appeared in 1618 than in 1591 or 1592 thus becomes disputable, although for the present it remains quite likely.

Pamphlets per year listed in the catalogue of the
Royal Library

		1591	2	1611	106	1631	67
1572	7	1592	2	1612	106	1632	103
1573	18	1593	7	1613	156	1633	39
1574	12	1594	27	1614	150	1634	18
1575	12	1595	19	1615	81	1635	51
1576	37	1596	22	1616	96	1636	62
1577	48	1597	37	1617	176	1637	86
1578	72	1598	53	1618	310	1638	40
1579	120	1599	57	1619	204	1639	65
1580	34	1600	43	1620	121	1640	60
1581	28	1601	21	1621	161	1641	74
1582	45	1602	31	1622	100	1642	108
1583	50	1603	33	1623	111	1643	141
1584	45	1604	46	1624	67	1644	110
1585	40	1605	24	1625	64	1645	101
1586	14	1606	38	1626	91	1646	141
1587	48	1607		1627	54	1647	229
1588	36	1608	215	1628	67	1648	192
1589	16	1609	128	1629	133		
1590	14	1610	129	1630	139		

[22]W. P. C. Knuttel, librarian and writer (1854–1921).

Reasoning thus from similar appearances, we can observe the first peak of production in the years 1576–79. The causes can be read directly in any chronology of Dutch history: the Pacification of Ghent,[23] the Union of Brussels,[24] the Cologne Peace Congress,[25] the Unions of Atrecht and Utrecht.[26] At that time the burning issues for everyone were war and peace, which increased the need for information. This can be confirmed in all phases of the struggle against Spain. Every time there was talk of peace negotiations we see the yearly totals of pamphlets go up, by comparison with the years immediately preceding: 1594, 1598, 1607–9, 1621, 1629–30, 1632–3, 1643–8. These figures are higher, and often much higher, than in times when the events of the war dominated the news. Victories were reported, celebrated in song and rejoicing; but peace negotiations always brought about a discussion of pros and cons. How much the flood of pamphlets increased the exchange of ideas can be seen particularly during the Twelve Years' Truce (1609–21).[27] Beginning in 1610, religion was the most commonly discussed subject. Only after the expiry of the truce was it driven from first place, but the religious question remained of central importance, and on a number of occasions—1626, 1630—it regained its leading position in the league table.

Ordinary wartime actions seemed to decline in importance by comparison, particularly at the beginning. The years of Maurice of Nassau's[28] great victories did not produce a rich harvest of pamphlets. Could this be an accident of preservation in the Knuttel collection? Indeed other collections offer a somewhat larger, but still not bountiful harvest. Was enthusiasm inspired only when Maurice proved his military leadership not just in siege warfare but also on the field of battle? In any case, Turnhout (1597) and Nieuwpoort (1600) received considerably more coverage than objectively more significant military events such as the conquest of Nijmegen or Coevorden. It seems as if the two battles brought about a lasting change, because after their time all great military events were always well represented in the reports: such examples include the sieges of Sluis (1604), Bergen op Zoom (1622), Breda (1625) and 's-Hertogenbosch (1629). Beginning with the Armada[29] of 1588, the high points of the war at sea were always covered

[23]Treaty of 1576 in which the seventeen provinces of the Netherlands united in order to expel the Spaniards.

[24]Pledge in 1577 by all seventeen provinces to continue the fight against Spain.

[25]Peace talks in Cologne in 1579 between the Spaniards and the Dutch. When the Spanish representative demanded the return to the status quo as it had existed in 1559—that is, when Spain had complete control over the seventeen provinces of the Low Countries—the talks failed.

[26]In the Union of Arras (Atrecht) in 1579, the southern provinces stayed with Spain, while certain towns and provinces agreed in the Union of Utrecht (also in 1579) to secure independence from Spain.

[27]Temporary end to the fighting between Spain and the Dutch, 1609–1621.

[28](1567–1625), Prince of Orange and a leader in the revolt for Dutch independence. His victories led to the Twelve Years' Truce.

[29]The Great Armada, the fleet Spain sent in 1588 in an unsuccessful attempt to invade and conquer England.

generously, in particular the action at the Downs in 1639, and to a somewhat lesser degree, the capture of the silver fleet[30] (1628) and the battle on the Slaak (1631).

There was remarkably great interest in foreign politics. The battle for the throne in France, the accession of James I[31] in England, and later the Gunpowder Plot[32] were the most frequently discussed events in 1589–90, 1603 and 1606, respectively. Disputes about religion temporarily overshadowed all others, but it still appears that in 1615, for example, there was definite interest in the civil war in France and the succession to Jülich. In the 1620's the war in Germany was sometimes better represented than the Netherlands' own struggle against Spain. Beginning in 1638 the same applies to the outbreak and course of the English Civil War.

Naturally one might ask to what extent these matters are relevant to our theme. After all, we are discussing popular culture: with such pamphlets, are we not reaching too high, or was there also a real demand for pamphlets among the popular classes? A first likely approach is through the prices, but little is known about them. A list, dated January 1610, of a number of then-current publications shows that the selling prices varied greatly, from twelve pennies—three-quarters of a stuiver[33]—to eighteen stuivers. That very expensive item costing eighteen stuivers, however, was an exception. The most frequently represented are prices between three and five stuivers— thus a price that neither strongly stimulated sales, nor could be regarded as downright prohibitive.

One thing must not escape our notice in any case: the pamphlet is a primary source for us, from which we can still learn about the events of the past. But for contemporaries pamphlets and printed newsletters formed only the second source of information, surely more exact and more detailed than the first, the oral rumours that preceded them in time. However quickly the printing press could work, it was not yet in a condition to provide immediate coverage of developments, particularly not in wartime. For the latest news people did not go to the bookstores, but to the market and the harbour. Hooft's letters teach us that he, the bailiff of Muiden, did not disdain the news that ferry-captains brought from Amsterdam. Foreigners in Holland could find themselves surrounded by a flock of curious questioners. The Swiss and Palatine delegates to the Synod of Dordt in 1618 had chosen Gorinchem as the last stopping place on their journey, but they quickly rejoined their ship, because the entire population of the little town swarmed around them.

---

[30]The fleet carrying precious metal from the New World to Spain.

[31]King of England, 1603–1625.

[32]A Catholic conspiracy in 1605 to blow up the English Parliament.

[33]Also spelled stiver, a Dutch coin of such little value that the word came to mean the smallest possible amount. First minted in the fifteenth century.

Not every rumour told the unvarnished truth. The message could be garbled in a hundred different ways, and sometimes turned into its opposite. That did not necessarily mean that people always had to doubt the good faith of the reporter. But in wartime news and propaganda easily blended together. The prior Wouter Jacobsz. had already learned this in the early years of the Revolt. We heard that Oudewater, Delft and Dordrecht have been recaptured by the Spanish, he wrote on the first page of his journal in August 1572, 'but alas, no matter how far and wide these tidings are spread, they always remain loose talk and fables'. The news reports about the war are filled with lies, this pro-Spanish cleric repeatedly declared, and he knew why: the rebels were deliberately falsifying the news. If the Spaniards achieved a battlefield success, there were always people who would immediately contradict and belittle the good news. Again and again they would try to rob the Catholics of their consolation, while they exaggerated their own power and congratulated themselves on the strength of their allies. The certain knowledge that rebels were always liars nonetheless allowed the devout to take heart. If they did receive bad news, they could encourage each other by blaming it on the malicious talk of their enemies, 'who always work toward that end, by the telling of wondrous tales to drive fear and anguish into the hearts of good Catholics'.

Wouter Jacobsz. seems to have believed there was a systematic campaign to drum up support on the home front for the military activities of the rebels. He probably overestimated the organisational ability of his arch-enemies, and he may have succumbed to a well-known temptation in sharply ideological conflicts: to blame every circumstance unfavourable to his own side on conspiracies by the opposition. No doubt some false rumours were indeed circulated in his time. In later years Alexander van de Capellen[34] incidentally gives us a peep at Frederick Henry's[35] kitchen, where they were concocted on his orders: 'Spread rumours that the enemy is beginning to gather troops at Wesel and Venlo'. This was only fitting for a captain-general: he had to make the States General believe that military action was necessary in the eastern part of the country. Thus the rumour had to be reported that the enemy was collecting troops there.

Rumours and suggestive reports were most easily spread by word of mouth. But if it was important to make a certain fact or insight known quickly to many people at the same time, other means had to be used as well. The simplest were the distribution of bills and the sticking of lampoons, the latter sometimes written by hand, and secretly stuck on the walls by night. Other instant productions included ballads, which not only gave information about events in one or two pages, but also interpreted them after a fashion. The English envoy complained in 1618 that an account of a sea-battle successfully

---

[34]Soldier and memoirist of the Dutch campaign in the West Indies (c.1590–1656).

[35](1584–1647), Count of Nassau and Prince of Orange (1625–1647), he led the Dutch forces against Spain after the Twelve Years' Truce.

won by Dutch whalers over their English competitors at Spitzbergen was being sung in the streets with open mouths and self-assured faces, as if it were a glorious victory over the enemies of the country.

Such ballads were perhaps comparable to our top of the pops, since the seventeenth century also had its popular melodies, although at that time they were based not on American but on French musical production. Charles Ogier[36] wrote in 1636 that all the roads and streets of The Hague were overflowing with French songs. It is possible that in courtly The Hague the population right down to the demi-monde carried a French veneer: the hawker Vroechbedurven (Spoil-quickly) in a farce by Biestkens[37] deliberately offered his wares in broken French to passersby in The Hague. But for the great Dutch public the foreign melodies were then also given a Dutch text. Some of the most beloved—'Si c'est pour omn pucellage' (If 'tis for my maidenhood), or the Dutch 'O schoonste personagie' (O most beautiful figure)—did yeoman service for countless rhymes. They also sold rather well. 'Comic rhymes were most in demand,' Van de Venne[38] tells us in passing about the sales of seventeenth-century bookstores. The demand for verses was so great that it could make even street-selling by pedlars worthwhile, although this work may have seemed the last remedy of shiftless folk and wastrels, who had landed on rock-bottom and could not find any other way of earning a living. They could still

> Walk around with almanacs, ballads, and sometimes with 'What wonder! What news!': There are so many lazy scoundrels who earn their bread in that way.

In those words, 'What wonder! What news!' we hear the cries of the street-vendors, who wanted to persuade the public to buy the news, and thus sold not only ballads, but also pamphlets. After our excursion into the realm of rumour, we return to the question of who really were the readers of pamphlets: quite often these were indeed destined precisely and particularly for the common man. It seldom happened that pamphlet-writers directed themselves only to the political elite. The small group of regents[39] could easily manage common discussions with the help of copied documents. The printing press was seeking a larger public. Proclamations that temporarily limited freedom of the press during a political crisis always tell us that misleading information is so damaging for 'the uninformed and inexperienced people, and the common man', who might be excited to riot by lying propaganda. Seldom did matters get so far out of hand. But it is possible that fear of rebellion could have made the regents sensitive to the wishes of public

---

[36] French traveler (1595–1654).

[37] Nicolaes Biestkens, playwright.

[38] Adriaen van de Venne, painter and poet (1589–1662).

[39] Leading merchants who composed a town's governing patriciate.

opinion. Writings for and against can never entirely be suppressed, Aitzema[40] declared, not even in a monarchy. 'But the worst is, that the approval or rejection of the community easily becomes so strong that it carries away the state itself.'

'The worst,' Aitzema said. This is the typical aristocratic style of thinking found in the regent oligarchy of Holland. A government must be independent of public opinion. Don't ask what the people think of your policy. The perceptions of the public must not prevent the administration from doing its duty. The first statement by Jacob Cats, the second by Johan de Witt.[41] Both of them were Grand Pensionaries of Holland,[42] one a perfect instrument of stadholderly autocracy, the other the incarnation of Loevenstein regentdom.[43] But Cats and De Witt both believed that the aristocracy should not share its power with the people. That was always the feeling of the ruling party in the Republic. The party in power preferred to retain safe custody of its majority, and would be responsible only to itself. Only the minority party had any interest in using the press to bring about discussion of the policies of its political opponents. The chance was thus always great that the opposition would be better represented in every pamphlet war, because it took the initiative and wanted to keep the flames burning brightly. Consequently, the pamphlet as such is not an exact measure of public opinion. A discussion in the press primarily showed that the minority saw no chance of becoming the majority in the regent's colleges through its own means. The reactions must then show whether it had appraised its chances correctly, and whether it would succeed in mobilising public opinion so that resistance to the regents' policies would become too strong.

The classic example of such an action remains the conflict between Remonstrants[44] and Calvinists during the Twelve Years' Truce. Conditions were then so favourable that the organisers of the action achieved a complete success. For an exemplary treatment within the framework of this study, however, this pamphlet war is less suitable because of its enormous magnitude.... We shall therefore choose another conflict, which was not entirely separate from the one just mentioned: the discussion about war, peace and truce during the years 1607–9. The victory in this case went to the government.

[40]Lieuwe van Aitzema, seventeenth-century Dutch historian, author of *Affairs of State and War, in and about the United Netherlands.*

[41](1625–1672), Dutch statesman, leader of the republican party, and opponent of the party of the Prince of Orange.

[42]Originally, the pensionary was the chief legal officer of a town or province. In the seventeenth century, the Grand Pensionary was the chief executive officer of the province of Holland.

[43]In 1650 the stadholder (provincial governor) had seven opponents, including Johan de Witt, imprisoned in Loevenstein castle. The Loevenstein faction was the name for those in the regents' party who supported the prisoners.

[44]Dutch Calvinist group that denied Calvin's doctrine of predestination, believing instead that people can influence their own salvation.

The truce came to pass, despite all the militancy of the pamphleteering opponents. It is true that the pamphlet war did have long-term consequences insofar as it helped to raise the climate of suspicion around Oldenbarnevelt,[45] which eventually made his downfall possible.

A glance at the list of titles shows us quickly that the flood of pamphlets that burst out in 1607 was intended to change the peace policy of Holland. There is indeed 'the *farmers' litany, or complaints of the peasants of Kempen about the miseries of this everlasting Netherlandish war'*. But the peasants of Kempen were not subjects of the Republic. Northern Netherlandish productions seldom appear in the list of pleas for peace: the *Testament of the war* was printed a couple of times, and it had a successor in the *Codicil of the Netherlandish war*. In the battle for public opinion, however, perhaps the most striking pamphlet is a rhyming *Small poetic tract concerning the fruits of war and peace*. Here a peace propagandist had his say, one who recognised that the question was winning popular support. It was no longer necessary to convince the regents. His arguments had to be directed toward the common man: they were intended to restrain him from mass protests against the peace. That is why he made the war party consist of profiteers, who wanted to continue the struggle because they made such good profits from it.

> *One is* commisaris[46] *or* commis,[47] *and the other I think*
> *Has an office of more station;*
> *In time of peace they would sit in poverty!*
> *They could barely get their living;*
> *Now they drink from gold and silver vessels,*
> *Not knowing, from luxury, what to do and endeavour.*

This was a typical seventeenth-century manner of playing on popular sentiment: the author did not merely say that the rich were profiting from the war. The terrible thing was that men of low origins had now landed in the lap of luxury. These *nouveaux riches* were neither great businessmen nor war profiteers, but civil servants who were living handsomely on the public purse. Public opinion in this time was much more sensitive to official corruption than to commercial profiteering; it did not regard the big businessman as public enemy number one, but rather despised the selfish judge or administrator, particularly when he was of humble origin, and thus still had to make his fortune. That sort of person sought only his own profit, and would never care about the ordinary man.

> *Disturbers of the peace, very strong in their nature,*
> *They are the worst, their particular welfare,*

---

[45] Dutch statesman (1547–1619) who negotiated the Twelve Years' Truce. He clashed with the Prince of Orange's party and was executed.

[46] Commissioner.

[47] Clerk.

Which they gladly prefer to the common good.
Not giving a thought to the damage war causes,
For the poor community that we see declining.

Such reasoning was the stock in trade of popular pamphlets. They were less likely to seek their persuasive force in reasoned argument than in appeals to popular feeling. The war propagandists were no different. They certainly did not go into the true motives of the supporters and opponents, but preferred to answer with their own demagogy. Naturally there were fortunate exceptions. Several pamphlets, for example, tried to discuss the issue of peace or war as a question of conscience. Should not a Christian always choose in favour of peace? The very word sounds 'completely loving, friendly and Christian' to our ears. But even these writers do not make it very complicated. One simply says that a just war is better than 'a false and evil deceitful peace', without explaining himself further as to what a just war might be, and whether the struggle against Spain in the year 1607 would fall under that definition. Another refers to Luke 22:36, where Jesus advises the disciples to sell their cloaks and buy swords. Nor did John the Baptist condemn the warrior's craft. He did not impose on soldiers a duty to choose another profession. It was enough if they did no violence to anyone and were satisfied with their pay. Here too one can think that the author was quickly satisfied, and that the question did not really depend on the responsibility of the soldiers, but on the government that took those soldiers into its service. Yet it did at least make sense to ask such questions in a discussions among Christians about war and peace.

This theme seldom appears, however. Most authors argued on another level. The core of their thinking was mainly that Spaniards could never be trusted anywhere. Of course they were able to support the point with ample historical evidence, and the best of them placed special emphasis upon the testimony of the past. The supporters of the war, one of the pamphleteers said, 'have not merely dreamed and guessed, but have experienced examples of it themselves in living memory'. The examples did indeed exist, and the pamphlet war gave them their classical expression in the form of a school textbook which has remained famous, the *Mirror of Youth*. But one can frequently notice that the authors were more interested in a purposive use of historical facts than in an exact account. Let us listen for example to the opening words of the *Catechism of the peace negotiations*, stated in question and answer form:

Q. Is there a monarch?
A. Yes, there is someone who would gladly become one.
Q. What is his name?
A. Io, el Rey.
Q. What kind of animal is that?
A. What? It is a saint.
Q. In which calendar can one find his name?

A. In the Roman one.
Q. In what letters does his name appear?
A. In black letters.
Q. Is he then a saint without a holy day?
A. Not at all, because he does much more than ordinary saints.
Q. Hey, what then?
A. He even makes saints.
Q. In what almanac can one find their names written?
A. In those of this country.
Q. In what letters are they listed?
A. In red letters.

Here we are listening to the true voice of a popular pamphlet. It is not concerned with objective information, but with influence. Events are not weighed in the balance; they are not even mentioned. They are only used, and interpreted in a manner that stays outside the discussion, because the interpretation is completely fixed. Spaniards are domineering and cruel. They lust for the blood of all Netherlands Protestants. That is the way it always has been and always will be. Convicted before the bar of history, the Spanish king has no more right to appeal and Philip III[48] must be measured by the same standard as his late father Philip II.[49] But haven't the Spaniards changed? They are even offering peace now! Yes, indeed, but such an offer cannot be more sincere than these prophets of peace themselves. Striving for a peace or truce does not mean a change of purpose; it only means a change of tactics. The purpose remains the complete subjugation of the Netherlands and the introduction of the inquisition. Only the means are new. The story that we find in *Respectable Conversations between the Pope and the king of Spain, concerning the peace to be made with us,* achieved great success. In that pamphlet the king played merely a supporting part. He only asks all the stupid questions, while all the answers come from the Pope, who has hatched a devilish plan to bring a hopeless struggle to an unexpected good end. It is impossible to conquer the Netherlands, he states. Spain has no more money for the task, and Rome cannot get any, because the bishops and cardinals would rather keep it for themselves. And even if a military campaign succeeded in pressing the Hollanders hard, the French would certainly come to their aid. Continuing the war would thus serve no useful purpose in any case. Therefore Spain must offer peace. Spain must do it on the most advantageous conditions possible, so that the allies will strongly pressure the Republic to accept. The peace will actually cost the king nothing, because he will not keep his promise. The Pope will grant him absolution in advance for the sin of breaking his word. Once the heretics have been lulled to sleep, 'then we shall come upon them unsuspected, attack them, destroy them, and uproot them from the earth, so that no memory of them remains'.

[48] King of Spain, 1598–1621.
[49] King of Spain, 1559–1598.

This pamphlet clearly shows the somewhat suspect contents of many works written to inform the public. It chooses as its starting point the bad faith of the opponent. This was no coincidental misfortune of wartime progaganda, for precisely the same tactic was used in the religious disputes of the Twelve Years' Truce. Then too the mutual casting of suspicion often took the place of pertinent argument. If the opponent cannot be trusted anyway, one need not take the trouble to refute his arguments. So it went in the debate over the truce. A discussion with the supporters of the peace was useless, because they were unable to see the cardinal fact of Spanish duplicity. They were too stupid to see through that falseness, or perhaps they had also been brought by Spanish gold. Spain saw no chance of conquering the Netherlands, we are told by the *True and short story of the great ambition and cruel tyranny of the king of Spain*. Thus the king had received advice 'that he should annually spend two or three hundred thousand guilders[50] in treasure on the pensionaries'. With this sentence the pamphlet ends. The writer was careful enough not to state that Spain actually paid any pensionaries, to say nothing of mentioning names. But he had done enough to set the reader thinking.

The power of Spanish gold was indeed a favourite theme of these writers. The Spaniard leaned on his golden stick, the Indies. Using this stick he could alternately strike or fondle his neighbours so adroitly that everyone would bow to his wishes. Only one person had always remained resistant to this treatment: 'the rarest thing that I ever heard or saw, is that *seignor* [the Spaniard] never knew how to deal with the Dutchman called Sailor'. Sailor had even firmly seized the stick at the eastern end, and now threatened to wrest it away from Spain. The message of this author is clear enough. Sailor could win the war by his own force, and would then acquire the golden stick for himself. As the booty promised to be his prize, could the prophets of peace in Holland honestly mean what they said? Surely they could not offer Sailor anything better?

In this manner the political information in the pamphlets could have poisonous effects, and be much more dangerous than the typical popular book despised by more enlightened spirits. Yet no serious measures were taken against either genre. A prohibition against printing or selling certain pamphlets always remained casual, and was loosely observed. In the Netherlands the rule was simply that everyone could say and write what he pleased, judged the Frenchman Charles Ogier. This fitted in well with the economic policy of the regents of Holland, who did not gladly restrict the free sale of goods if there was any chance of making a profit on them. An English prohibition against the import of books, enacted on the eve of the civil war, raised an official protest from the States-General.[51]

[50]Silver coins dating from 1601, each worth twenty-eight stuivers (stivers).

[51]Central governing body for the provinces of the Netherlands. Controlled by a merchant oligarchy, its power was limited because all provinces had to agree on policies.

One simply had to accept that not all printed matter was of superior quality. Pamphlets could slander, deceive and indoctrinate with shameless lack of sensitivity for the interests of others. The virtues of modern mass-media, but no less their vices also, were already present in seventeenth-century pamphlet literature. Then too the dregs often remained in the bottom of the sieve of news-distribution. The titles of many pamphlets still cry out to us: *Horrible murder happened at Delft! Pitiful fire at Wilda! Amazing haunting at Brussels!* Come and read how three students in Kloppenburg raped two girls and murdered four! See how sixty-four witches killed more than a thousand people and six thousand animals! Son murders his mother and father! Innocent girl beheaded at Steenwijk!

When a new pamphlet appeared three years later about a young daughter at Vlissingen, who met her end in the same sad way, the question does arise whether a clever businessman simply reheated the old stew in a new pot. Sometimes indeed the actual event was so minor, and described so broadly on the title-page, that the publisher simply mixed some leftovers with the main course: 'here is added a case of haunting, which happened earlier at Rotterdam, by which a great murder was caused'. The printer of the sentence against Claes Jeroensz.—'for the abominable crimes and incest done by him'—had so little to report besides the actual sentence that he brought up one murder case after another, in a general commentary on the wickedness of the times.

The wickedness of the times, indeed . . . because the exploiters of sensationalism generally justified themselves with unctuous moralising conclusions. 'This is, dear reader, short but true, what we have wanted to tell you about these two so gruesome murders. Hoping that such will serve as an example for everyone to guard against similar things.' Anyone who had a desire to commit murder, should murder his desires. The three boys from Danzig, robbers and murderers who had endangered the city and surrounding area for seven years, were specially cited to parents as a warning. 'Will you discipline your children when the twig is still green? Because once they begin to wither, it's too late.' Then perhaps it was best to let the children themselves read these pamphlets as lessons in life, just as the reporter of the murder at Heusden in 1609 urged them to buy and read:

Buy me, famous youth
[You'll find] in me the murder is so explained,
[That] I am always well worth the money.

Thus far everything was for consumption. The people read what they received. The lower class did, however, also have its own group of producers, in the chambers of rhetoric or drama companies. Every city had at least one such company, and often there were more. In the villages, particularly in what is now South Holland, this form of active recreation enjoyed great popularity. In Bergsenhoek, Overschie and Bleiswijk; in Ooltgensplaat, Zwartewaal and Goeree; in Kethel, De Lier and Scheveningen; in Hazerswoude, Stompwijk, or Katwijk aan de Rijn—wherever one went, the dramatists were to be found. Their prize questions and performances attracted the attention of hundreds of interested folk. On festive days for the theatre, such as the celebration of the raising of the siege of Leiden, it was possible to rent balconies and windows for then-fabulous sums, even as much as eighteen gulden—the monthly income of a craftsman. But he could not work then anyway, because in a village in Holland an extended fest would stop all work completely:

> *Who can still think of haying and threshing and milking,*
> *When it's the annual feast of the dramatists in these parts?*

In these colourful popular festivals, the dramatists themselves found a re-ward for their lengthy efforts. Their ambitions, however, extended some-what further than performing highly coloured spectacles as occasions for public enjoyment. The chamber of Kethel, for example, pretended to find its origin in the circumstance, 'that the youth within the village and sur-rounding area of Kethel had little or no exercise directed toward any good works or edification'. Their purpose, as they themselves described it, was spiritual education of youth in the broadest sense of the word. Besides the occasional Bible-study groups under church supervision, the chambers of rhetoric were indeed the only organisations that could be compared to pre-sent-day church or secular youth-clubs. This purpose was often expressed in ambitious programmes. The seventeenth-century rhetoricians upheld old traditions from the time of the Reformation by setting prize questions and performing plays that treated current religious problems. While the general public attended their performances for the sake of the farce that was offered as an encore, the chambers strove to reach as high as possible:

> *What they show is all taken from scripture and antiquity:*
> *One might just as well go to school or to church.*

Disheartened spectators who expressed their disappointment in this fash-ion did not, however, represent the feelings of preachers and church coun-cils. The provincial synod of South Holland had noted in 1592 that the Leiden players wanted to present a biblical message on the stage. Far from rejoicing, they brought the dramatists under their watchful eye, 'since their profession was not to speak God's word to the people'. Aggravation in-stead of edification would be the unavoidable result. Thereby the chief objection to such plays was stated. Anyone who would publicly expound and explain the Bible must have a calling from God, and the church must have confirmed this calling. The rhetoricians had received nothing by which they could legitimate themselves as exponents of the scriptures: their Bible plays were a form of false prophecy. Moreover, the players did not shy away from representing sacred things, as if it did not go be-yond human theatrical skill to appear on stage in the form of Jesus Christ or even God the Father. Thus in 1605 the Southland players performed the conversion of Paul, whereby the central character baptised several fellow players on stage. In the same village the company had once played the parable of the rich fool, 'in which one [actor] portrayed the person of God our Heavenly Father'. At Oude Tonge a player had taken on the role of Christ, and had himself baptised by the prophet John the Baptist.

That the church most strongly opposed precisely these plays must have given the rhetoricians the feeling that their noble intentions were misunderstood. Thus it may have been out of pure peevishness that in 1606 the chamber of De Lier 'played a very scandalous piece, full of blasphemies against Christ and the teachings of the truth, to the praise of its so-called rhetoric, to the slander of preachers and godly persons'. It was certainly not prudent to express feelings of rancour in this way. The *classis*[52] of Delft brought the case forthwith to the Deputised Councils and the Court of Holland, and these governing institutions generally showed themselves very sympathetic to objections from the church, as long as the matter involved nothing more than rhetoricians. Only a few chambers were so fortunate as the Corenbloem (Cornflower) of The Hague, which enjoyed subsidies from the magistrate for its performances. Much more often it happened that church and government worked hand in glove to fight the rhetoricians, in principle for the same reasons. Thus the Deputised Councils of Holland prohibited a performance at Maassluis at Easter in 1621, 'because we understand that the said days and all feast days should be employed only to serve the Lord God with thanks and praise, and not spent in lewdness, levity and profanation of the same'. In 1608 the Court of Holland prevented plays at Zoetermeer and Zegwaard because 'such plays are mostly directed toward misuse of God's Word, and scandalous abuse of the government of the country'. Naturally the last-mentioned motive carried a great deal of weight with the magistrates. Had not the chamber of Maasland at the *kermis*[53] of 1605 staged a play 'which was condemned not only for offence to mortality, but also for harm to the common good of the country'? And had not the demand for this play been so great that shortly afterwards it was performed in Nootdorp as well?

No effective prohibition of all rhetoricians' plays was ever enforced, although there were sometimes general proclamations issued against 'public plays of rhetoric, whether they be interludes, burlesque plays or others'. But to all appearances the public was too strongly attached to this form of amusement: thus restrictions were limited to casual injunctions, or warnings that under no circumstances was the stage to 'introduce the acts of kings and princes'. Indeed the government would certainly not encourage the formation of new chambers, because they caused nothing but aggrava-

---

[52]The presbytery, the organization of pastors and elders responsible for governing the local churches.

[53]Fair.

tion and scandal anyway—according to the official answer given in 1603 to 'some young villagers and other persons ill-disposed to the common good' at Voorschoten. Nevertheless, their evil intentions appear to have received approval, because twelve years later a chamber did exist in the village.

The reformed church thankfully received support from the government, but on its own it went somewhat further. Donteclock,[54] preaching from the pulpit in Delft in 1582, had already branded the rhetoricians' activities as one of the foremost sins for which the United Netherlands were being punished; yet he was not stricter than the overwhelming majority of his colleagues. In 1606 the *classis* of Leiden considered the question of whether a known rhetorician, who after having shown repentance now again wanted to participate in plays, should also be allowed to take communion. The meeting decided that the man would have to choose between the stage and the sacrament. Participation by church members in a chamber of rhetoric was almost entirely ruled out. The shoemaker of Delft in 1578 who tried the combination by becoming emperor of the rhetoricians while maintaining his membership in the church was presented with the same choice—and two years later he decided to leave the religious community. The rector of Naaldwijk, who had translated a piece for the rhetoricians, 'a dishonest comedy of Terence',[55] no less, was only readmitted to the communion after a confession of guilt. The tailor Cornelis Jansz. at Kethel also got into difficulties with the church council in 1606, when he had accepted an order from the chamber of rhetoric and prepared the costumes for the players who would participate in the Haarlem regional drama festival. And naturally it was quite logical that the church council of Schipluiden should also take action against those who had attended even one performance, and thus tasted the forbidden fruit.

Thus here too church and state had their concerns about popular culture. It may appear that the ordinary Hollander must have seen these two institutions as his opponents, who time and again wanted to prevent him from realising his heart's desires. . . .

[54]Regnerus Donteclock, preacher and author, d.1627.
[55]Publius Terentius Afer (c.190–159 B.C.), Roman comic poet.

Guilds

MACK WALKER

The guild, an economic and social association of practitioners of a specific craft or trade, was a prominent and characteristic feature of medieval and early modern urban life. Guilds regulated the quality and output of goods and limited competition in order to maintain prices and so guarantee guild members a secure living. Additionally, guilds offered a social life and took care of their members and of their widows and children. Traditionally, historians have argued that guilds decayed in the early modern period, weakened by capitalism and state centralization, until the Industrial Revolution finally swept them away. Recently, however, historians have reexamined guilds and have come to believe that they continued to exercise significant social and economic functions even as late as the eighteenth century. Mack Walker examines the guilds in the eighteenth-century German home towns (those towns, with a population no greater than ten to fifteen thousand, that were relatively independent of outside authority and that, unlike larger cities, did not have a patrician class). He finds the guilds to have been active, powerful, and cohesive.

The selection opens with an account of a tinsmith's attempt to force his guild to approve his marriage, which the guild considered indecent. Why was the guild steadfast in its refusal to recognize the marriage? The guild, after all, fought the marriage for many years and ostracized the offending tinsmith, probably for as long as he lived. Why did guilds pay so much attention to the personal lives of their members, going even so far as to investigate the legitimacy of grandparents? What was guild morality? How did guild moralism define and defend the community?

To become a master in a guild, one had first to become an apprentice and then a journeyman. Exactly how did a man successfully pass through those stages? Why did so many fail to attain the coveted status of master? Why were guilds so suspicious of those from outside the town? Masters had both obligations and privileges: their widows and children likewise had certain rights. Here the economic and social functions of the guild came together, as the guild performed roles later taken over by modern governments. Why did the guilds become so much more important in the eighteenth century than they had been earlier?

The tinsmith Flegel, citizen of Hildesheim, was in love, and he wished to marry. That he should marry was in itself seemly, for the proper pursuit of his trade required a solid domestic establishment supporting and surrounding the workshop: a wife to help out and meet customers, and to provide relatives; a decent home for apprentices and a gentling influence on journeymen; an assurance of Flegel's own diligence and reliability as a valuable member of the community. The trouble was that Flegel had set his heart, not wisely but too well, on the daughter of a fellow citizen named Helmsen; and when he went to register his intention to marry with the tinsmith's guild he was barred from doing so on grounds of indecency. The prospective bride's father—not she herself—had been born out of wedlock and then subsequently legitimized.... Helmsen's legitimacy was recognized by the territorial law of the Bishopric of Hildesheim, in which the community was located, but that did not make him legitimate in the eyes of the Hildesheim guildsmen. Indeed the citizen status of the sometime bastard Helmsen suggests that outside influence had forced him on the community, ensuring the unending rancor of the real Hildesheimer. The guild constitution, to which Flegel had subscribed, provided that wife as well as master must show proof of four irreproachable grandparents; and inasmuch as a master's children were automatically eligible for guild acceptance and support, Flegel's determination to marry the Helmsen girl demanded of the tinsmiths that they sponsor the grandchildren of a bastard before the community.

Flegel had become engaged in 1742. Eleven years before, in 1731, an imperial edict had appeared which provided, among other things, that legitimacy established by "the authorities" should be recognized as valid by the guilds. Accordingly Flegel appealed to the Hildesheim Town Council against the guild decision, citing the imperial decree. But who were the authorities in Hildesheim? The important guilds of the town were directly and constitutionally involved in town government, ostensibly as representative of the citizenry: the *Ämter*[1] of the butchers, the bakers, the shoemakers, the tanners, and the *Gilden*[2] of the tailors, the smiths, the wool weavers, the retailers, and the furriers. Moreover the first four, the *Ämter*, had a special relation with the bishop which they used as leverage against the Council when they felt need of it. The Council therefore... turned the case over to its committee for artisans' affairs; and there nothing was decided. After a year, Flegel took the extraordinary step of marrying Fräulein Helmsen anyway, in a ceremony held somewhere outside Hildesheim. When the guildsmen heard of it they were enraged: never before, they said, had a Hildesheim master artisan thus defied his guild's jurisdiction in marital matters. For Flegel to get away with it would violate one of the most important sanctions the guild had for controlling the composition and the behavior of its membership. And it would make the Hildesheim tinsmiths look bad, and with them all the other Hildesheimer. The guild excluded Flegel from its meetings and functions, and it goes without saying that it imposed economic and social boycott against him, master tinsmith though he was.

For three years, Flegel appeared repeatedly before the Town Council asking that the imperial decree be enforced in his favor; repeatedly he was

---

[1]Councils.
[2]Guilds.

turned away. In 1745 he appealed to the episcopal government, declaring that the guilds in their defiance of the law sought only after their own "gloire."[3] Also, inasmuch as they were represented in the town government and thus in the highest town court, they were acting in their own case against him. Here he was entering on dangerous ground, for if the guild-influenced town government indeed constituted "the authorities" with the right to establish legitimacy, then his case was lost. But locally it was lost anyway, and his appeal to the bishop invited the episcopal government to assert that they, not the Town Council, were "the authorities" in Hildesheim. The bishopric demanded that the Council issue formal judgment; but the Council, caught between state on one side and guilds on the other, found a temporary way out in a request for an opinion from the faculty of law at the University of Halle: Was the requirement of four legitimate grandparents legal? Was Helmsen legitimate (as book law said) or not (as the Hildesheimer said)? The Halle professors decided for Flegel and against the guilds, and the Council announced that decision. The smiths thereupon countered with the argument that the Halle faculty was not learned in Hildesheim local law and circumstance: community law breaks book law. Flegel was not reinstated nor his wife recognized. In 1747, five years after his marriage, he asked the Council to enforce the Halle decision; the Council issued the order, but nothing else happened. The Council then urged all concerned to try "good will" as a means to solution, and still nothing happened; but finally the bishopric ordered enforcement within two weeks. The Council summoned a meeting of the guild to admit Flegel, fearing military intervention by the bishop, but the hall remained empty; not a single master tinsmith appeared. Finally the Council ordered the guild to readmit Flegel and acknowledge the validity of his marriage lest episcopal soldiers and bureaucrats put an end to the privileges and autonomies of Hildesheim. The guild officers all resigned, and then there was nobody for the law to talk to.

Probably that is enough about the tinsmith Flegel. Eventually he was formally readmitted and his marriage registered, but that did not settle the case; after dragging on for several more years it disappeared into the episcopal courts. It is safe to say that Flegel never found a peaceable life in Hildesheim, for he had defied the procedures upon which community peace was founded. . . . Defense of their honor against incursions like Flegel's was nothing new to the citizen-guildsmen of Hildesheim: they had defended it before against a master shoemaker who wanted to marry a piper's daughter, against a tailor who turned out to have a wet nurse for a mother, and against a smith who tried to register a miller's daughter as his wife. The social prudery and political stubbornness of the Hildesheim guilds were part of the character of every hometown community, and a role of guild organization was to lock those characteristics institutionally into the community as a whole. "For their functions," wrote Wolfram Fischer [*Handwerksrecht und Handwerkswirtschaft um 1800* (Berlin, 1955), 15], "extended far beyond the economic, and their

[3]Glory.

legal status placed them as integrating constituents of the political and social order of the old Empire. Only when we start with the social location of the guild and bring all its functions into consideration do we see the true role of the economic in the guild system." That "social location" was the home town; only there—not in the city and surely not the countryside—could the guilds assume so broad a role and still remain basically economic institutions. Only in the context of the home town is it comprehensible how the time of the notorious "decay" of the early modern German trades guilds should have been the period probably of their greatest power to impress their values and goals upon the society of which they were components.

To begin to describe them it is useful to separate out the several ways in which the hometown guilds entered into community life: economic regulation, political organization and representation, and guardianship of social or domestic standards.... As occupational groupings within the community— of butchers, shoemakers, carpenters, and the rest—guilds supervised the recruitment, training, and allocation of individual citizens into the community's economy, and their economic character placed its stamp upon hometown morality and the nature of citizenship itself. As primary political organizers of the citizenry..., they bore political and civic factors into economic practice and moral standards. And finally as moral and social watchdogs they saw to the quality of the citizenry—the *Ehre*, the honor, of the hometown workman and Bürger.[4]

Still in the exercise of all these linked functions they worked as economic media; their special influence on the community and its membership rested ultimately on that role....

The hometown guild artisan ordinarily sold his own products, on the same premises where he produced them; or he performed skilled services within the specifically defined limits of the community. The customs and statutes that governed his training and regulated his activities were quite similar from one place to another.... Craft guild rules which assumed a local but diversified economy set him apart from the merchant guildsmen of the cities (although some small towns had retailers' guilds entitled to sell certain imported goods locally), and set him apart also from the state-licensed or unorganized rural artisan. The rules were usually set down in written articles, statutes or charters prepared by each guild and confirmed or tolerated by some authority, much as the statutes of the towns themselves.... [U]sually confirmation came at the instance of the guild from the local magistracy or a local court. The guild's formal authority rested on that confirmed or acknowledged statute, which outlined its training program, the regulations governing the exercise of the trade, its powers to elect and to limit membership, the specific economic activity over which guild members held local monopoly..., and the geographical area... within which the monopoly prevailed.... [R]ules to implement training programs were used to serve

---

[4]Citizen, townsman.

the economic and familial interests of the guildsmen, by holding down membership and excluding outsiders; conversely the economic interests of the trade were subject to pressure upon the guildsmen as members of the community to see to the useful education and social incorporation of the citizenry....

Guild statutes often set forth rules of guild life in remarkable detail, although of course much guild activity took place informally and unrecorded ...and in conjunction with the cousins and brothers on the town councils and in the other trades.... In the countryside, in professionally governed or mercantile cities like Hamburg and Nürnberg, and in the Prussian centralized country, incorporated craft guilds either did not exist or their structure was used as the channel for government regulation of the economy. But craft guilds within the hometown communities could not be reached by that kind of legislation or control because the civic community of uncles and brothers lay between, and because the guilds themselves were part of the communal system of authority.

A guild's affairs were administered by a collegial body of from two to four Overmasters...chosen by a process incorporating both the will of the membership and the choice of the civic authorities.... The Overmasters decided internal conflicts, spelled out rules, levied fines and imposed minor punishments, administered guild finances and properties, saw to the inspection of masterworks prepared by candidates for mastership (though this might be done by a specially appointed inspector), and generally represented the interests of the trade, within the community and to the outside if need be. A guild court composed or dominated by these officials could expel any member who did not accept its decisions, and thus foreclose his practice of the trade; and frequently such a court punished members for civil or criminal misdeeds like theft or adultery, on the grounds (if anybody asked) that the transgression had brought the trade into disrepute, so that the trade must punish the offender to clear its name....

The Overmasters were custodians of the Guild Chest,... repository of its official documents and secrets, ceremonially opened on the occasion of meetings of the membership. Plenary meetings... were supposed to be held regularly—quarterly as a rule—but extraordinary meetings might be called to consider special problems, like a serious infraction of the rules by one of the members or some action by the authorities or by another trade that threatened the interests of the guild....

The several aspects of guild life converged on the master's estate, as citizen, head of household, and independent craftsman. The process of selection and induction began with apprenticeship. Active masters were expected to undertake the training of the sons of fellow townsmen as apprentices; apprentices were required to be Christians of honorable estate and parentage. After a trial period of a few weeks in a master's shop, petition was made to the Overmasters for formal registration of the apprentice with the guild; if his birth was properly certified and his other credentials met conditions set by the guild, he was admitted upon payment of a registration fee . . . to the guild and a training fee . . . to the master. . . . The apprentice was bound to serve the master loyally for a stated period, some three or four years, during which time the master for his part was obliged to give the apprentice real training and practice in the trade—not just use him as an errand boy—and a decent place in his domestic establishment. Now: often the sons of masters within the guild were forgiven the fees, or paid reduced fees, or were excused from apprenticeship altogether, or signed in and out on the same day without the regular period of training. The grounds were . . . that a boy already knew what went on in his father's trade as well as an ordinary apprentice from another trade was expected to learn it; but it amounted to group favoritism and encouraged inbreeding within the trades. . . .

When the apprenticeship was done the young man paid another round of fees, usually underwent some convivial hazing, and thus was promoted to journeyman. The journeyman was presumed to have learned the basic skills of his trade, but he was not yet ready to carry it on independently. First he was to go on a round of travels, working at a wage for other masters in other places, and getting the behavior of late adolescence out of his system, away from home but still free of the responsibilities and encumbrances of a domestic establishment of his own. His training and good reputation were certified by the guild in which he had served his apprenticeship, so that the guild, its reputation at stake, was careful with the certification; similarly the journeyman relied on the good name of his home guild (or absence of a bad name) for his acceptance abroad. . . .

When a journeyman arrived at a new town he went to the journeymen's hostel sponsored by his trade there, and applied to the host . . . for work. The host directed him to a local master looking for help if there was one; if no work could be found within a stipulated short period, probably no more than a day and a night, the journeyman was sent on his way with the help of a small grant from the guild treasury. . . . If he stayed in town without work he was treated as a vagrant, for that is what he was; strange unemployed journeymen meant beggars and thieves to the home town.

There at the hostel he ordinarily lived, while he was locally employed; and his papers were deposited in the guild chest controlled by the Overmasters. Only a master or a master's widow in his learned trade could legitimately employ him: if he valued his prospects as master and Bürger he would not enter the service of a noble, nor of the state, nor work at a factory, nor go as a soldier or a servant. After a given minimum term of employment in one place the journeyman might leave to resume his wandering, or be dismissed by his employer, when proper notice was given and the piece he was working on was finished. . . . His papers were endorsed by the local guild to show that he had worked there, and how he had behaved. . . .

. . . [T]wo or more years of attested wandering was a customary condition for application for mastership. Far and away the best place for a journeyman to apply for mastership—barring a palatable widow or orphan—was in his home town, so there he usually returned when his wanderyears were done. His application was filed with the Overmasters of the guild to which he sought entry, and after their evaluation it was laid before the assembled masters and usually before the civil authorities as well. He had to provide certification of apprentice training that the local masters would accept, proof of his travels to proper places and of proper behavior when he was there, and of course above all he had again to prove legitimate ancestry. All of these conditions were more easily met by a local boy, unless there was something wrong with him, than by an outsider.

The examination of all these qualifications offered plenty of opportunities to exclude the candidate if the masters so chose, and if they could exclude him without offending colleagues, relatives, neighbors, and customers. Yet another hurdle was the masterwork, an exhibition of the candidate's skill prepared in the place where he applied. ... It was easy to assign a difficult piece of work or an expensive one, and then if need be still to reject it in the name of the guild's high standards: where, young man, did you learn to make things *that* way? If the trade was over-filled ... then the candidate might be rejected on that ground, or told to wait; and there was no guarantee that he might not later be bypassed for a more recent candidate who found greater favor. Another economic condition was that the candidate must prove he had the resources to establish his shop and assume the burdens of citizen and family head, some combination of tools and cash, perhaps; and often he was obliged to commit himself to the community by building or buying a house. Guilds commonly denied mastership to any bachelor, a practice that not only enjoined domestic commitment but helped the marital prospects of guild widow and orphan, not to mention unplaced daughters of the community as a whole: thus marriage ordinarily coincided with admission to mastership. ...

The stranger upon whom these conditions were imposed was a stranger no more by the time he had fulfilled them all: proof of family background and domestic intent, locally produced masterwork, material resources in the town and a place in its economy, and time to learn about the community and for the community to learn about him. Familiarity and community acceptance was the real purpose of it all. That is why waiving the rules for local boys of respectable family made perfect sense to the hometownsmen, though to anyone from outside the home town, to anyone who thought of guilds purely as economic instruments, the communal working of the system smelled—and still does—of corruption, decadence, and economic malfunction.

The new master now shared in the local guild monopoly and agreed to abide by its rules. The guild monopoly made good economic sense within the community insofar as it maintained an appropriate balance and relation in and among the trades without exposing any citizen to ruinous competition, and assured that only skilled and responsible practitioners would pursue each of them. It was, to be sure, a system of mutual defense by guildsmen-citizens. But any guild that showed itself so restrictive as seriously to undersupply the local economy..., or to exclude citizens' sons without economic justification, incurred community pressure to erase entries into the trade, and it invited breaches of its monopoly which the community and its authorities would consider justified. If a trade grew very rich, it would attract sons of influential families who could not easily be excluded by numerical limitations. The hometown guild monopolies were enforcements of the rules whereby the community kept its soundness and autonomy, directed first of all against outsiders but also against any citizen who failed to go along with the rules.

Outside trespassers were mainly non-masters who produced or sold articles within the area where the guild claimed monopoly.... A glover who made a wallet might have his windows knocked out by the bag-makers, and then a carpenter be hazed by the glaziers for repairing them. The boundaries between respective trade monopolies made for endless controversy when they were not clearly understood in local custom and abided by. Within the trade, a master was punished by his guild or suspended if he stole customers from his colleagues, sold from door to door instead of working and waiting in his shop, cut prices or departed from standard materials and method, hired too many journeymen, or otherwise introduced disturbing elements of competition and conflict within the trade. The aforesaid tailor even if he was licensed might be using an improper stitch or improper cloth in his attic; or worse yet, he might try to sell clothes ready-made for pay by somebody outside the town....

Only a master might take on apprentices and journeymen, and even he only so many, and only so often, as the guild allowed: the rules differing among trades and places but usually on the order of one apprentice at a time and no more than two journeymen. Masters' widows had important status and rights within the guild (recall the insistence on respectable backgrounds for wives), and the guild had a responsibility for their welfare. A widow could continue the operation of her husband's shop; if she had no journeyman she could demand one from one of the masters; if she married a journeyman of the same trade he was made master promptly, cheaply, and free of limitations on membership because she was already one of the admitted number. She did not attend meetings or vote, for there was no place for women there, nor could she take on an apprentice; but she was freed of most guild obligations and fees. A master's blood son usually enjoyed, along with the special dispensations of fees and training, a presumptive right by birth to enter his father's guild. A master's daughter possessed in a latent way much the same rights, transferring them with marriage to a journeyman of the same trade as her father and working in his shop, so that the journeyman became in effect a son; if she was orphaned those guild rights were her main inheritance. The social and familial appurtenances of mastership were very important, where there was no life insurance and no state social security system; but they pertained only within the familiar home community; nobody recognized them anywhere else. . . .

The structure and working sphere of the guilds show the place of economic institutions in hometown life. There is no doubt that the guild system was unsuited to economic growth and social mobility. . . . But that was the obverse of the guild's vital function in communal society and politics. Their close oversight of membership and their social and moral restrictiveness, their preservation of economic security for citizen-members: the very practices that made them such valuable and effective components of the community are what historians and others have meant by the decay or the decline of the early modern German guild. What appears as decadence by general economic standards was really the absorption, into these economic structures, of the important social and political functions they had in the stable communities of postmedieval and preindustrial Germany. . . . [T]he guild assumed the character described in this chapter sometime around the seventeenth century. . . . The guilds of the economically livelier medieval towns apparently did not behave that way. . . . There the guild seems to have functioned as a system of economic regulation and training, and indeed as a frame for political action, but without the character of social exclusiveness, communal integration, and the enforcement of morals that it has in this story. It may be that the isolation and stability (stagnancy) of the later hometown economies is what made the difference, compared with the flourishing medieval towns. . . . If so, that would be to say that the guild system, like any other economic system, worked more freely and more flexibly at times of economic vigor and expansion than at times of weakness and contraction. Yet it may remain a distinctive characteristic of the communal guild system that it responded to the pressure of bad times or of change by shrinking into conservative exclusiveness, rather than by the adaptation or renovation that might be expected of freely individualistic or of state-controlled economic systems. That characteristic came to matter a great deal.

In histories of the early modern German trade guild an inconsistency crops up that is very like the one that appears in the histories of the towns themselves. "Decadence," though agreed upon, takes two contrary forms. On the one hand guild decline appears as degeneration at the hands of the absolutist state which, by converting guilds into its own economic instruments or undercutting their powers, robbed them of their truer older functions; on the other hand guild decline is shown in stubborn, selfish behavior *contrary* to the interests of the whole population and the state, defying the common welfare and the public economy the state sought to further. . . . [T]he period of guild decline was precisely that at which guilds were best able to defy state or public policy broadly conceived. . . .

[T]he hometown guild was formed and stabilized in the quieter times that followed the wars of religion and empire; it was post-Westphalia.[5] . . .

---

[5]The Peace of Westphalia in 1648 ended the Thirty Years' War.

The extremes and the eccentricities of guild moralism remain puzzling. . . . One explanation is that the notion of honorable status, of *Ehrbarkeit*, with which they were intensely concerned, was so broad and vague a slogan that it provided no reasonable or functional limits. . . . Its imprecise character led the guildsmen into absurdities of prurience and persecution when they tried to judge and act upon it. There was no check on their eagerness to show their own morality by the severity with which they judged others.

The main preoccupation with legitimacy of birth, which extended by easy stages into questions of sexual behavior and social background, had a reasonable foundation in the domestic character of community and economy: the importance of knowing who somebody was, and the soundness of his family circumstances. The guild encompassed the citizen-master's life, not just his occupation. His family was part of his occupation and his guild; his widow and his orphans were cared for by it and his sons were specially privileged within it. . . . *Ehrbarkeit* meant domestic, civic, and economic orderliness and these were undermined by the promiscuity and irresponsibility implied by illegitimate birth. Legitimate childbirth resulted from sober and responsible intention to have a child, whose conception bore the community's sanction; illegitimacy implied the contrary. . . .

It might be argued that moral sanctions were directed less against loose sexual behavior as such than at its social consequences: the foisting upon the community of persons with uncertain origins and uncertain qualifications for membership. The hometownsman's pride was closely involved in the guild's quest for purity. More mobile elements of German society were held by hometownsmen to be sexually and maritally promiscuous, so that sexual and marital purity were a caste mark that guildsmen-citizens employed to set themselves apart. It was important to be different from lower elements especially, from the rooting peasantry with its servile origins and style. Then there were the merchants and peddlers, traveling salesmen of their day, trying like cuckoos to pass off their bastards into the artisanry; and loose-living aristocrats had to be watched for that too. . . .

No doubt the guilds used ostensibly moral grounds to exclude persons held undesirable for reasons not strictly moral—not directly concerned with sex or marriage, that is, but exclusion for economic or civic reasons. . . . Put moralism for the sake of exclusion together with sexual purity as the hometownsman's mark of caste, and guild moralism becomes a specific instrument for excluding unwanted social elements from the community, and as such its use was stretched to the borders of credibility. It helped screen out unwanted outsiders, regardless of social estate, because it was so much harder for them than for natives to prove honorable family background. In other moral questions too, not only did the outsider have little evidence to offer for himself, his very arrival at the gates made him suspect of having become *persona non grata* elsewhere, and chances are he had. Why hadn't he applied in his own home town, where people knew him? ...

The taint of illegitimacy lasted for generations; the same was true of other dishonorable estates. The list of dishonorable occupations ... is almost without limit because each guild and each place had to show itself more discriminating than the rest, and no one could dissent from any instance without jeopardizing his own honor. Hangmen first of all: the usual taboo of the executioner, but hometown hangmen got a lot of other disgraceful work as well: clearing carrion, burying rotten fish. ... Skinners worked with dead bodies too. ... The line between what skinners did with carcasses and what butchers and tanners did with meat and hides was elaborately guarded, but not well enough to keep the tanners free of taint. Barbers and surgeons worked with wounds, a disgusting and servile business. So did bathers, and doubtless besides there were promiscuous goings-on at the baths. The lofts of mills were morally suspect too, and millers swindling middlemen and speculators to boot. Shepherds were contemptible everywhere. What kind of a man would be a shepherd? They skinned dead sheep ... , and the same stories about a shepherd's relations with his sheep seem to have been told that I heard in New England as a boy. The weaving of linen was another primitive occupation, and like shepherding had suspect rural overtones and connections. Musicians and players moved from place to place, like itinerant peddlers and beggars. And officials of the state: their sons were adjudged dishonorable by the guildsmen. ... It was a mark of dishonor to have worked as a peasant, or for a noble, or in a factory. ...

Guild morality equated the outsider with dishonor; those two factors of repulsion multiplied together to produce guild moralism's intensity and its righteousness. It is important to note here that guilds, economic institutions, bore this spirit in the hometown community. The fervid moral preoccupation of the guilds, like their social and economic restrictiveness, seems mainly to have developed in the seventeenth and eighteenth centuries. There had been dishonorable occupations for long before that ... , but little sign that moral fervor had been an important part of guild life. It was a part of the multiplication of their role beyond the custody of economic standards and training. That role was multiplied by the maintenance of social continuity and stability, and that by the guardianship of civic standards, and finally all united into morality in the sense of personal justification, of the kind traditionally in the hands of religious institutions—*moral* morality, the morality of conscience. The curious stock expression, "The guilds must be as pure, as if they had been gathered together by doves," seems to have originated in the seventeenth century. It may be that in the background of the early modern German craft guild's moral guardianship was the weakening and dispersal of religious institutions after the wars of religion: institutions perhaps with more experience and discrimination in moral questions than the home town. Civic authority had taken up moral custody first: not only state laws but seventeenth-century town statutes were full of religious and moral exhortations. But these had nearly disappeared by the mid-eighteenth century. And when the guild assumed the moral role, it adapted moral questions, unsurprisingly, to its economic structure and interests and to its place in the civic community. The guild, first habitat of the hometown Bürger, blended economic and civic and personal standards together into the moral quality of honor, in such a way that a man's personal morals—and his ancestors'—determined his economic competence and his civic rights; at the same time economic competence was prerequisite for civic and moral acceptance; and at the same time responsible civic membership was requisite for economic rights and personal justification. Such a combination might be called bourgeois morality, but like the political standards mentioned before it was the morality of the hometownsman, not the mobile and sophisticated high bourgeois. Hometownsmen did not have the multiple standards and compartmentalized lives that so many modern moral and social critics deplore: one set of standards for church on Sunday, another for relations with friends, another for business relations. They were whole men, integrated personalities, caught like so many flies in a three-dimensional web of community.

The totality of the web made the moralism with which the hometownsman defended his economic interests, and the righteousness he brought to his politics; it provided the aura of depravity and evil he attributed to rivals and strangers. The guilds in their connective functions—between citizen and community, and among compartments of life we incline to treat separately—were vital institutions of communal defense and also main determiners of what it was that would be defended, and against whom.... The hometown community rested on the guild economy, and fell only when the guild economy was overwhelmed.

The Peasants

JEROME BLUM

In the eighteenth century, approximately 90 percent of Europe's population were peasants, though some areas, such as northern Italy and the Rhineland, were relatively urbanized. The peasantry was not a homogeneous social group, as Jerome Blum takes care to demonstrate. What different types of peasants were there? Which areas of Europe had the greatest concentration of free peasants?

Although serfdom existed throughout Europe, there were pronounced differences between the condition of serfs in eastern Europe and those in western Europe. How, for example, did the lives of serfs in France differ from those in

Russia? What, exactly, did serfdom entail? What obligations did a serf owe to his lord? How did a peasant become a serf? Serfdom was not slavery, but the cruel treatment and oppression accorded many serfs and their families distinguished them little from slaves. In Old Régime Europe, the many worked and suffered so that the few could live well, and all over Europe the few, the elite, looked upon the peasants as contemptible inferiors put on earth to serve their lords. What cultural and intellectual assumptions lay behind these attitudes?

Blum depicts the peasants as an unenviable lot, leading wretched and difficult lives. It is no wonder that peasants drowned their misery in heavy drinking.

With the ownership of land went power and authority over the peasants who lived on the land. There were a multitude of variations in the nature of that authority and in the nature of the peasants' subservience to their seigniors[1] in the compass of the seigniors' supervision and control, and in the obligations that the peasants had to pay their lords. The peasants themselves were known by many different names, and so, too, were the obligations they owed the seigniors. But, whatever the differences, the status of the peasant everywhere in the servile lands was associated with unfreedom and constraint. In the hierarchial ladder of the traditional order he stood on the bottom rung. He was "the stepchild of the age, the broad, patient back who bore the weight of the entire social pyramid . . . the clumsy lout who was deprived and mocked by court, noble and city."

In all of the servile lands there were peasants who enjoyed full or partial freedom from seigniorial authority. Many of these people traced their free status to forebearers who had settled as colonists in newly opened regions, drawn there by the promise of freedom for themselves and their dependants. Others owed their liberty to emancipation freely given by the seigniors or purchased by the peasants. In the Swiss cantons of Uri, Schwyz, Unterwalden, Appenzell, Glarus, the Toggenberg district of St. Gall, and the uplands of Bern, the peasants had never paid servile obligations, or had freed themselves of these payments long ago. In France an undetermined but not extensive amount of peasant land, located especially in the center and south, had managed to evade the seigniorial net, despite seigniorial and governmental efforts to enforce the rule of *nulle terre sans seigneur*.[2] In western Germany there were settlements of free peasants called imperial villages. Created centuries before, these villages, like the imperial cities, recognized only the Holy Roman Emperor as their lord. By the eighteenth century, however, most of the imperial villages had fallen under the control of local rulers and had lost their special status. Other free peasants lived along the French-German border. In medieval times, lords had freed these people to keep them from leaving to become colonists elsewhere, or because

[1] Lords.
[2] "No land without its lord."

as borderers they had special military value. All together, the free peasantry made up a small fraction of the rural population of western Germany, and despite their free status most of them had to pay dues and fees to seigniors who had established authority over them.

Eastern Germany, and especially East Prussia, had a much larger free peasant population than did the west. In 1798 in East Prussia 12,790 (21 percent) out of 61,301 peasant holdings belonged to free peasants. . . .

. . . Those freemen who rented land from private seigniors sometimes had to pay dues in kind and labor in addition to a money rent. They often lived in their own villages or on isolated farmsteads. Increasingly, however, manorial land encircled their holdings, they became fellow-villagers of the seigniorial peasants, and by the eighteenth century some of the *Kölmer*[3] had lost much of their freedom to the lords in whose villages they now lived. . . .

In Denmark, too, free peasants often found themselves at the mercy of seigniors. Their number, never large, fell sharply after the establishment of royal absolutism in 1660. By the end of the seventeenth century they made up less than 1 percent of the peasant population in most of the kingdom. . . .

Most of the Austrian Monarchy had only a sprinkling of free peasants. In the Slav provinces of Bohemia, Moravia, and Silesia they comprised scarcely 1 per cent of the rural population. . . . Liberty came typically through individual acts of emancipation, usually in return for a money payment by the peasant. Other so-called free peasants actually were runaway serfs. . . .

Hungary had about 250,000 free peasants in the 1820's out of a rural population of about nine million. Some of these freemen were prosperous farmers, others had no land at all and earned meager livings as hired workers of noblemen and of landed peasants. . . .

In eighteenth- and nineteenth-century Russia serfs won freedom by voluntary emancipation by their seigniors, or by purchasing their freedom, or by military service. A handful of wealthy peasants, who had gained their riches through trade and industry and who paid heavy prices for their emancipation, became members of the bourgeoisie. The others, once freed, were enrolled in the category of state peasants and so remained in an unfree status, albeit one not as constraining nor as degrading as that of the serf. In the second half of the eighteenth century the government offered special privileges to foreigners to persuade them to colonize unpeopled regions of European Russia. The colonists, most of them Germans, whose descendants numbered nearly half a million by the 1850's, had much more freedom than did state peasants but still had certain external restraints placed upon them. . . .

Among all the servile lands, Poland and the Danubian Principalities had the largest proportions of free peasants in their populations. In Poland at the end of the eighteenth century between 20 and 30 per cent of about one million holdings were held by freemen. Many of these people came

[3]Freemen in East Prussia.

from neighboring lands, especially runaways from Pomerania and Silesia. They were welcomed by Polish landowners, who asked no questions and demanded only a small quitrent[4] of the newcomers. Others were residents of towns that in the sixteenth and seventeenth centuries had received city privileges. This allowed the townsmen to hold land on free tenures.... Still other freemen were runaway serfs who enjoyed freedom in their new places of residence so long as their owners did not reclaim them. Not all free peasants, however, remained in that status. Many of them voluntarily became serfs of a lord. Some did this in return for the seignior's assumption of the debts of the peasant, some to find peace and security or seigniorial protection from criminal prosecution, but by far the largest number became serfs because they married a serf and thereby acquired the status of their spouse.

An estimated 107,000 or about one-fifth of the more than 500,000 peasant families in the Danubian Principalities were free. Most of these people lived in the hill country, where they owned their land and where they had rights to the use of forests and pastures. The Principalities also had peasant colonists who cleared and settled seigniorial land in return for special privileges stipulated in written agreements.... They agreed to do only three to six days of labor a year for the seignior and most of them had the right to commute this small obligation into a cash payment. They received the right to the perpetual use of the land they cleared. The state levied a reduced tax on their land and allowed them to pay it directly to the state treasury, and thereby escape the extortions inflicted on other peasants by the agents of the treasury. In a land where official extortion and corruption was a way of life that was a valuable concession.

The peasants of western Europe, save for a relatively small number, had long ago thrown off the bonds that held them in serfdom. Nonetheless, they still owed servile obligations to seigniors, and they were still subject, to a greater or lesser extent depending upon the locality, to the jurisdiction and punitive authority of seigniors. Some historians have made much of the fact that the dependence or servility of these peasants was not attached to their persons (as it was to the person of a serf). Rather, they argue that the dependence adhered to the land. It became part of the price the peasant paid for the use of his holding to the seignior who had the superior ownership of the land. Since nearly all of the land in these societies belonged to seigniors—whether prince, nobleman, institution, or burgher—nearly all of the peasants owed servile obligations. It seems to me to be a matter of little practical consequence, except perhaps to nationalistic historians, whether the servility and dependence adhered to the person or to the land. If, however, the argument must be pursued, there is much that shows that servility often did adhere to the person. Thus, peasants who were landless and who earned their livings as hired farm laborers or as artisans were under seigniorial

---

[4] A rent paid in lieu of labor services.

jurisdiction and had to pay servile obligations, albeit in smaller amounts than peasants with land. In many parts of central and western Europe, peasants owed services and obedience to other seigniors in addition to the seignior who had the superior ownership of the land on which the peasant lived. Indeed, in some places the payments owed to the superior landowner counted among the lesser obligations of the peasant. The other seigniors could include a lord who had jurisdiction over the peasant, another to whom he had to pay a share of his produce, and a so-called *Vogtherr*, or patron. It was quite common to have one or more of these seigniorial roles divided among several people who had acquired their partial ownership through purchase, inheritance, gift, or exchange. Usually, one individual filled several of these roles, or joint owners consolidated their claims through exchange or purchase, so that probably few peasants had a different person in each of these seignioral roles. Two or three seemed the usual pattern, though in southwestern Germany it was not uncommon for a peasant to have four separate seigniors....

The fact was that peasants in the western lands were dependent upon seigniors and stood in a servile relationship to them. Surely it made no difference to the individual peasant whether that dependence was acquired by birth into the peasantry, or by virtue of occupation of a certain piece of land. The dependence was still there. Even peasants who were recognized as fully free and who were alodial[5] proprietors of their holdings had to pay obligations to seigniors that were not demanded of property owners who belonged to other orders.... The peasants themselves recognized their unfreedom and servility. The *cahiers*[6] of grievances they sent to Paris on the eve of the Revolution were filled with complaints and anger at the servile obligations and the seigniorial privileges that oppressed and confined them. The judgment...that "the principle of the absolute freedom of the human person was not generally recognized" before the emancipations of the peasantry was true not only of his homeland, but of all the servile societies of western Europe.

The relatively small number of serfs in western Europe were called *mainmortables* in French-speaking lands and *Leibeigene* or *Eigenhörige* in German-speaking ones. Their serfdom was vestigal, a remnant of the serf-dom once so common in western Europe, and with little resemblance to the far harsher serfdom that prevailed in eastern Europe. Peasants acquired the stain of serfdom in several ways. One, of course, was through inheritance—in Germany through the mother's side only. Residence in certain towns and villages automatically converted people into serfs of the local seignior, who in some instances was the town itself as a corporate entity.... People became serfs, too, after they had occupied for a specified period, such as a year and a day, a holding that carried with it the status of serf. This kind of serfdom, found

[5] Free lands (without a lord).
[6] Lists.

in parts of Swabia, Hannover, northwest Lorraine, parts of Luxembourg, and in Franche-Comté, was called *Realleibeigenschaft* or *mainmorte réelle*, because the serfdom adhered to the land.

Some regions held a high concentration of serfs, others had smaller numbers or none at all. In France about 400,000 of the estimated one million *mainmortables* in that country lived in Franche-Comté, where in 1784 a contemporary estimated that they made up half of the population.... In Savoy the majority of the peasants were *mainmortables*. Among the German states, Baden and Hannover had relatively large concentrations.... Lesser densities occurred in other states of western Germany; central Germany had almost no serfs. Several of the Swiss cantons had *mainmortables* among their population....

Serfs could legally be bought, sold, exchanged, or given away by their owner. Nearly always such transactions involved the alienation by the serfowner of his seigniory, and with it his rights over the serfs who lived there. The only effect this sale had on the serfs was that now they had a new lord to whom they owed their obligations. There were instances, however, in which serfowners sold or exchanged their serfs without land, as if they were chattels. The serf then had to move to the seigniory of his new owner. Such sales remained legal in a number of German principalities up to the end of the servile order, though in practice they seem rarely to have taken place.

The western European serf could own land in his own name, or hold land on hereditary tenure from a lord of whom he was not the serf. Like other peasants, he could have several seigniors to whom he owed obligations. Like other hereditary tenants, he could buy, sell, exchange, mortgage, or bequeath his land at will. However, none of these conditions applied to land he held from the seignior whose serf he was. He had to have his master's consent to alienate or mortgage the holding, or face confiscation and eviction. When lords gave their serfs permission to alienate, they demanded a fee. In Franche-Comté the charge was one-twelfth of the sale price, but sometimes seigniors demanded as much as one-half. The serf could not bequeath his holding and his personal property to whomever he pleased. Again he had to have his master's consent. In France and in Savoy he could leave his property only to those children who lived with him. Failing such heirs, all of his property escheated to the seignior. Some serfowners in France and Savoy even claimed as their own the property of those of their serfs who lived away from the lord's seigniory and who died leaving heirs. A royal decree of 8 August 1779 ... ordered the end in France of this practice....

In southwest Germany the lord once had claimed all of the property of a deceased serf on the ground that all which the serf possessed belonged to the lord, who out of grace had permitted the peasant to own and use the property during his lifetime. Traces of this persisted into the eighteenth century, when the seignior claimed all of the property at the death of a childless serf. In general, however, the lord took only a set percentage of the serf's property, or his best animal, or his best garment, or a small cash payment, and allowed the serf to bequeath the rest of his property as he wished. In northwest Germany the lord customarily took half of the movables of the decedent and his second best animal. . . .

In principle the serf could not leave the seigniory of his owner, but it had been a long time since lords had been able to enforce that rule. Now the serf could leave if he received permission from the lord and met certain conditions. In Franche-Comté and in Lorraine if the serf left without authorization the lord could take the income from the departed peasant's hereditary holding. If he did not return within a specified period—ten years in Franche-Comté—the holding escheated to the seignior. In many places the peasant who wanted to leave had to pay an exit fee to his lord By paying the exit fee the peasant freed himself from serfdom. If he left without paying the fee, he remained a serf and his lord had a claim on his property when he died. If the departing peasant who left without paying was a woman, she not only remained a serf, but in the Germanic lands her children were legally serfs of her lord, no matter where they were born or where they lived.

Serfs did not have to leave the seigniory in order to gain their freedom. They could purchase it if their owner was willing, and remain in their homes. The price was set by agreement between lord and serf, although in some places it was a fixed amount. On occasion an entire village bought its liberty at what must sometimes have been a great financial sacrifice. The people of Pusey in Franche-Comté paid their lord 50,000 livres and ceded a meadow to him in return for their emancipation from serfdom and from the obligations they owed him. In Bavaria, and after 1701 in Lorraine, serfs who entered the priesthood or who married a noble or who were ennobled (these two latter events must have been most unusual) were automatically freed.

Nearly everywhere seigniors required their serfs, male and female alike, to make a small annual payment, usually presented in person, as an acknowledgment of their serfdom. Sometimes, too, the serfs had to do homage and take an oath of loyalty to the lord, either periodically or when the serf became the occupant of a holding. . . .

The degree of freedom enjoyed by the serfs of western Europe, especially when compared with that of the serfs of eastern Europe, has persuaded some historians to maintain that their serfdom was "nothing more than a special kind of taxation" and a device to increase seigniorial revenues. It is said that their obligations were no more onerous, and sometimes less onerous, than those of other peasants, and that their status was neither degrading nor socially incapacitating, so that serfs rose to high rank in church and state and remained serfs. If, indeed, the obligations and status of serfdom made so little difference, it becomes difficult to understand why serfs bothered to redeem themselves from it, at sometimes excessively heavy prices. It is worth noting, too, that as a rule serfs who rose to high office were allowed to redeem themselves. . . . The fact that legally serfs could be bought, sold, exchanged, or given away certainly distinguished—and degraded— their status as compared with other peasants of western Europe. And it seems clear that serfs themselves considered their position as both demeaning and intolerable. They ran away to escape it and they entered lawsuits against their lords. . . .

In general the status of the peasantry worsened as one moved eastward across the continent and it reached its nadir in the lands that lay on the other side of the Elbe River. Most of the peasants there were held in a serfdom that was far more onerous and far more degrading than the vestigal serfdom of western Europe. In the last part of the eighteenth century the term *Leibeigenschaft*, slavery, came into use in German-speaking lands as the name for serfdom, instead of the more accurate *Erbuntertänigkeit*, hereditary subjection. It was employed especially by reformers in the hope that the use of the odious word "slavery" would lend force to their arguments for change. Actually, serfdom in eastern Europe was not slavery (though sometimes it seemed scarcely different from it), if only because the serf was recognized as a legal individual, within certain limitations could initiate and participate in court actions, and possessed certain individual, albeit severely restricted, rights.

There were, of course, differences among the eastern lands in the extent to which the peasants were "servile subjects of the manor." . . . In Russia, Livonia, Poland, Schleswig-Holstein, Denmark, and in much of eastern Germany, especially in Mecklenburg, Swedish Pomerania, and Upper Lusatia in Electoral Saxony, the law placed few limits upon the authority of the seignior. Often the only effective restraint on the lord was his knowledge that his demands might reach the point at which his serfs would run away to escape them. The peasants in the Austrian Monarchy and in Electoral Saxony (except for Upper Lusatia) and other lands of east-central Germany were considerably less dependent upon the will and whim of their seigniors. Reforms of the second half of the eighteenth century had given the peasants of the Hapsburg realm many rights they had not before possessed. They still bore "the marks of the yokes and chains of their earlier slavery," for they remained the hereditary servile subjects of their lords. But now the central government had established norms that curbed the powers the lord once had over his peasants. For example, he could not now demand more labor services than the laws specified, nor could he prevent his peasants from leaving, providing they complied with the complex provisions set out in the legislation, nor could he evict them from their holdings without proper cause. . . .

Serfdom in the Danubian Principalities differed from the serfdom of the other eastern lands, notably in that the seignior had neither civil nor criminal jurisdiction over his peasants. In practice, however, the serf there had no real protection against excessive demands and harsh treatment by his seignior. . . .

The alienation of serfs without land, often involving the breakup of families, reveals the depth of the degradation to which serfs had been reduced in many of the eastern lands. They were sold, mortgaged, exchanged, and gambled away. This concept of the serf as a chattel, a thing that could be made over to another person, apparently was a phenomenon largely of the seventeenth and especially of the eighteenth century. The practice assumed especially large proportions in Russia. The law code of 1649 had forbidden the sale of serfs, but serfowners quickly and freely disregarded the ban. The central government did nothing to stop them. Instead, it gave its tacit recognition by such legislation as a ban on the use of the hammer by auctioneers at public sales of serfs, or in 1833, and again in 1841, outlawing the separation of parents and their unwed children by sale or gift. In 1761 the Livonian diet gave legal sanction to the sale of serfs without land, though it forbade their sale for export and the separation of a married couple. A contemporary in the 1770's reported that serfs and their children were exchanged for horses and dogs. When famine struck in the winter of 1788–1789, seigniors in one district of Livonia, in order to save on the support they had to provide their serfs, were reported to have sold orphan girls of six to twelve for a pittance and even given them away. In Mecklenburg, where peasants probably suffered worse treatment than anywhere else in Germany, there was an active and open trade in serfs from the mid-seventeenth century on, though it did not receive official sanction from the government until 1757....

...In 1759 the government ordered an end to the active commerce in serfs in Prussian Silesia. The ban seems not to have been entirely effective, since sales continued there until as late as 1795. By a decree of 8 November 1773 Frederick II[7] expressly forbade the sale of serfs without land in East Prussia. In contrast, in Swedish Pomerania as late as the 1780's legislation specifically permitted the sale of serfs without land and mortgaging and exchanging them. A writer in 1784 compared the traffic there in serfs with the African slave trade. In Schleswig-Holstein the law forbade the sale of serfs without land, but serfowners paid no heed to the prohibition. Reports told of a lord who exchanged a serf for two dogs and of serfowners who used their serfs as stakes in gambling at cards.

In Poland the law was silent on the right of lords to sell their serfs without land, and eighteenth-century jurists decided that they did have the right.... Some of the transactions broke up families. Some were made on the condition, insisted upon by the church, that the serfs had to remain Catholics. If they did not, the seller had the right to demand back his serfs. Most of the sales were to nearby lords, but sometimes the serfs were sold to more distant masters and even to buyers from Germany.

In Hungary and Transylvania, too, the laws said nothing about the sale of serfs without land. Lords there bought, sold, mortgaged, exchanged, and gave away serfs from the sixteenth to the late eighteenth centuries. The last known sale of a serf without land in Hungary occurred in 1773 and in Transylvania in the 1780's....

[7]Frederick the Great, King of Prussia, 1740–1786.

In Russia there were servile peasants other than the serfs of private proprietors. By far the most numerous of these people were the state peasants. Early in the eighteenth century Peter[8] had created the state peasantry as a separate legal and social category, as part of his program to simplify administrative procedures such as the collection of taxes and other obligations. He formed the core of the new category from peasants who had never been enserfed, the *odnodvortsy*, descendants of minor servitors who had been settled on the frontiers, migrants to Siberia, and the non-Slavic peoples of the Volga basin and beyond. Later rulers added other groups, notably the peasants of the church after the secularization of the church's lands in 1764, and the peasants who lived on the manors owned by the tsar and his close kinsmen. By 1858, on the eve of the emancipation, state peasants actually outnumbered the serfs; a contemporary estimate put the population of state peasants at 27.4 millions and that of the serfs at 22.8 millions.

The state peasants lived on land that belonged to the government. . . . The peasants were subject to the will of the government, which put them under the supervision of bureaucrats. They had far more autonomy over their lives and activities and far more personal freedom than serfs had. Their obligations to the state were considerably less than the obligations that serfs had to pay their owners, and the compulsory labor service that bore so heavily upon the serfs did not figure among their obligations. However, theirs was an insecure status, for the tsar could give them and their land to private persons, whose serfs they then became. That happened to many thousands of state peasants. The government also assigned them to full or part-time employment in state-owned and privately owned industrial enterprises, especially in mining and metallurgy.

After the state peasants, the appanage peasants were the most numerous category of non-seigniorial peasants in Russia. They lived on the estates owned by the imperial court. . . . By 1860 there were over 800,000 male appanage peasants. . . . Like the state peasants, the appanage peasants paid only a money fee and did not have other obligations in kind or labor. . . .

The gypsy slaves of the Danubian Principalities were the last true thralls in Christian Europe. In the mid-nineteenth century there were about 200,000 of them, or between 5 and 6 per cent of the estimated population of the Principalities. They were the property of monasteries and private persons who used them principally as domestics, though monasteries sometimes assigned them to work in the fields. Others, in return for payments to their owners, were allowed to go off and earn their livings as nomads, or as sedentary artisans in towns and villages. Being slaves, they had no legal personality and so possessed no civil rights. . . . They were bought and sold like beasts of the field, and because they were poor workers they usually did not command good prices. And, like a beast, they could never acquire freedom or a legal personality because it was not possible to enfranchise

[8]Peter the Great, Tsar of Russia, 1689–1725.

them any more than it was possible to enfranchise a beast. If their owner did release them, another person could claim ownership, just as he could of an ownerless animal or object.

There was also a smaller group of gypsies who theoretically belonged to the sovereign (initially all the gypsies had belonged to the ruler who had alienated them to monasteries and private persons). These gypsies, numbering around 37,000 in 1837, had nearly complete personal freedom, paid only a small fee to the ruler, lived the traditional tribal nomadic life of the gypsy, and earned their living in traditional gypsy fashion as artisans, bear trainers, musicians, beggars, and thieves....

The subservience of the peasant and his dependence upon his lord were mirrored in the attitudes and opinions of the seigniors of east and west alike. They believed that the natural order of things had divided humankind into masters and servants, those who commanded and those who obeyed. They believed themselves to be naturally superior beings and looked upon those who they believed were destined to serve them as their natural inferiors. At best their attitude toward the peasantry was the condescension of paternalism. More often it was disdain and contempt. Contemporary expressions of opinion repeatedly stressed the ignorance, irresponsibility, laziness, and general worthlessness of the peasantry, and in the eastern lands the free use of the whip was recommended as the only way to get things done. The peasant was considered some lesser and sub-human form of life; "a hybrid between animal and human" was the way a Bavarian official put it in 1737. An eyewitness of a rural rising in Provence in 1752 described the peasant as "an evil animal, cunning, a ferocious half-civilized beast; he has neither heart nor honesty...." The Moldavian Basil Balsch reported that the peasants of his land were "strangers to any discipline, order, economy or cleanliness...; a thoroughly lazy, mendacious...people who are accustomed to do the little work that they do only under invectives or blows." A counselor of the duke of Mecklenburg in an official statement in 1750 described the peasant there as a "head of cattle" and declared that he must be treated accordingly....

A few were more understanding. Stanislaus Leszczy (d. 1766), twice elected king of Poland and twice deposed, wrote that in that country "the nobleman condemns his peasant to death without any legal ground and even more frequently without legal proceedings and without any ceremony. We look upon the peasant as a creature of an entirely different sort, and deny him even the air which we breathe with him, and make hardly any distinction between him and the animals who plow our fields. Often we value them even lower than the animals, and only too often sell them to cruel masters who compel them to pay for their new servitude by excessive toil. I shudder when I mention the law which imposes a fine of only 15 francs on the noble who murders a peasant."...

The conviction of their own superiority harbored by the seigniors was often compounded by ethnic and religious differences between lord and peasant. In many parts of central and eastern Europe the masters belonged to a conquering people who had established their domination over the native population. German seigniors ruled over Slavic peasants in Bohemia, Galicia, East Prussia and Silesia, and over Letts and Estonians in the Baltic lands; Polish lords were the masters of Ukrainian, Lithuanian, and White Russian peasants; Great Russians owned manors peopled by Ukrainians and Lithuanians and Poles; Magyars lorded it over Slovaks and Romanians and Slovenes—to list only some of the macro-ethnic differences. Few peoples of the rest of the world can match Europeans in their awareness of and, generally, contempt for or at least disdain for other ethnic and religious groups.... The dominant group, though greatly outnumbered, successfully maintained its cultural identity precisely because it considered the peasants over whom it ruled as lesser breeds of mankind, even pariahs....

Schooling for most peasants was, at best, pitifully inadequate and usually entirely absent, even where laws declared elementary education compulsory. ...[B]y far the greatest part of Europe's peasantry lived out their lives in darkest ignorance.

The peasants themselves, oppressed, contemned, and kept in ignorance by their social betters, accepted the stamp of inferiority pressed upon them. "I am only a serf" the peasant would reply when asked to identify himself. They seemed without pride or self-respect, dirty, lazy, crafty, and always suspicious of their masters and of the world that lay outside their village. Even friendly observers were put off by the way they looked and by their behavior. One commentator complained in the 1760's that "one would have more pity for them if their wild and brutish appearance did not seem to justify their hard lot." ...

A few thoughtful people recognized that the responsibility for the misery and ignorance of peasant existence lay not in the nature of the peasant himself, but in the nature of the social and economic order in which he lived. J. C. Schubart (1734–1789) ... a distinguished German agriculturist ... explained that "the more industrious the poor peasant the more miserable; for almost everyone wants to refresh himself from his sweat and fatten himself from his blood; he is thereby beaten down, discouraged, and in the end becomes slothful because he realizes that he is more tormented and more ill-treated than a beast of burden." ...

In their hopelessness, their desperation, and perhaps their self-hate, peasants everywhere, men and women and often children, drank heavily and even passionately. In many lands their addiction was encouraged by their seigniors, who had the monopoly on the manufacture and sale of spirits, who owned or leased out the village inn, and for whom these activities provided an important source of income. Some Polish seigniors even paid their hired labor in scrip redeemable only at the village tavern for drinks. Contemporaries frequently commented on the endless drinking and on its destructive effects. An account in an official publication in Silesia in 1790 that told of the crushing poverty and misery of the Polish peasants of Upper

Silesia, reported that "Brandy or the mere thought of it transports these people from laziness, sluggishness and slackness to lightheartedness, happiness and exuberance.... They consume it with a frenzy.... The consequences of their intemperance are to be expected, the destruction of their health, disorder, neglect, need, confusion, discord, and sometimes murder."...

In light of their subservience and of their lowly condition, it could be expected that the peasantry would be politically powerless. Unlike the other orders of the traditional society, most peasants did not have institutionalized instruments, specifically representation in assemblies and estates, by which they could express their interests and voice their demands. Peasants were represented as an order in the diets of some of the lesser German principalities ... and in the Austrian provinces of Tyrol and Vorarlberg, where the peasants were free.... In the rural cantons of Switzerland, the free peasantry dominated the cantonal assemblies; in other cantons, urban oligarchs ruled over townspeople and country people alike. In some parts of France, peasants had sometimes been allowed to participate in the choice of delegates to the Estates General, the national assembly, which had last met in 1614. When the Estates General were summoned on the eve of the Revolution, representatives of the third estate were chosen by the system of indirect elections in which all heads of peasant families were allowed to participate.

Peasants did have scope for political activity and for some degree of self-government at the village level. Nearly everywhere seigniors had allowed their peasants much autonomy in the management of their village communities. In the eighteenth and nineteenth centuries, however, communal autonomy declined significantly as seigniors, for their own private reasons, intervened increasingly in the internal operations of the peasant community....

The Commercialization of Fashion

NEIL McKENDRICK

As Neil McKendrick points out, not all societies have been fashion conscious; indeed, most societies have not experienced abrupt changes in fashion and have not desired them. Why have the style and material of clothes been so static through the centuries? Why until recently have people been immune to the dictates of fashion?

This lack of novelty in fashion did not apply to the most powerful groups in Western civilization. Why, for instance, were the clothes of kings, queens, and emperors so luxurious, ornate, and varied? What was the relationship between fashion and political power? What social functions did differentiation in costume serve?

By the eighteenth century, the situation had begun to change. Two hundred years earlier, people had desired to copy the fashions of the social elite; now they could do so. What happened by the eighteenth century to enable the middling sorts of people to adopt different and varied fashions? McKendrick argues that a revolutionary commitment to fashioned occurred, that fashion had became a big business, and that fashion finally affected people of various social levels. To what extent was there then a fashion revolution parallel to the eighteenth-century agricultural, industrial, and demographic revolutions? What does McKendrick mean by a western European fashion pattern? Why did it emerge first in England?

Did the population's demand for fashion give rise to frequent and regular changes in costume, or did those who manufactured clothes deliberately stimulate people's desire for change? Which people were responsible for disseminating news about the latest fashions? What role did the capital city, London, play in this fashion revolution?

On what basis does McKendrick claim that the "commercialization of fashion in eighteenth-century England can be encapsulated in the history of the fashion doll"? How did the doll influence the English in matters of fashion? What social impact did the doll have?

This essay also stresses the economic foundations of developments in fashion and decisions about fashion. Do you agree that entrepreneurs could manipulate the public in matters of fashion?

In England the several ranks of men slide into each other almost imperceptibly, and a spirit of equality runs through every part of their constitution. Hence arises a strong emulation in all the several stations and conditions to vie with each other; and the perpetual ambition in each of the inferior ranks to raise themselves to the level of those immediately above them. In such a state as this fashion must have uncontrolled sway. And a fashionable luxury must spread through it like a contagion.

N. Forster,[1] *1767*

...The concept of fashion is now deeply embedded in Western European society, and its importance in modern industrialized economies is difficult to overlook. Whole industries are built around, and dependent upon, design changes and the public reaction to them. There are even explicitly named *fashion industries* which exploit man's—and more particularly, in some societies, woman's—constant need for variety and change. But it would be a mistake to think—as so many moralists have done—that the importance of fashion is a constant of the human condition. Man has not always hungered for fashionable change, and even in those societies in which they *have* hungered they have often been unable to satisfy their appetites.

An anthology of quotations concerning fashion might seem to point to both its age and its universal influence. Proverbial wisdom was recorded in classical Latin to the effect that 'Fashion is more powerful than any tyrant', and the poets of antiquity were as specific as they were prolific on the subject. Ovid,[2] as early as the year A.D. 8, wrote in *The Art of Love,*

[1] Nathaniel Forster (1726[?]–1790), writer on political economy.

[2] Latin poet, 43 B.C.–A.D. 17

I cannot keep track of all the vagaries of fashion,
Every day, so it seems, brings in a different style.

...Even English literature can provide a respectably antique pedigree. Chaucer[3] in 'The Knight's Tale' confirmed the truism that 'There's never a new fashion but its old'; Shakespeare in *Much Ado About Nothing* affirmed that 'The fashion wears out more apparel than the man', and in *Henry VIII* complained that 'new customs, Though they be never so ridiculous (Nay, let 'em be unmanly), yet are followed.' But such quotations do not encompass all societies and, even in those they do include, they are often more relevant to a history of attitudes than to a history of material possessions.

It may be a constant of the human condition to want to be in fashion. It is certainly not a constant of that condition to be able to be so. Nor has being in fashion entailed frequent changes for many societies and most classes.

For if one takes a long enough view and a sufficiently international one, the history of costume is a remarkably stable one. Fashion, in the clothes worn by most men and women in most societies, has been remarkably static.... The fashionable tumult over the last two hundred years or so is the chronological exception not the rule; and geographically, until very recently, only the West experienced the full frenzy of fashionable excess. For much of human history most people have been virtually immune to the effect of fashion. Most were born to immunity through poverty; some acquired immunity through the scarcity of objects to indulge their fashionable whims upon—in such a consumer vacuum the propensity to spend is effectively held in check; some had immunity thrust upon them by royal edict or sumptuary laws.[4]

Recent work in social history has reminded us forcibly that there are fewer constants in the human condition than we have usually imagined, or has often been assumed. The sex drive, for instance, was not constant. It could be severely repressed by hunger, hard work or an inadequate diet (not to mention the effect of changing cultural norms and expectations); it could be intensified by leisure, prosperity and ample nutrition. The age of marriage is not constant either. The average age at first marriage—or the proportions of any given society who marry at all—can vary remarkably in the face of varying social and economic restraints and inducements.... The marriage *rate* can also fluctuate alarmingly with changing opportunities: ranging from the modest choice of marriage partners offered by eighteenth-century Lisbon where one-third of the women were nuns, to the ubiquitous marriage of prosperous twentieth-century America where some 90 per cent of women marry. Illegitimacy rates can vary from the remarkably low average of one or two per cent in the face-to-face society of pre-industrial Europe to 73 per

---

[3] Geoffrey Chaucer (c.1345–1400), author of the *Canterbury Tales*.

[4] Sumptuary laws regulated and restrained personal extravagance, especially in dress and food.

cent in some parts of the West Indies of the mid-twentieth century. The age at which different societies characteristically give birth to their children is also more flexible than many historians have imagined. All such phenomena have proved to be very sensitive to economic circumstance and cultural expectations.

When the basic human drives to marry, to make love and to raise a family can vary so markedly in the face of social, cultural and economic restraints, so *a fortiori* can the less basic but nonetheless pressing human need to be dressed in the latest fashion.

It is not difficult to recognize the importance of diet, housing and medical breakthroughs in allowing so many more people to live to the full the age-old assumed life-potential of three score years and ten. It is not difficult to grasp that as a result the average expectation of life at birth has risen in Europe from less than thirty to nearly seventy in little more than three hundred years. It has not so far been so readily realized and accepted that man's potential to consume has also only very recently undergone a revolution of similar dimensions.

The historical forces working against fashion were many. Poverty was the most important. Custom and tradition were powerful allies. A stable society was a further buttress against change: established hierarchies, which prevented or severely restricted vertical social mobility, remained remarkably faithful to the costumes which distinguished men's place in that hierarchy....

Museums of costume can be deceptive. Richness and grandeur which strike us as strange, even 'fantastical' may have been the unchanging costume of kings and priests for centuries: splendour and variety in the dress of a queen may well have been the result of conspicuous consumption by a single individual operating within the bounds of a single hardly varying fashionable mode.

Power often needs display and ornament. The divinity which 'doth hedge about a king' has usually needed more tangible expression to impress most of his subjects. The 'Emperor's clothes' would be seen through by more than the innocent eye of a child, unless they were of a splendour and magnificence which could not be overlooked. Clothes in the past were 'used to set apart men and women, enhance their glory, touch them with a divinity to which these men who toiled and worked, or bought and sold, could never hope to aspire'.

Sumptuary laws forbidding imitation were designed to reinforce their élite status, to restrict the grandeur to the few, and to guarantee their sense of separateness. In its simplest but most extreme form, the great simply monopolized a single colour. The Sons of Heaven, the Chinese Emperors, wore yellow, reserved to them alone: the Roman emperors wore the imperial purple preserved for them and their immediate family. In societies in which such restrictive devices could not be enforced, separateness has been insisted on by wealth. The famous extravagance of Queen Elizabeth's[5] wardrobe fulfilled a very political need. It was the visible external proof of her divinity; it buttressed her political power; and her courtiers were expected to buttress it further with a spectacular display of satellite finery....

But such a picture, accurate as it is, should not deceive us into thinking that the eighteenth century, by the end of which monarchs were much more soberly dressed, saw a decline of the power of fashionable excess. For where in the sixteenth century men longed to be able to follow fashion and ape the nobility and gentry, in the eighteenth century they were able to do so. Of course, the attractions of fashion were not new to the eighteenth century. 'Since in every age fashions beguile all ages and classes in varying degrees, ordinary folks lower down the social scale were susceptible too, and strained their resources to ape their betters. As the proclamation of 1562 bewailed "such as be of the meaner sort, and be least able with their livings to maintain the same" felt that they must follow the fashion'.

...[S]ixteenth-century fashion is 'full of baleful comment upon the dictates of fashion, which first seized the rich in thrall and then their servants'.... 'I have known divers [serving men]', wrote William Vaughan[6] in 1600, 'who would bestow all the money they had in the world on sumptuous garments'. But that pride, that curiosity, that desire to 'bestow their money' and strain their resources was not allowed its full expression until the eighteenth century. Just as some individuals lived their natural span to the full in previous centuries, so some succumbed happily to the tyranny of fashion. But just as the evidence of geriatric Elizabethans is no evidence of a high expectation of life in the late sixteenth century, so these quotations prove only the existence of the desire to follow fashion and the ability of a few to do so. It is only... since the eighteenth century that fashion approached its full potential and was accepted by contemporaries as exercising 'uncontrolled sway'....

In one sense, of course, the poets and the proverbs are right. Such is the biological display function of clothes, such are the possibilities for displaying status, rank, wealth and class, that some form of costume differentiation can be found in most societies and most ages. But fashion in the sense of rapid change in shape, material and style is something quite different....

Such are the social and sexual potentialities of fine costume that there will always be examples to be found of inventive exploitation of it. Such is the perverse nature of mankind that sumptuary laws will always intensify the desire of some of those legally deprived in this way to wear the banned material. Such is the ingenuity of men and women that even in the most inauspicious circumstances some will contrive to indulge them-

---

[5]Queen of England (reigned 1558–1603).
[6]British poet (1577–1641).

selves in fashion. But more than that is needed to bring about the revolutionary commitment to fashion, the commercial hold over fashion and the widespread social dispersion of fashion which I want to describe and explain. It was no longer a matter of the aspiring few wanting to be in fashion. In the late eighteenth century large numbers in society felt that they *must* be in fashion, whether they liked it or not, even to the point of ridicule. It was no longer forbidden fruit or an atypical social need. It was now *de rigueur*,[7] socially required of one to be in fashion. As the *Town and Country Magazine* asked plaintively in 1785, 'What can a man do?'

> Banyans[8] are worn in every part of town from Wapping to Westminster, and if a sword is occasionally put on it sticks out of the middle behind. This however is the fashion, the ton, and what can a man do? He *must* wear a banyan.

By the end of the eighteenth century the first signs of a surfeit of fashion can be seen, as commerce increasingly took over the manipulation and direction of fashion. Men and women increasingly *had* to wear what commerce dictated, had to raise or lower their hems and their heels at the dictates of the cloth manufacturers and the shoe sellers. . . .

In my view the Western European fashion pattern (and indeed the more general Western European consumer pattern) is as marked, as important and as worthy of attention as the much studied 'European Marriage Pattern'.[9] If and when they are both recognized, the well advised historians will eventually wish to look back to the sixteenth century at least, just as they will certainly need to look at Holland in the early eighteenth century and France in the later, but for the first full efflorescence of the new fashion and consumer patterns they will need to concentrate on eighteenth-century England. There they will find not just one or two isolated comments on annual fashion but a multiplicity, not just the occasional foreign visitor describing his admiring reactions to English fashion but dozens expressing their astonishment, not just a few burgesses' wives desirous of following fashion but virtually all the middle class, many of the tradesmen, mechanics and more prosperous working classes. There too, they will find the statistical backing of rising aggregate demand, there they will find that before 1780 most of the increased demand came from the home consumption of manufactured goods. The other necessary supporting evidence will also be found there: the well-evidenced cases of commercial manipulation of fashion and the well-substantiated cases of major industrialists building their fortunes on fashionable goods. The vital agents in the spread of fashion can be found too: not only the traditional fairs and pedlars, but the Manchester Men, the Scotch Drapers, Scotch Hawkers and the provincial shopkeepers. The vital agents in the transmission of accurate fashion intelligence were also for

---

[7]Obligatory.

[8]Also spelled banian, a loose gown, jacket, or shirt of flannel.

[9]Late marriages, with a high percentage of people remaining unmarried.

the first time available—the fashion magazines, the fashion plates and the English fashion doll. In addition there were the advertising columns of the press, both of the provinces and London. The role of London, indeed, swelled to a quite new significance as the radiant centre of the fashion world and conspicuous consumption, transmitting through its season, its exhibitions, its shops and their trade cards, new patterns of consumption more widely than ever before. They were transmitted along the new turnpike roads, by the more efficient coaching system, along the new canals, and through the new satellite centres of fashion and commerce in the province. The process was by 1800 unmistakable, the evidence overwhelming.

Where in the sixteenth century, for instance, we have a composite image of the Tudors...[10] for the eighteenth century it would be difficult to confuse the products of one reign with another. The accelerating pace of fashion change can only be accommodated by referring to the styles of George I,[11] George II,[12] the 1760s, the 1770s, the 1780s and 1790s, and with many fashion goods even that is insufficient and anyone with scholarship worthy of the name would have to refer to individual years....

This fashion revolution did not happen by accident. The social and economic circumstances were immensely favourable, but fully to realize its great economic potential required careful guidance and skillful exploitation. The role played in this by the process of commercialization was of vital importance....

The commercialization of fashion in eighteenth-century England can be encapsulated in the history of the fashion doll. The doll may seem, to some, to be a curious, even a trivial, expression of the commercial techniques and the emergent consumer demand which underlay the Industrial Revolution. But as a vivid symbol of both the extension of the market and the means by which that market was extended, it dramatically exemplifies the change from fashion which was expensive, exclusive and Paris-based, to a fashion which was cheap, popular and London-based. Most dramatically of all it exemplifies the change from a fashion which was royal in origin, limited (essentially aristocratic) in its immediate influence, and very slow to filter through to the rest of society, to a fashion which was directly aimed at the popular market, indeed which was specifically intended to extend it further into a *mass* one. This fashion promoter was not only immediately available to the new consumer market, it was also capable of responding very rapidly to its needs, its growth, and its fluctuations. Where the French fashion doll of the first decades of the century served only an *élite*, the English fashion doll of the last decades of that century served a mass consumer market. Perhaps even more significantly, where the former was court controlled the latter was controlled by business. Entrepreneurs had taken over the

[10]Ruling dynasty of Britain, 1485–1603.

[11]King of England, 1714–1727.

[12]King of England, 1727–1760.

fashion doll and committed it to the service of commerce. Its role was now the manipulation and extension of consumer demand. Its dramatic metamorphosis in the course of the century nicely confirms the change from a world where fashion was not only designed to serve the few but was designed to mark them off from the rest of society, to a world where fashion was being deliberately designed to encourage social imitation, social emulation and emulative spending, a world which blurred rather than reinforced class divisions and allowed the conspicuous lead of the fashion leaders to be quickly copied by the rest of society. By the end of the eighteenth century the competitive, socially emulative aspect of fashion was being consciously manipulated by commerce in pursuit of increased consumption. This new fashion world was one in which entrepreneurs were trying deliberately to induce fashionable change, to make it rapidly available to as many as possible and yet to keep it so firmly under their control that the consuming public could be sufficiently influenced to buy at the dictate of *their* fashion decisions, at the convenience of *their* production lines. Those fashion decisions were increasingly based on economic grounds rather than aesthetic ones, on the basis of what the factories could produce and what the salesmen could sell rather than on what the French court dictated. Commerce was now pulling the strings in control of the fashion doll. They still needed the co-operation of the exclusive world of the fashionable aristocrary. The fashionable few remained what Wedgwood called 'the legislators of taste', but they were no longer the sole beneficiaries of its pleasures, and the fashionable lead they provided was increasingly under the manipulative control of entrepreneurs seeking a quicker access to a mass market.

The changing face of the fashion doll reveals the extent to which this change occurred in the course of the eighteenth century.

At the beginning of the eighteenth century the fashion doll came over every year from Paris. Even war could not hinder its progress. For as the Abbé Prevost[13] wrote...'by an act of gallantry, which is worthy of being noted in the chronicle of history, for the benefit of the ladies the ministers of both Courts granted a special pass to the mannequin; that pass was always respected, and during the times of greatest enmity experienced on both sides respected, and during the times of greatest enmity experienced on both sides the mannequin was the one object which remained unmolested'. Addison[14] was outraged at the import of 'the wooden Mademoiselle' at the height of war, and in his anger claimed that one came carrying the French fashions every month. Other evidence suggests that one a year was the normal ration. It also makes clear that the doll was sent first to the English court and then, when the Queen and the ladies of the court had absorbed its fashionable lessons, it made its way to the leading London fashion makers. Advertisements announcing that 'Last Saturday the *French doll for the year 1712* arrived at my house in King Street, Covent Garden', suggests

[13] French novelist (1697–1763).
[14] Joseph Addison (1672–1719), English essayist.

that those who believed that 'for a twelvemonths this remained the dress-makers' model' were right.

Variously known as 'pandoras', 'mannequins', 'dolls of the Rue St. Honoré' (the centre of French fashion) and 'grand courriers de la mode'[15] the fashion dolls could be extremely elaborate and very expensive. Many were made 'lifesize in order that the clothes with which they were dressed might immediately be worn'; they were to be models for hairstyles, head gear, and all the accessories of fashion—even down to the details of 'how they wore their underclothing'.

Such was their influence that after the Queen, her ladies-in-waiting, and the London fashion shops had had their fill, the dolls spread further abroad. One was advertised in *The New England Weekly Journal* in 1733 where it was announced that for two shillings[16] you could look at it, and for seven shillings take it away.

Eventually the geographical spread of the fashion doll's influence was very great. But its immediate social impact was small, and it was too expensive to influence directly the mass market. To transmit fashions in quantity (cheaply and quickly, and yet accurately) something less ponderous was needed than the life size, fully dressed, elaborately coiffured French mannequin. The answer was the English fashion doll which has been described as 'a revolutionary invention conquering the market from 1790 onwards'. It was a flat fashion model cut out of cardboard. It cost only three shillings in 1790 and later only a few pence.[17] It was printed by the thousand. It was, in the words of a contemporary commentator in 1791, 'about eight inches high', with 'simply dressed hair', and 'complete with underclothing and corset'. With it went

> six complete sets of tastefully coloured, cut-out dresses and coiffures, which means summer—and winter—clothing, complete dresses and négligés, caracos, chemises, furs, hats, bonnets, poufs, etc. Each dress and hat is made in such a way that the doll can easily be dressed in it, giving a fully dressed or décolleté effect while the dress fits perfectly in either case. Hat or bonnet can be adjusted freely to be pulled over the face or set back. They can be put straight or at an angle, suiting the hairstyle in a tasteful manner or otherwise. In short: dress and coiffure can be varied, and by trying, each given its particular 'air'. This dressing and undressing, being able to set up and change again, makes for the uniqueness of the English doll. One might obtain even more changes by having some extra dresses designed and painted. The whole is packed in a neat paper envelope, and can easily be carried in portfolio or working bag.

In 1791 it was described in Germany as 'a new and pretty invention' from England from which 'mothers and grown women' could observe and

---

[15]Great messengers of fashion.

[16]A former unit of British currency; one-twentieth of a pound.

[17]Penny; English coin worth one-twelfth of a shilling.

even study 'good or bad taste in dress or coiffure'. Very soon hundreds of different sheets of the dolls were available, specifically aimed at different classes and professions, as it was realized how quickly it could spread new fashion ideas.

It was original, cheap and effective. It was capable of almost endless variety. It could penetrate many different social levels. As an advertisement it had good survival value, for even when discarded by mothers it was taken up by children as a toy, and so could begin the indoctrination of the next generation of fashion consumers—teaching even in infancy the importance and intricacies of fashion awareness. Those who produced the English fashion doll did not rely simply on the accidents of parental dispersal—they marketed the fashion doll separately as a toy aimed specifically at children.

The original fashion doll continued to serve the upper end of the market, while the English one publicized the latest fashions to the rest of society, until Napoleon finally ordered that the export of French dolls should cease.

After over four hundred years the French fashion doll was dethroned by a popular usurper. The first record of the fashion doll dates back to 1396 and the English royal court. The purpose it had so expensively, so exclusively and so ponderously served was now to pass to a mere paper cut-out—so humble and so ephemeral as to be beneath the notice of most historians but symptomatic of the rapid changes in the diffusion of fashion views which had occurred in the eighteenth century. For by the time of its appearance, the fashion manipulators had a host of other means by which they could spread the latest fashions down through the ranks of English society.

Some of them have fortunately proved more durable than the little paper cutouts. For few English fashion dolls have survived to offer us visible proof of the extension of the market. Their more imposing, more impressive, more collectable ancestors have displayed a greater ability to survive, and in doing so have helped to obscure the popular influence of their ephemeral, if popular, descendants. Like so many of the commercial techniques of the eighteenth century, the fashion doll has a tradition which long predates its commercial apotheosis. Its use by the French as a popular means of propaganda for centuries has long been recognized: 'At a time when as yet the press was non-existent, long before the invention of such mechanical means of reproduction as the woodcut and the copper plate, . . . the doll was given the task of popularizing French fashions abroad'. The English version of this means of spreading their fashions has received less attention, but it was certainly effective. Its almost infinite variety deservedly earned it the contemporary description of 'the protean figure'. It provided a direct channel to those who wished to be in fashion. It offered an effective means by which artisans, craftsmen and even labourers—and more especially the wives of all of them—could be sucked into the thrall of fashion. The wives of the newly prosperous artisans . . . now knew what to spend their money on.

Fortunately there were other sources of fashion intelligence to satisfy the growing appetite for accurate information which grew in step with the rising demand for consumer goods. The fashion plate and the fashion magazine and the advertisements of fashions in the newspapers were effective allies of the fashion doll, and have survived in sufficient numbers to demonstrate clearly both their quality and the period in which they revealed their importance.

For although the first fashion magazine appeared in France in the 1670s, ... 'it was in England that the systematic and ... widespread production of fashion prints began'. The time was the last three decades of the eighteenth century.

The Lady's Magazine brought out its first fashion print in 1770, and it was at this time that an enterprising advertiser started to insert a page of the latest hats and dresses into ladies pocket books and almanacs. These were specifically devised for the guidance of 'ordinary young gentlewomen, not the extravagant few'....

There were many traditional agents of fashionable change operating throughout the eighteenth century, and even earlier. Many had been highly effective, and there is ample contemporary comment to testify to their powers. According to *The London Tradesman* of 1747 such was the power of the fashionable tailor that 'to some he not only makes their Dress, but ... may be said to make themselves'....

In fact by 1747 *The London Tradesman* in its catalogue of 'all the TRADES' had already recognized the pervasive impact of fashion on the most diverse employment. Trade after trade was said to require 'a fruitful Fancy, to invent new Whims, to please the Changeable Foible of the Ladies'; or 'a quick Invention for new Patterns ... to create Trade'....

By mid-century most of the commercial benefit of fashion was felt to accrue to London: the shoes made in the provinces sold in the London 'Saleshops', the cutlery of Birmingham and Sheffield furnished the 'great Demand' for cutlery sold in the London shops who 'put their own Marks upon them and sell them as *London* made'; and yet London was still regarded as being heavily dependent on Paris for new fashions in 'Wigs, Perukes and Fans'.

It was to take longer for London to take over from Paris, for the provinces to adopt the fashions of London, and for the full battery of commercial practices designed to exploit fashion to be developed. Trusler[18] was convinced that the fashionable contagion, or what he called 'the infection of the metropolis', had spread. In his view, published in 1777, 'The great degree of luxury to which this country has arrived, within a few years, is not only astonishing but almost dreadful to think of. Time was, when those articles of indulgence, which now every mechanic aims to be in possession of, were enjoyed only by the Lord or Baron of a district'. As the result of the increase of trade and riches 'men began to feel new wants'. They 'sighed for indulgences they never dreamed of before'. The 'wish to be thought

---

[18]John Trusler (1735–1820), priest and author of *The Way to Be Rich and Respectable* (1777).

opulent ... led them into luxury of dress. The homespun garb then gave way to more costly attire, and respectable plainness was soon transformed into laughable frippery' and 'every succeeding year gave way to fresh wants and new expences'.

The spread down the social scale was explicitly described: 'the infection of the first class soon spread among the second', 'a taste for elegancies spread itself through all ranks and degrees of men'. The influence of London was explicitly blamed: 'The several cities and large towns of this island catch the manners of the metropolis ... the notions of splendour that prevail in the Capital are eagerly adopted; the various changes of the fashion exactly copied'.

The ever increasing speed of change was also widely noted. Mandeville[19] had actually supplied a convenient contemporary index by which to measure the spread of fashionable change in the early eighteenth century. For he wrote in 1723 that 'Experience has taught us, that these Modes seldom last above Ten or Twelve Years, and a Man of Threescore must have observ'd five or six Revolutions of 'em at least'. By the 1770s contemporary observers found the pace of change so accelerated that they regarded fashions as annual, and amongst the super-fashionable as monthly. As the pace of fashionable change stepped up, not everyone could keep up. The costume museums of eighteenth-century dress are very revealing as to the skilful feminine subterfuges that were employed to keep a single dress in line with the demands of fashion. For even the museum pieces show repeated signs of alterations as their wearers struggled to keep up with the shortlived modes of the eighteenth century. Not even the fashionable could always afford to buy new clothes when the whirligig of fashion was spinning as rapidly as it did in the reign of George III,[20] and the rest of society had to make constant use of the needle and their own ingenuity. But however ingenious the changes they devised, the evidence of increased spending suggests that the eighteenth-century fashion manipulators made them buy more than ever before.

Fortunately, contemporary comment has left a uniquely rich record of the chronology and nature of changes in fashion in the eighteenth century. Not surprisingly, those comments are dominated by a concern with contemporary costume. Fashion and dress are often used almost interchangeably. From Mandeville onwards special attention was given to the role of clothes in this process of social and economic change.

Fashion was the key used by many commentators to explain the forces of social imitation, social emulation, class competition and emulative spending. These were the motive forces which made fashion such a potent commercial weapon in the eighteenth century. Mandeville had specifically identified them as such in *The Fable of the Bees*. He knew that consumption occurred for motives very different from everyday utility. He knew that consumption

[19]Bernard Mandeville (1670–1733), English satirist and author of *The Fable of the Bees* (1723).
[20]King of England, 1760–1820.

could serve as the visible evidence of wealth. . . . He recognized that elegant clothes could serve as an overt statement of social superiority.

In this he anticipated Veblen.[21] For if, in Veblen's language, good repute rested on pecuniary strength, then one of the best means of displaying that strength, and thereby retaining or enhancing one's social standing, would be to indulge in conspicuous consumption of goods. The most obvious, the most socially visible way of doing this in early eighteenth-century society lay in displaying the clothes one wore. As Mandeville wrote, 'People . . . are generally honour'd according to their Clothes . . . from the richness of them we judge their Wealth . . . It is this which encourages every Body, who is conscious of his little Merit, if he is any ways able, to wear Clothes above his Rank.' He even recognizes the way in which a growing and more mobile population, either congregating in, or merely visiting, more 'Populous cities', would intensify 'the Veblen effect'. The desire to dress above one's rank would operate, he argued, 'especially in large and populous Cities, where obscure men may hourly meet with fifty Strangers to one Acquaintance, and consequently have the pleasure of being esteem'd by a vast Majority, not as what they are, but what they appear to be'. . . .

Clothes were the first mass consumer products to be noticed by contemporary observers. It is often forgotten that the industrial revolution was, to a large extent, founded on the sales of humble products to very large markets—the beer of London, the buckles and buttons of Birmingham, the knives and forks of Sheffield, the cups and saucers of Staffordshire, the cheap cottons of Lancashire. Beer was arguably the first mass consumer product to be mass produced under factory conditions and sold to the public for cash at fixed prices by pure retailers. But the sales of mass-produced cheap clothes understandably excited more attention. When *The British Magazine* of 1763 wrote that 'The present rage of imitating the manners of high life hath spread itself so far among the gentle folks of lower life, that in a few years we shall probably have no common folks at all', it was the imitation of fashionable dress that it was complaining of.

Dress was the most public manifestation of the blurring of class divisions which was so much commented on. Social expectations rose with family income. The standards of what Veblen later called 'pecuniary decency' rose too as succeeding layers of English society joined the consuming ranks. The effects excited much comment, 'It is the curse of this nation that the labourer and the mechanic will ape the lord', wrote Hanway,[22] 'the different ranks of people are too much confounded: the lower orders press so hard on the heels of the higher, if some remedy is not used the Lord will be in danger of becoming the valet of his Gentleman'. . . . The *London Magazine* for 1772 reported that the classes were imitating one another so closely that 'the lower

---

[21]Thorstein Veblen (1857–1929), American sociologist, author of *The Theory of the Leisure Class* (1899).

[22]Jonas Hanway (1712–1786), English traveler and philanthropist.

orders of the people (if there are any, for distinctions are now confounded) are equally immerged in their fashionable vices'....

Writer after writer notes the 'absence of those outward distinctions which formerly characterized different classes'. Somerville,[23] writing in the early nineteenth century, reflects on the changes which had taken place in his lifetime. 'At that time various modes of dress indicated at first sight the rank, profession and the age of every individual. Now even the servants are hardly distinguishable in their equipment from their masters and mistresses'....

All the historians of fashion record the change in fashion tempo in the middle of the eighteenth century....

On every side contemporaries rushed into print to explain the phenomenon. It was the result, they all agreed, of the downward spread of fashion, and of the imitation by the poor of their social superiors. As early as 1750 Fielding[24] complained that 'an infinite number of lower people aspire to the pleasures of the fashionable'. In 1755 *The World* complained of 'this foolish vanity that prompts us to imitate our superiors ... we have no such thing as common people among us ... Attorneys' clerks and city prentices dress like cornets of dragoons ... every commoner ... treads hard on the heels of the quality in dress'.

But whereas Fielding was full of admiration for the way the fashion leaders used their arts 'to deceive and dodge their imitators ... when they are hunted out in any favourable mode', *The World*, writing five years later, saw the result of the 'perpetual warfare' as defeat for 'the nobility'. For they 'who can aim no higher, plunge themselves into debt to preserve their rank'. They were 'beaten out of all their resources for superior distinction; out of innumerable fashions in dress, every one of which they have been obliged to abandon as soon as occupied by their impertinent rivals. In vain have they armed themselves with lace and embroidery and intrenched themselves in hoops and furbelows; in vain have they had recourse to full-bottomed perriwigs and toupees; to high heads and low heads and no heads at all'....

Part of the increased consumption of the eighteenth century was the result not only of new levels of spending in lower ranks, but also new levels of spending by those in the higher ranks who felt for the first time threatened by the loss of their distinctive badge of identity. At the beginning of the century Steele[25] had written 'each by some particular in their dress shows to what class they belong', at the end of the century Wenderborne,[26] in contrast, declared 'Dress is carried to the very utmost, and the changes it undergoes are more frequent than those of the moon ... this rage for finery and fashion spreads from the highest to the lowest; and in public places ... it is

---

[23]Thomas Somerville (1741–1830), divine and historian.

[24]Henry Fielding (1707–1754), English novelist.

[25]Richard Steele (1672–1729), English essayist, dramatist, and politician.

[26]Gebhard Friedrich August Wenderborne (1742–1811), author of *A view of England towards the End of the Eighteenth Century*.

very difficult to guess at [people's] rank in society or at the heaviness of their purse'.

The situation was unique as well as novel. It had never happened before in Britain. It had not yet happened anywhere else in the world.... [I]n other countries the vulgar imitate the higher ranks, [in England] on the contrary, the great are solicitous to distinguish themselves from the mob'.

Finally, as the pace of fashion changes accelerated ever more rapidly, we find the rich moving into subtleties of cut rather than competing (as they did in the 1750s and 1760s and even more so in the 1770s and 1780s) in ever greater extremes of fashion. And finally a kind of fashion truce was called. 'For the first time in our history the Gentleman began to adopt the styles of dress and the actual garments of the working man.' It was, in fact, part of the change from 'a crude to a subtle method of expressing social superiority'—a change which finally triumphed in Beau Brummel's[27] doctrine that 'a gentleman's clothes should be inconspicuous in material and exquisite only in cut'. This process still had a long way to go. Distinctions in dress, of course, survived—very marked ones to our eyes—but they were much less obvious, particularly in male costume, in the eyes of contemporary observers.

Although fashions changed rapidly, there was greater social uniformity in the changes. All of which, of course, suited those producing and selling fashion. Demand could be controlled to suit their needs. A larger and more homogeneous market was the basis of mass-produced factory output.

As a result of this increased homogeneity, each year is seen as having a distinctive stamp, and experts can date fashion prints with almost the same certainty that one can read the hallmarks of Georgian silver. 'Fashion in hats and hair dressing changed so rapidly in the last quarter of the eighteenth century that...dating offers no great difficulty'. The changes in colour, shape, material and style were immensely various, but the changes were sufficiently marked and sufficiently widespread to be dateable. Contemporaries even referred to the in-colour of each year. In 1753 purple was the in-colour—'all colours were neglected for that purple: in purple we glowed from the hat to the shoe'. In 1757 the fashion was for white linen with a pink pattern. In the 1770s the changes were rung even more rapidly—in 1776 the fashionable colour was 'couleur de Noisette',[28] in 1777 dove grey, in 1779 'the fashionable dress was laycock satin trimmed with fur'. By 1781 'stripes in silk or very fine cambric-muslin' were in; by 1785 steel embroidery on dress was all the rage; by 1790 'the fashionable colours were lilac and yellow and brown and pale green'. So although at the end of the century men complained that 'fashions alter in these days so much, that a man can hardly wear a coat two months before it is out of

[27]English dandy, 1778–1840.
[28]Hazel.

fashion', the pattern of change was now more uniform, and more than ever at the behest, and for the convenience, of commerce....

The fashion doll, the fashion print, the fashion magazine, the fashion advertisement, the fashion shops, the great manufacturers making fashion goods and the hordes of those selling them were all agents in pursuit of new levels of consumption from an ever-widening market.

Those manufacturers who produced goods for mass consumption needed to reach markets never previously tapped. One must not forget that the prosperity of Lancashire cotton manufacturers, London brewers, Sheffield cutlers, Staffordshire potters, the toy makers of Birmingham—and the fortunes of the woollen, linen and silk industries—were based on sales to a mass market. Fashion was an essential, if not sufficient, key to open up the necessary access to that market....

If we...see fashion as an important key to understanding both society and the economy, then a study of the tumult of fashion of late eighteenth-century England may help to unlock some of the mysteries still surrounding that period's remarkable economic growth. Certainly those concerned with selling and marketing and distributing their goods gave it their concerned and concentrated attention. 'Fashion' was seen by many of them as being 'far more important than merit'. So it commanded as much of their time and energy as did the traditional preoccupations with capital, labour and production. They were fully convinced of the commercial potential of fashion and they were determined to exploit it in their sales campaigns....

The Devils of Toulon: Demonic Possession and Religious Politics in Eighteenth-Century Provence

B. ROBERT KREISER

In Europe of the sixteenth and seventeenth centuries, courts executed perhaps 100,000 accused witches, most of them convicted for having allegedly signed a pact with the devil to cause evil and overturn Christendom. Both intellectuals and the populace were united in proclaiming the terrible danger that witches posed; only a few skeptics dared to protest the torture and execution of those hapless women designated as Satan's agents. The witch craze in France differed from that in other parts of Europe in having a number of spectacular trials involving sorcerer-priests accused of bewitching nuns. The trials regularly concluded with notoriety for the nuns' convent and flames for the priest. In this article, B. Robert Kreiser examines the last case of such a sorcerer-priest in the southern French town of Aix in 1730–1731. Although social historians often study aggregate groups, sometimes a case study can illuminate collective mentalities. This witchcraft trial thus exposes popular beliefs and politics and helps us understand the decline of witchcraft accusations.

Like the earlier trials of the seventeenth century, this one quickly gained notoriety. It had all the necessary ingredients: an accomplished priest, a beautiful and religious girl, sexual improprieties, and the involvement of outside groups that had more than a casual interest in the outcome of the trial. Kreiser's detailed look at the forces and issues at play raises several questions. What, for example, does the Cadière-Girard affair say about the nature of popular religion? How does one explain the difference between the view, on the one hand, of the judges and other educated persons toward the lurid accusations of witchcraft and the attitude, on the other, of the populace? Why did the priest, Jean-Baptiste Girard, not burn for his alleged crimes?

On the night of 17 November 1730 and continuing for much of the next day, the streets of the Provençal port city of Toulon buzzed with excitement over news that an exorcism was in progress at the apartment of the Cadière family. The dramatic ritual was being performed in the presence of numerous awestruck witnesses by the abbé Francois Cadière, a novice priest, over the prostrate body of his younger sister, Marie-Catherine, the alleged victim of demonic possession. Although unauthorized by the bishop of Toulon, the ceremony was conducted in general conformity with the rules prescribed in the Roman Ritual and included the recitation of long, solemn prayers, the pronunciation of words from Scripture, sprinklings with holy water, repeated signs of the cross, adjurations addressed to the devil, and invocations to God for His protection against malign powers—all designed ostensibly to drive out the demonic personality from Mlle. Cadière and deliver her from her various torments. Between spells of unconsciousness and seizures of violent convulsions, Catherine rolled about the room and spat at the crucifix in her brother's hands; her face contorted, her eyes "fixed in a piercing and unnatural stare," she burst forth with loud screams and torrents of blasphemy and obscenity which could be heard by the huge throng gathered in the streets below. Upstairs, speaking in Latin (a language Catherine did not know), the abbé Cadière asked his sister to reveal the identity of the sorcerer presumed responsible for her condition. Replying in a mixture of Latin and Provençal, in a strange, almost disembodied voice, she repeatedly declared that the source of her possession was Jean-Baptiste Girard, a well-known Jesuit priest who until two months earlier had served as her confessor and spiritual director. This dramatic public accusation, which another Cadière brother took pains to announce from the window to the crowds outside, marked the final break in the bizarre relationship which had developed between the Jesuit and his young, hitherto socially obscure female penitent and launched the notorious Cadière-Girard affair on its way to becoming a major witchcraft trial—the last such trial in French history....

The Cadière-Girard relationship had not always been so strained or irregular as it must have appeared on that mid-November night in 1730 when the exorcism was under way. At the outset their relationship had been perfectly innocent and proper.... The highly respected Jesuit priest had arrived in Toulon in April 1728.... His transfer to Toulon was intended to improve the position of the Society of Jesus in that city and to win back souls from the pro-Jansenist[1] Carmelites[2] and the Oratorians,[3] the Jesuits' chief rivals in the spiritual life of Provence. Girard was at this time aged forty-eight, gaunt, physically unattractive, but with a reputation as a celebrated preacher and talented confessor who had already directed several of his previous penitents on the path toward saintliness. Catherine Cadière, eighteen years old, "ravishingly beautiful," uneducated, and extremely naive and impressionable, had been raised by her widowed mother in an atmosphere of almost obsessive religiosity and rigid moral discipline. With her family's encouragement she had determined from a very young age to devote herself to an intensive regime of strict observance—a decision she repeatedly confirmed and strengthened and eventually expanded into a resolve to lead a wholly ascetic life.... Catherine gradually came to believe that she was an "elect soul," particularly favored in heaven, and that she had received a divine command to serve and suffer for others. Her guiding ambition was to become a saint, and in her single-minded determination to achieve this goal she assiduously studied the lives of several celebrated mystics, endeavoring to emulate, if not to surpass, their spiritual feats. Her own exemplary piety and selfless acts of charity, her frequent religious transports and remarkable gifts of prayer, lent some credence to these pretensions to divine inspiration. But it was not until the arrival of Father Girard that she finally found a director of conscience sympathetic to her spiritual aspirations.

...Girard was just as eager to enhance his own reputation as a "maker of saints" as Cadière was to attain recognition for her holiness. Within a short time she had become the Jesuit's star adept, singled out from among his many penitents to be the object of his special attention. She also reportedly began to display gifts and perform feats—clairvoyance, divination, levitation, stigmata—which, though later shown to be of dubious authenticity, for a long time afforded further support for her claims to saintliness.... Indeed, under Girard's influence and guidance Catherine's

---

[1]Jansenism was a Catholic theological and political movement that stressed the sinfulness of man.

[2]Members of a Catholic religious order established in the twelfth century.

[3]Members of the French Oratory, a Catholic order that emphasized the training of priests in seminaries.

fame and popularity spread rapidly throughout Provence. Once word of her remarkable religious achievements had reached the public, the people of Toulon, believing Catherine to be truly inspired, began to venerate her as a saint and to invoke her intercession with God in order to effect a variety of cures. Many persons, including a number of Jesuits besides Girard, testified to the "salutary effects" of her "holy prayers," But no one was more taken with the saintly ecstatic than the bishop of Toulon, . . . Louis de La Tour du Pin de Montauban. Anxious for the prestige which he and his diocese would gain from the presence of a future saint, he was quick to extol Catherine's virtues, publicize her marvels, and take her under his protection. By the middle of 1730, therefore, Catherine's status as a living saint and a celebrated local heroine appeared to be quite securely established—a fact which helps to explain much of the popular support she would later receive in her legal battles with Girard.

In the meantime, however, even while Girard was promoting Catherine as a would-be saint, and enhancing his own reputation in the process, their relationship had not remained entirely innocent. According to evidence brought out by the partisans of the Cadières during the course of the trial, toward the end of 1729 (after having served some eighteen months as her confessor) Father Girard began to display an unseemly interest in his young, attractive penitent, though he managed for a long time to keep his allegedly unholy designs and his illicit behavior discreetly hidden from the outside world, even from Catherine's own family. The Cadières naturally insisted that the responsibility for initiating this affair lay completely with Girard. They claimed that Catherine had been the reluctant victim of his sexual advances, coerced into immorality against her will. They alleged, in fact, that the "wanton Jesuit" had resorted to magic and sorcery in order to seduce and corrupt his innocent, unsuspecting penitent. According to the later testimony of Mlle. Cadière herself, Girard first bewitched her in November 1729, literally casting a spell by breathing into her mouth and blowing on her forehead, "in a way that had something very peculiar about it"—an act he was said to have performed frequently in the course of the following year. From that point on Catherine was completely infatuated with her confessor. She reported feeling strange sensations whenever she was in his presence, "something like a finger moving about my entrails and making me feel quite wet." To complicate matters even further, in March 1730, when Cadière feared she had gotten pregnant—a claim that was never actually substantiated—Girard reportedly forced her to drink a potion which resulted in an abortion.

By exploiting his position as a director of conscience and perverting the holy sacrament of confession for diabolic ends—at least according to the Cadières—Girard had violated the very laws of God and thus stood charged of the crime of "spiritual incest." Worse, to justify this irregular behavior and to overcome his penitent's often-expressed misgivings about her own "evil thoughts" and "shameful immodesties," Girard allegedly had recourse to the heretical mystical doctrines of Quietism,[4] which reportedly held that an individual filled with or illuminated by the Holy Spirit could not commit a sin and which also taught the total disregard of bodily acts in achieving a complete purity of soul. When Catherine continued to display great anxiety about the extraordinary abuses and "discipline" to which Girard was daily subjecting her body, the Jesuit sought to allay her fears, repeatedly reassuring her that it was "the will of God" that she endure such "humiliation" in order to advance on the path to saintliness. "My dear child," he supposedly told her, "I want to lead you to [the highest stages of] perfection; do not be disturbed by what happens to your body; banish your scruples, your fears and doubtings. By this means, your soul will become stronger, purer, more illuminated. It will acquire a holy freedom." In their private correspondence Father Girard frequently urged Catherine, "Do not have any will of your own, and do not feel the least repugnance. Do everything I tell you, like a good [little] girl who finds nothing difficult where her father asks for [something]." This combination of Catherine's complete and utter devotion to her extremely solicitous confessor and his insistence on her obedience and submission to his "paternal" authority had come to characterize their relationship by the summer of 1730. . . .

The last year of Mlle. Cadière's association with Father Girard was also marked by the onset of classic "hysterical" symptoms. From November 1729 onward, despite periods when she experienced a sense of spiritual peace and "an abundance of divine grace," she felt persistently besieged and harassed by demons, overwhelmingly powerful discarnate forces which troubled her imagination and disturbed her every action. During these prolonged periods of torment she heard sinister voices and was assaulted by sordid visions and erotic fantasies. In addition to these hallucinations, she suffered a variety of psychomotor disturbances and fell repeatedly into ecstatic trances, during which she suddenly gave out with howlings and unwonted profanity and blasphemed against the Eucharist, the saints, and the mysteries of the faith. On occasion she displayed a complete aversion to sacred things and an inability to pray or to take part in religious exercises. For many months Girard, apparently still convinced that his penitent was a likely candidate for eventual beatification, succeeded in convincing Catherine that she was suffering from only a temporary "state of obsession," which had actually originated with God as a way of testing her commitment and her faith. He also persuaded her that she would have to endure these demonic assaults for a period of a year. Before the year was over, however, Catherine had begun to interpret her torments—and her strange relationship with Girard—in a wholly different light.

---

[4]A seventeenth-century French Catholic movement, condemned by the papacy, that stressed the inadequacy of human effort. Quietism held that a person should maintain complete passivity, including indifference toward salvation, and abandon himself to God.

Already increasingly ambivalent in her feelings toward Girard, Mlle. Cadière had a falling-out with the Jesuit in the late summer of 1730, owing in large part to his refusal to allow her to leave the gloomy, secluded convent at Ste.-Claire d'Ollioules in which he had placed her several months earlier. In September, after Girard had attempted to transfer his penitent to another convent outside the diocese, the bishop of Toulon, Catherine's self-appointed protector, decided to place her under a new spiritual guide. On the urging of Mlle. Cadière's Dominican brother, the bishop appointed to this position Father Nicolas Girieux, a virulently anti-Jesuit Carmelite priest and a prime mover in the subsequent developments in this affair. Following the break with Father Girard and the change of confessors, Catherine began to reveal the details of her association with her former director of conscience. These stunning revelations led Father Nicolas to conclude that Catherine's sensational physical and moral afflictions went far beyond a "state of obsession" and were, in fact, incontrovertible evidence that she was actually the victim of demonic possession. He also contended that Father Girard was responsible for sending the invading spirits which had been dominating her entire personality and impelling her to act contrary to her reason and against her will. According to Father Nicolas even the marvelous feats Catherine had claimed to perform and on which her reputation for saintliness had rested very likely came not from God, but rather from the devil.

But even under Father Nicolas's spiritual direction . . . fearsome demonic torments continued to plague Mlle. Cadière. . . . By mid-October, acting with episcopal authorization, Father Nicolas had privately exorcised Catherine and two other former penitents of Father Girard, both of whom claimed to have endured states of obsession and seduction experiences similar to Mlle. Cadière's.

In the meantime, however, Girard's numerous allies had managed to convince the bishop of Toulon that Cadière and her entire family were publicity-seeking impostors and that their attempts to discredit the virtuous Girard were motivated by revenge and were all part of an anti-Jesuit plot. On 10 November, therefore, the bishop suddenly revoked the priestly powers of Father Nicolas and Father Etienne Cadière, Catherine's Dominican brother, thus setting the stage for the dramatic events which took place in the Cadière apartment only a week later.

The nature and purpose of the spectacular, unauthorized, semi-public exorcism of Catherine Cadière on 17 November now become fully intelligible. When Catherine experienced a violent "hysterical crisis" on that day, her brothers and Father Nicolas were only too anxious to exploit it. Their main object in undertaking this theatrical ritual, which they apparently staged to achieve maximum publicity, was as much to indict Girard as to dispossess Catherine. Although they no doubt hoped to effect her "disenchantment," they also wished to demonstrate, supposedly out of the mouth of the devil himself, that the Jesuit priest was a sorcerer and that he had bewitched his former penitent into immorality and blasphemy.

In the days following the exorcism, Catherine and her family lodged a formal complaint with the civil authorities and delivered a barrage of charges—sorcery, "spiritual incest," Quietism, procurement of an abortion— against Father Girard. They spoke, in particular, of the numerous spiritual and physical torments Catherine had allegedly been forced to endure for over a year at the hands of her former confessor, whom they depicted as a depraved and hypocritical voluptuary and as a vainglorious, ambitious "monster of degradation." The fantastic revelations and titillating allegations of sexual exploitation, heresy, and bewitchment provoked a sensational scandal and piqued the curiosity of countless individuals. For at least a week the crowds in the vicinity of the Cadière house were so large as to render the nearby streets virtually impassable. The exorcism had thus brought the seamy affair into public view and stimulated a great deal of idle gossip about the "satanic immorality" and "evil reputation" of Father Girard, increasingly identified in the popular mind as a suspected agent of the devil. The portrait of Girard which had already begun to emerge in the writings of several pro-Cadière polemicists came more and more to involve the highly conventional, even stylized representation of a "type": the debased, smooth-tongued sorcerer-priest, instrument of Satan and traitor to God and to his conscience—a familiar figure in the history of French witchcraft. Indeed, in preparing their stereotyped portrait of Girard, his detractors combed through the records of previous French witchcraft trials and pored over the rich demonological literature in a conscious effort to establish direct parallels between Father Girard and such notorious sorcerer-priests as Louis Gauffridy (Aix-en-Provence, 1611), Urbain Grandier (Loudun, 1634), and Thomas Boullé (Louviers, 1647), all three of whom had been convicted of and executed for crimes similar to those alleged against Girard....

The fact that a highly regarded member of the Jesuit order was now under such a cloud practically guaranteed that the affair would quickly become embroiled in the contemporaneous controversies of French ecclesiastical politics. To the Jansenists, self-proclaimed champions of a pure, uncorrupted form of Christianity who were fighting for their survival after a century-long conflict with the formidable Society of Jesus, Girard's "heinous crimes" offered a welcome opportunity to launch a major assault against the dominant theological and moral position of their powerful rivals. Although they questioned Catherine's innocence in the sordid affair, certain Jansenist controversialists eagerly took up her cause as a convenient vehicle for indicting the entire Jesuit order. In their view Father Girard exemplified the longstanding moral bankruptcy of his Society, which they held ultimately responsible for his perversions; in accomplishing the disgrace of Girard, therefore, they hoped to heap discredit upon all of his fellow Jesuits as well....

Forced on the defensive, Father Girard and his Jesuit colleagues fought back. While the friends and relatives of Mlle. Cadière were carrying their charges to the police lieutenant of Toulon, Girard acted to save his honor and protect his order from further embarrassment by appealing Catherine's "vicious calumnies" to his bishop. At the same time the Jesuits closed corporate ranks and brought their considerable influence to bear in an effort to stifle the entire affair. . . .

On 16 January 1731, after parallel investigations by the civil and ecclesiastical authorities in Toulon had proved inconclusive, an *arrêt du conseil*[5] transferred the entire affair to the *Parlement*[6] of Aix, in the hope—and expectation—that the sovereign court would dispose of the matter with great dispatch. In turning the case over to the Parlement, however, the government was placing it in the hands of a judicial body that could be quite fractious and even unruly, especially where issues of religious politics were concerned. . . . As a precaution, therefore, the government, anxious for a favorable outcome in the case, placed the actual conduct of the inquest in the hands of two magistrates who were staunch allies of the Jesuits. . . .

. . . [T]he conduct of the investigations was far from even-handed. From the outset, in fact, the authorities appear to have countenanced a host of procedural irregularities designed to favor Girard. Alleged violations of the customary investigative process as well as abuses of ecclesiastical authority were already reported to have occurred during the preliminary inquest carried out by diocesan officials in Toulon. The Cadière family charged these officials with suppressing evidence, rehearsing and prompting many witnesses, suborning others into perjury, and taking down depositions only from persons who were predisposed to defend the conduct of Father Girard. Individuals whom Mlle. Cadière called to testify on her behalf were faced with threats of reprisals; those who persisted in giving testimony later discovered that their remarks had not even been entered into the record. Several other former penitents of Girard who came forward to corroborate Catherine's allegations against the Jesuit faced harassment and intimidation. . . .

. . . Throughout the diocesan hearings and during the subsequent parlementary investigations, Catherine was treated as though she, and not Girard, were the accused. The authorities kept her interned in convents under Jesuit control, refused to allow visits from her family, and denied her access to a confessor of her own choosing. The *commissaires*[7] assigned to the Parlement's inquest subjected her to a series of relentless interrogations and allegedly went so far as to extort from Catherine a drug-induced retraction of all the charges pending against Father Girard. When she later withdrew the retraction, they reportedly threatened her with various forms of judicial torture if she did not recant. Even with all the official efforts at browbeating and coercion, she would manage to persist in her original accusations to the end of the trial. As for Girard, despite the seriousness of the allegations made

---

[5] A decree of the king's council.

[6] A sovereign judicial court.

[7] Commissioners.

against him, he not only remained free during most of the inquest, but was also allowed to perform his various priestly duties unimpeded. . . .

While the authorities did everything within their power to influence the proceedings, Girard's lawyers also mounted a strong counterattack on the Jesuit's behalf, categorically denying as unsubstantiated all the charges pending against him. They depicted Girard as a honorable priest of solid faith, exemplary virtue, and saintly piety—a far cry from the monster of degradation portrayed by the Cadières. His only faults during his two years as Catherine's director of conscience, they contended, had been an imprudent excess of credulity and zeal, as a result of which he had failed to act quickly and decisively to disabuse his penitent of her monstrous delusions or to stifle her overwrought sensuality. His accusers, by contrast, were vengeful partisans and conniving schemers, who had deliberately distorted and even fabricated evidence, with the aim of publicly dishonoring the name and defaming the character of Father Girard. The Jesuit's partisans charged Catherine with having faked and cynically manipulated the various "supernatural" phenomena she had earlier claimed in trying to pass herself off as a saint. . . . In fact, they insisted, the charges of sorcery and bewitchment which the Cadières had brought against the maligned Girard were a tissue of lies and absurd inventions, designed to deflect attention from Catherine's own misdeeds and indiscretions. As for her exorcism, that had been staged by Catherine's brothers, who had carefully rehearsed their sister to act out a role, counterfeiting the signs of possession in conscious imitation of several notorious demoniacs before her.

Confronted by these countercharges, polemicists and lawyers on the Cadière side replied with a torrent of impassioned pamphlets and legal briefs of their own. Dozens of such works appeared in 1731 and served to arouse a general revulsion against Girard and the Jesuits and gave new life to the Jansenist cause. . . . Where the pamphleteers left off, the clever song writers and crude versifiers joined the fray, endlessly repeating one another in their caustic vilification of Girard and derisively chanting of his imminent conviction. Verses, epigrams, and songs circulated in manuscript and in print, frequently accompanied by explicitly pornographic *estampes*.[8] At the same time, the rumor mills were grinding out lurid stories about Father Girard's allegedly scandal-ridden past. A proliferation of allegorical fables and scurrilous lampoons contributed further to Girard's disgrace. Like some of the tracts, many of these other propaganda pieces exploited the theme of Girard as a sorcerer-priest and played on popular fears of the devil and of demonic forces operating in the world.

Where public opinion was concerned, the pro-Cadière propagandists seem to have correctly gauged the mood and temper of the time. If most of those in positions of authority favored Girard, the Cadière side could count on increasingly strong and vocal support from other levels of society, especially

[8]Prints.

from among the *menu peuple*,[9] many of whom had come to revere Catherine as a saint. In taking their case to the streets, therefore, the proponents of Mlle. Cadière found an extremely receptive audience, only too eager to rally to her cause. The people of Provençe had been following the trial very closely and were ready to believe the allegations made against Father Girard, particularly those which portrayed the Jesuit as an instrument of Satan. Throughout the spring and summer of 1731 they held frequent demonstrations to show solidarity with their beleaguered saint and to express their indignation at Girard, whom they repeatedly denounced as a scoundrel, a devil, and a sorcerer.... By the end of August 1731 most of Provençal society, from the great *gens de qualité*[10] to the lowliest of the laboring poor, was caught up in the furious debates. With almost everyone forced to take sides, it became virtually impossible to remain neutral. What is more, growing agitation on behalf of Mlle. Cadière had begun to have an important impact on the conduct of the trial, as Catherine's ardent supporters came increasingly to look to the judges in the Parlement of Aix to save her and punish the accused sorcerer—already convicted in the court of public opinion.

It was in this highly volatile, intensely partisan atmosphere that the Parlement of Aix attempted to conduct its deliberations.... So sharp were the divisions and so heated were the discussions that several sessions erupted into shouting matches; some especially zealous and short-tempered magistrates traded insults with each other, and on more than one occasion a few judges almost came to blows....

Similar tensions and differences of opinion existed within the *parquet*,[11] whose five members had responsibility for reviewing the collected evidence, determining guilt or innocence, and proposing appropriate penalties.... On 11 September 1731, speaking for a majority of three, the *procureur-général*,[12] Boyer d'Aiguilles, delivered a stunning pronouncement. He recommended that the court find Catherine Cadière, the initiator of the original complaint, guilty of false accusations, calumnious slander, abuses of religion, profanations of the faith, and the feigning of saintliness and possession—all the charges which Father Girard, the accused, had levelled against her.... Boyer further proposed that Catherine be subjected to "the question,"[13] both "ordinary" and "extraordinary," in order "to extract the complete truth concerning her accomplices," and that she then be turned over to the public executioner for hanging. Boyer also recommended a series of lesser punishments for the Cadière brothers, Father Nicolas, and Catherine's *avocat*,[14] Chaudon. Concerning the fate of Girard, the *procureur-général* was completely silent. After

[9]The "little people," the common people.
[10]People of quality.
[11]The collective name for the king's representatives in Parlement.
[12]The Attorney General, the king's primary representative in Parlement.
[13]Torture. "Extraordinary" was more intense than "ordinary" torture.
[14]"Advocate" or barrister.

publishing his conclusions, he turned over the case to the *Grand'Chambre*[15] for final review and adjudication. A tumultuous four weeks were to pass—including final interrogations of and confrontations between Cadière and Girard—before the court was to deliver its verdict....

...Fearing the worst, many of her partisans began pouring into Aix from all over Provence to protest the *parquet*'s conclusions and to mount a campaign to dissuade the magistrates in the *Grand'Chambre* from upholding the *procureur-général*'s judgment. Some particularly ardent supporters, meanwhile, were even preparing to take up arms to save Catherine if that became necessary. With emotions and public suspicions running higher every day, rumors of Jesuit intrigues and plots were rampant. Reports began circulating that the Jesuits were planning to poison Father Girard and kidnap Mlle. Cadière in order to put an immediate end to the whole affair. Though unfounded, such reports prompted some of Catherine's alarmed partisans to establish an around-the-clock vigil near the convent in which she was being held captive. Any member of the Jesuit order seen on the streets could expect to be insulted, threatened, or even beaten.

On 10 October, the day the Parlement was at last to render its verdict, the magistrates of the *Grand'Chambre* entered the Palais de Justice[16] around 7:00 a.m. Even as the judges were filing into the court, huge, noisy, increasingly restive crowds, no doubt hopeful of influencing the Parlement's deliberations, had begun to gather in the public square outside.... The judges finally published their verdict just before nightfall. And a confusing and paradoxical verdict it was! To begin with, none of the magistrates, not even the most ardent partisans of the Jesuits, was prepared to follow the harsh conclusions of the *procureur-général*. But beyond general agreement on that point, the judges voting on the case were sharply divided. Twelve held that Father Girard should be burned and Catherine Cadière released; twelve others voted to acquit the Jesuit while condemning his former penitent to penalties ranging from two years confinement in a convent to life imprisonment. Forced to break the tie and cast the deciding vote, First President Lebret (who was also the intendant[17] of Provence) determined on what essentially amounted to a double acquittal, returning Girard to the ecclesiastical authorities for judgment of his irregular conduct as a priest and sending Mlle. Cadière back to her mother. The court voted to drop the charges against Father Nicolas and the brothers Cadière, though the Cadière family was left to pay all court costs.

The Parlement rendered its verdict without publicly commenting on any of the various charges which had been raised during the course of the trial. It is nevertheless clear that, at least where Girard was concerned,

---

[15]The most important chamber of the Parlement.
[16]The Palace of Justice, the seat of the Parlement.
[17]The chief royal agent in a province.

the decision as to his guilt or innocence rested not on the accusations of demonopathic sorcery, but rather on the charges of priestly malfeasance. Indeed, the allegations of sorcery and bewitchment, which had seemed so central to the case against the Jesuit (at least in the public's mind), did not even figure in the court's final deliberations, since the judges, adhering to strict standards of evidence, and skeptical about charges that were predicated on the unacceptable premise of diabolic intervention or possession by an evil spirit, set them aside as not proved. Even among the dozen magistrates who voted to convict Girard there was no willingness to give any credence to these charges, which several of the pro-Cadière jurists openly disparaged. In declining to sanction the accusations of sorcery and possession, the court was explicitly acknowledging its acceptance of the royal edict of 1682. That decree, which was designed to establish judicial uniformity throughout the kingdom for such alleged offenses, had marked the monarchy's official abandonment of criminal prosecutions for witchcraft. It was this point of view which the Parlement's verdict of 10 October 1731 had thus reaffirmed.

But the announcement of the court's highly equivocal verdict produced a mixed reaction. The decision satisfied neither the Jesuit partisans of Father Girard, eager to see their colleague completely exonerated and his accusers convicted for their "vicious calumnies," nor the supporters of Catherine Cadière, convinced of their saintly heroine's total innocence and equally certain of Girard's guilt. To be sure, the allies of Mlle. Cadière, having come to expect that her execution might be imminent, were overjoyed at her acquittal. The crowds stationed outside the Parlement burst into loud applause for the twelve judges who had voted to set her free and raised her lawyer on their shoulders in triumph. When Catherine was released from her convent prison, hundreds of her supporters rushed to touch and embrace her or to kiss the hem of her dress. Others had to be satisfied with catching only a glimpse of their heroine as she was escorted through the streets of Aix. Similar celebrations went on in every corner of Provence. But the indignation many of Catherine's adherents felt over Girard's virtual acquittal soon overcame much of the joy they experienced on hearing of her release.

All over France—and beyond—pamphleteers and songwriters joined in the chorus of criticism.... The protests sometimes became quite unruly. In Aix crowds of Cadière's supporters hurled rocks at the carriages of pro-Girard magistrates and hooted and jeered at Girard himself when he appeared in public for the first time in months. In Toulon the local agitation went on for three days and nights. Effigies of Father Girard were dressed to represent the figure of the devil, paraded around town, and then burned in a spectacular ceremony. Royal troops had to be called in to prevent one aggressive mob from setting fire to a Jesuit religious house. Similar acts of vandalism and minor riots occurred throughout Provence. This violent behavior served not only as a means of venting the public's anger at the Parlement's "craven action" in allowing Girard to go unpunished, but also as a ritualized expression of popular justice and as a symbolic purging of the demonic influences and polluting elements in their midst; for to their way of thinking the court's release of the Jesuit priest had let loose on the community a potentially dangerous sorcerer.

In an effort to quell these disturbances the intendant Lebret ordered a regiment of royal troops into Aix. In addition, he secured scores of *lettres de cachet*[18] which authorized the arrest or exile of Cadière partisans in Toulon, Aix, and Marseille, including a significant number of magistrates, lawyers, merchants, and clergy. Others suffered the loss of royal pensions. The harshest treatment was reserved for members of the Cadière family, all of whom were subjected to intense persecution and harassment. Catherine herself, within a short time of her release, had been ordered to leave the city of Aix at once or face arrest. From that day on she mysteriously disappeared from sight, never to be heard from again.

As for Father Girard, he made haste to escape from Provence entirely. . . . [H]e retired to his native Dôle in February 1732. That same month the ecclesiastical authorities in Toulon formally absolved him of all the crimes imputed to him. In the meantime, the Jesuits, determined on a clear-cut vindication, had embarked on a vigorous campaign to rehabilitate the reputation of Girard and refurbish the image of the Society of Jesus. Several writers concentrated their efforts on extolling Girard's heretofore neglected merits. One apologist went so far as to compare Father Girard to Jesus Christ, since they had both allegedly suffered similar trials and tribulations. By the time Girard died, on 4 July 1733, allegedly in "the odor of sanctity," his colleagues already deemed him worthy of veneration as a future saint and were even preparing to propose him for beatification. In the long run, however, their efforts proved unsuccessful.

Although the authorities had managed to restore relative calm in Aix and Toulon by the end of 1732, the memory of the Cadière-Girard affair would linger on long after all the protagonists in the case had passed from the scene. Despite Girard's apparent "rehabilitation" the notorious scandal had badly tarnished the image and reputation of the Society of Jesus and would continue to plague the order until its expulsion from France in 1764. No amount of influence, corporate solidarity, or casuistry had been able to deliver the Jesuits from the embarrassment, popular distrust, and increasingly low public esteem which their colleague's alleged improprieties had brought them. In large part this situation resulted from the fact that the Jansenists had conducted a very successful campaign to exploit this episode to their own advantage. . . . Portraying Mlle. Cadière—and themselves—as innocent victims of injustice and arbitrary authority, they managed not only to mobilize public opinion behind her, but at the same time to attract considerable popular support for their own cause as well. In the process they contributed much to bringing the larger debates of religious politics within

---

[18]Sealed letters addressed to private persons that usually ordered imprisonment or banishment.

the public's purview and to raising the political consciousness of groups and individuals who were not ordinarily or traditionally "political."

The Cadière-Girard affair . . . thus reveals the deep divisions which were beginning to rend the very fabric of the Gallican Church and which were to undermine public respect for and confidence in the established authorities. Equally important, however, the Cadière-Girard case also discloses the growing cultural cleavage in early eighteenth-century France between the two traditions of belief in witchcraft, the popular and the learned, whose convergence in the late Middle Ages had been a significant precondition of the great sixteenth- and seventeenth-century witch hunts. Since the mid-seventeenth century an increasing proportion of the educated had come to display a more sophisticated understanding of and a greater sensitivity to the basic psychological and physiological processes which lay behind the unusual manifestations and abnormal organic and mental states displayed by Catherine Cadière and others. Ever greater numbers of learned doctors, lawyers, judges, philosophers, and theologians were directly challenging the very notions of sorcery and demonic possession, ascribing the strange phenomena and deviant behaviors which were usually associated with diabolic intrusions to various natural causes: hysterical passions, vapors, melancholia, derangement, insufficiently controlled imagination, or pure trickery. For these critics the alleged demoniac was more in need of medical attendance and/or incarceration than exorcism or the prayers of the Church. Although their "natural" explanations remained tentative and uncertain, their vision of the world and of man had reduced dramatically, if not completely, the domain of the supernatural.

But this "structural change in human mentality" among the learned elite still had not, of course, penetrated to the uneducated masses. While skepticism was becoming the dominant view among the educated, popular mental structures and traditional habits of belief remained essentially untouched. The terrifying fantasies and hallucinations reported by Catherine Cadière made a strong impression on these people, for whom the world was still dominated by innumerable benign and malevolent forces. Intervention by unseen powers in the natural order of things remained for them an ever-present reality and a constant source of apprehension. Along with their belief in the devil's continual surveillance over and intrusion in their daily lives, they continued to place great credence in the reality of human witches and sorcerers who willfully chose to act as agents of a lustful, destructive devil in order to cause the possession of their helpless victims. For the people of Provence the traditional stereotype of the sorcerer-priest was still very much alive, and they were thus quite prepared to believe that Jean-Baptiste Girard had had "commerce with demons" and ought therefore to have been executed for his despicable and dangerous crimes. But despite the tenacity and continued vitality of these traditional beliefs, especially among the unlettered, the view embodied in the royal edict of 1682 was the one which came to prevail.

Even more than the declaration of 1682, however, it was the Cadière-Girard case which, as the first (and only) major test of this decree . . . , clearly marks the end of witchcraft as a justiciable crime. The refusal of the Parlement of Aix to convict Father Girard for sorcery and bewitchment, and its outright dismissal of these charges as not proved and not credible, reaffirmed the official view—gaining strength since at least the middle of the seventeenth century—that witchcraft no longer represented a threat to the established religious, political, or social order. In the last analysis, it is far less important whether Girard was actually guilty of any of the numerous crimes of which he stood accused or, for that matter, whether he died "in the odor of sanctity" or in disgrace. What is significant is that, unlike Urbain Grandier and other accused sorcerer-priests of the previous century, Jean-Baptiste Girard died in his bed, and not at the stake.

Death's Arbitrary Empire

JOHN McMANNERS

The eighteenth century is known as the Enlightenment, the Age of Reason, or the Age of Voltaire. John McManners reveals the underside of that epoch of cultural achievement, a world where, for most people, death triumphed early. When McManners reviews the history of eighteenth-century France in terms of medicine, disease, and mortality, he finds ill health, violence, and misery to have been as characteristic of the age as enlightened reason and Voltarian wit.

How long could one expect to live in the eighteenth century? The high rate of infant mortality was the primary reason for such a low life expectancy. Why did so many infants and children die? Did people do all they could to ensure their children's health and long lives? Orphans were less likely to survive childhood than any other group. The presence of orphanages suggests that society attempted to care for orphans. If that is true, why did so many die so young?

Which diseases were most deadly? McManners paints a bleak picture of physicians and their ability to treat illness and disease. Why were medical doctors so ineffective? Surely we cannot place the blame on physicians, for their patients, even in the best of times, were models of poor health. Living conditions in towns (such as overcrowding and the lack of sanitation), an insufficient and poor diet, the dangers of the workplace, even the clothing, all made people easy prey for disease. And where could one be safe? Not in an institution, for hospitals, army barracks, and asylums, for example, were dangerous places.

Nothing, not even youth and robust health, could give security from suffering or early death, for eighteenth-century France was a violent society. Highwaymen, domestic violence, wild animals, and rural conflicts were omnipresent. Often hungry, cold, sick, and frightened by forces seemingly beyond their control, the overwhelming majority of people had little time to marvel at Voltaire's wit.

In eighteenth-century France, 'death was at the centre of life as the graveyard was at the centre of the village'. Speaking in averages, and confounding in one the diversity of the whole country and the fortunes of all classes, we find that something like a quarter of all babies born in the early years of the century died before reaching their first birthday, and another quarter before reaching the age of eight. Of every 1,000 infants, only 200 would go on to the age of fifty, and only 100 to the age of seventy. A man who had beaten the odds and reached his half-century would, we may imagine, have seen both his parents die, have buried half his children and, like as not, his wife as well, together with numerous uncles, aunts, cousins, nephews, nieces, and friends. If he got to seventy, he would have no relations and friends of his own generation left to share his memories. If this is a description of the average, what can we say of the unfortunates whose sombre ill luck weights down the figures to this mean?...

A new understanding of the eighteenth century comes to us when we review its history in terms of disease and mortality. In narrow fetid streets and airless tenements, in filthy windowless hovels, in middens and privies, in undrained pools and steaming marshes, in contaminated wells and streams—and, for that matter, in the gilded corridors of Versailles, where excrement accumulated—infections of every kind lurked. The files of the administrators, more especially those of the Royal Society of Medicine at the end of the *ancien régime*,[1] are full of information sent in by medical experts about local epidemics and peculiar illnesses, but it is often difficult to deduce from their accounts what the specific diseases were. They spoke essentially of symptoms. Fevers were 'bilious', 'putrid', 'autumnal', 'red', 'purple', 'intermittent', 'malignant', 'inflammatory'. The spitting of blood so often mentioned could have been the result of cancer of lungs or larynx, infection of the trachea, or pulmonary tuberculosis; their 'scurvy', deduced from bleeding gums and painful joints, could include arthritis and pyorrhoea. An autopsy frequently produced a report of 'worms' in lungs or stomach, without any other evidence to bring precision.... 'With their bodies assaulted on all sides, these people were carried off before the more subtle disorders had a chance to strike.' The main killers were influenza and pulmonary infections, malaria, typhoid, typhus, dysentery, and smallpox, striking in waves across a debilitating pattern of routine afflictions—mange, skin disorders, gout, epilepsy. The grimmest scourge of all was smallpox, which seems to have

[1] Old Régime, the period before the French Revolution of 1789.

become a more common and more virulent disease from the late seventeenth century. A doctor of Montpellier in 1756 described it as being 'everywhere', as it were 'naturalized' and 'domesticated', especially at Paris, 'where it never relaxes its grip'.... Not surprisingly, then, the army records on new recruits continually speak of marked faces.... This was, indeed, a disease which destroyed the beauty of so many of those it did not slay....

... There were two seasons when mortality was at its highest, winter and early spring on one hand, and autumn, especially the month of September, on the other. In some places, winter was the cruellest season, in others autumn. From December to March, pneumonia and pulmonary afflictions abounded, and the sheer cold took its toll of those who were ill-clothed and lacked the means to keep warm. And these were numerous. Wood was in short supply in the cereal-growing plains and in the cities. Heating arrangements were rudimentary; even in Versailles, wine froze at the royal table in winter, and the heavily padded and decorated coats of courtiers were not just for display. Clothing passed from upper to lower classes and from older to younger generations, getting more and more threadbare on its journey. The poorer streets of cities were a motley pageant of rags, anonymous or with prestigious social origins. There were peasants who never changed their linen, and when they discarded it, it was too worn to be sent to the paper-mills. Even the more prosperous peasants... made do with two shirts and two coats a year, and a cloak every five. There was not much in the wardrobe to keep them warm and dry in the snow or rain of winter. In August, September, and October, dysentery would strike, and before illnesses encouraged by the excessive heat had declined, there would come the onset of those which flourished in the ensuing dampness.... These were fevers—malaria (coming, as contemporaries noted, with the floods), typhoid, and 'purple fever' which was often confused with the ubiquitous scarlatina or measles. Generally, it was adults, especially the aged, who succumbed in winter, and the younger children in the autumn—though there were exceptions: the cold in some places carried off more babies under the age of one than the intestinal infections of the hotter weather. Superimposed upon this yearly cycle of menace was the arbitrary onslaught of great epidemics, sometimes driving the death rate up to double and treble the monthly average; there was the dysentery in Anjou in 1707 and 1779, highly infectious and lethal within two or three days, the influenza in the same province which caused devastation in 1740, the typhoid and enteric fever in Brittany from 1758 onwards which was largely responsible for reducing the population of that province by 4 per cent; there were more localized outbreaks, like the military fever in Pamiers in 1782 which killed 800 people.

Being born was a hazardous business for both mother and child. 'Don't get pregnant and don't catch smallpox' was Mme de Sévigné's[2] advice to her married daughter... although she had only simple ideas of how

---

[2] Famous writer of letters, 1626–1696.

to avoid either. The proverbial pride in pregnancy of primitive societies was overwhelmed, in eighteenth-century France, by fear. Medical manuals considered a pregnant woman to be suffering from an illness, and even cited Scripture in ascribing the pains of childbirth to the transgression of Eve. Many women, especially those of the poorer classes, came to their ordeal in wretched health, and the prevalence of rickets caused deformities which made delivery difficult. There were hardly any hygienic precautions, the technique for arresting haemorrhages was not yet developed, and the manipulation of forceps (supposed to be limited to qualified surgeons alone) was clumsy. Until the reign of Louis XVI, there was hardly any attempt to train midwives. In reporting to their bishops or to the secular authorities, parish priests described how the office of midwife came to be filled in their parish.... A *curé*[3] in the diocese of Boulogne in 1725 said that his midwife inherited the job from her mother—'the women have a reasonable amount of confidence in her.' Another *curé* said that 'ours has worked here for thirty years: she took up the office of her own accord, the women of the parish accepted her, and it has not been thought fitting to oblige her to undergo further training.' Horror stories about midwives abound—beating on the stomach to 'hasten delivery', cutting the umbilical cord too close or failing to tie it, forgetting the placenta, crippling babies by rough handling, and— even—showing off by turning the infant round so that the feet emerged first. Louis XIV made a clean break with tradition when he called in a man, the surgeon Jacques Clément, to the *accouchement*[4] of the Dauphine in 1686.... But were surgeons much more use than midwives? Clément bled his patient, wrapped her in the skin of a newly flayed sheep, and kept her in a dark room for nine days without so much as a single candle. And how good was the gynaecologist whose advertisement in Paris has been preserved as a curiosity?—'Montodon, ci-devant pâtisseur, boulevard Bonne Nouvelle, est actuellement chirurgien et accoucher.'[5] In fact, there was little that even the most expert practitioner could do if things went wrong. If the baby's head stuck, there would be a week of agony and the vileness of gangrene before inevitable death. The Caesarian section without anaesthetics left one chance in a thousand for the women.... Many babies were stillborn, or died within a few days, or were maimed for life. A memoir to an intendant in 1773 describes young people coming out of a parish mass, marked by inexpert deliveries—atrophied, hunchbacked, deaf, blind, one-eyed, bandy-legged, bloodshot of eye, lame and twisted, hare-lipped, 'almost useless to society and fated for a premature end'. Many women too were killed, or crippled, or mentally scarred; a *curé* blames the rise of contraceptive practices in his parish on the neurotic determination of so many women never to undergo the experience of childbirth again.

[3]Chief parish priest.

[4]Parturition.

[5]Montodon, former pastry-cook, boulevard Bonne Nouvelle, is currently a surgeon and obstetrician.

... Between 20 and 30 per cent of babies born died in their first year: in a particularly wretched hamlet in the early part of the century, over 32 per cent died in their first year and over 22 per cent in their second. There were, of course, healthy and unhealthy areas, depending on the peculiar combination of advantages and disadvantages in food supplies, geographical features, and climate. The national average in the eighteenth century for children surviving to the age of ten was, roughly, 55 per cent; at Crulai in Normandy it was 65 per cent; in poverty-stricken villages amidst the stagnant malarial pools of the Sologne or of the Mediterranean littoral, it was 40 per cent.... The deadly season of the year for infants was early autumn, when heat, humidity and flies, and unhygienic ways of living brought the intestinal infections for which no remedy was known. These visitations were facilitated by the custom, prevalent among richer people and town dwellers, of sending infants away to be nursed by foster mothers. Towards the end of the century, of the 21,000 babies born each year in Paris, only 1,000 were fed by their mothers, another 1,000 by wet-nurses brought into the home, 2,000 to 3,000 were sent to places near the city, and the rest to more distant localities—concentric circles within which the proportion of deaths became higher as the distance from home increased.... For families of the urban working class, like small shopkeepers or the silk workers of Lyon, it was an economic necessity to get the wife back to counter or loom quickly. For the leisured class, a satisfactory explanation is harder to find; a certain harshness of mind, an unwillingness to become too attached to a pathetic bundle whose chances of survival were so limited, the desire to resume sexual relationships as soon as possible, the belief that loss of milk diluted the quality of the blood of the mother, a reliance on the therapeutic qualities of country air to give the baby a good start or (very doubtfully) some subconscious reaction against an infant's 'oral sadism'—whatever the reasons, a compelling social custom had arisen. In 1774, a reformer, appealing to have children 'brought up in the order of Nature', described the sensation when a mother declares her intention of breast-feeding her first child: protests from her parents, and all the ladies lamenting to see her risking her life for a new-fashioned theory. Given the demand, around the cities a wet-nursing 'industry' had arisen. In some villages near Limoges, girls married earlier to qualify. Such glimpses as we get of this peculiar interchange between town and country show an unfeeling and mercenary world—women who take on two or three babies in addition to their own, knowing that there will be competition for survival, who go on drawing their pay when they know their milk is drying up and their client's infant will have no chance.... These practitioners are preying on legitimate children, with parents to look after their interests and hoping against hope that they will be trundled back home in nine months' time. What then of the illegitimate ones, the multitude of foundlings, the *enfants trouvés*?[6]

---

[6]Orphans, foundlings.

The fate of these unhappy infants throws a harsh, cold light on the cruel underside of the century of crystalline wit and rococo delicacy. Increasing numbers of children were being abandoned. An average of 2,000 a year came to the Enfants Trouvés of Paris in the 1720s, rising to a record total of 7,676 in 1772; thereafter, royal edicts forbade the bringing-in of foundlings from the provinces, and the Parisian total stabilized at about 5,800 a year. In Bordeaux at the mid-century, there were about 300 admissions annually; in Metz, in the winter of 1776, no less than 900. . . . These numbers swamped the organizational abilities of the *ancien régime*, . . . and the hopeless problem they presented deadened the charitable instincts of those who cared. A Genevan doctor reports a nun of the Parisian foundling hospital taking refuge in the reflection that these innocent souls would go straight to eternal bliss, since the revenues of her institution could not feed any more of them anyway. There was a prejudice against making immoral conduct easier by spending money on those 'unhappy fruits of debauchery' (though it is true that some children were abandoned by married parents who were too poor to maintain them). Many illegitimate children were doomed before ever they reached the shelter of an institution—physically impaired by the mother's attempts to conceal her pregnancy or to produce an abortion, infected with venereal disease, or hopelessly weakened by a journey from some distant place, crowded in baskets on the back of a donkey, or of a porter travelling on foot, or jolting in a wagon. The infants who got through the crucial first week in which so many died had to survive the grim and crowded conditions in the hospital, and the rigours of the system of putting out to nurse (with private families paying more to preempt the healthiest and most reliable foster mothers). Only one foundling in ten lived to reach the age of ten: nine had perished. Such survivors as there were would live gloomily learning a trade in some institution full of prostitutes, layabouts, and madmen, or in some ruthlessly disciplined orphanage; a very few might be found again by their parents or left with some sympathetic country family—but the chances of a decent existence were infinitesimal. One who did get through the hazards and succeeded was the *philosophe* and mathematician d'Alembert,[7] left as an infant on the steps of the church of Saint-Jean-la-Ronde. An expert on the calculus of probabilities, he must often have reflected on the odds that he had beaten.

Driven to despair by poverty, some parents abandoned their children: there were suspicions that others did not strive officiously to keep them alive. The synodal statutes of various dioceses ordered the *curés* to warn their flocks against the dangerous practice of putting children to sleep in the beds of their parents, where so often they were suffocated. . . . A surgeon described the injuries suffered by babies in the vineyard country around Reims: while their mothers toiled among the vines they were sometimes attacked by

---

[7] Jean le Rond d'Alembert, 1713–1783.

animals—eyes pecked by turkeys, hands eaten off by pigs. And for the healthy grown-up, the ordinary routines of life were precarious. Society was ill-policed, unable to take effective measures to suppress highwaymen and discipline vagabonds. Rural life was violent. Wife-beating was common. Unpopular *curés* were kept awake by nocturnal *tapages* [8] which could degenerate into riots. There were affrays with cudgels and clubs at fairs. In Languedoc, where the hunting rights of the lords had been bought off, peasants went around with guns; poachers returned the fire of gamekeepers; and pot-shots were taken at *seigneurs* [9] and other unpopular local worthies. The youths of villages were organized, quasi-officially, into bands, the '*garçons de paroisse*',[10] who fought pitched battles with those from other places at fairs, marriages, and the draw for the *milice*,[11] or when communities quarrelled over boundaries or grazing rights.... In towns, the police force was inadequate to maintain order at festivals or to organize precautions against accidents. A panic at the fireworks in Paris for the marriage of the Dauphin in 1770 led to more than 1,000 being trampled to death; two years later, the great fire at the Hôtel-Dieu claimed many victims. There were, indeed, few precautions against fire—for long the only Parisian fire brigade was the Capuchin friars, swarming into action in frocks and cowls, with axes and ladders. Narrow streets, ramshackle buildings, and an abundance of wooden construction made the old parts of cities hopelessly vulnerable, tinder dry in summer, and underpinned with extra fuel in winter when the cellars of the rich were crammed with firewood and grain.... Buildings, especially the parish churches for whose maintenance a local rate had to be levied, were often left unrepaired and dangerous; every year there were floods from unbanked rivers, wreaking devastation and leaving legacies of fever. In the streets and in the countryside, savage dogs, some with rabies, wandered; in remote areas wolf packs hunted—there was a government bounty for each one killed, the parish priest to issue a certificate on the production of the ears; in 1750, 126 were killed in the province of Anjou alone. Our modern concept of 'accident' as some technical failure—burnt-out wire, slipping flange, broken lever—obtruding into well-organized habitual comfort, was almost unknown in the eighteenth century. Life was hazardous throughout....

Up to the last two decades of the *ancien régime*, hardly anything was done to regulate dangerous trades or to prevent industrial accidents.... Even so, though nothing was being done, contemporaries were becoming aware of the terrifying hardships which crippled industrial workers and abbreviated their lives.... Conditions in French mines were grim enough: twelve hours a day underground, in continual danger from explosions (because fires were burning to suck air along the galleries) and from flooding (if the horse-turned

[8] Rows.
[9] Lords.
[10] Boys of the parish.
[11] Militia.

pumps failed). The workers who polished mirrors, their feet continually in water and hands continually getting cut, were worn out by the interminable pushing to and fro of the heavy weight; printers received fractures and bruises from the levers of their presses; candle makers stifled in the heat around the furnaces; hemp crushers invariably got asthma; gilders became dizzy within a few months from the mercurial fumes which eventually poisoned them; workers who handled unwashed wool were recognizable by their pale and leaden countenances, upon which would be superimposed the permanent stains of the colours used in dyeing. Alarming examples of the effect of bad conditions of working and living on mortality rates can be studied in the armed forces. In war, few sailors were killed by cannon-balls. The seventy-four-gun ship *Ajax* patrolled in the Atlantic and Indian Oceans from February 1780 to June 1784; during that period 228 of her crew of 430 died. Battle accounted for only thirty (and of these half perished from the explosion of one of the ship's own cannon); nine were drowned . . . ; no less than 185 were killed by diseases: scurvy, dysentery, malaria—infections that ran riot among men cooped below decks for most of their time afloat, and living on food lacking in indispensable vitamins. . . . It could be said that war killed soldiers, but essentially indirectly. The mortality rate in a particular regiment from 1716 to 1749 was five times higher in war years than in those of peace, but the deaths occurred principally from December to April, when the troops were in winter quarters. In the barracks built in the eighteenth century (always at the expense of the local authorities, not of the Crown), the standard size for a room was 16 by 18 feet, to contain thirteen to fifteen men crammed into four or five beds. These stifling conditions, rampant epidemics, the cold outside, and venereal disease killed many more in winter quarters than the shot and steel of the enemy in the summer campaigning season. It was a rule under the *ancien régime* that life in State institutions was abbreviated. When *dépôts de mendicité*[12] were set up in 1767 to clear vagabonds off the roads, the inmates died off rapidly. . . . At Rennes, of 600 initially arrested, 137 died within a year, though it is true there were a lot of infections about at the time. At Saint-Denis, the death rate in the *dépôt* was consistently double that for the town, not excepting the high infant mortality from the latter total.

. . . [D]eath was not without deference to rank and possessions, to the well-to-do with their log fires, warm clothing, protein diet, and spacious houses. . . . True, in this age of multitudinous servants, it was difficult to erect effective barriers of unofficial quarantine—in the last resort, infections got through. . . . No doubt there were special afflictions to descend upon the self-indulgent; moralists (with some injustice to the sufferers) liked to instance apoplexy, paralysis, and gout. Cynics would add the dangers from the medical profession; the peasant, who distrusted blood-letting and could not afford to pay the surgeon to do it, was at least free from his attentions. Even so, the life expectancy of the rich was much better than that of the poor,

---

[12]Workhouses.

and the men of the eighteenth century knew it. In statistical terms, we might guess that the advantage was something like ten years above the average and seventeen years above that of the very poor. Peasants, living crowded together in single-roomed cottages, were very vulnerable, and even more so were the poor of the towns, whose debilitating conditions of working were allied to crowded, insanitary accommodation. Disease spread quickly where there was only one bed for a family. A doctor in the countryside complained of the way in which people 'occupy the beds of those who are dead of the malady [typhoid] on the same day the corpse is taken out of it', and it was well known that the communal bed was one of the reasons why the great plague of 1720 in Provence so often swept off a whole family. . . . The church-wardens of the poverty-stricken parish of Saint-Sauveur in Lille complained that the death rate of their parishioners in the epidemic of 1772–3 had been much higher than in the wealthy parish of Saint-André. 'The higher num-bers here', they said, 'can only be because the inhabitants are poor, more numerous and crowded into little houses, often occupied by many families, and situated in very narrow streets called alleyways . . . , they breathe the less pure air here, and because of the dirt which is virtually inseparable from poverty, they propagate all the diseases which catch a hold among them.' In Lyon, the silk workers lived twelve to fifteen in a garret, forty to fifty families in a house in the tall buildings around sunless courts, stinking of the chickens, pigs, and rabbits that they reared, and of latrines. . . .

When the Royal Council on 29 April 1776 set up its commission to investigate epidemic diseases in the provinces, one of the questions it posed was: 'Why do epidemics sometimes seem to spare a particular class of citizens?' Probably, the intention was not to look at the obvious overcrowding of the slums, but at the food and water supplies and at the dietary habits of the different classes. Seventy years earlier, during the misery at the end of the reign of Louis XIV, the economist Boisguilbert, in a burning tirade, had censured the maldistribution of food supplies which cut short so many lives. There are men, he said, who sweat blood in their toil, with no food other than bread and water, in the midst of a land of abundance, who 'perish when only half their course is run', and whose children are 'stifled in their cradles'. . . . Estimates . . . —at Arles in 1750, by the agricultural society of La Rochelle in 1763, by the owner of a carpet factory in Abbeville in 1764—show that the poorer peasants and urban workers, though far from being reduced to bread and water, lived all their lives on the margins of danger: any loss of working days had to be paid for by starvation later. There was a cycle of illness, debt, and hunger which made death almost certain on the next round of visitation, and it was not unusual for wretches who had struggled fiercely against starvation to give up on hearing that they had caught some disease, knowing that the future had little hope.

Most people in France lived on cereals, because this was what they could afford. A modern attempt to work out a typical budget for a family of the poor majority in an ordinary year, suggests 50 per cent of expenditure on bread, 16 per cent on fats and wine, 13 per cent on clothing, and 5 per cent on heating. So far as the proportion on bread is concerned, eighteenth-century estimates studied more recently confirm the generalization. The ration in hospitals was one and half *livres* a day, and this was the amount an employer generally allowed to a servant in Paris.... Judged on the scale of calories, in a fair year, the workers of France were fed efficiently, so far as potential energy was concerned, but, as more than 90 per cent of these calories came from cereals (including maize porridge in the south and beer in the north), the dietary deficiencies are obvious. The food consumption of the inmates of the hospital of Caen (bread, and the unusual advantage of plenty of Norman cider), of the conscripts doing guard duty at the citadel of Saint-Malo in the mid-century (unimaginative bread, biscuits, and salt meat, with none of the coastal fish which ought to have diversified their diet), of the peasants of Périgord (chestnuts and maize in fearful stews kept simmering all day), of the peasants of Basse-Auvergne (bread, soup of nut oil, and water tinctured with wine)—all show the same deficiencies: a lack of meat, fish, dairy produce, and fresh vegetables. That meant a deficiency of vitamins, animal fats, calcium, and trace elements, leaving the way open for rickets, scurvy, skin eruptions, loss of teeth, the breaking down of the natural power of resistance to cold, and the stunting of growth, both physical and mental. It was a matter for wonder that men from mountain areas (where the pastures offered milk and meat) were so tall—as in Auvergne, where they towered over the puny inhabitants of the cereal-growing plain.... The ill effects of the inevitable deficiencies were increased by ignorance.... [T]here was little knowledge of what constituted a balanced diet. Even the rich did not know what was good for them. They ate a large amount of meat.... But an analysis of the meals eaten by a magistrate of Toulouse and of the pupils at a boarding-school for young nobles shows, even so, a lack of calcium and some vitamins. The food available to ordinary people was not always wisely used. The regulation stew-pot of the peasants boiled away the vitamins.... Fresh bread was unusual, since for economy, huge loaves which lasted for two or three months were baked in communal ovens. The oft-recorded obstinacy of peasants in refusing to eat unusual food like potatoes, even when starving, is paralleled by the refusal of the Parisians to accept the government economy bread of wheat, rye, and barley, invented during the dearth of 1767. And of course, the people were spendthrift; living on crusts and onions all week, they would go to drinking booths on Sunday night, or swig a tot of *eau-de-vie*[13] on their way to work in the mornings. But statistics of vitamin, calcium, and trace-element deficiencies can prove too much. Like the analysis of wages in eighteenth-century France, they go to show that half the population ought not to have been alive at all. Life, for these people, was 'an economy of makeshifts', patching up a living by all sorts of incongruous combinations of earnings; no doubt they supplemented their food supplies by tilling odd

---

[13]Brandy.

corners, keeping animals in hutches, gleaning in hedgerow and common, begging, poaching, and pilfering. That was why it was so dangerous to become institutionalized, whether shut up in a *dépôt de mendicité*, a hospital, a madhouse, or on shipboard. Survival became difficult when there was no scope for enterprise.

Whatever mysterious and useless medicines they prescribed, the doctors of eighteenth-century France knew the primary importance of sound nourishment to aid the sick to recovery. Meat soup was the standard prescription for all convalescents.... 'Remedies and advice are useless unless there is a foundation of solid nourishment,' said a physician called in to investigate the outbreak of dysentery in Anjou in 1707, and he asked for 'bouillons' to be dispatched daily to all who had been afflicted. 'Bread, wine, and blankets' were the prescriptions of the doctors of Anjou who dealt with epidemics of dysentery in 1768 and typhus in 1774. In times of dearth, the poor were driven to eat contaminated or unripened grain, and were poisoned in consequence.... Officials in Brittany in 1769 and 1771 reported diseases (one called them of an 'epileptic' kind) which were sweeping the provinces because the crop failures had driven the people to eat grain that had been damp when stored and had fermented and grown musty.... In the Sologne, there were outbreaks from time to time of ergotism caused by infected grain—the disease was called 'St. Anthony's fire' and 'dry gangrene': it led to the loss of fingers, noses, or whole limbs, and eventually to madness. And the greatest killer of all was contaminated water. Springs and wells would become infected as they dried up or floods overflowed them from dubious catchment areas, or were permanently dangerous because of defective masonry in cisterns, or because animals had access to them. Typical complaints concern effluent from flax-crushing or animal manure getting into drinking supplies, or froth from the oxen's mouths still floating on the top of buckets brought in for domestic consumption. In some villages without a well, water was collected in shallow holes dug here and there and had to be filtered through linen. And any Parisian who gave a thought to where his water supply came from would confine himself to drinking wine always—if he could afford it.

Certain seasons of the year brought the shadow of food shortages. There were the dangerous months... from April to July, when the previous year's grain was being used up, and before the new crop was harvested. There was a danger period too in winter, especially for townspeople, for freezing weather might ice up the canals along which the supply barges came, or stop the water-mills from grinding the flour. And, worst of all, the crop might fail, damaged by unseasonable cold or rain or hail; rumour would race ahead of truth, encouraging the hoarding which transformed fear into the first instalment of grim reality.

It is generally said that the era of great famines ended in 1709; thereafter came shortages, serious indeed, but not deadly.... 'In the seventeenth century people died of hunger: in the eighteenth they suffered from it.' This is true so far as dying as a direct result of starvation is concerned, though local historians can always find a catastrophic year to form an exception worthy to qualify as the last of the crises.... A common-sense review of the probabilities of dying might suggest a logical sequence: famine, hunger weakening the resistance of the population, the resort to contaminated food causing illness, the onset of some killing disease, and the starving poor forced into vagabondage acting as carriers for the infection. In practice, in the eighteenth century this proposed pattern of death's operations is only occasionally borne out by comparisons of the graphs of corn prices, illness, and mortality. At Dijon in the 1740s, it seems clear that famine must have been the essential cause of the increase in the number of deaths, though an epidemic could strike at a particular place with an overwhelming impact only explainable by its own virulence....

It has been argued, with eighteenth-century England as the example, that malnutrition does not weaken resistance to disease, except in the case of afflictions arising directly from deficiencies of diet, and tuberculosis and dysentery. A historian who has never known what it is to be hungry for very long instinctively feels inclined to doubt this assertion. True, studies of the Third World today show how deprived peoples can sometimes maintain themselves in calorific and protein balance on a diet that would mean starvation to the inhabitants of advanced countries. While bodily size and appearance are affected by the food supply, the same does not necessarily apply to resistance to infection. But there is a distinction to be made. While the nutrition taken by individuals seems not to have much effect on their chance of becoming infected with most diseases, it is of the utmost importance in deciding what their ultimate fate will be. 'Malnutrition does not particularly favour or impede the acquisition of infection, but it goes a long way to determine the course of the resulting disease.' The relationship between dearth and epidemic among the poorer classes of eighteenth-century France is not so much a short-term correspondence, but a general pattern of attrition by the alternations and the accumulated onslaughts of hunger and disease. The point may be taken, however, that pathogenic bacteria and viruses do not need to wait to find a human population weakened by famine before they strike; some apparently hopeless human groups may have built up an immunity, while some apparently flourishing ones may be unprotected. One disease may fade out, leaving the weak as predestinate victims for another; thus the plague vanished from Languedoc after 1655, and malaria took over, its victims forming a new reservoir of infection to pass on to future generations. We may picture death as vigilant but unhurried and patient. Sometimes hunger served its purposes, as in the terrible dearth in the spring of 1740 in Auvergne, where a *curé* reported that the women let their children die so that the adults could live, and the men, to avoid conceiving children, resorted to unnatural practices with animals. Sometimes some overwhelming contagion, like the plague of Marseille, swept away all human defences. It could be, in these disasters, that the swift succumbing of the physically weak was a precondition for a widespread pattern of infection which trapped the rich, who might otherwise have escaped.... More often, the continuing cycle of disease, hunger, renewed disease, and despair brought life to an end. There is a story of Louis XV encountering a funeral procession and asking what the man had died from. 'Starvation, Sire.' It was an indictment of his government, and the answer would have been true, indirectly, of many other deaths from infections and accidents. 'C'est de misère que l'on meurt au dix-septième siècle'.[14] ... Though the situation was changing in the eighteenth century, this grim generalization was still broadly applicable. Particular diseases were the indispensable infantry in Death's dark armies, but his generals were Cold and Hunger.

[14]"It was destitution that brought on death in the seventeenth century."

The Sans-Culottes

ALBERT SOBOUL

One of the great watersheds in history, the French Revolution signaled the passing of the Old Régime. Monarchy, hierarchy, and privilege, all pillars of the social order, came under attack, not only in France, but through much of Europe. French armies crisscrossed the Continent, attempting to spread revolutionary ideals of "liberty, equality, and fraternity," and in the process inadvertently awakened the most potent of nineteenth-century ideologies, nationalism. Historians have entered seemingly interminable debates concerning the French Revolution, questioning, among other things, whether or not it was favorable to liberty, or to capitalism, and which social groups benefited the most from the Revolution.

Albert Soboul was a Marxist historian. As such, he argued that the Revolution opposed what was a feudal society, virtually destroying the old nobility, and so prepared the triumph of a capitalist economy. For Soboul, class conflict was an integral part of the Revolution. Soboul gained fame with his magisterial study of the Parisian sans-culottes, *a fascinating, if ephemeral, social group that influenced political events in Paris and supported vociferously the Terror of 1793–1794.*

The sans-culottes *were workers, artisans, and shopkeepers, distinguishable, according to Soboul, by their dress, behavior, and attitudes (political, economic, and social). Why did the* sans-culottes *detest aristocrats, abhor merchants, and loathe the rich? What did the* sans-culottes *want from the Revolution? What political ideas did they espouse? We should not romanticize the* sans-culottes *as virtuous workers out to cleanse society of oppressive noblemen, exploitative businessmen, and other enemies of the "people," for the* sans-culottes *often resorted to pillaging, frequently hailed violence, and cheered the guillotine as it lopped off thousands of*

heads. Why did they favor execution—so many executions—as an instrument of
state policy? Ironically, many of the sans-culottes *themselves fell victim to the*
guillotine.

    Soboul's study is valuable not only as an example of Marxist historiography
but as a thorough examination of the sans-culottes, *as well. Thus he depicts their*
violent behavior without neglecting what motivated them to indulge in it.

If we are to attempt to discern the social characteristics of the sans-culottes,
it is important first to draw attention to the manner in which they defined
themselves....

Ostensibly, the sans-culottes were recognizable by their costume, which
set them apart from the upper strata of the former Third Estate. Robespierre[1]
used to differentiate between *golden breeches* and *sans-culottes*. The sans-
culottes themselves made the same distinction. Noting the intrigues that
undermined the Sceaux Committee of Surveillance, the observer Rousseville,
in his report on 25 Messidor, year II,[2] stresses the antagonism between the
"silk-stockings" and the sans-culottes. Conventions of dress also pitted sans-
culottes against the *muscadins* [royalist sympathizers]. Arrested on 4 Prairial,
year III, for having said that "the blasted muscadins'll soon have a spade
up there...", and questioned as to what he meant by these words, Barack, a
clockmaker's assistant of the *Lombards* section,[3] replied that "as far as he was
concerned, muscadins were those who were well dressed."...

Costume was accompanied by particular social behavior. Again, on
this subject, the sans-culottes declared their stand through opposition. In
the year II, the manners of the ancien régime were no longer acceptable.
The sans-culottes refused to adopt a subordinate position in social relations. Jean-Baptiste Gentil, timber merchant, arrested on 5 Pluviôse, year II,
for not having fulfilled his duties toward the Republic, was reprimanded
for his public demeanor: "One had to approach him with hat in hand,
the word *sir* was still used in his household, he retains an air of superiority."... The principal charge against Gannal, iron merchant from the
Réunion section, arrested on 7 Frimaire, was his "haughty manner toward his
workers."...

The sans-culottes often estimated a person's worth by external appearance, deducing character from costume and political convictions from
character; everything that jarred their sense of equality was suspect of being
"aristocratic." It was difficult, therefore, for any person of the old regime
to find favor in their eyes, even when there was no specific charge against
him. "For such men are incapable of bringing themselves to the heights of our

---

[1]Maximilien Robespierre (1758–1794), leader of the most extreme political faction during
the Terror of 1793–1794.

[2]The French Revolution introduced a new calendar on October 5, 1793, and dated the year
I from 21 September 1792, the beginning of the Convention.

[3]In June 1790, Paris was divided into 48 sections, which held regular meetings.

revolution; their hearts are always full of pride and we shall never forget their former grandeur and their domination over us."

...The sans-culottes tolerated neither pride nor disdain; those were aristocratic sentiments contrary to the spirit of fraternity that existed between equal citizens and implied a hostile political stand toward democracy as practiced by the sans-culottes in their general assemblies and in their popular societies. These character traits appeared frequently in reports justifying the arrest of suspects.

On September 17, 1793 (Fructidor, year I), the committee of the *Révolutionnaire* section decided to arrest Etienne Gide, clock merchant, who had supported the Brissotins;[4] he was also accused of being haughty and proud and of often speaking *ironically*. On October 12, one bourgeois, a solicitor, was arrested by the revolutionary committee of *Réunion:* he had risen to support aristocrats in the general assemblies; more particularly, he demonstrated a "haughty manner toward the sans-culottes."...

Even more serious, according to the sans-culottes, than a haughty or disdainful manner toward themselves or straightforward indifference were statements referring to them as being of a lower social order. In its report of 8 Frimaire on Louis-Claude Cezeron, arrested for being a "suspect," the committee of the *Poissonnière* section made a particular case of a statement made during a meeting of the general assembly on the preceding May 31 (12 Prairial): "that the poor depended on the rich and that the sans-culottes were never any more than the lowest order possible." Bergeron, a skin merchant from *Lombards,* said that "although he understood that the sans-culottes were fulfilling their duty as citizens ... it would be better for them to go about their work rather than meddle in politics." He was arrested on suspicion on 18 Pluviôse.

The sans-culottes refused to tolerate others taking advantage of their social or economic status to impose upon them.... Anthéaume, a former abbé, ... was arrested on 16 Brumaire: he was reprimanded for "pride and intolerable pedagogy contrary to equality and the simplicity of a good republican."

The sans-culottes had an egalitarian conception of social relations. Their behavior also concealed realities which were more specific. To what extent were they seized upon and expressed?

The most clearly stated social friction in popular awareness was that which pitted aristocrat against sans-culotte: it was against the aristocrats that the sans-culottes addressed themselves from July 14[5] to August 10,[6] and against whom they continued to battle. The address of the sans-culottes

---

[4]Followers of Jacques-Pierre Brissot de Warville, who in 1791 advocated that France go to war against European monarchies.

[5]14 July 1789, fall of the Bastille in Paris.

[6]10 August 1792, overthrow of the French monarchy.

society of Beaucaire before the Convention[7] of September 8, 1793, is significant: "We are sans-culottes... poor and virtuous, we have formed a society of artisans and peasants... we know who our friends are: those who freed us from the clergy and from the nobility, from feudalism, from tithes, from royalty and from all the plagues that follow in its wake...."

The nature of the class struggle was even more clearly stated in the address of the Dijon Popular Society on 27 Nivôse, year II: "We must be one people, and not two nations, opposed... all recognized aristocratic individuals without exception should be condemned to death by decree." According to mechanic Guyot..., "all the nobles, without exception, deserve to be guillotined."

At this point, the aristocracy was the main enemy of the sans-culottes. Ultimately, they managed to include in this term all their adversaries, although these might not necessarily belong to the quondam nobility, but to the upper echelons of the former Third Estate. In this way the role of the sans-culottes is imprinted upon the Revolution, and further demonstrates the autonomy of their action.

On July 25, 1792, the *Louvre* section announced the fall of the King, at the same time denouncing the hereditary aristocracy, "the ministerial, financial and bourgeois aristocrats, and particularly the hierarchy of recalcitrant priests." By the year II, the meaning of the word "aristocrat" was extended to embrace all the social classes against which the sans-culottes were struggling.... Hence the specifically popular definition, coined by an anonymous petitioner in the year II, which has both political and social connotations: the aristocrat was one who regretted the passing of the ancien régime and disapproved of the Revolution, did nothing to further its cause, did not swear his allegiance to it, did not enlist in the National Guard,[8] one who did not purchase expropriated land, although he might have had the means to do so; one who left land uncultivated without selling it at its true value, or leasing it, or giving a half share in the produce. The aristocrat was also he who did not give work to laborers or journeymen, although he might be in a position to do so, and "at a wage commensurate with food prices"; did not subscribe to contributions for the volunteers; and had done nothing to improve the lot of his poor and patriotic countrymen. The real patriot was he who took a contrary attitude on every possible occasion. The term aristocrat in the end, therefore, designated all the opponents of the sans-culottes, bourgeois as well as noble, those who formed "the class of citizens from whom one should take the billion we have to levy throughout the Republic." The most extreme sans-culottes did not use the term "aristocrat" for the old nobility, but for the bourgeoisie. On May 21, 1793, a popular orator from the *Mail* section

---

[7]Name of the governmental assembly that first met on September 21, 1792, and established a republic.

[8]Citizen militia organized in Paris after the fall of the Bastille.

declared that "aristocrats are all the people with money, all the fat merchants, all the monopolists, law students, bankers, pettifoggers and anyone who has something."

The economic crisis had contributed to bringing social clashes to a head: to the fundamental hostility between sans-culotte and aristocrat was added that of the sans-culottes and the upper sectors of the Third Estate.... A note sent to the Public Safety Committee in Pulviôse, year II, pointed out the existence of two parties in the *Brutus* section: that of the people, the sans-culottes, and the other consisting of "bankers, money changers, rich people." An address delivered before the Convention on 27 Ventôse mentioned the brave sans-culottes, who were opposed not only to the clergy, the nobility, royal coalitions, but also to attorneys, lawyers, notaries and also all "those fat farmers, those egotists, and those fat, rich merchants: they're at war against us, and not against our tyrants."

Was this the "haves" against the "have-nots"? Not precisely. As far as the sans-culottes were concerned, artisans and shopkeepers belonged to the propertied classes. More particularly, the friction was between those who believed in the notion of limited and controlled ownership and the partisans of total ownership rights such as were proclaimed in 1789. Or the opposition between those who believed in controls and taxation, and those in favor of economic freedom; the opposition between consumer and producer.

Contemporary documents, over and beyond these basic reactions or distinctive statements, also allow us to explore the nuances of the social antagonisms expressed by the sans-culottes with some accuracy. They denounced "respectable people," meaning by this those who possessed, if not riches, then at least leisure and culture, the better-educated citizens, the better-dressed, those conscious if not proud of their leisure and their education. They denounced the propertied classes, that is to say, those who had unearned incomes. Finally, they denounced the rich in general, not only the propertied classes or the "haves," but also the "big men" as opposed to the "little men," which they were. The sans-culottes were not against property already owned by artisans and shopkeepers, and which journeymen aspired to possess, provided that it was limited.

The expression "respectable people" was first heard after June 2 (13 Prairial), when sans-culottes and moderates opposed one another on political and social platforms. The term was first applied to the bourgeoisie opposed to equality, but ended by having as wide a connotation as the term "aristocrat," and embracing all the enemies of the sans-culottes.... A certain Lamarre, lemonade vendor from the *Bon-Conseil* section, was arrested on 5 Prairial, year III; he consistently raised his voice against "respectable people," demanding before the assembly that they all be guillotined. As for washerwoman Rombaut, she stated that every single one of those so-called "respectable people" should be guillotined.

If the sans-culottes ironically called their adversaries "respectable people," the latter did not fail to treat them as rabble; thus, with two expressions, the lines for social clashes were drawn. On September 25, 1793 (4 Vendémiaire, year II), carpenter Bertout was arrested on the orders of the committee of the *République* section: he had declared a desire for "another government being established to oppose the rabble, because respectable people were lost." . . .

This opposition was further expressed in the animosity between the sans-culottes and those who possessed unearned incomes, a situation that came to a head during the autumn of 1793, when the economic crisis and the difficulties of daily living resulted in increased class antagonism. The fact of being independently wealthy gave cause for suspicion. On September 18, 1793 . . . , the revolutionary committee of *Mucius-Scaevola* ordered the arrest of Duval, first secretary of the Paris Police, on two counts: for contempt toward the assemblies of that section, and for enjoying an income of 2,000 livres. . . . On 2 Germinal, the revolutionary committee of the *Mont Blanc* section issued a warrant for the arrest of Jean-François Rivoire, formerly a colonist in Santo Domingo: he had not signed the Constitution, he had never contributed to the funds, nor had he served in the Guard. Further, he had an income of 16,000 livres. In one extreme case a certain Pierre Becquerel from *Guillaume-Tell* was arrested on 19 Ventôse during a raid by the police in the Gardens of Equality, simply for having said he had a private income. On the preceding 2 Frimaire, the *Lepeletier* popular society adopted a petition to exclude from all government posts not only former nobles, the sons of secretaries to the king, brokers and dealers, but also all persons known to possess incomes of more than 3,000 livres. Posts vacated by this measure would be reserved for sans-culottes. These latter were not therefore opposed to all forms of income from investments, but only to the very wealthy. . . .

The sans-culottes' hostility toward those with large private incomes was merely one particularly stressed aspect of their instinctive opposition to the rich. Extreme sans-culottes like Babeuf[9] in the year IV were not far from considering the Revolution as a declared war "between the rich and the poor." The nature of this clash to a large extent characterized Terrorist sentiments. . . . When sectional power was in the hands of the sans-culottes, full of animosity or hatred toward the rich, they did not fail to take discriminatory action against them. Wealth was often the motive for suspicion. Although wealth was rarely the only motive invoked, it often lent support to vague accusations. . . .

This deep-rooted tendency among the sans-culottes to speak against the rich was encouraged in the year II by the ruling politicians of the time. "Herein lies the revolution of the poor," wrote Michel Lepeletier in the National Education Project which Robespierre read before the Convention on July 12 and 29 of 1793 (Messidor/Thermidor, year I). . . . Saint-Just[10] said: "The unfortunate are the powerful on earth; they have the right to speak as

---

[9]François Babeuf (1760–1797), firebrand who formed the "Conspiracy of Equals" and attempted to overthrow the government in 1797.

[10]Louis-Antoine Saint-Just (1767–1794), a revolutionary leader during the Terror.

masters to governments who neglect them." . . . The crisis of the Revolution from the spring to the autumn of 1793 made the popular alliance necessary: the sans-culottes formed the cadre that was to permit the most advanced faction of the bourgeoisie to quell the aristocracy and its allies. "The hidden danger," wrote Robespierre in his diary during the June 2 insurrection, "lies in the bourgeois; in order to conquer the bourgeois, it will be necessary to rally the people." . . . Those who did not belong to the government openly exploited the antagonism between the rich and the sans-culottes for political ends. . . .

The differences between the sans-culottes and the rich were rounded out by the former's hostility toward business enterprise, and this hostility constituted one of the fundamental currents of popular opinion during the year II.

Being urban consumers, the Parisian sans-culottes were naturally against those who controlled staple food supplies. Retailers, they blamed the wholesalers. Artisans or journeymen, hardly workers in the actual meaning of the word, they remained essentially small independent producers, hostile toward those who had interests in commercial capital. The economic crisis and political struggles intensified this inherent antagonism among the sans-culottes. Scarcity and high prices spiraled, and every merchant was soon suspect of being a monopolist or a shark. The struggle against the Girondins[11] and subsequently, after May 31, against the moderates, was often, at least on the sectional level, turned into a struggle against the merchant bourgeoisie. The sans-culottes were insistent upon taxation and controls, and the conflict deepened; to the extent that they defended freedom of enterprise, the merchants became suspect. Henceforth, the sans-culottes included with the noble aristocracy and the religious hierarchy the mercantile aristocracy as well. . . .

In 1793 and in the year II, popular hostility against the merchants was marked, in its moments of paroxysm, by violence and pillage. It was also marked by a constant desire for repression. . . . In March of 1793 (Ventôse/Germinal, year I), during the recruitment of troops for the Vendée campaign, collections for volunteers were often an occasion for the sans-culottes to confirm their hostility toward the merchants. In *Lombards*, Jean-Baptiste Larue, journeyman mason and member of the revolutionary committee, declared that the volunteers were "idiots if they left without each having a hundred pistoles[12] in their pockets, that we should cut off the heads of all these buggers, those merchants, and that after this operation, the sums of money required would soon be found."

Once popular power was on firm ground, the title of merchant alone was often reason enough for suspicion on the part of revolutionary committees.

[11]Name given to a group of moderate republican deputies. They were purged in 1793 from the Convention.

[12]Gold coins.

They were encouraged by the Commune,[13] whose arrests of the nineteenth of the first month ranged among their suspects "those who felt sorry for needy farmers and merchants, against whom the law must take measures." Certain committees had not expected this encouragement. After September 14, the committee of *Lombards*, where hostility toward the merchants was particularly strong, arrested a certain Dussautoy; he was reprimanded simply for being a wholesale grocer.... In *Bon-Conseil*, the committee justified the arrest on 25 Brumaire of Jean-Louis Lagrave, wholesale grocer, merely because of his social behavior: "He spends his time among business people, snobs like himself, not consorting with any patriot... always flaunting his rank among the wholesalers, censuring and even molesting citizens, like most wholesalers."...

The hostility of the sans-culottes toward business was not restricted to measures against individuals; this was a war against an entire social class that, although it did not seek to eliminate that class from politics, at least sought to curb its powers, to put a halt to its prejudicial activities....

The reaction set in finally after the year III, and the merchants made the most of their revenge against former Terrorists for the maltreatment to which they had been subjected. During Germinal and Prairial, a simple remark was sufficient motive for arrest. The food shortage, worse because the "maximum"[14] had been abolished, once again increased hostility toward commerce among the sans-culottes. The dossiers of the anti-Terrorist repression offer ample evidence, allowing us to determine the precise nature of public opinion on this subject; this varied, circumstances permitting, from a simple expression of hostility to a suppressed desire for the elimination of a social class.

For having said, in year II, "Neither the merchants nor the rich are worth sparing," Davelin, a feather dealer from *Amis-de-la-Patrie*, was disarmed on 5 Prairial, year III. Jacques Barbant, from *Arsenal*, was arrested: he had made certain vague derogatory remarks about merchants....

From hostility toward commerce, the more aware or the more violent among the sans-culottes went on to justify pillage....

During the upheavals of February 25 and 26, 1793 (Ventôse, year I), cobbler Servière, revolutionary commissar of the *Muséum* section in the year II declared before the general assembly, in what was formerly the Germain church, "that he thoroughly approved of pillage and would be very much against having to oppose it."... In *Bonne-Nouvelle*, water carrier Bergeron was arrested on 6 Pluviôse, in the year III, when "as a result of his provocations he incited the pillaging of the wood merchants." In some ways..., pillage corresponded to the fundamental egalitarianism of the

---

[13]Government of the city of Paris, 1789–1795, divided into 48 sections and dominated by radical factions.

[14]Name applied to two laws in 1793 that set maximum levels for wages and prices. The ceiling on wages, but not that on prices, was stringently enforced. Thus the *sans-culottes* were not satisfied.

sans-culottes: individual action was legitimated by the inequality of living conditions.

Beyond the offensive remarks or the exhortation to pillage, Terrorist exaltation and the desire for punitive measures show the deep-rooted hostility of the sans-culottes toward the commercial bourgeoisie. Many militants considered the threat of the guillotine in times of shortages an excellent remedy. To oblige farmers to sell their grain according to the official price, they insisted upon the creation of a revolutionary army. When this army was created, the sans-culottes constantly demanded that it be accompanied by a mobile guillotine, in order further to insure its efficaciousness. This outlook can be traced throughout all the Terrorists' abusive remarks made in the year II against the merchants. Widow Barbau, from *Indivisibilité,* a veritable harridan according to her denunciators, had the habit of declaring "that until the snobbish merchants, the aristocrats, the rich, etc., are guillotined or dispatched en masse, nothing will work out properly." Widow Barbau quite naturally placed the merchants before the aristocrats. In *Unité,* a certain Roux asked for the erecting of guillotines "on every street corner in Paris, on the doorsteps of every merchant, so that, he said, we can have cheap merchandise." . . . In *Invalides,* the clockmaker Fagère declared that "when the aristocrats are finished, we'll take up with the merchant class again. . . . "

In the year III, shortages and misery still exacerbated sans-culottes' hatred of the merchants. Terrorist remarks abound in the dossiers of the repression. On 19 Ventôse, Jacques Rohait, a job printer from the *Panthéon-Français* section exasperated by the high cost of meat, said that "all those wretched merchants deserve to swing." . . .

During those Prairial days, frenzied offensive remarks were not unusual. Nicolas Barrucand, dyer, former revolutionary commissar of *Arsenal,* declared that on the feast day of Corpus Christi "the streets should be carpeted with the heads of merchants." . . .

The still vivid memories of the year II suggested to many sans-culottes the need for a return to organized terror in order to put an end to the merchants, as they had done to the aristocrats. Ferrier, a hatter from *Gardes-Françaises,* remembering the uprisings in Lyons, Marseilles and Bordeaux in 1793, and the repression which followed, declared that "the large communes composed entirely of merchants and the wealthy must be destroyed, their inhabitants humbled and put down." . . .

These texts reveal that the sans-culottes identified themselves by opposition to the aristocracy, riches, and to commerce—antagonisms that account for the imprecise nature of the social distinctions within the former Third Estate and the difficulty of defining the sans-culottes as a social class. The sans-culottes can be clearly defined only when compared to the aristocracy; when compared to the bourgeoisie, the distinction becomes less clear. Composed of many socially disparate elements, the sans-culottes were under mined by internal dissent, which explains both their inability to establish a coherent program and, in the last analysis, their political defeat. . . .

The sans-culottes considered violence to be the ultimate recourse against those who refused to answer the call of unity. This stand was one of the characteristics of their political behavior. Popular violence had allowed the bourgeoisie to carry out its first attacks against the ancien régime; indeed, the struggle against the aristocracy would not have been possible without it. In 1793 and in the year II, the sans-culottes used that violence not solely against the aristocrats, but also against the moderates who were opposed to the establishment of an egalitarian republic.

Doubtless we should at times seek the biological roots of this recourse to violence, of this exaltation. Temperament offers some explanation. The reports of Prairial, year III, on the former Terrorists often mention their irascible, passionate nature and their tendency to fits of rage; "Their outbursts were usually the result of being in a position to make malicious remarks without thinking of the consequences." Their reactions were the stronger because the sans-culottes were often frustrated, poor, uneducated, inflamed by awareness of their misery.

In the year III the reactionaries indiscriminately labeled all Terrorists drinkers of blood. Although one must be careful not to generalize and take denunciations and police reports literally, one must nevertheless concede that, for certain individuals, violence did mean the spilling of blood. . . . Bunou, from the *Champs-Elysées* section, who was arrested on 5 Prairial, demanded in the year II that a guillotine be erected in the section, "and that he would act as executioner if there was none to be found." Lesur, from the *Luxembourg* section, was arrested on 6 Prairial for having made a similar suggestion: "that the guillotine was not working fast enough, that there should be more bloodletting in the prisons, that if the executioner was tired, he himself would climb the scaffold with a quarter loaf to soak up the blood." In the *Gardes-Françaises* a certain Jayet was arrested on 6 Prairial for having declared in the year II, "that he would like to see rivers of blood, up to the ankles." On leaving the general assembly of the *République* section, another declared: "The guillotine is hungry, it's ages since she had something to eat." Women shared this Terrorist exaltation. A certain Baudray, a lemonade vendor from the *Lepeletier* section, was arrested on 8 Prairial for having said "she would like to eat the heart of anyone opposed to the sans-culottes"; she intended to raise her children on the same principles: "You hear them talk of nothing but cutting, chopping off heads, not enough blood is flowing."

Nevertheless, temperament alone does not sufficiently explain the fact that the majority of the popular militants approved of if they did not exalt violence and the use of the guillotine. For many, brute force seemed the supreme recourse when a crisis had reached its paroxysm. These same men, who did not hesitate to make blood flow, were more often than not ordinarily quite calm, good sons, good husbands and good fathers. Cobbler Duval from the *Arsenal* section was condemned to death on 11 Prairial, year II, for his role during the uprising of the first; his neighbors testified that he was a good father, good husband, good citizen, a *man of probity*. The feeling that the nation was threatened, the belief in the aristocratic plot, the atmosphere of turbulent days, the tocsin and the issuing of arms made these men beside themselves and created in them something like a second nature. According to the civil committee of the *Faubourg-du-Nord* section, Josef Morlot, a house painter, arrested on 5 Prairial, year III, was a man with two distinct personalities. "One of these, guided by his natural bent, was gentle, honest and generous. He has all the social virtues, which he practices in private. The other, subjugated by present threats, manifests itself in the bloody colors of all the conjoined plagues in their utmost virulence."

This violence was not gratuitous. It had a political aim and a class content; it was a weapon which the sans-culottes were forced to use in their resistance to the aristocracy. A teacher by the name of Moussard employed by the Executive Commission of Public Instruction, was arrested on 5 Prairial, year III. "Yes, I was carried away," he wrote in his defense. "Who wasn't during the Revolution? ... They say I am fanatical: yes; passion burns within my breast, I am intoxicated with the idea of liberty and I shall always rage against the enemies of my country."

The guillotine was popular because the sans-culottes saw in it an instrument whereby they could avenge the nation. Hence the expressions *national cleaver, national ax;* the guillotine was also known as the *scythe of equality.* Class hatred of the aristocracy was heightened by the belief in an aristocratic plot which since 1789 had been one of the fundamental reasons behind popular violence. Foreign war and civil war further strengthened the popular notion that the aristocracy would only be exterminated by the Terror and that the guillotine was necessary for consolidating the Republic. Becq, a clerk in the Navy Department, a good father, a good husband and well thought of, but extraordinarily impassioned according to the civil committee of the *Butte-des-Moulins,* turned his impassioned nature against priests and noblemen, whom he *usually* recommended for assassination. Jean-Baptiste Mallais, cobbler and revolutionary commissar of the *Temple* section, was the same: he did not hesitate to use clubs when arguing with noblemen and priests considered enemies of the people; he spoke of arming the wives of patriots "so that they in turn can slit the throats of the wives of aristocrats." ... Even more indicative of the political aims which the sans-culottes hoped to achieve through violence and through the Terror were the words recorded by the observer Perrière on 6 Ventôse, year II: "Is the guillotine working today?" asked a dandy. "Yes," replied an honest patriot, "there is always somebody betraying somebody or something."

During the year III violence became even more important for the sans-culottes. The Terror had also been an economic aspect of government; it had sanctioned the application of the "maximum," which had guaranteed the people their daily bread. Whereas the reaction coincided with the abolition of price-fixing and the worst shortages, certain among them came to identify the Terror with abundance, in the same way as they associated popular government with the Terror. Cobbler Clément from the *République* section was denounced on 2 Prairial for having declared "that the Republic cannot be built without blood flowing." . . . Mistress Chalandon from the *l'Homme-Armé* section declared, "Nothing will really work properly until permanent guillotines were erected at every street intersection in Paris." Carpenter Richer, from the *République* section, touched the heart of the matter when he said, on 1 Prairial: "There will be no bread unless we spill some blood; under the Terror we didn't go without."

Whatever specific aims the Parisian sans-culottes had in mind, the Terror and popular violence to a great extent swept away the remnants of feudalism and absolutism for the bourgeoisie. They nevertheless corresponded to a different form of behavior, in the same way as popular political practices, essentially characterized in 1793 and in the year II by voting by acclamation and by fraternity, expressed a concept of democracy that was fundamentally different from that of the bourgeoisie, even of the Jacobins.[15]

Doubtless the revolutionary bourgeoisie, during the critical moments of its struggle against the aristocracy, also resorted to violence; they, too, made use of certain popular practices; for example, during the course of the Convention elections, in Paris, they used the roll-call vote. Events justified this departure from the usual concepts of liberal democracy, and also class interests. Once the revolutionary government was in power, neither these interests nor the events would allow these practices to continue. Although these practices were in accord with the popular temperament, they were incompatible with the behavior and political ideas of the bourgeoisie. They also threatened its sovereignty. . . .

---

[15]Members of republican political clubs during the French Revolution. Originally containing moderates, the Jacobins became increasingly radical and dominated the government during the Terror.

II

THE NINETEENTH CENTURY

Historians generally count the nineteenth century as lasting from the end of the Napoleonic Wars (1815) to the beginning of World War I in 1914. Nineteenth-century Europeans appeared to possess a confident optimism, if not arrogance, that rested on European scientific achievement, industrial advance, and imperial conquest. The great world fairs of the period—London, 1851; Paris, 1900—which displayed all the world's art and manufactures, and which asserted European superiority over the rest of the world, suggest how rich, powerful, self-assured, and nation-proud were the times. In short, the nineteenth century was an era of seeming greatness as Europe flexed its industrial and political muscles, until World War I, the "war to end all wars," demonstrated the terrible consequences of modern technology joined with rampant nationalism and militarism.

Not all Europeans, of course, could revel in the power exercised by the leaders and the social elite of various nations. The power and wealth were not evenly distributed, and most people continued their never-ending struggle for food, work, and a modicum of security.

The major socioeconomic development in this century was the Industrial Revolution, whose effects were felt throughout society. The factories and machines of the Industrial Revolution altered relations among social classes, gave rise to new types of work and workers' organizations, inspired original ideas about the reorganization of society, raised the standard of living, contributed to the formation of immense urban centers, and made change rather than stability the expected fact of life. This unequal distribution of the new riches helped to spawn class conflict, manifest in the programs of socialists, communists, and anarchists, as well as in mass political parties that gathered in the laboring poor.

One of the themes of nineteenth-century history is the development of worker consciousness (aided perhaps by growing literacy and the penny press) and the increasing politicization of the masses, who could easily resent the lifestyles and power of the bourgeoisie. These changes occurred in the midst of the new urban landscape, transformed by technological wonders such as steel and electricity. Great new industries arose in chemicals, oil, and pharmaceuticals. At the same time, millions of Europeans left their homes to colonize and rule other cultures. The *nineteenth century was the heyday of European imperialism and the great age of European power. Textbooks might stress nineteenth-century intellectual and cultural movements such as Romanticism or political developments such as the unification of Italy and of Germany, all important in their own right, but these must be set against the background of rapid and unsettling change in the human relationships, values, and beliefs that concerned the vast majority of the population.*

Factory Discipline in the Industrial Revolution

SIDNEY POLLARD

The nature of work and leisure time changed dramatically with the Industrial Revolution. Previously, workers could proceed at their own pace, determining when to rest or to cease their labors for the day. After all, who would care if a woman at a loom in her own home suddenly decided to take a fifteen-minute break? But, as Sidney Pollard shows, the entrepreneurs who were the early factory owners consciously endeavored to change the more relaxed work habits of pre-industrial England. In the process, they aimed at nothing less than the reformation of the workers' morals and character.

What exactly was the new factory discipline? How did it operate? The need to alter the employees' concept of work derived from the machinery. In what ways did machinery make it imperative for workers to conform to factory discipline? What does Pollard mean by the concept of "time-thrift"?

For the owners to demand factory discipline was not enough; they had to force or cajole their workers to relinquish patterns of behavior that were, after all, centuries old. The owners used three methods: the carrot, the stick, and "the attempt to create a new ethos of work order and obedience." What did each of these methods consist of? How effective were they? Surely some of the problems of factory-operative behavior—problems from the owners' point of view, that is—still persist today. Child workers presented a special problem for the owners. What methods helped ensure that the very young would become accustomed to factory discipline?

It is interesting that Pollard claims that the carrot, a favored method of enlightened factory owners, was successful, but was not copied very much. Why? What did the owners think of the workers' character? How do you explain the owners' great concern to prohibit swearing and indecent language? Did they usually treat their workers with respect, or did they view them as mere cogs in the wheels of production? What conclusions does Pollard draw about the imposition of factory discipline?

It is nowadays increasingly coming to be accepted that one of the most critical, and one of the most difficult, transformations required in an industrializing society is the adjustment of labour to the regularity and discipline of factory work.... [T]he first generation of factory workers will be examined, irrespective of its appearance at different times in different industries.

The worker who left the background of his domestic workshop or peasant holding for the factory, entered a new culture as well as a new sense of direction. It was not only that 'the new economic order needed ... part-humans: soulless, depersonalised, disembodied, who could become members, or little wheels rather, of a complex mechanism.' It was also that men who were non-accumulative, non-acquisitive, accustomed to work for subsistence, not for maximization of income, had to be made obedient to the cash stimulus, and obedient in such a way as to react precisely to the stimuli provided.

The very recruitment to the uncongenial work was difficult, and it was made worse by the deliberate or accidental modelling of many works on workhouses and prisons, a fact well known to the working population. Even if they began work, there was no guarantee that the new hands would stay. 'Labourers from agriculture or domestic industry do not at first take kindly to the monotony of factory life; and the pioneering employer not infrequently finds his most serious obstacle in the problem of building up a stable supply of efficient and willing labour.' Many workers were 'transient, marginal and deviant', or were described as 'volatile.' It was noted that there were few early manufactures in the seaport towns, as the population was too unsteady.... Thus it was not necessarily the better labourer, but the stable one who was worth the most to the manufacturer: often, indeed, the skilled apprenticed man was at a discount, because of the working habits acquired before entering a factory....

... [I]n Scotland even the children found the discipline irksome: when the Catrine cotton mills were opened, one of the managers admitted, 'the children were all newcomers, and were very much beat at first before they could be taught their business.' At other mills, 'on the first introduction of the business, the people were found very ill-disposed to submit to the long confinement and regular industry that is required from them.' The highlander, it was said, 'never sits at ease at a loom; it is like putting a deer in the plough.'

In turn, the personal inclinations and group *mores* of such old-established industrial workers as handloom weavers and framework knitters were opposed to factory discipline. 'I found the utmost distaste', one hosier reported, 'on the part of the men, to any regular hours or regular habits.... The men themselves were considerably dissatisfied, because they could not go in and out as they pleased, and have what holidays they pleased, and go on just as they had been used to do....'

As a result of this attitude, attendance was irregular, and the complaint of Edward Cave,[1] in the very earliest days of industrialization, was later re-echoed by many others: 'I have not half my people come to work to-day, and I have no great fascination in the prospect I have to put myself in the power of such people.' Cotton spinners would stay away without notice and send for their wages at the end of the week, and one of the most enlightened firms, McConnel and Kennedy, regularly replaced spinners who had not turned up within two or three hours of starting time on Mondays, on the reasonable presumption that they had left the firm: their average labour turnover was 20 a week, i.e. about 100 per cent a year.

---

[1] Printer, 1691–1754.

Matters were worse in a place like Dowlais, reputed to employ many runaways and criminals, or among northern mining companies which could not guarantee continuous work: 'the major part of these two companies are as bad fellows as the worst of your pitmen baring their outside is not so black', one exasperated manager complained, after they had left the district without paying their debts. Elsewhere, ironworks labourers, copper and tin miners and engineering labourers deserted to bring in the harvest, or might return to agriculture for good if work was slack.

'St Monday' and feast days, common traditions in domestic industry, were persistent problems. The weavers were used to 'play frequently all day on Monday, and the greater part of Tuesday, and work very late on Thursday night, and frequently all night on Friday.' Spinners, even as late as 1800, would be missing from the factories on Mondays and Tuesdays, and 'when they did return, they would sometimes work desperately, night and day, to clear off their tavern score, and get more money to spend in dissipation', as a hostile critic observed. In South Wales it was estimated as late as the 1840's that the workers lost one week in five, and that in the fortnight after the monthly pay day, only two-thirds of the time was being worked.

As for the regular feasts, 'our men will go to the Wakes', Josiah Wedgwood[2] complained in 1772, 'if they were sure to go to the D—l the next. I have not spared them in threats and I would have thrash'd them right heartily if I could'. . . .

Employers themselves, groping their way towards a new impersonal discipline, looked backwards sporadically to make use of feasts and holidays, typical of the old order in cementing personal relationships and breaking the monotony of the working year. . . . The Arkwrights and the Strutts, standing on the watershed between the old and the new, had feasts in Cromford in 1776, when 500 workers and their children took part, and annual balls at Cromford and Belper as late as 1781, whilst in 1772 the Hockley factory had an outing, led by the 'head workman' clad in white cotton, to gather nuts, and be regaled to a plentiful supper afterwards.

Other examples from industries in their early transitional stages include Matthew Boulton's[3] feast for 700 when his son came of age, Wedgwood's feast for 120 when he moved into Etruria, . . . and the repast provided by the Herculaneum Pottery at the opening of its Liverpool warehouse in 1813. Conversely, the Amlwch miners organized an ox-roast in honour of the chief proprietor, the Marquis of Anglesea, when he passed through the island on his way to take up the Lord-Lieutenancy of Ireland. 600 workmen sat down to a roasted ox and plenty of liquor at the Duke of Bridgewater's expense to celebrate the opening of the canal at Runcorn, and feasts were usual thereafter at the opening of canals and railways, but within a generation it was the shareholders that were being feasted, not the workers, whose

[2]Owner of a pottery factory, 1730–1795.
[3]Inventor (1728–1809), along with James Watt, of an efficient steam engine.

relationship with the employers had by then taken on an entirely different character.

Once at work it was necessary to break down the impulses of the workers, to introduce the notion of 'time-thrift.' The factory meant economy of time and . . . 'enforced asceticism.' Bad timekeeping was punished by severe fines, and it was common in mills such as Oldknow's or Braids' to lock the gates of the factory, even of the workrooms, excluding those who were only a minute or two late. 'Whatever else the domestic system[4] was, however intermittent and sweated its labour, it did allow a man a degree of personal liberty to indulge himself, a command over his time, which he was not to enjoy again.'

By contrast, in the factories, Arkwright,[5] for example, had the greatest difficulty 'in training human beings to renounce their desultory habits of work, and identify themselves with the unvarying regularity of the complex automaton.' He 'had to train his workpeople to a precision and assiduity altogether unknown before, against which their listless and restive habits rose in continued rebellion', and it was his great achievement 'to devise and administer a successful code of factory diligence.' 'Impatient of the slovenly habits of workpeople, he urged on their labours with a precision and vigilance unknown before.' The reasons for the difference were clear to manufacturers: 'When a mantua maker chooses to rise from her seat and take the fresh air, her seam goes a little back, that is all; there are no other hands waiting on her', but 'in cotton mills all the machinery is going on, which they must attend to.' It was 'machinery [which] ultimately forced the worker to accept the discipline of the factory.'

Regular hours and application had to be combined with a new kind of order in the works. Wedgwood, for example, had to fight the old pottery traditions when introducing 'the punctuality, the constant attendance, the fixed hours, the scrupulous standards of care and cleanliness, the avoidance of waste, the ban on drinking'. . . .

Finally, 'Discipline . . . was to produce the goods on time. It was also to prevent the workmen from stealing raw materials, putting in shoddy, or otherwise getting the better of their employers.' It allowed the employer to maintain a high quality of output. . . .

Works Rules, formalized, impersonal and occasionally printed, were symbolic of the new industrial relationships. Many rules dealt with disciplinary matters only, but quite a few laid down the organization of the firm itself. 'So strict are the instructions,' it was said of John Marshall's[6] flax mills

---

[4] Also known as the putting-out system, whereby a merchant provided raw materials to workers, who then worked in their own homes.

[5] Richard Arkwright (1732–1792), inventor of the water-frame, a spinning machine that led to the creation of large cotton mills.

[6] Textile magnate.

in 1821, 'that if an overseer of a room be found talking to any person in the mill during working hours he is dismissed immediately—two or more overseers are employed in each room, if one be found a yard out of his ground he is discharged ... everyone, manager, overseers, mechanics, oilers, spreaders, spinners and reelers, have their particular duty pointed out to them, and if they transgress, they are instantly turned off as unfit for their situation.'

While the domestic system had implied some measure of control, 'it was ... an essentially new thing for the capitalist to be a disciplinarian.' 'The capitalist employer became a supervisor of every detail of the work: without any change in the general character of the wage contract, the employer acquired new powers which were of great social significance.' The concept of industrial discipline was new, and called for as much innovation as the technical inventions of the age.

Child work immeasurably increased the complexities of the problem. It had, as such, been common enough before, but the earlier work pattern had been based on the direct control of children and youths, in small numbers, by their parents or guardians. The new mass employment removed the incentive of learning a craft, alienated the children by its monotony and did this just at the moment when it undermined the authority of the family, and of the father in particular. It thus had to rely often on the unhappy method of indirect employment by untrained people whose incentive for driving the children was their own piece-rate payment.

In the predominantly youthful population of the time, the proportion of young workers was high. In the Cumberland mines, for example, children started work at the ages of five to seven, and as late as 1842, 200–250 of the 1,300–1,400 workers in the Lonsdale mines were under eighteen. At Alloa collieries, 103 boys and girls of under seven were employed in 1780. In the light metal trades, the proportion was higher still. Josiah Wedgwood, in 1816, had 30 per cent of his employees under eighteen, 3.3 per cent under ten years of age. The greatest problems, however, were encountered in the textile mills.

The silk mills were dependent almost exclusively on child labour, and there the children started particularly young, at the ages of six or seven, compared with nine or ten in the cotton mills. Typically from two-thirds to three-quarters of the hands were under eighteen but in some large mills, the proportion was much higher: at Tootal's for example, 78 per cent of the workers were under sixteen. Adults were thus in a small minority.

In the cotton industry the proportion of children and adolescents under eighteen was around 40–45 per cent. In some large firms the proportions were higher: thus Horrocks, Miller and Co. in 1816 had 13 per cent of their labour force under ten years of age, and 60 per cent between ten and eighteen, a total of 73 per cent. The proportion of children under ten was mostly much smaller than this, but in water mills employing large numbers of apprentices it might be greater: New Lanark, under David Dale in 1793, had 18 per cent of its labour force nine years old or younger.

In the flax and the woollen and worsted industries, the proportions of workers under eighteen were rather higher than in cotton, being around 50 per cent. Again individual large works show much higher figures. In John Marshall's Water Lane Mill in 1831, for example, 49.2 per cent were under fifteen, and 83.8 per cent altogether under twenty-one. Further, in all the textile branches the children were largely concentrated in certain sections, such as silk throwing and cotton spinning. In such departments, the difficulties of maintaining discipline were greatest.

These, then, were the problems of factory discipline facing the entrepreneurs in the early years of industrialization. Their methods of overcoming them may be grouped under three headings: the proverbial stick, the proverbial carrot, and, thirdly, the attempt to create a new ethos of work order and obedience.

Little new in the way of the 'stick', or deterrent, was discovered by the early factory masters. Unsatisfactory work was punished by corporal punishment, by fines or by dismissal. Beatings clearly belonged to the older, personal relationships and were common with apprentices, against whom few other sanctions were possible, but they survived because of the large-scale employment of children. Since the beating of children became one of the main complaints against factory owners and a major point at issue before the various Factory Commissions,[7] the large amount of evidence available is not entirely trustworthy, but the picture is fairly clear in outline.

Some prominent factory owners . . . prohibited it outright, though the odd cuff for inattention was probably inevitable in any children's employment. More serious beatings were neither very widespread, nor very effective. . . . [L]arge employers frowned on beatings, though they might turn a blind eye on the overlookers' actions. 'We beat only the lesser, up to thirteen or fourteen . . . we use a strap', stated Samuel Miller, manager of Wilson's mill in Nottingham, one of the few to admit to this to the Factory Commission, 'I prefer fining to beating, if it answers . . . (but) fining does not answer. It does not keep the boys at their work.' The most honest evidence, however, and the most significant, came from John Bolling, a cotton master. He could not stop his spinners beating the children, he stated, 'for children require correction now and then, and the difficulty is to keep it from being excessive. . . . It never can be in the interest of the master that the children should be beaten. The other day there were three children run away; the mother of one of them brought him back and asked us to beat him; that I could not permit; she asked us to take him again: at last I consented, and then she beat him.'

Dismissal and the threat of dismissal, were in fact the main deterrent instruments of enforcing discipline in the factories. At times of labour shortage they were ineffective, but when a buyers' market in labour returned, a

[7]Royal commissions established to investigate working conditions.

sigh of relief went through the ranks of the employers at the restoration of their power. Many abolished the apprenticeship system in order to gain it, and without it others were unable to keep any control whatsoever. Where there were no competing mill employers, as at Shrewsbury in the case of Marshall and Benyon's flax mills, it was a most effective threat.

In industries where skill and experience were at a premium, however, dismissals were resorted to only most reluctantly....

Fines formed the third type of sanctions used, and were common both in industries employing skilled men, and in those employing mostly women and children. They figure prominently in all the sets of rules surviving, and appear to have been the most usual reaction to minor transgressions. Where the employer pocketed the fine there was an additional inducement to levy it freely, and in some cases, as in the deductions and penalties for sending small coal or stones up in the corves from the coal face, these became a major source of abuse and grievance.

Their general level was high and was meant to hurt. Typically, they were levied at 6*d*. to 2*s*. for ordinary offences or, say, two hours' to a day's wages. Wedgwood fined 2*s*. 6*d*. for throwing things or for leaving fires burning overnight, and that was also the penalty for being absent on Monday mornings in the Worsley mines. At Fernley's Stockport mill, swearing, singing or being drunk were punished by a fine of 5*s*. and so was stealing coal at Merthyr. Miners were fined even more heavily: average weekly deductions were alleged to be as high as 1*s*. or 2*s*. out of a wage of 13*s*.

Deterrence as a method of industrial discipline should, strictly, also include the actions taken against workers' organizations.... The law could usually be assumed to be at the service of the employer, and was called into service for two types of offence, breaches of contract and trade-union organization and rioting. Workmen's combinations were widely treated as criminal offences in employers' circles, even before the law made them explicitly such, and in turn, the legal disabilities turned trade disputes easily towards violence, particularly before the 1790's. In the Scottish mines, serfdom was only just being eradicated, and in the North-East the one-year contract, coupled with the character note, could be used also to impose conditions akin to serfdom; opposition, including the inevitable rioting, was met by transportation and the death penalty not only in the mines, but even in such advanced centres as Etruria as late as 1783.

Where their powers permitted, employers met organization with immediate dismissal: 'any hands forming conspiracies or unlawful combinations will be discharged without notice' read one rule as late as 1833. More widespread, however, was the use of blacklists against those who had aroused the employer's disfavour. Little was heard of them, even in contemporary complaints by workmen, but their importance should not be underrated:... it is increasingly obvious that they were a most important prop of that reign of terror which in so many works did duty for factory discipline.

By comparison with these commonly used examples of the 'stick', more subtle or more finely graded deterrents were so rare as to be curious rather than significant. John Wood, the Bradford spinner, made the child guilty of a fault hold up a card with his offence written on it; for more serious offences, this punishment was increased to walking up and down with the card, then to having to tell everyone in the room, and, as the highest stage, confessing to workers in other rooms. Witts and Rodick, the Essex silk-mill owners, made their errant children wear degrading dress. These measures presuppose a general agreement with the factory code on the part of the other workmen which today few would take for granted. . . .

Employers were as conservative in the use of the carrot as they were in the use of the stick. For a generation driving its children to labour in the mills for twelve to fourteen hours a day, positive incentives must indeed have been hard to devise and, for the child workers at least, were used even less than for adults. Much better, as in the case of at least one flax mill, to give them snuff to keep them awake in the evenings. The extent of the predominance of the deterrent over the incentive in the case of the factory children is brought out in the returns of the 1833 Factory Commission, in replies to item 57 of the questionnaire sent out: 'What are the means taken to enforce obedience on the part of the children employed in your works?' . . . Bearing in mind that most respondents were merely concerned to deny that they beat their children, and that many replied with the method they thought they ought to use, rather than the one actually in use, the following proportion may appear even more surprising:

Number of firms using different means to enforce obedience
among factory children, 1833

Negative		Positive	
Dismissal	353	Kindness	2
Threat of dismissal	48	Promotion, or higher wages	9
Fines, deductions	101	Reward or premium	23
Corporal punishment	55		
Complaint to parents	13		
Confined to mill	2		
Degrading dress, badge	3		
Totals	575		34

The contrast is surely too strong to be fortuitous, especially since the bias was all the other way.

For adults, there were two positive methods which formed the stock-in-trade of management in this period. One was sub-contract, the transference of responsibility for making the workers industrious, to overseers, butty-men, group leaders, first hands and sub-contractors of various types. But this solution, which raises, in any case, questions of its own, was not a method of creating factory discipline, but of evading it. The discipline was to be the older form of that of the supervisor of a small face-to-face group, maintained by someone who usually worked himself or was in direct daily contact with the workers.

The other method was some variant of payments by results. This provided the cash nexus symbolic for the new age. It was also a natural derivation from the methods used in earlier periods in such skilled and predominantly male trades as iron-smelting, mining, pottery or the production of metal goods. In 1833, of 67,819 cotton-mill workers in 225 mills, 47.1 per cent were on piece-work and 43.7 per cent were paid datally,[8] the method of payment for the remainder being unknown. Labourers, children and others under direct supervision of a skilled pieceworker, and some highly skilled trades in short supply, such as engineers and building craftsmen, did, however, remain on fixed datal pay.

In many enterprises the 'discovery' of payment by results was greeted as an innovation of major significance, and at times the change-over does seem to have led to marked improvements in productivity....

Many of the older systems of payment by results, as in copper or tin mines, or in sinking colliery shafts, consisted of group piece-work, in which the cohesion and ethos of the group was added to the incentive payment as such to create work discipline. The newly introduced systems, however, were typically aimed at individual effort. As such, they were less effective ...and they were often badly constructed, particularly for times of rapid technological change. There were many examples of the usual problems of this type of payment, such as speed-up and rate cutting, as at Soho and Etruria, loss of quality, and friction over interpretation and deductions. Nevertheless, it represented the major change and forward step in the employer's attitude towards labour, not only because it used cash as such but more specifically because it marked the end of the belief that workers were looking for a fixed minimum income, and a rate of earnings beyond this would merely lead to absenteeism...and the beginning of the notion that the workers' efforts were elastic with respect to income over a wide range.

The rise in the belief in the efficacy of incentive piece payments coincided with a decline in the belief in the efficacy of long-term contracts. These contracts were largely a survival of the pre-industrial age, adopted by many employers even during the Industrial Revolution at times of acute shortages of labour. In the north-eastern coalfield, the one-year binding had become almost universal since the beginning of the eighteenth century and it had spread to salters, keelmen, file-workers and others. Ambrose Crowley[9] bound his men for six months, Arkwright for three months,...some potteries for

---

[8]Daily.

[9]Iron smelter who pioneered the large-scale importation of Swedish ores.

seven years, some cotton mills for five up to twenty-one years and the Prestonpans chemical works for twenty-one years. But any hope that these indentures would ensure discipline and hard work was usually disappointed, and the system was quickly abandoned as a disciplinary method, though it might be continued for other reasons.

A few employers evolved incentive schemes with a considerable degree of sophistication. In their simplest form, overseers bribed children to work on for fourteen or fifteen hours and forgo their meal intervals, and John Wood[10] paid them a bonus of 1*d*. weekly if they worked well, but hung a notice of shame on them if they did not. At Backbarrow mill, apprentices received a 'bounty' of 6*d*. or 1*s* ., to be withdrawn if offences were committed, and in silk mills articles of clothing were given to the children as prizes for good work; at one silk mill, employing 300 children aged nine or less, a prize of bacon and three score of potatoes was given to the hardest working boy, and a doll to the hardest working girl, and their output then became the norm for the rest. Richard Arkwright, in his early years, also gave prizes to the best workers.

Later on, these bonuses were made conditional on a longer period of satisfactory work, or modified in other ways. In the early 1800's the Strutts introduced 'quarterly gift money'—one-sixth of wages being held back over three months, and paid out at the end only after deductions for misconduct. At John Marshall's the best department received a bonus each quarter, amounting to £10 for the overlooker and a week's wage for the hands, and some Dowlais men, at least, also received a bonus of £2 every quarter, conditional upon satisfactory performance. At the Whitehaven collieries, the bonus to the foremen was annual and was tied to net profits: when these exceeded £30,000, the salary of the two viewers was nearly doubled, from £152 to £300, and those of the overmen raised in almost like proportion from a range of £52–82 to a range of £90–170—a particularly effective and cheap means of inducing industry. In other coal mines, the ladder of promotion to overmen was used effectively as an incentive. . . .

Compared with the ubiquity of financial rewards, other direct incentives were rare and localized, though they were highly significant. Wedgwood at times appealed directly to his workers, in at least one case writing a pamphlet for them in which he stressed their common interests. . . . Arkwright gave distinguishing dresses to the best workers of both sexes and John Marshall fixed a card on each machine, showing its output. Best known of all were the 'silent monitors' of Robert Owen.[11] He awarded four types of mark for the past day's work to each superintendent, and each of them, in turn, judged all his workers; the mark was then translated into the colours black-blue-yellow-white, in ascending order of merit, painted on the four sides of a piece of wood mounted over the machine, and turned outward according to the worker's performance.

[10] A worsted manufacturer who began the movement for a ten-hour day.

[11] Industrialist and social reformer, 1771–1858.

There is no doubt that Owen attached great importance to this system, entering all daily marks in a book as a permanent record, to be periodically inspected by him. There is equally no doubt that, naive as they might seem to-day, these methods were successful among all the leading manufacturers named, Robert Owen, in particular, running his mills, both in Manchester and in Scotland, at regular high annual profits largely because he gained the voluntary co-operation of his workers. Why, then were these methods not copied as widely as the technological innovations?

The reasons may have been ignorance on the part of other masters, disbelief or a (partly justified) suspicion that the enlightened employers would have been successful with or without such methods, enjoying advantages of techniques, size or a well-established market; but to limit the reasons to these would be to ignore one of the most decisive social facts of the age. An approach like Owen's ran counter to the accepted beliefs and ideology of the employing class, which saw its own rise to wealth and power as due to merit, and the workman's subordinate position as due to his failings. He remained a workman, living at subsistence wages, because he was less well endowed with the essential qualities of industry, ambition, sobriety and thrift. As long as this was so, he could hardly be expected to rise to the baits of moral appeals or co-operation. Therefore, one would have to begin by indoctrinating him with the bourgeois values which he lacked, and this, essentially, was the third method used by employers.

In their attempts to prevent 'Idleness, Extravagance, Waste and Immorality', employers were necessarily dealing with the workers both inside the factory and outside it. The efforts to reform the whole man were, therefore, particularly marked in factory towns and villages in which the total environment was under the control of a single employer.

The qualities of character which employers admired have, since Weber's[12] day, been to some extent associated with the Protestant ethic. To impart these qualities, with the one addition of obedience, to the working classes, could not but appear a formidable task. That it should have been attempted at all might seem to us incredible, unless we remember the background of the times which included the need to educate the first generation of factory workers to a new factory discipline, the widespread belief in human perfectibility, and the common assumption, by the employer, of functions which are to-day provided by the public authorities, like public safety, road building or education.... [O]ne of their consequences was the preoccupation with the character and morals of the working classes which are so marked a feature of the early stages of industrialization.

Some aspects of this are well known and easily understandable. Factory villages like New Lanark, Deanston, Busby, Ballindalloch, New Kilpatrick, Blantyre, and ... Antrim, had special provisions, and in some cases full-time staff, to check the morals of their workers. Contemporaries tended to praise

[12]German sociologist (1864–1920), author of *The Protestant Ethic and the Spirit of Capitalism.*

these actions most highly, and it was believed that firms laying stress on morals, and employing foremen who 'suppress anything bad' would get the pick of the labour. Almost everywhere, churches, chapels and Sunday Schools were supported by employers, both to encourage moral education in its more usual sense, and to inculcate obedience. Drink and drunkenness became a major target of reform, with the short-term aim of increasing the usefulness of scarce skilled workers... who were often incapacitated by drink, and the long-term aim of spreading bourgeois virtues.

In this process much of the existing village culture came under attack. 'Traditional social habits and customs seldom fitted into the new pattern of industrial life, and they had therefore to be discredited as hindrances to progress.' Two campaigns here deserve special mention.

The first was the campaign against leisure on Saturdays and Sundays, as, no doubt, examples of immoral idleness. 'The children are during the weekdays generally employed', the Bishop of Chester had declared solemnly in 1785, 'and on Sunday are apt to be idle, mischievous and vitious.' This was not easily tolerated. Thus Deanston had a Superintendant of streets to keep them clear of immorality, children and drink. Charles Wilkins of Tiverton formed an 'Association for the Promotion of Order' in 1832 to round up the children and drive them to school on Sundays. All the hands at Strutt's and Arkwright's under twenty had to attend school for four hours on Saturday afternoons and on Sundays to 'keep them out of mischief.' Horrocks' employed a man 'for many years, to see that the children do not loiter about the streets on Sundays.' At Dowlais the chapel Sunday school teachers asked J.J. Guest in 1818 to order his employees to attend, otherwise there was the danger that they might spend the Sabbath 'rambling and playing.' Even Owen expressed similar sentiments: 'if children [under ten] are not to be instructed, they had better be employed in any occupation that should keep them out of mischief', he asserted.

The second was the prohibition of bad language. At the beginning of the eighteenth century, Crowley's 'Clerk for the Poor', or teacher, was to correct lying, swearing, 'and suchlike horrid crimes'; while at the same time Sir Humphrey Mackworth, at Neath, fined 'Swearing, Cursing, Quarrelling, being Drunk, or neglecting Divine Service on Sunday, one shilling', and the Quaker Lead Company, at Gadlis, also prohibited swearing in 1708. Later this became quite regular, wherever rules were made: at Darley Abbey, in 1795, the fine was 9d or 1s.; at Mellor, 1s.; at Nenthead, 6d.; at Galloway's where 'obscene and vulgar language' was prohibited, the men themselves levied the fines. At Marshall and Benyon's also, according to Rule 4 of 1785, a jury of seven was to judge the offence of striking, abusing or harming another workman.

Again, the rules of Thomas Fernley, Jr., Stockport, cotton mills, stated: 'while at work... behaviour must be commendable avoiding all shouting, loud talk, whistling, calling foul names, all mean and vulgar language, and every kind of indecency.' Swearing, singing, being drunk were fined 5s.; overlookers allowing drink in the mills were fined 10s. 6d. . . .

This preoccupation might seem to today's observer to be both impertinent and irrelevant to the worker's performance, but in fact it was critical, for unless the workmen *wished* to become 'respectable' in the current sense, none of the other incentives would bite. Such opprobrious terms as 'idle' or 'dissolute' should be taken to mean strictly that the worker was indifferent to the employer's deterrents and incentives. According to contemporaries, 'it was the irrationality of the poor, quite as much as their irreligion, that was distressing. They took no thought of the morrow.... The workers were by nature indolent, improvident, and self-indulgent.'

The code of ethics on which employers concentrated was thus rather limited. Warnings against greed, selfishness, materialism or pride seldom played a large part, sexual morals rarely became an important issue to the factory disciplinarians (as distinct from outside moralists) and, by and large, they did not mind which God was worshipped, as long as the worshipper was under the influence of some respectable clergyman. The conclusion cannot be avoided that, with some honourable exceptions, the drive to raise the level of respectability and morality among the working classes was not undertaken for their own sakes but primarily, or even exclusively, as an aspect of building up a new factory discipline.

Any conclusions drawn from this brief survey must be tentative and hesitant, particularly if they are meant to apply to industrial revolutions in general.

First, the acclimatization of new workers to factory discipline is a task different in kind, at once more subtle and more violent, from that of maintaining discipline among a proletarian population of long standing. Employers in the British Industrial Revolution therefore used not only industrial means but a whole battery of extra-mural powers, including their control over the courts, their powers as landlords, and their own ideology, to impose the control they required.

Secondly, the maintenance of discipline, like the whole field of management itself, was not considered a fit subject for study, still less a science, but merely a matter of the employer's individual character and ability. No books were written on it before 1830, no teachers lectured on it, there were no entries about it in the technical encyclopaedias, no patents were taken out relating to it. As a result, employers did not learn from each other, except haphazardly and belatedly, new ideas did not have the cachet of a new technology and did not spread, and the crudest form of deterrents and incentives remained the rule. Robert Owen was exceptional in ensuring that his methods, at least, were widely known, but they were too closely meshed in with his social doctrines to be acceptable to other employers.

Lastly, the inevitable emphasis on reforming the moral character of the worker into a willing machine-minder led to a logical dilemma that contemporaries did not know how to escape. For if the employer had it in his power to reform the workers if he but tried hard enough, whose fault was it that most of them remained immoral, idle and rebellious? And if the workers could really be taught their employers' virtues, would they not all save and borrow and become entrepreneurs themselves, and who would then man the factories?

The Industrial Revolution happened too rapidly for these dilemmas, which involved the re-orientation of a whole class, to be solved, as it were, *en passant*. The assimilation of the formerly independent worker to the needs of factory routine took at least a further generation, and was accompanied by the help of tradition, by a sharply differentiated educational system, and new ideologies which were themselves the results of clashes of earlier systems of values, besides the forces operating before 1830. The search for a more scientific approach which would collaborate with and use, instead of seeking to destroy, the workers' own values, began later still, and may hardly be said to have advanced very far even today.

[13]Casually, in passing.

The Industrial Bourgeoisie

J. F. BERGIER

The Industrial Revolution transformed Europe and the world in the nineteenth century. With the Industrial Revolution the bourgeoisie gained preeminence. In this article J. F. Bergier seeks to understand that section of the bourgeoisie responsible for the stupendous industrial expansion in England in the late eighteenth century and subsequently in western Europe in the nineteenth century.

The history of the bourgeoisie is a long one. Where and when did it originate? Who were the bourgeoisie? How did someone become a member of the bourgeoisie? After a person had successfully risen to the bourgeoisie, he attempted to acquire land as soon as possible. Why was there such a great attraction for land, even among urban businessmen?

By the eighteenth century, the bourgeoisie was rent by internal divisions. What different groups of bourgeoisie existed and what characterized each one? How did the group that concerns Bergier, the industrial bourgeoisie, emerge? In the nineteenth century, the bourgeoisie as a whole secured political power. But why, despite its possessing the material means to do so, did the industrial bourgeoisie shy away from politics? Why did various groups in the bourgeoisie distrust one another?

The industrial bourgeoisie preferred then to concentrate on the accumulation of wealth through industrial production. How was the industrial bourgeois an entrepreneur? What traits did the early industrialists share? Why did they appear first in the cotton and iron sectors of the Industrial Revolution? How did they raise the capital to finance their industries?

If there were different sorts of bourgeoisie, there were also various types of industrial bourgeoisie. For much of the nineteenth century, the industrialists had no unity; they were too diverse in social origins, education, wealth, and outlook. Eventually, Bergier contends, the industrial bourgeoisie did coalesce as a social group. How did the industrialists manage to do this and to overcome those obstacles that had impeded cohesion? To what extent might a historian challenge Bergier's contention that the industrial bourgeoisie had "won the day"?

At the dawn of the industrial age, the bourgeois was no newcomer to the social scene. Indeed, he had existed for centuries, ever since the urban renaissance that almost all Europe experienced between the eleventh and fourteenth centuries. Originally, the bourgeois was the burgher or town dweller active as a merchant, official, artisan, lawyer or man of letters and enjoying certain rights conferred by the charter of his borough. But this original, legal notion of the bourgeoisie gradually became more complex.

On the one hand, the bourgeois enjoyed real social and material privileges with regard to the rest of society, particularly vis-à-vis the mass of peasants. They were therefore increasingly reluctant to share those privileges with newcomers, and laid down conditions of entry. The strictness of these conditions varied from one town to another, or one period to another. In Paris, a stay of a year and a day was all that was required for a man to acquire bourgeois status, as well in the eighteenth century as in the Middle Ages. But other towns imposed a longer period of residence: five years in Bordeaux, ten years in Lyons, Marseilles, and Périgueux. In Bordeaux, bourgeois also had to be householders, which created a kind of property discrimination between bourgeois and non-bourgeois. Elsewhere it was more common for access to the bourgeoisie and its privileges to be subject to the payment of a tax, which was sometimes low, sometimes very high: being free to fix the amount of this tax as they chose, the bourgeoisie could allow or refuse entry to their group just as they saw fit, thereby giving it the characteristics of a self-conscious and selective class. Thus, in Geneva, an independent city-state whose bourgeois were in some sort their own seigneur, a register was begun as early as the fifteenth century for recording the names of newly-admitted bourgeois; their descendants gradually came to form a real bourgeois aristocracy of *citoyens*.[1] In the eighteenth century, this aristocracy had become so inaccessible that it provoked a reaction from those who had failed to gain admission. . . .

On the other hand, the bourgeois did not confine themselves to the cramped precincts of their towns. In a society which remained fundamentally rural, at least up to the threshold of the nineteenth century (and often much later, in Germany, or Russia, for example), and in which the social prestige pertaining to the nobility was linked with land-ownership, the townsfolk felt

[1]Citizens.

rather left out of things. They had an ardent desire to acquire land and have it worked by tenants. This brought two advantages: the prestige and authority conferred by the ownership of land; and ground rent, which generally yielded lower profits than business or industry, but which had the merit of being more stable. Hence, by the fifteenth or sixteenth centuries, the original meaning of the word bourgeois began to be lost, and by the eighteenth century it was no more than a remembrance of things past. On the eve of the Revolution, the French bourgeoisie, which was certainly not the wealthiest, held more than thirty per cent of the cultivated land. In Switzerland or certain regions of western Germany, almost all the land was in bourgeois hands. By contrast, in those countries where great domains were formed at a very early date and the towns' hold on the country was correspondingly weaker (northern Germany, central and eastern Europe, the Iberian Peninsula), the vast majority of land was held by the nobility or the church. England, where the bourgeoisie and the gentry were much more closely interdependent—to say the least—than elsewhere, stood halfway between the two extremes. But there too the acquisition of land was a constant aim of the early industrial bourgeoisie, whose members remained extremely attached to their largely rural origins.

At all events in this slow, uneven but unmistakable transformation the bourgeoisie very gradually lost the unity originally secured by its status in law. True, even in the eighteenth century the condition of 'bourgeois' still conferred certain privileges. But the privileges were increasingly losing their value because all kinds of divisions were occurring within the bourgeoisie. These divisions were due to the separation of the bourgeoisie into professions and to the emergence of discrepancies in the wealth of its members.

Without going into detail, and ignoring the innumerable regional differences, we can readily distinguish between four broad groups of bourgeois. The first comprises the rentiers, comparatively few in number (in France, around ten per cent of the total 'bourgeois' effective) and generally not very powerful within the bourgeoisie. Their role in the rise of industry was minor; and what share they had in it came generally late in the day: they had no profession, in most cases lacked drive and initiative, and for a long while remained distrustful of industrial investment, preferring the proven profits of ground rent, commercial income, or government loans. The second group comprises the members of the learned professions, the magistracy, or the administration: neither their duties nor their incomes led them to take much interest in industry. There were exceptions, however: there is evidence to show that the French notaries played a role as purveyors of capital (in small amounts) to small, recently-founded enterprises; but this role remained marginal and rarely led them to become industrialists themselves.

The two remaining groups are more interesting from our point of view. The first consists of the *bourgeoisie d'affaires*,[2] the men who held all the reins

[2] Businessmen.

at the close of the ancien régime. Their incomes were often higher than those of the nobility, whose equals they believed they were in many respects. This group produced the best State officials, and in places where the nobility was lightweight, the city republics for instance, it *was* the State—indeed, this was an ancient tradition in the great commercial cities of London, Paris, Lyons, Amsterdam, Geneva, or Frankfurt. These bourgeois were big merchants or bankers (the two pursuits were henceforth rarely combined as they had been during the Renaissance): a few families in the largest cities, closely linked by marriage and often linked from one city or country to another. The family connections of the Protestant bankers of Geneva, Paris, or Amsterdam, the shipowners of Marseilles, Bordeaux or Nantes, and so on were as wide as their business connections, and the solidarity that they created was astonishingly efficient. This tiny minority, then, held a large majority of the financial power and actual wealth of the European nations and their colonies. Hence this bourgeoisie also controlled the main manufactories—the nearest thing to what we would call industry. For, on the very threshold of the industrial revolution, the manufacturing bourgeoisie had still to acquire a personality of its own. The masters of the enterprises were the wholesale dealers. Either they already brought together wage-earning workers in their mines or factories . . . or, more often than not, they resorted to the old *Verlag-System*,[3] providing home workers with all or part of the tools and the raw materials and buying back the finished product at a price fixed by the dealer that virtually amounted to a wage.

The fourth and last group within the bourgeoisie, by far the most numerous, was that of the artisans and shopkeepers, the innumerable minor trades that were practised more or less independently. The separation between this group and the previous one is, of course, imprecise. When does an artisan become a manufacturer, or a shopkeeper a dealer? Yet on the whole the differences are glaringly obvious. Income, to start with, was much lower in this last group; and the way of life in each case was strikingly different. The man of affairs draws his profits from his investments, from the risks that he takes; his job is to direct, to calculate, and to take decisions. The artisan or shopkeeper lives mainly off their own manual labour: the only difference between them and their employees is that they give the orders, while continuing to perform part of the work themselves.

These differences within the bourgeoisie, though obvious, are essential. For they ruled out all coherence between the groups, all sense of speaking the same social language, recognisably distinct and foreign to other social languages: in other words, the bourgeoisie had not yet become a class. Even if in some places it enjoyed certain juridical privileges which marked it off and conserved it—we have given the example of the Geneva bourgeoisie—it had no unity.

---

[3] Domestic, or putting-out system.

This accounts for all that was in store for the bourgeoisie: the difficulties that it was to encounter before it achieved complete political dominance; and the emergence of a new economic group, the industrial bourgeoisie, whose presence swiftly revolutionised the traditional structures that we have just been summarising.

...[T]he 'conquering bourgeois'...is an admirable description of the bourgeois onslaught on all the levers of political and economic power, an onslaught that began as early as the eighteenth century and spread, with varying degrees of delay, from one country to another.

This is not the place to discuss the bourgeois seizure of political power. Besides, the circumstances, motives, and results differed appreciably from one country to another. The main thing is that everywhere, with or without violence and institutional discontinuity (very marked in France, barely apparent in England), the bourgeoisie took control. In some places it did so directly; in others it merely had to act upon the traditional framework of government. True, it did not meet with unqualified success everywhere. In those countries where industrialisation was early and rapid (Great Britain, France, Belgium and the Netherlands, Switzerland, Scandinavia), the success was clear and uncontestable. Elsewhere, it was slower and less effective, because the bourgeoisie still had to contend with either the dispersion of government (Germany, Italy) or the inertia of the economic and social structures, which gave predominance to the large domains (Austria, Hungary, Poland, Russia, Spain). Despite this diversity of attainment, however, there can be no denying that here was a universal trend of considerable force.

It is remarkable that, in a general way, the political bourgeoisie, which furnished all or part of the members of the governments, the parliaments, or the main administrations, did not merge for a very long while with the industrial bourgeoisie, whose climb was largely parallel and whose interests would seem at first sight to have coincided with those of the government and its officials. There were exceptions—Robert Peel,[4] for instance. But the industrial entrepreneurs seem to have preferred to mind their own affairs rather than the affairs of state.

The question arises why. In the early phase of industrialisation, most of the entrepreneurs came from environments...which were largely unprepared for political activity. They did not have the kind of prominence needed to win votes; and indeed, in those countries where the franchise was based on property, many of them would not have been eligible to stand in the first place. By the second or third generation, the more successful industrialists had largely attained the local prestige and acreage they needed to enter politics, yet they rarely did so. Biographies of industrialists are still far too few for us to form a satisfactory notion of the reasons for this abstention. It is probable, however, that it was due more to a lack of ambition in this field and to a lack of

---

[4](1788–1850); British prime minister, 1834–35 and 1841–46.

experience in or even taste for this kind of activity than to any lack of interest in government as such, on which, after all, the prosperity of the enterprises depended in two respects: in a general way, with regard to legislation (on labour, external trade, and so on) and taxation; and in a more particular way, in respect of government orders placed with the factories. The entrepreneurs did not stand aloof altogether, however. They had agents and spokesmen in the parliaments and occasionally even in the governments; though devoted to the cause of industry, these men were rarely industrialists themselves.

It is clear, then, that the industrial bourgeoisie merged neither with the upper bourgeoisie of the parliaments and administrations nor with the traditional upper bourgeoisie of trade and finance. The latter kept to themselves. They usually distrusted the parvenu industrialists, whose recent wealth seemed to flout theirs and to challenge the status quo that they were determined to defend. For several generations there was virtually no collusion or association between merchants and bankers on the one hand and industrialists on the other. The capital held by the former did not find its way into industry for a long while (in England and France, not until the middle of the nineteenth century; in the other countries, guided by the experience of the pioneers, the hesitation did not have to be so prolonged). In this respect, the absence, up to around 1850, of adequate banking structures and industrial credit institutions says much about this compartmentation of the bourgeoisie.

What, then, were the origins of this industrial bourgeoisie? Where did the entrepreneurs come from? We may start by asking what is meant by an entrepreneur.

The word can mean two things, only one of which concerns us here. In its most usual sense, dating from the industrial revolution, the term 'entrepreneur' applies to anyone who directs, for his own account, an industrial undertaking (or even an enterprise producing nonindustrial goods or services), and who employs labour. But recent writers . . . have limited the meaning of the word to the creator or rejuvenator of an enterprise—the man whose personal drive, inventiveness (in matters of management as much as—and often more than—production technique), and taste for competitive risk-taking results in 'progress': progress for his enterprise, if he is considered individually, in which case 'progress' is measured in terms of his profits; or, taking him as part of a collective effort, in the context of an industrial sector or a nation, progress in the material welfare of society as a whole.

In this precise sense in which we shall be using the word, the entrepreneur is a man with an original mental, not to say moral, make-up. For indeed the emergence of the entrepreneur class and the achievement by them—and by their workers—of the industrial revolution resulted from the historically exceptional combination of these personal qualities and the demographic, economic, social, and technical circumstances that are held to have been the prerequisites of the take-off. The entrepreneur sees everything in terms of profitability: ever since the earliest days of industrialisation he has possessed in the highest degree that spirit of capitalism that Max Weber,[5] rightly or wrongly, associated with protestantism....

The spirit of capitalism had, of course, existed among the merchants and financiers before the industrial entrepreneurs came along. What the latter added, with help of circumstances that became particularly favourable to them, was their sense of adaptation and their genius for innovation that enabled them to appreciate the practical implications of the latest technical discoveries: their first aim was to get rich, but their second aim was to contribute to the progress of society by turning out a product that was cheaper, or better, or both.

Hence the entrepreneur was very different from the big capitalist that preceded him. If his thrift recalls the frugality of his predecessor, his kind as a whole imported an imaginativeness that the man of affairs before him (and for a long while alongside him) only displayed individually and in a much smaller way. All was grist to the entrepreneur's mill, everything counted, everything was possible; his only limitations were those of his market—and even these did not hamper him, since his innovations enabled him constantly to broaden the market, the global limits of which were still imprecise (and remained so at least until the first half of the twentieth century).

All this meant that the industrial entrepreneur broke free from the social limitations that capitalists before him had imposed upon themselves. This partly explains the social clashes that industrialisation was not long in producing. But was the entrepreneur's freedom with regard to social conventions a deliberate disregard for 'breeding' or merely a lack of it? This brings us back to the question of where the entrepreneurial class or group came from in the first place.... [T]he entrepreneurs of the industrial revolution, wherever it occurred, were obviously not all like the type that we have been portraying. The fact that they were not is clear from the splits that occurred within the industrialists' own social group—another question to which we must now turn.

Before the appearance of the industrial entrepreneurs, from 1760–80 in England then gradually elsewhere in Europe, 'industrialists' were, of course, already to be found. But some of them, wholesale dealers often called manufacturing merchants, merely organised commercially the output of a host of wage-earning artisans, without ever attempting to modify or rationalise the methods and techniques involved; their manufactories were more like communities of workers than industrial enterprises. The other 'industrialists', small independent artisans, mostly lacked sufficient means and (especially) sufficient imagination and breadth of mind to make significant innovations—from which they would constantly have been precluded in any case by the strict rules of the guilds.

---

[5]German sociologist (1864–1920), author of *The Protestant Ethic and the Spirit of Capitalism*.

Hence neither the manufacturing merchant group, through lack of interest, nor the artisan group, through lack of wherewithal, was able to mutate outright into an industrialist group. Not surprisingly, therefore, the other social and professional categories (nobility, peasantry, learned professions, and so forth) stood aloof from this great economic and social movement. So what we find is not a change of activity on the part of a group, but the quasi-spontaneous generation of a new group whose members came from every section of society. It was not birth, trade, or fortune that made the first industrialists, but initiative, ambition, and luck—if they succeeded, for the emergence of this new group was an affair for the fittest or luckiest; those who could not keep up helped to form the nucleus of the future proletariat.

The first industrialist groups gathered in the peak sectors of the industrial revolution: cotton and iron. It was there that needs were greatest and the demand seemingly insatiable; it was there also, in industries as new as spinning or as unorganised as ironworking, that the structures were most flexible and the prospects brightest. Hence these were the two fields in which enterprises proliferated—very rapidly in England, especially after 1785, rather more slowly but around the same time in France, and not much later in Switzerland (from 1801 onwards). Progress went ahead by leaps and bounds rather than constantly, with the braking effects and recessions provoked by the conjuncture as a whole (political and military events as much as the purely economic cycles).

In this mad rush, particularly in the cotton industry, almost anyone could set himself up as an industrialist. All that was needed to install a spinning frame was a small amount of capital (which could be got from a money-lender) and the services of a workman sufficiently acquainted with the technique to act as foreman. In almost every case, the biographies of these early industrial entrepreneurs show them to have started out from modest circumstances: shopkeepers, rural artisans, inn-keepers, farmers. Arkwright,[6] the most famous (or at least the most typical) of them, who died in 1792 with a knighthood and worth a million, was a barber; whether or not he really invented the water-frame, he exploited it with the genius that others applied to the various new techniques. The Peels, who also built up a considerable fortune before one of them turned his hand to politics, had been well-to-do farmers; Sir Robert's grandfather had begun by dabbling in hand-spinning and cotton printing in the time left over from the land: from this he launched out into power-spinning and calico printing. . . .

Things were much the same in France: many of the great spinning or weaving dynasties began as humble artisan (rather than farming) families: the Peugeots, who built their fortune in textiles well before the motor-car, had been successively farmers, innkeepers, and millers before establishing a calico works near Montbéliard in 1759. But there were also a few former

---

[6]Richard Arkwright (1732–1792), inventor of the water-frame, a spinning machine that led to the creation of cotton mills.

merchants among these entrepreneurs: 'dealers as long as the work was done by hand, they became industrialists as soon as mechanisation made it possible to set up spinning frames or power looms at little cost,... In Switzerland, the first spinning mills, very modest affairs, were also opened by well-to-do farmers or artisans (they were usually both at once), before being taken over as early as 1800 by merchants... who were in a better position financially and commercially to acquire the already complicated and more costly English machines, or patents to build them on the spot.

The same can be said of the ironmasters. Many of them were of country extraction, such as... Richard Crawshay,[7] the 'iron king', whose father was a small farmer; John Wilkinson's[8] father was a countryman before signing on as a labourer in an ironworks. But others belonged to an artisan milieu that naturally guided them towards the iron and steel industry....

Outside England, the iron industry was perhaps generally more 'bourgeois' in its origins: beginning rather later, it necessitated a larger initial investment. In France, it was the main *maîtres de forges*[9] traditionally established in the richest ore regions who became great industrialists. Here it was not so much the kind of activity that changed as the methods and scale of production. We find the same thing occurring in Saxony and the Rhineland later on (1820–40). It would seem, however, that the later industrialisation began, the greater was the contribution of the upper strata of the bourgeoisie, with occasional financial aid or even direct participation from the landed aristocracy.

In spite of the undeniable diversity of the social and professional origins of the industrial pioneers in individual countries, the dominant trend was for them to come from the land. The towns—the large pre-industrial cities devoted to trade and the traditional crafts—made little contribution to industrialisation.... Further, the industrialist willingly returned to the land (in England more than elsewhere, perhaps): as soon as the fortune that he had built up allowed him to do so, he hastened to buy land (if possible the land formerly worked by himself or his ancestors) and to have it worked, in his turn, by tenants.

These industrialists were not technicians, still less scholars, but improvisers. They brought their inventiveness to bear, not on production techniques, but on their application, that is to say the internal organisation of the enterprise and the commercialisation of the products. An enquiry into the British cotton industry in 1803 showed that, despite the simple nature of the machinery, most of the entrepreneurs were incapable of taking their own technical decisions: 'The reason of it is, that the master was never acquainted with the art of weaving, he just puts in a man who understands the trade, invests his

[7] Owner of an ironworks, 1788–1867.
[8] Owner of iron foundries, 1728–1808.
[9] Iron-master.

capital, and when he gets the price of the market, he goes forward'.... Hence a kind of division of labour was called for, not only in the appropriation of labour but in the management itself. It diminished, however, after a generation or two, when the heirs to an enterprise had managed to acquire specialist training. As we know, this division of technical and commercial responsibilities within the mangement reappeared at the end of the nineteenth century and from then on spread to all large and medium-sized enterprises.

In any case, the entrepreneurs had quite enough worries as things stood, without having to bother about actual production. They had to gather together a labour force, which was rarely as simple as the romantic tradition of a permanent host of unemployed would have us believe. (Right from the start of industrialisation the labour market underwent frequent variations that were not always to the workers' disadvantage.) The entrepreneurs had also to organise the commercial side of their enterprises—buying and selling. They had continually to cope with increasing competition, and, in order to do so, keep up with the needs and tastes of their customers and with the technical innovations that they had to be among the first to exploit if they were not to be crushed. Lastly,... they had to make the best possible arrangements for financing their enterprises.

A great deal of ink has flowed on the question of capital for industry. Marx believed that the start of the process of industrialisation depended on the prior accumulation of capital.... Yet this view is nowadays contested both by a number of economists and by historians. The former who... have been making a careful scrutiny of the prerequisites for industrialisation, have come to the unanimous conclusion—though with some disagreement over priorities—that other factors were more decisive than the availability of capital: a prosperous agricultural system capable of feeding the people who quit the land for the factories; an infrastructure of trade and communications guaranteeing the supply of raw materials and the disposal of the products; an adequate level of technological development; and so forth. The historians, for their part, have established: (i) that the 'original accumulation' of capital that Marx traced back to the sixteenth century in fact went through many vicissitudes between then and the industrial period: the eighteenth or early nineteenth centuries were not 'wealthier' than the sixteenth; and (ii) that the initial investment of the industrial revolution, at least in those countries where it occurred first, remained very low.

The basic technical innovations—almost exclusively the work of amateurs or artisans of slender means—were characteristically very simple and therefore comparatively inexpensive. A frame or loom for working cotton, wool, or flax, even a steam engine or a blast furnace, did not involve enormous expenditure. The business became expensive when many looms, frames, or engines were used at once. Almost all the entrepreneurs started out with a small plant that they built themselves or bought, and with a correspondingly small labour force. They set themselves up on funds of their own or money loaned to them by a small circle of relatives, friends, or connections. They could not have done otherwise, moreover, since the large amounts of capital held by the bankers, merchants, or big landowners were only very rarely available to them. To expand or renew their plant, they had to rely on reinvestment of their profits.

Self-financing was the rule at the start of industrialisation. (The later-developing countries differed in this respect. Northern Italy, Russia, and so on, with their great agricultural domains, got less negligible aid from the landed capitalists and from the investments of foreign capital.) And in the second generation, self-financing enabled the large enterprises to expand and increase at the expense of the smaller and less profitable ones. The fact is that, even then, the men of affairs were still chary about industrial investment; and the banking system remained inadequate for industrial needs up to and beyond 1850.

Yet after 1800 in England, 1820 in France and Switzerland, self-financing in the strict sense ceased to be the rule entirely. The entrepreneurs had swiftly realised that it was in their interests to invest in other enterprises besides their own. It could be advantageous to take out interests in rival enterprises, already equipped but less successful, in order to gain more or less direct control of them: examples of this were frequent in the textile industry. Investment in other, complementary industries could enable the entrepreneur to improve his supply of raw materials (e.g. an ironmaster assigning assets to a mining concern) or his outlets (many owners of spinning mills gave financial aid to the weavers).

This soon led to concentration, vertical as much as horizontal. (The phenomenon was probably more accentuated in France or Switzerland than in England, and in ironworking more than any other branch.) But this concentration was also simultaneously a cause and effect of the severe selection process which... eliminated large numbers of particularly ill-prepared industrialists and practically put them at the mercy of their more successful competitors. Concentration in industry had the further effect, which helped to shape the new bourgeoisie, of creating company enterprises with varying numbers of partners. Even if one or other of the partners emerged as a leader and acted the part of the 'entrepreneur' more than the others, all the active partners (as distinct from sleeping partners) took their place in the developing industrial bourgeoisie.

... The industrial bourgeoisie was not the agent, but the product of the industrial revolution. It arose as the result of an identity of interests among a number of individuals whose social origins differed widely (despite certain dominants that emerge), and a common orientation in their activity.

But even though this industrial bourgeoisie shared the characteristic features of the entrepreneur, it had no self-awareness and no awareness of its collective role in society. It had no unity, no solidarity: it had no existence as a class. Too many differences stood between the individuals of whom it was composed: differences as regards social origins and hence education, and differences, fairly rapidly accentuated, as regards wealth. At the time of the group's emergence, cohesion was also obviated by the geographic spread of the different ventures within each nation. This obstacle was generally soon overcome, however, as the industrialists conglomerated in zones that were particularly favourable with regard to the availability of raw materials, communications, labour, and so on. The industrial towns that resulted—Manchester, Birmingham, Lille, Saint-Etienne, Zurich, Turin, the Ruhr cities, and so forth—were not merely the overcrowded and insanitary seats of the working masses; they were also the rallying points of the industrial bourgeoisie. This development had a share in setting the industrial bourgeoisie apart from the other groups of bourgeois, who generally stayed on in the towns where they conducted their affairs, notably in the capitals of trade and traditional industry: London, Paris, Lyons, Milan, Berlin, etc. A final obstacle to the cohesion of the group was the keen competition among its members; and this obstacle was never completely overcome.

Gradually, however, this cohesion was achieved, at least partially. Two main factors which transcended national frontiers were largely responsible for this: (i) the development of an ethos, a culture peculiar to the industrial bourgeoisie; and (ii) the historical necessity, existing before it was felt or understood, for solidarity within the group—a kind of defence mechanism against the animosity of the rest of society, whose structures the industrial bourgeoisie, however small it was in actual numbers, had already wrecked.

... [A]t the outset, the industrial bourgeoisie necessarily had no culture of its own; that is to say, it produced no artifacts, and transmitted no ideas, bearing the mark of its personality (of which it had none) or its inventive genius, its dynamism. Indeed, its contribution to the cultural effort and progress of society as a whole was but a very humble one. In this respect also it differed considerably from the traditional bourgeoisie. Many, if not most, of the early industrial entrepreneurs had never got beyond the rudimentary schooling consistent with their station. Very few of them bothered to better their knowledge of things outside their profession; and sensibility was even rarer among them than knowledge. True, the refinement and taste of Wedgwood,[10] for instance, are often justly praised: indeed such qualities were the famous potter's stock-in-trade. Boulton,[11] the great entrepreneur, was a skilful mechanic, an art-lover, and the friend of many men of letters and science. The Mulhouse spinning-mill owners were highly educated and cultured. But those of the industrialists who belonged to the cultural élite of their day were still the exceptions (which made for further divisions within the group). The vast majority were self-made men whose stocks of knowledge, even technical knowledge, were very rudimentary. Owen,[12] a

---

[10]Josiah Wedgwood (1730–1795), owner of a pottery factory.

[11]Matthew Boulton (1728–1809), inventor, along with James Watt, of an efficient steam engine.

[12]Robert Owen (1771–1858), industrialist and social reformer.

notable exception in this respect, had harsh things to say around 1820 about the 'cotton barons': they were generally 'plodding men of business, with little knowledge and limited ideas, except in their own immediate circle of occupation'....

Nonetheless, progress in this field was more or less rapid, depending on the country considered. It was particularly rapid in Switzerland, whose industrialised regions had long enjoyed a higher degree of literacy than most other countries. Gradually, the industrial countries (France was rather slow in this respect) opened higher institutions and trade schools in an attempt to make good the technological advance gained by England. As a rule, these innovations were not put forward by the industrialist group and do not appear to have had its support at the outset. But they were ultimately of service to it. Trained engineers capable of assuming increasingly complex professional responsibilities came to dominate the group; and thanks to their broader culture the group as a whole gained in refinement and maturity. And this attempt to form a body of qualified industrial managers contributed, of course, to the reinforcement of economic growth.

Having acquired a higher degree of education and culture, the industrial bourgeoisie of the time of Louis-Philippe[13] or Robert Peel was proportionately more powerful and effective as a social force. But its potential remained limited by the fact that it had still not formed itself into a coherent group; before it did so, it had to encounter obstacles which only a united onslaught could overcome.

The first obstacles were political ones. As we have seen, the entrepreneurs were reluctant to get involved in politics. But it was important to them that government policy should suit their interests. When necessary, they managed to agree among themselves and put forward proposals, indeed demands....

But these political obstacles revealed a latent conflict between the newcomers and the traditional bourgeoisie. This covert yet unremitting 'class struggle' within the bourgeoisie was fought over proposed legislation, economic doctrines (with the industrialists successfully disseminating the principle of laissez-faire), and social status....

At all events, there can be no doubt that sooner or later, in every country, the industrial bourgeoisie won the day.... 'The time has come,' wrote Isoard in 1834, 'for our industrialists to occupy the positions held since 1789 by successively, the priests, the soldiers, the lawyers, and the men of letters.' And did not Marx himself also stress the historically decisive role played by the entrepreneurs? But, for him, that role had already been fulfilled by 1848....

For indeed behind the employers were the workers. From being an unorganised mass, the proletariat became conscious of its destiny, meaning its size and its strength. Faced with this challenge, the industrial bourgeoisie

---

[13]King of the French, 1830–1848.

in its turn finally became conscious of itself and the privileges that the proletariat was beginning to contest. Just as the word capitalism would be coined some time later to answer its predecessor socialism, the industrial bourgeoisie became a 'class' in the full meaning of the word to resist the growing pressure of the working class.

Lantern Smashing in Paris

WOLFGANG SCHIVELBUSCH

Individual and collective protest take different forms in different cultures and periods. Moreover, acts of social complaint take aim at objects and values whose symbolic importance is sometimes difficult to fathom. Thus the historian must investigate the various meanings that material objects held for social groups. Here, in the case of lantern smashing, Wolfgang Schivelbusch seeks to uncover what the stringing of lanterns meant to Parisians and to other urban dwellers in Europe and why they resorted to the destruction of technological developments in lighting that one might think would have made cities better places in which to live.

In the Middle Ages, darkness immersed cities when the sun went down. Social life ground to a near standstill as people huddled in their homes for warmth and protection. Both city gates and individual houses were locked. The night was given over to night-watchmen, lawbreakers, and supernatural creatures and forces.

By the sixteenth century, city governments had begun tentatively to install artificial lighting, though it was not until the late seventeenth century at least that major European cities had conquered the night to any appreciable degree. Paris, renowned as the "city of light" because of its cultural brilliance, took the lead in applying artificial light to its streets. The city strung cables so that lanterns hung above the middle of the streets. In 1760 a new and more powerful type of lighting, the reflector lantern (réverbère) turned nighttime into day, as contemporaries noted (and imagined). In reality, even this innovation did not illuminate the streets fully (this was not technologically possible until the late nineteenth century) because the lanterns shone brightly over limited areas only. Paris was still a mixture of patches of light and of darkness. Still, it is significant that more sources of light illuminated more of the city than ever before and that the state and not individuals took responsibility for the increased illumination. Previously, individuals had carried their own sources of light as a means of identification as well as for illumination. Now, just as the state had asserted its control over the military and the police, it laid claim to a monopoly of the dispensation of light.

Why did the state insist on public lighting? Why did the populace smash lanterns and so plunge streets back into darkness? Who performed the lantern smashing? What psychological and symbolic functions did lantern smashing serve? Why did the city governments of Paris and London administer different punishments for the crime of lantern smashing?

Why did crowds during the French Revolution choose to hang people from lanterns? How did the act of lantern smashing change in the French Revolution and in the nineteenth century from what it had been before then? Why did poets often write of paving stones together with lanterns? That is, what linked paving stones to street lighting? What transformation occurred in the city when lanterns had been smashed?

When and why did lantern smashing decline? According to Schivelbusch, crowds brought on darkness by lantern smashing but then had festive illuminations that ended the darkness. Why did the crowds do this and why did the police oppose the festive lighting as they had contested the smashing of lanterns?

'After midnight, every street light is worth a host of watchmen'. . . . This was one of the principles of maintaining law and order in late-eighteenth century, pre-revolutionary Paris. By day, 1,500 uniformed police were on the streets. By night, 3,500 lanterns (*réverbères*) achieved the same result.

The police budget shows how important public lighting was in the security apparatus. Lighting accounted for 15 per cent of the total, making it the largest single item in the police budget apart from the watch (Le Guet). Mercier,[1] who defines the police apparatus as a *machine* for maintaining order in Paris, lists its most important components as 'the street lights and *réverbères*, the various guard units...and the torch bearers'. In this picture of order and security, illumination meshes seamlessly with the whole range of police methods; indeed, lanterns almost seem to dominate everything else.

It comes as no surprise, therefore, that from the start the street lanterns of Paris provoked aggression from below. 'Drunkards and debauchees, wandering through the streets at night, amused themselves by smashing them with their sticks, if they could reach high enough'. Where the *réverbères* were hung so high that they were out of reach of sticks, a new method of destroying them became popular. It consisted of cutting the ropes on which the lanterns hung, letting them smash on the pavement.

Whatever the details and methods, smashing lanterns was obviously an extremely enjoyable activity. Here, there is only room for a brief sketch of its psychological significance. Its main appeal was putting out the light. The act of extinguishing a fire (the psychoanalytical archetype is urinating on the fire) confers a feeling of omnipotence. Destroying lanterns in the seventeenth and eighteenth centuries offered the additional satisfaction of symbolically unseating the authority they represented: the darkness that prevailed after the lanterns had gone out stood for disorder and freedom. Added to this visual experience of omnipotence was a no less pleasurable aural one. The sound of breaking glass is like an explosion. Something that a moment ago was solid, an object with a highly symbolic significance, is suddenly wiped out. The desire to wreak such destruction and also to experience a symbolic sexual release in the loud splintering of breaking glass were probably the deeper motives behind lantern smashing.

[1] Louis-Sébastian Mercier (1740–1814), dramatist, critic, and commentator on life in Paris.

Every attack on a street lantern was a small act of rebellion against the order that it embodied and was punished as such. In Paris, destroying lanterns was not treated as disorderly conduct (*contravention aux ordonnances*) but as a criminal offence not far short of lese-majesty. 'If any Man break them', an English travel writer reports in the late seventeenth century, 'he is forthwith sent to the Gallies; and there were three young Gentlemen of good families, who were in Prison for having done it in a Frolick, and could not be released thence in some Months; and that not without the deligent Application of good Friends at Court'. In London, where street lanterns did not symbolise an absolute monarchy, punishments for the same crime, or rather offence, were correspondingly milder: a fine of twenty shillings for the first offence, forty shillings in case of recurrence, and three pounds for a third offence.

During the Paris revolutions and rebellions of the nineteenth century, lantern smashing—until then an individual, libertine phenomenon—became a collective, plebeian movement. But before it reached this stage, there was an unforeseen and lethal interlude. In the summer of 1789, the meaning of the French verb *lanterner* changed. Mercier describes this change as follows: 'Originally, this word meant "to do nothing" or "to waste one's time". At the beginning of the Revolution, it meant "to hang a man from a lantern".' This is how popular revenge vented itself in the first weeks of the Revolution, before the Committee of Public Safety[2] and the guillotine imposed their order on revolutionary justice. The first victims were two of the most hated representatives of the *ancien régime*,[3] Foulon[4] and Berthier,[5] who, on 22 July 1789, were strung up on a lantern fixed to the front of the Hôtel de Ville.[6] Unlike most lanterns, which hung from ropes stretched across the street, this one was attached to the wall by means of a gallows-shaped fixture. This unusual feature can be explained by the fact that the lantern was not in a street but on a square, the Place de Grève[7] (the traditional execution site), which could not be spanned by a rope.

The most obvious reason for using this particular fixture for an execution was that it was shaped like a gallows. But something else must have been at work too, as the streets of Paris were full of objects just as well suited to the purpose—there were many trees, for example, and sign-boards of shops

[2]Created on 6 April 1793, the Committee of Public Safety had wide powers and was in large part responsible for the Reign of Terror (1793–1794).

[3]The Old Régime, the government and society existing before the French Revolution of 1789.

[4]Joseph François Foulon (1715–1789), Old Régime administrator who organized military resistance to Paris in 1789 and was lynched because it was believed he had attempted to starve the city.

[5]Louis Bénigne François Berthier de Sauvigny (1737–1789), intendant (agent of the crown) of Paris, lynched along with his father-in-law Foulon.

[6]City hall.

[7]Square in front of the city hall.

and inns were still sufficiently numerous and quite strong enough. This was more likely a case of settling accounts in a manner both real and symbolic. Hauling down the lantern and replacing it with a representative of the old order bloodily reversed the ancient symbolism. If lanterns represented the *ancien régime*, then a hanged Foulon and a hanged Berthier represented the unleashed power of the people. There may have been a further symbolic reason for using that specific lantern on the Hôtel de Ville: a bust of Louis XIV[8] was mounted in a niche above it. There, popular justice could take place right under the eyes of the king.

This by no means complete account of the prelude to lantern smashing shows that lanterns were not chosen accidentally. Rather, long-pent-up grievances vented themselves in this choice. The literature and folklore of the period, which immediately took up the theme, show us the extent to which the Revolutionary masses of 1789 were obsessed with the image of the lantern. Camille Desmoulins[9] called his famous speech in the summer of 1789 'Discours de la lanterne aux Parisiens',[10] and he was nicknamed 'Procureur de la lanterne'.[11] And the chorus of the revolutionary song 'Ça ira',[12] which preceded *La Marseillaise*[13] in the same way that the lantern foreshadowed the guillotine, goes, 'Les aristocrates à la lanterne!'[14] ...

Hanging people from lanterns played no further part in the Paris revolutions and rebellions of the nineteenth century. This activity was replaced by lantern smashing, which at first glance looks like a revival of the seventeenth- and eighteenth-century tradition. According to the forces of the state, attacks on lanterns were nothing short of wanton vandalism by nocturnal rowdies. Maxime Du Camp[15] describes such attacks from the perspective of the Second Empire:[16]

> During the rebellions, of which there were many in the Restoration period[17] and under Louis Phillipe,[18] street lanterns were like a red rag to a bull for all those good-for-nothings who are glorified in literature these days. Whenever a crowd gathered, that lot—all they deserved was the whip—would appear and swarm around like bees around a honeypot. They would throw stones at

[8]King of France, 1643–1715.

[9]Lucie-Camille-Simplice Desmoulins (1760–1794), lawyer and then revolutionary, who advocated killing those who opposed the Revolution and voted for the execution of King Louis XVI. He later called in his newspaper for a relaxation of the Terror and was guillotined.

[10]The lantern's (lamp-post's) speech to the Parisians.

[11]The lantern's attorney.

[12]Things will work out, a revolutionary song dating from 1790, to which anti-aristocratic verses were later added.

[13]This song became the French national anthem in 1795.

[14]Hang the aristocrats on the lamp-post!

[15]French journalist, poet, and novelist (1822–1894).

[16]Period of the reign of the French Emperor, Napoleon III (1852–1870).

[17]Period of the reestablished monarchy after the Revolution and Napoleon (1814–1830).

[18]King of the French, 1830–1848.

lanterns, breaking the glass. The worst of them would climb onto the shoulders of their comrades and cut the ropes on which the lanterns hung. Then they would make off as quickly as they could, before the police patrol, alerted by the noise of the lantern smashing on the pavement, could get there. Sometimes they would reduce a whole street to complete darkness in no more than fifteen minutes.

Lantern smashing appeared as an adjunct to general revolt for the first time in July 1830. Contemporary reports give a different impression of it from Du Camp. A German eye-witness, for example, described it as follows: 'The populace, furious, runs through the streets, smashing lanterns, challenging the bourgeoisie to fight, and swearing that it will have vengeance'. Or to quote a French report: 'In the midst of these horrors [the street fighting of 27 July, the first day of the July Revolution][19] night fell over the city, and now the populace began smashing the *réverbères*. . . . Along with the *réverbères*, all other symbols of the treacherous king's authority were destroyed—they did not want anything to remind them of him'. This was no longer a case of a few mischievous nocturnal revellers destroying a lantern or two; now the 'populace' was involved, and its aim was to extinguish *all* lanterns. The fact that lanterns are mentioned in the same breath as the other hated emblems of domination shows that the old symbolism was still very much alive. We even find a new variant on the reversal of the lantern's symbolic significance—a further development on the 1789 practice of hanging people from the ropes holding up lanterns. Here it is, as observed by a German visitor: 'The populace vented its anger on all the signs of royal power: escutcheons, at first draped with black crape, were taken down or smashed and hung on lantern cords'.

But it was not just that the rebels had a gift for symbolic gesture. Lantern smashing was above all a practical strategy in street fighting against the forces of the state. The darkness that spread as lanterns were smashed created an area in which government forces could not operate. The eye-witness we have just quoted wrote: 'As lanterns were smashed and darkness descended, the streets were too unsafe for royal troops to be allowed to stay there. They retreated, behind their cannons and with constant skirmishes, to Louis XIV Square. From there, they dared to send out patrols, but only to the main roads and *quais*'.[20]

Lantern smashing erected a wall of darkness, so to speak, protecting an area from incursion by government forces. It went hand in hand with another technique of nineteenth-century street fighting: the erection of real walls, or barricades. The barricade acted as a physical impediment matching the visual one provided by the unilluminated night. 'Streets where attacks were expected, or that the rebels wanted to hold, were blocked with wooden implements, planks and stones, the lanterns were removed or smashed, and weapons were collected and cartridges prepared'. The result of this double

[19]French insurrection in July 1830 that overthrew the authoritarian and reactionary King Charles X and ushered in the reign of the moderate king, Louis Phillipe.

[20]Quays; embankments of the river.

barricading has been described as follows: 'Stripped of all its lanterns and completely barricaded, Paris was made impregnable within a few hours'. With the simultaneous appearance of barricades and smashed lanterns in July 1830, the repressed returned in a classical way. These revolutionary acts reversed the order that absolutism had imposed on the street 150 years earlier. Tearing up the paving stones and re-assembling them as barricades freed the earth to return to its 'natural' state, which had disappeared in the seventeenth century; extinguishing the artificial light of the lanterns restored the natural darkness of the night. The soil below the pavements, and the clear, dark night sky above the smashed lanterns—so goes, more or less, a poetic description, reissued in May 1968,[21] of nature and society liberated by revolution.

In the wake of the July Revolution, the paving stones of Paris became a powerful literary motif. . . . 'After the three days, paving stones are ubiquitous'. He points out that the word *pavé*[22] occurs forty-three times in poems written between 1830 and 1833—in the poetry written between August and December 1830 alone, it appears eighteen times. Most praised of all was the transformation of pavements into barricades. Victor Hugo[23] noted in his diary: 'The pavement is the most splendid symbol of the people. One tramples on it until it dashes one's head to pieces'. He is also the author of the line 'Under the living pavement, that rumblingly assembles'. Adolphe Dumas[24] wrote:

Les Pavés! les Pavés!
D'eux-mêmes, en remparts, comme soldats, levés
Arrêtent les assauts . . .[25]

Apolitical poets as well as revolutionary ones wrote of the pavements. Here the pavement appears as the street's armour, intact, not yet broken open by revolution, a symbol of 'ugliness, hardness, colourlessness—in short, unnaturalness'. This poetry shows pavements and street lighting as historically interlocked. The reflection of lantern light on the pavement became a poetic motif for loneliness, sorrow and coldness.

Pour soleil des lanternes
Qui de leurs reflets ternes

[21] A period of massive student demonstrations in Paris.

[22] Paving stone.

[23] Novelist, poet, and essayist (1802–1885), the leading French literary figure of the nineteenth century.

[24] French poet (1806–1861).

[25] "The paving stones! the paving stones! Piled up in bulwarks, like soldiers, they halt attacks." (Original author's note.)

Baignent les pavés gris[26]
(Gautier).[27]

Sur le pavé noirci les blafardes lanternes
Versaient un jour douteux plus triste que la nuit[28]
(Musset).[29]

La lumière glacée aux vitres des lanternes
Miroitait tristement sur le pavé boueux[30]
(Esquiros).[31]

... 'The lights of Paris, so often a symbol of brightness and cheerfulness, seem to be darkened and soiled, as it were, by contact with the pavement'.

... Alphonse Esquiros, for whom lantern light and pavements evoke sadness, sees the light playing over the Seine quite differently: 'I love the reflection of the *réverbères* on the waves'. Similarly, Musset writes:

Que j'aimais ce temps gris, ces passants, et la Seine
Sous ses mille falots assise en souveraine.[32]

The river, symbol of the restless life, is the opposite of the pavement—a piece of freely flowing nature in the middle of the city that can reflect even artificial light naturally.

But let us go back to the smashing of lanterns. What sort of darkness spread when lanterns were broken?

Descriptions read like illustrations of what Mercier had predicted fifty years earlier when he wrote, referring to the police *machine* (that could not have been a machine without lighting), 'if it were ever brought to a halt, then Paris would be exposed to all the terrors of a captured city'. To the contemporary observer, the city stripped of light and the military seemed like a medieval city after dark: 'It is difficult to imagine the total darkness into which this big city was plunged when its lighting was destroyed. Locked doors of shops and houses, and lowered blinds in the windows conveyed the impression of a deserted city, visited by the plague. A terrible silence

---

[26]"Lanterns as suns, that flood the grey pavements with their lustreless light." (Original author's note.)

[27]Théophile Gautier, French poet and novelist (1811–1872).

[28]"On to the blackish pavement the leaden lanterns cast their uncertain light that was more melancholy than the night." (Original author's note.)

[29]Alfred de Musset, French romantic poet (1810–1857).

[30]"The cold light of the lanterns was reflected sadly in the dirty pavement." (Original author's note.)

[31]Henri Alphonse Esquiros, French politician and poet (1814–1876).

[32]"How much I loved this grey hour, the strollers and the Seine, lit up by its thousand majestic torches." (Original author's note.)

completed the picture of horror and threat'. State power, impotent in the darkness created by the rebels, reacted by repeating a call it had already issued in the sixteenth century. Once again, citizens were urged to identify themselves by displaying lights, thus bringing the situation under control. 'Inhabitants of Paris', goes an appeal made by the Chief of the Paris police in July 1830, 'keep your distance to these wretches; do not let an imprudent curiosity mislead you into taking part in these riots. Stay inside your houses; put lights in your windows at night to illuminate the street; prove, by your prudence and your sober behaviour, that you have nothing to do with scenes that would put you to shame'.

In Victor Hugo's novel *Les Misérables*,[33] the play, or rather the struggle between light and darkness during a rebellion, unfolds in two scenes that seem like a distillation of history. Let's start with the scene in which Gavroche, the street urchin (*gamin*) breaks a lantern. The chapter is called 'A boy at war with street-lamps'. As the scene begins, Gavroche strays into a street where the lanterns are still burning in the middle of a rebellion. ' "You've still got lights burning in these parts", he said. "That's not right, mate. No discipline. I'll have to smash it." He flung the stone, and the lamp-glass fell with a clatter which caused the occupants of the near-by houses, huddled behind their curtains, to exclaim, "It's '93[34] all over again!" "There you are, you old street." said Gavroche. "Now you've got your nightcap on." ' If light represents the order of the old society, then darkness is the counter-order of the rebellion—this is the lesson drawn from the Paris revolts in *Les Misérables*. It is elaborated in another scene, in which the young hero Marius leaves the part of Paris where normal conditions prevail and goes to the area held by the insurgents. His path takes him from light to darkness. The closer he gets to the rebel area, the darker it gets. 'At the end of the Rue des Bourdonnais the street-lamps ceased'. This is where the no-man's-land begins, and it is completely dark. From a bird's-eye view—Hugo's favourite perspective on the city—it presents itself as

> a huge patch of darkness in the centre of Paris, a black gulf. Owing to the breaking of street-lamps and the shuttering of windows, no light was to be there, nor was any sound of life or movement to be heard. The invisible guardian of the uprising, that is to say, darkness, was everywhere on duty and everywhere kept order. This is the necessary tactic of insurrection, to veil smallness of numbers in a vast obscurity and enhance the stature of every combatant by the possibilities which obscurity affords. At nightfall every window where a light showed had been visited by a musket-ball; the light had gone out, and sometimes the occupant had been killed. Now nothing stirred; nothing dwelt in the houses but fear, mourning and amazement; nothing in the streets but a kind of awe-struck horror.

---

[33] *The Wretched* (1862), Victor Hugo's masterpiece, one of the world's greatest novels.

[34] A seminal year of the French Revolution that saw war, internal riots and revolt, the execution of the king and queen, and the Terror, when many were guillotined.

Eighteen years later Hugo's description would not have applied. At first sight, the old, well-known scenes of lantern smashing seemed to be repeating themselves in the February Revolution of 1848.[35] 'In the centre of Paris', writes Garnier-Pagès,[36] chronicler of this revolution, 'the populace is destroying the *réverbères* and the gaslights. Shops are closed and dark. The darkness is total. Under its cover, armouries are being plundered and barricades erected'. And Victor Hugo, this time writing as an eye-witness, not as a novelist, noted on 23 February: 'The Marais[37] presents a dismal sight. . . . The *réverbères* are smashed and their lights extinguished'. On closer inspection, however, it seems that in 1848 lanterns were not destroyed to the same extent as they had been in 1830 and in the numerous revolts of the 1830s. In any case, these two quotations are the only ones that could be found in contemporary accounts of the 1848 revolution. But if lantern smashing was no longer what it had been, this was simply because lanterns were no longer what they had been either. Between 1830 and 1848, a technical revolution had taken place in the street lighting of Paris. The old oil *réverbères* had gradually been replaced by gaslights. Compared to London, this change took place very slowly in Paris. In 1830 Paris was lit exclusively by oil *réverbères*, with very few exceptions. By 1835 less than 5 per cent of the total, that is only 203 lanterns, were fed by gas. Gaslight did not become the dominant form of lighting until the 1840s, although even then, there were still many oil *réverbères* around.

Owing to this new technology, street lanterns not only spread a new type of light, but they themselves—metaphorically speaking—appeared in a new light. While the individual oil lantern with its fuel reservoir was a self-contained, autonomous apparatus, the individual gaslight was part of a big industrial complex. The oil lantern was perceived to a certain extent as something individual, whose light could also be extinguished individually. Meting out the same treatment to one of the new gaslights would have been a quixotic act, for each of these was merely an offshoot of the true centre, the far distant gas-works. A new way of putting out the light, appropriate to the new technology, had to aim at shutting down the gas-works. This possibility appears as a threat for the first time in the February Revolution. Perhaps it is no coincidence that it was an American observer who found this technical change worth commenting on: 'Great anxiety was felt as night fell, relative to the gas, which it was feared would be cut off by the insurgents; but by the concentration of a large military force round the works this fear was removed, and the lamps were all lit, with the exception of those on the Champs-Elysées which had been broken by the rioters'.

Unlike Paris, the other revolutionary capitals of Europe kept their street lanterns unbroken. Vienna and Berlin did not witness scenes like those that

[35] Revolution that caused the abdication of King Louis Phillipe and the creation of a republic.

[36] Louis Antoine Garnier-Pagès, French politician and historian (1803–1878).

[37] Area on the right bank of the Seine River in Paris that originally was marshy land, then an aristocratic neighborhood, and, in the nineteenth century, a commercial district.

took place in Paris in July 1830 simply because they did not have a revolution then. When the spark of the February Revolution spread in 1848, street lighting remained intact—with one spectacular exception. On the night of 13 March, on the former glacis of Vienna (the area between the old city and the suburbs, which later became the 'Ring'), 'all the gas lamp-posts [were] destroyed, so that the gas flared up to the height of a man, creating a fantastic, new type of lighting in the night, one that had never been seen before'.

The motives for this act of lantern smashing remain obscure. The light was not extinguished in order to envelop the rebels in protective darkness; on the contrary, gaslight was set free to leap up into the air as a giant flame that illuminated the night more brilliantly than any lantern. This can be chalked up to the lack of revolutionary experience that distinguished the rebels in Vienna and Berlin from those in Paris. During street fighting at night in Berlin, many windows were illuminated—not by loyal citizens who wanted to identify themselves as such to the authorities (remember the Paris police chief's appeal) but by the rebels. The commanding general describes in his memoirs how easy this made it for the advancing armed forces: 'The lights and the full moon, shining brightly in a clear sky, were a great disadvantage for the rebels. Because all the windows were illuminated, none of the shots fired by the soldiers missed, while those fired by the rebels, who were dazzled by the moonlight and by the lights in the houses opposite, were inaccurate and often went astray'.

However irrational and disastrous these lights were, they completed the circle described by the revolutionary use of light. For the Paris revolutions ended not in darkness but in blazing festive illuminations. Victory—or what was perceived as victory—was celebrated in the light and with the light. The street urchins who had smashed street lanterns now turned out in force to activate the new lighting. Garnier-Pagès writes: 'Gangs, consisting mainly of street urchins, roamed the streets and forced residents to illuminate their houses immediately. People obeyed this command either willingly, or most reluctantly, with much grinding of teeth. The well-known cry of "Lampions! Lampions!"[38] rang out in voices of all pitches until a dazzling brightness satisfied the demand'. The same picture emerges for Vienna: 'The people celebrated their victory with impressive torchlight processions and magnificent illuminations—no window in the city or the suburbs remained dark, it was unprecedented splendour—it was a genuine expression of joy'. And in Berlin

the victory of the people was celebrated at night with a magnificent illumination; people were firing off guns with joy all night long.... The American envoy, Donelson, took part in the illumination with warm enthusiasm.... A gang of armed burghers and workers turned up at the Russian legation, too,

[38] A lampion is a small lamp, usually an oil lamp with tinted glass, used as street lighting (or on carriages).

demanding that it be lit up. Meyrendorff[39] agreed, not exactly willingly, but the consequences of a refusal would have been serious.

In the eyes of the police, these festivals of light soon became as threatening as the darkness that had preceded them. After all, these lights were neither surveillance lights nor lights of royal displays as in the festive illuminations of the *ancien régime*—they were a revival of the ancient bonfire. Thus the following public announcement appeared on 17 March in Vienna: 'As the residents of Vienna have for several days displayed their delight at the rights conceded to them by His Majesty by means of general rejoicing and illuminations, in response to a general desire we ask that, in order to avoid any disturbances and to restore the peace at night, no illuminations take place in the city and the suburbs from today on'.

[39] Freiherr Peter von Meyrendorff (1796–1863), Russian minister in Austria.

The Potato in Ireland

K. H. CONNELL

Why did the Irish, unlike any other Western people, depend upon the potato for so long and almost exclusively? So does K. H. Connell begin this essay. Implicit in the question is the realization that seldom has a single food, other than grain, so shaped a culture. Connell sees the widespread use of the potato originating in the Irish landholding system and influencing, perhaps more than any other element, the fate of the Irish in the seventeenth, eighteenth, and nineteenth centuries.

Introduced in the sixteenth century from the New World, the potato quickly took root in Ireland. Why there and not to the same magnitude elsewhere in Europe? It is interesting that the reasons have nothing to do with the potato's taste nor with the population's desire for that vegetable itself. The potato was the right food at the right time and situation. Connell blames the English for their rapacious presence in Ireland, for their milking and bilking of the land and its people. To what extent, then, were the English responsible for Irish adoption of the potato? Note that for Connell, the causes of change were fundamentally economic.

Yet, even so, the potato had certain qualities that other foodstuffs did not. What attributes did the potato possess that convinced or compelled the Irish to grow it so extensively? What was the Irish diet like? Did the potato make the Irish a healthy people? How did the Irish compare with the peasantry of western Europe?

How did the potato affect population growth in Ireland? Fertility? Age of marriage? While the potato may have had beneficial effects, it proved to be a fragile prop to the millions of Irish in the nineteenth century. As a food crop, what were some problems with the potato? Considering the perils that attended strict reliance on the potato, did the Irish simply make a mistake, one that cost at least 500,000 lives? What might the Irish have done to ward off the disaster that finally came with the potato famine?

What caused the famine? What explanations did contemporaries offer? Does Connell feel England was to blame for the catastrophe? Why, as Connell asks, did much of the populace return after the famine to the potato, knowing that it might fail once more? What finally motivated the Irish to vary their diet?

Connell begins this article with landholding practices; he concludes by underlining the importance of land legislation in the late nineteenth century. How did land acts affect the lives and foods of the peasantry?

According to Arthur Young,[1] writing in the 1770s, "The food of the common Irish [is] potatoes and milk." Many of the uncommon Irish of Ulster and parts of Leinster ate as much oaten bread or porridge as potatoes; they were familiar with the taste as well as the look of butter and eggs; and in good times they expected a daily meal with fish or bacon, even a weekly meal with meat. But for the greater part of the country, for a century before the Famine,[2] Young's generalization will serve: the great mass of the population had, in effect, a single solid foodstuff: stirabout, or an oatmeal loaf, was an occasional treat: weeks or months separated the red-letter occasions when meat was eaten: day after day, three times a day, people ate salted, boiled potatoes, probably washing them down with milk, flavouring them, if they were fortunate, with an onion or a bit of lard, with boiled seaweed or a scrap of salted fish.

No other western people, generation after generation, has starved or survived with the bounty of the potato: why did the Irish depend on it so long, and so nearly exclusively?

The tradition is that the first Irish potatoes were grown by Sir Walter Raleigh[3] in 1588: certainly, by the following decade, he or another had introduced this new crop and food. An agricultural community, isolated and backward, is likely to be conservative in both its farming and its eating. Nonetheless, when the potato reached Ireland the traditional foods were already being displaced—and by forces whose persistence made the potato almost inevitably their successor. Formerly, milk and its derivatives had bulked large in the Irish dietary. No other food may be as readily available to a nomadic, pastoral people; but a settled society, practising tillage, is likely to retain milk as its staple only while land is abundant. But land in the sixteenth century was made scarce by confiscation, the redistribution of population and the landlord's demands. Some alternative was needed to livestock produce, some foodstuff more economical of land. Traditionally, only grain had been available, and dairy produce had given way to oaten bread and porridge. But once the potato was known, not only milk, but grain also rapidly receded in the popular dietary. The potato, in much of

[1] Agriculturist and traveller, 1741–1820.

[2] Of 1845–1849.

[3] English soldier and explorer, 1554–1618.

the country, was a more rewarding crop than oats. An impoverished people, ill-provided with granaries, mills and ovens, welcomed a food that could be stored in earthen clamps and made edible simply by boiling. Troubled times, too, favoured the potato: it had a briefer growing season; it remained relatively safe underground while grain might be carried away, burned or trampled underfoot; and when people took to the hills with their cattle, potatoes they might grow, but hardly grain.

These, however, are incidental recommendations of the potato: essentially, it displaced the traditional foods because it provided a family's subsistence on a smaller area of land. Still, in the seventeenth century, the pressure on land was maintained by the dislocation of war; and later, in more tranquil times, by the growth of population: continuously, however, and most insistently, land was made scarce by the landlord's demands.

Irish property was rooted, much of it recently, in confiscation: sudden gains might be suddenly lost: principles of estate-management were sharpened, therefore, by the owner's desire to get the most from his property while it remained his. The grantees, moreover, might be landlords already, attached to their English estates, administering them with feeling for their tenants as well as for their rents. The Irish, if they accepted the popular view, were a barbarous people, amongst whom it was foolhardy to live: certainly they were a people alien in language, loyalty and religion. Little, therefore, induced a man with ties in England to settle on his Irish estate, to get to know his tenants and sympathize with their problems. More often, they were reduced simply to a source of rent, the landlord's refuge when creditors encroached on his English property or his thriftless living. But duty, as well as necessity, turned the screw. England, the mother-country, reckoned to profit by her colony: a landlord's leniency lightened his country's purse as well as his own. The Irish, moreover, were disaffected and lazy: they needed punishment and reform: a sharp rent was a blend of both, perhaps of more lasting benefit to the man who earned it than to the man who spent it.

The institutions of Irish landlordism were as predatory as the spirit. Land-agent, middleman and rack-renting: many a head-landlord felt ill-served by this apparatus of exploitation—but rarely because it failed to impoverish his tenants. Few of them ever had the chance of getting a living in the Irish towns; emigration became a likely escape only in the nineteenth century: land, therefore, a man must have to feed his family—and for a foothold on land he offered an extravagant rent. Commonly, in the topsy-turvy Irish economy, the more onerous the rent, the less productive the farm, the landlord who exacted an elastic rent was no improver; and the tenant who paid it was neither inclined nor able to better his farming.

Spurred on, then, by the fear of eviction and the loss of his livelihood, the tenant struggled to increase his rent. But, with a stagnant technique of farming, to earn more rent meant earmarking a larger proportion of his land for rent crops—a smaller proportion, in consequence, for his family's subsistence. And the less land on which a family must grow its food, the more imperatively was the potato its staple—for on no other crop could it live more economically of land. Where landlord-tenant relationships were milder—as in Ulster—there might be supplements to the potato; where, incessantly, they were harsh, people lived, not simply on the most prolific crop, but on its most prolific varieties.

Now, if the elasticity of rent tended to make people live on the potato, it tended also to reduce them to the bare quantity that would keep them alive and working. But, in fact, until the two or three decades before the Famine, the potato was lavishly consumed: people retained more potato-land than their subsistence required. But we have not, I think, made too much of the landlord's exigence, too much of the expansiveness of rent-land. There were kind-hearted landlords; landlords restrained by leases, by the fear of violence, even by the realization that profits were related to a tenant's productivity as well as his promises. So bountiful, moreover, was the potato, that a couple of acres, even less, gave a family all it could use, and conveniently waste: a little more gave real abundance. Then there was much land, doubtfully capable of earning rent, but available for the people's subsistence: it might grow potatoes well enough, but so bulky a crop was hard to sell when most country families grew their own, and communications were poor. On the whole, too, potato harvests were good until towards the 1820s; and in the occasional bad year the pig, not his master, pulled in his belt.

Certainly until the 1820s the monotony of the Irishman's diet was usually offset by its abundance. There are scores of accounts from the late eighteenth and early nineteenth centuries of the quantity of potatoes people ate. A small farmer from co. Down told a royal commission in the 1830s that "a stone of potatoes is little enough for a man in a day, and he'd want something with it to work upon".... There is little doubt that, day in day out, except when the crop was poor, the adult Irishman ate some ten pounds of potatoes a day. If he ate nothing else and drank only water he was hardly disastrously undernourished: if, as commonly happened, he had a cupful of milk with each meal, to the biochemist, if not the gourmet, he was admirably nourished: he had some 4,000 calories a day, compared with the required 3,000; he had enough protein, calcium and iron; he had a sufficiency, or a superabundance, of the listed vitamins.

The Irish, then, burdened with predatory landlords, practised a primitive farming: food, clothing and shelter were about the extent of their material comfort; the potato was their food; they were clothed in rags; their hovels, not infrequently, they shared with their animals. But for all their wretchedness, they were admirably nourished—better, maybe, than the mass of the people of any other country during any recent century.

Now, for much of the time that they lived on the potato, the number of the Irish increased with astonishing vigour. The population of Ireland in 1780 was probably something over four million—much what it is today. But, sixty years later, on the eve of the Famine, the four million had doubled to eight million—and contributed nearly another two million to the population of Britain and North America. Probably in no other western country has so rapid a rate of natural increase been so long sustained. Was it fortuitous that an extraordinary dependence on the potato was accompanied by an extraordinary excess of births over deaths?

During the years of this coincidence, and drawing partly on Irish experience, Malthus[4] evolved a theory of population growth plausible enough to come rapidly into vogue: population, his contemporaries agreed, tends to increase more rapidly than the resources needed for its sustenance: unless births are checked, population is limited by premature death—the result of scarcity of food or some like calamity. Was it, then, simply the lifting of this traditional restraint that caused the population of Ireland to bound upwards towards the end of the eighteenth century; was it that a people, formerly ill-nourished, lived longer as they were plentifully fed on the potato?

We lack the statistics to answer this question with assurance. But the presumption is that the potato facilitated the growth of population less by reducing mortality than by increasing fertility—and helping then to forestall an off-setting increase in mortality. Acceptance of the potato tended, no doubt, to improve physique and lessen the incidence of deficiency disease. But, advancing piecemeal over more than a century, the potato in much of the country was all but fully accepted by the 1730s: it tended, that is, to reduce mortality too gradually and too early to be the direct cause of a sharp increase in population in the 1780s.

More probable, in the 1780s, than any reduction in mortality was an increase in fertility, the result of more-youthful marriage than had been customary. Today, the Irish marry later than any other people whose statistics are available. And latest of all to marry is the would-be farmer. He is expected to have "a hold of the land" before he thinks of marrying: a farm, that is, must be his or earmarked for him. Farms, however, are rarely divided; there is little reclamation: typically, in consequence, the only land a man can acquire is his father's, but fathers are rarely anxious to give up the reins. The transfer of the land is probably put off until the old man is in his seventies: his eldest son, by then, is probably in his mid-thirties—and 38 is the average age at which farmers' sons marry in the Republic.

Now it is plausible to argue that this kind of restraint to marriage was also felt during much of the eighteenth century—though less severely than today, for fathers, no doubt, died younger. The critical change towards the end of the century was that land became more readily available—and, therefore, youthful marriage more readily possible. By the 1780s and 1790s holdings were less commonly passed intact from father to son. It was possible, often imperative, for a father to mark off a piece of his land and make it over to a still-youthful son, and later, maybe, provide for a second, even a third, son. Essentially, this subdivision of holdings was a consequence of the extension of arable farming.

---

[4]Thomas Malthus (1766–1834), English economist, author of *An Essay on the Principle of Population*.

Irish patriots had long pleaded for legislation to encourage corn-growing. But the Irish towns were a useful market for surplus British grain; and Irish supplies would have been resented in Britain. There was, therefore, no effective legislation until the second half of the century. By then the growth of Britain's own population was turning her from an exporter to an importer of corn; by the 1780s constitutional changes allowed Irish patriots to try their hand at moulding the Irish economy. Foster's[5] corn law of 1784 imposed duties on the import of grain and offered bounties on its export; war, from 1793, further inflated corn prices—the more effectively after 1806 when, at last, Irish grain entered Britain duty-free. Between the 1780s and the early years of the new century oat prices more than doubled: on more and more estates the tilling tenant could pay most rent; he, therefore, was preferred by the landlord.

But more tilling tenancies meant smaller tenancies: the grassland a family could conveniently manage was embarrassingly large to cultivate by spade or plough; there was no class of people with the capital and the skill to manage large arable farms; tillage, moreover, needed the labour of the larger population subdivision induced.

By the closing decades of the eighteenth century, then, tenant farmers, anxious to provide for their sons, were encouraged by their landlords to divide their holdings. Their sons—and daughters—were scarcely aware of the inducements in other societies to postpone marriage: with an elastic rent, there was little reward for industry, little opportunity for thrift—almost no hope that by deferring marriage a family might be reared on a firmer foundation. Living conditions were wretched and hopeless: marriage could hardly make them worse; it might make them more tolerable.

When, therefore, land was within their grasp, young people seized the opportunity it offered of marrying younger than had been customary. Few of them knew of the possibility of restricting family size: almost none wanted to do so; it cost little to rear a child; even young children helped on the land; and, in a country without a poor law, a numerous family was some assurance against a destitute old age. The earlier a girl married, therefore, the more children was she likely to have; the sooner a new generation was added to the old.

Largely, then, the impetus to the rapid growth of population seems to have come from earlier marriage facilitated by subdivision, and followed by larger families. But where does the potato come in?

The incidence of sterility and still-birth varies, no doubt, with the nutrition of husbands and wives—and of their parents. Insofar, then, as the potato was improving nutrition—even before 1750—it tended to increase fertility in the closing decades of the century. And, without the potato, subdivision could hardly have persisted for some three generations until, on the eve of the Famine, half of all holdings were of five or fewer acres. Much hilly

---

[5]John Foster (1740–1828), Chancellor of the Exchequer in Ireland.

land, mountain and bog was included: holdings so small and unrewarding could earn a rent, and support a family, only if it lived on the potato. Had the popular dietary been more varied, subdivision would have halted earlier; marriage, presumably, would have been delayed and fertility reduced. Already by the 1820s and 1830s, some farms were so reduced in size that nothing could be pared from them for a son wishing to marry: increasingly he was tempted to emigrate; but sometimes he settled in Ireland on a scrap of waste, otherwise of little use, but able to grow potatoes.

The potato, then, tended to increase fertility; but its significance in population history is more for what it prevented than for what it did. Malthus was an accurate observer: population in his time pressed on resources: rising fertility tended to make food scarce, and to be offset, therefore, by rising mortality. But Ireland, for some sixty years, was exceptional: not only were additional children born, but many of them survived and contributed to the astonishing rapidity of population growth: crucial to their survival was the abundance and nutritional excellence of the potato.

The effects of the potato mentioned so far—its tendency to keep mortality down and, indirectly, to increase fertility—these tendencies depended on its being steadily and abundantly available. But the perils of living on a single food are more than usually acute when this food is the potato. Its yield, maybe, is more erratic than that of oats or wheat; yet it keeps so badly that the surplus of one year does nothing directly to make good the deficiency of the next; it is bulky, too, difficult, if communications are poor, to move from areas of abundance to areas of scarcity. It is planted late—lest it be damaged by frost: usually, therefore, the season is advanced when its failure becomes apparent, too advanced for other foods to be grown. Nor, in all probability, can its victims buy a substitute: growing their own potatoes, they have no money earmarked for food; reduced to the most frugal of foods, they hardly have money at all; their society, too, will have needed—and reared— only a rudimentary food trade. And even if there is public or charitable provision of grain, their troubles are not at an end: accustomed to a crop prepared simply with a pot and a fire, they are ill-equipped with the mills to grind corn; with the ovens and skills to bake it—even with the stomachs to digest it.

The potato, then, is a capricious staple, liable to fail and hard to replace. Yet not until after 1815 were the perils of Ireland's potato economy persistently demonstrated. In 1740—and again in 1807—early and severe frost destroyed much of the crop while it was still undug: 1800 and 1801 were lean years for Ireland as for much of the rest of Europe. By and large, however, from the middle of the eighteenth century until after 1815, the Irishman had his fill of potatoes.

Why was the precariousness of life on the potato so long concealed? It is hardly respectable to attribute more than incidental movements in economic development to shifts in the weather. Over three-quarters of a century, nevertheless, few seasons disagreed with the potato; partly, too, it yielded well because year after year, as more people depended on it, it was planted on land, not all of it poor, on which it had never grown before. But it is easier to explain the frequency and severity of failures after 1815 than their rarity before. Again, it seems, the weather played a part: year after year, between 1820 and the Famine, the potato succumbed to cold, wet seasons; it may have succumbed also to diseases unknown in Europe until steam navigation brought them across the Atlantic. Inherently, too, it probably became less resistant to disease as old varieties degenerated, and the new were chosen for their prolificness more than their vitality. And its yield became even less certain as it was grown on old land, starved of manure and exhausted by over-cropping; on new land, recently waste and ill-adapted to its needs—on so much land that once disease appeared, it quickly spread.

In the 1820s and 1830s the potato failed, partially or locally, at least as often as it yielded well. No longer, almost certainly, was rising fertility unaccompanied by rising mortality. But, it seems, there was little slackening in the rate of natural increase. The fickleness of the potato may have been countered by increasing the area on which it was planted: certainly the agrarian troubles and the unpaid rents of these years suggest an unwonted encroachment of subsistence-land on rent-land. It is probable too—for vaccination was spreading—that rising mortality from malnutrition was offset by falling mortality from smallpox. Marriage in these decades was postponed—as subdivision reached its limits, as the supply of food became less certain: but later marriage did not necessarily mean fewer births; the abnormal number of births in the previous twenty years was followed now by an abnormal number of potential parents.

Rapid natural increase, then, depended no longer on the bounty of the potato. But more and more its effects within Ireland were offset by mounting emigration, motivated, much of it, by the treachery of the potato. It was not until after 1845 that population began to decline: then, with three failures of the potato, two of them virtually complete, the population, in five years, was reduced by a fifth: half a million, perhaps more, died of starvation and associated diseases; a round million fled, like refugees.

The victims of so vast a catastrophe speculated, of course, on its cause. Was it brought by the fairies, the weather or atmospheric electricity; by the people's saintliness or sinfulness—by God's spreading the faith by spreading the Irish, or by his chastening a people who wasted the potato in its abundance, violated their pledge of temperance, emancipated the Catholics and subsidized Maynooth?[6] In the most pervasive of the popular explanations, the Famine was the work of the British government: "the Almighty . . . sent the potato blight, but the English created the Famine".

At the time this explanation had a rational and an emotional appeal. It is true enough that there was no escape from famine unless the government

---

[6] A Roman Catholic seminary in Ireland, the permanent endowment of which was controversial in the 1840s and 1850s.

provided it; and there was the ring of salvation neither in allowing the export of Irish grain, nor in public works more obviously penal than benevolent. And a people, so beset by catastrophe, shied from the further agony of self-incrimination: if England, indeed, created the Famine, its victims had no call to dwell on their own defects; not even on their tolerance of the landlordism that made them idle and improvident.

Commonly, the historians of the Famine have reiterated the indictment of England. Their sympathies, very often, have been nationalist: nationalism in Ireland has been reared less on the rights of man than on historical wrongs, and the most grievous wrong was England's murder of a million. . . .

The scholarly studies of the Famine sponsored by the Dublin government and the Irish Committee of Historical Sciences enable us to re-assess England's guilt. . . . Mr. Thomas P. O'Neill allows us to believe no longer that the government, by staying the export of grain, could have staved off the famine: there was, he makes clear, an acute shortage of food, and it was relieved, not aggravated, by trade with Britain and the outside world.

Other measures of relief failed, not because the government so willed, not even because it was callous or negligent, but simply because the Famine was an intractable problem, an insoluble problem in the knowledge and opinion of the time. Once famine was imminent, epidemics of typhus and relapsing fever were all but certain: the doctors, backed however fully by the state, could do little to arrest their spread, or cure their victims. Famine—and therefore fever—could be averted only if the potato were saved, or if, by some administrative miracle, five million people were otherwise fed. The government, without delay, sought scientific advice on the potato; but the botanists knew nothing of the cause of the blight, nothing of how its spread might be arrested or its recurrence prevented. Nor were the economists and political theorists more effectual. The rotting of the potato was no excuse for corrupting their "scientific" poor law; and it was on their principles that Russell's[7] relief works foundered, their faith in unproductivity, central control and payment by results. Their insistence on free trade ruled out what relief there was in a ban on the export of Irish grain; and back of Russell's laggardly and niggardly import of food lay their refutation of state intervention, their certainty that it must aggravate more than alleviate.

A native government, it is true, might have deferred less to politics and economics more plausible in England than in Ireland. But no government could have contained the Famine: given the dominance of the potato, some such disaster was all but inevitable; given the growth of population, the more it was delayed, the more malevolent it must be. If, indeed, "England created the famine", it was not . . . in pursuit of a "deliberate policy of extermination": it was because, centuries earlier, she had geared the Irish economy to the

---

[7]Lord John Russell (1792–1878), Whig prime minister from 1846–1852, an exponent of free market economics.

elastic rent which ensured the diffusion of the potato and the unbridled growth of population.

No survivor of the Famine forgot the perils of life on the potato: fifty years later, the sight of a bowl of floury potatoes could bring tears to an old man's eyes. Yet in much of the country, as the blight receded, as seed became available, the potato was restored almost—but not altogether—to its former eminence. The yellow meal, eaten at first to save life, soon was enjoyed; and turnips and cabbage also became more familiar: none of these foods strained much more than the potato the peasant's resources, or his wife's cooking: all, therefore, encroached on the potato, or eked it out in the bad year, or before the new crop was dug. In north-eastern Ulster the potato was forsaken more rapidly—because, no doubt, it was never so firmly established. But elsewhere, its real relegation began, not in the 1840s, but in the 1870s and 1880s: "it was spuds, morning, noon and night", an old Donegal man recalled of his boyhood in the 1870s: a dozen years earlier, Clare families still lived on potatoes and sour milk; still in Cork and Limerick people reckoned on their ten pounds a day. And from the western seaboard, into the present century, the smaller holders "have nothing else to rely on: potatoes are their sole support".

Now for long, in the Médoc, it had been the custom to give grapes by the roadside an unappetizing appearance by spraying them with a mixture of copper sulphate and lime. But it was not until the 1880s that a passing botanist noticed that the sprayed plants were healthier than the rest, and, after some experiments, advocated Bordeaux mixture as a preventive of blight on the potato. In the following decade the Royal Dublin Society organized tests in Ireland, and, together with government agencies, landlords, teachers and doctors, it endeavoured to overcome the peasant's reluctance to spray. Spraying, some of course thought, was "going against nature": others, having started to spray, were lulled by a good season or two; or they lost faith because their mixture was adulterated or improperly prepared; or because, too poor or too unmechanical to use a knapsack, they had ineffectively shaken the mixture from a broom, or a handful of heather. By the time of the first war, the resistance was mostly overcome; spraying was all but universal. Before then the only safeguard against the blight was to plant a resistant variety; but the resistance even of the Champion had proved to be partial and diminishing. As long, then, as the hold of the potato persisted, famine recurred: several times in the second half of the nineteenth century scenes were enacted reminiscent, if not of the forties, at least of the twenties and thirties. But by the end of the century, the failure of the potato brought acute suffering only to the poorest families, most of them in the worst-congested districts: almost everywhere else the potato—with the milk that went with it—was yielding to stirabout (made increasingly of oats, instead of Indian corn); to bread, oaten and soon wheaten; to American bacon; to sugar, jam and tea—perhaps, where smuggling survived, to coffee in place of tea. The potato, of course, has never been ousted; but, in the words of its devoted historian, "it is eaten because it is liked, not because it is necessary".

There are two problems: why, after the Famine, did people revert so largely to a food they knew might fail again; and why, by the last quarter of the century, had they reduced it to one of several staples?

For all the agony that followed its failure, there was feeling still for the potato. People accustomed to stomachs distended three times a day by three or four pounds of potatoes, felt hungry and uncomfortable, though nourished enough on porridge or bread; or they complained of their difficulty in digesting grain stuffs. After the Famine, then, they welcomed the potato; and it was, very probably, a better food than any alternative widely available. And the people sensed also that, though the potato should fail again, they would hardly suffer as in the forties: the relieved (not only the relievers) learned by their mistakes; publicity and politics increasingly loosened the purse-strings: American relatives were a growing resource; and to join them became the conventional response to hardship at home.

The potato, before the Famine, meant more than nutriment; and people were drawn back to it by more than the need for food and bodily comfort. The open door and a meal for all-comers was a custom that sprang from the heart, but depended on the potato: hearts were hardened when the potato rotted—and any traveller might bring the fever. But when famine was past, it was good once more to disregard the cost of food—to return to the potato.

In reality, no doubt, as well as in the novels and travellers' tales, the Irishman was an indolent creature—not surprisingly if his family were large and his holding small; if industry, in his society, were robbed of its reward. For the lazy man there was no crop like the potato: it needed merely a few days' planting in the spring, possibly earthing up in the summer, and some more days' digging in the winter: with another week, cutting and carrying turf, a family might be fed and warmed for the year. By reverting to the potato, people with the taste for travel could take to the road soon after St. Patrick's Day, return temporarily to cut the turf, and settle down eventually to a leisurely winter with all the comfort they knew: the restless, ambitious man could spend his summer lifting the English harvest—even hewing stone in an American quarry; his family he might send out to beg, or leave at home to win the turf—and earn the rent if there were butter to be made.

But like its original diffusion, the re-establishment of the potato after the Famine probably owed more to the landlord's exigence than to the people's inclination. In the years of unpaid rents, and heavy taxes, the debts of already-embarrassed landlords piled up. In 1848, accordingly, the Encumbered Estates Act eased the transfer of Irish property—and patriots looked to it for the return, at last, of native, benevolent landlords. Much land changed hands under the act—a third of the whole country, it is said, in three years. The buyers, too, were mostly Irish; but Irish who were the patriots' despair. Few of their countrymen in 1849 had the money and the will to play the landlord and the assurance that they could make it a paying game. Much encumbered property was bought by petty shopkeepers and land agents, by gombeen men and publicans, men, it might be, who had done well in the Famine, selling grain to a people unused to buying food, buying land from a people forced to abandon it. The central tradition of Irish property was safe in their keeping—perhaps, indeed, more rigorously applied, for their properties, by and large, were smaller than their predecessors'; more of them lived on the spot, and, stemming very often from the people they exploited, they were better informed of their hidden resources. There was probably no real relaxation of the pressure of rent-land on subsistence-land until the organized withholding of rent: for every peasant, then, who willingly returned to the potato after the Famine, others went back to it willy-nilly.

In the 1870s and 1880s, the land war was followed by the land legislation. In many respects it is this, not the more spectacular Famine that divides the nineteenth century: until then the social and economic life of the countryside was geared to an elastic rent; but the land acts first stabilized rent, then made it a dwindling real charge. With industry and its reward at last united, there was point in farming more productively. Costlier foods were now within the peasant's reach: no longer must he live on whatever supported him with the greatest economy of land. Sometimes, it is true, the tenant-at-will, blown up to be head of a landowning family, shied too far from his old improvidence: his family must eat potatoes so that he might buy more land, make a priest of his son, or dower his daughter beyond her station. But prudence so extreme was not typical: an owner-occupier had his status to think of: he looked with "modest shame" not just on the potato, but on home-baked bread: commonly, moreover, he had relatives "in emigration", brothers and sons who mocked at his potatoes and milk, who expected when they came home to find baker's bread and jam and tea.

Victorian England:
The Horse-Drawn Society

F. M. L. THOMPSON

In this study of Victorian horses, F. M. L. Thompson contrasts the myth of the "railway society" with the reality of the growth of the horse population in nineteenth-century English society. His basic interest is to understand the social and economic functions of the horse in an industrial society.

What specific role did the horse and carriage have in Victorian England? What evidence does Thompson present to show that the horse was expensive and inefficient as a commercial means of transportation? Moreover, the horse was an exceptional pollutant whose droppings made urban life nasty. We hear much today about the pernicious effects of automobiles on the urban landscape, but Thompson's analysis of the noxious contributions of horses to atmospheric stench, street muck, and noise level of the last century makes our cities appear to be centers of pristine tranquillity by comparison.

Even modern complaints about traffic congestion must be muted when contemplating the Victorian street, prey to the chaotic mixture of horses and horse-drawn vehicles. How did city governments attempt to cope with the numerous and unpleasant problems that horses caused?

Another stereotype (in addition to the one holding modern cities to be dirtier than those in the past) Thompson lays to rest is that railroads made horse-drawn transport obsolete. Why did railways in fact require horses and how did the railroads stimulate transportation by horse-drawn vehicles?

Along with horses, carriages constituted a prominent feature of the Victorian city. What social functions did carriages serve? How did carriages affect urban life and space?

Finally, what conditions led to the demise of horse-drawn transport? We have moved from the omnipresence of horses to that of cars. Thompson does not bemoan the world of horses that we have lost. Yet, were cities in any way better off with horses than with automobiles?

Horses are hard work. Their food is bulky, heavy, and they demand enormous quantities of it. It all has to be manhandled.... Two and a half tons for one horse for one winter. In this they differ sharply from the motor car, whose food comes expensively but effortlessly out of a pipe. I would assert, but not offer to demonstrate, that stoking a horse is almost as hard and almost as continuous a labour as stoking a locomotive. Horses also work hard. So hard for so long, historically, that of course horsepower naturally became the measure of the strength of the steam engines and internal combustion engines which eventually replaced them. Animal horsepower was most versatile in its applications. Anything a petrol[1] or diesel engine can do a horse can do, worse.... At one time anything on wheels had a horse in front of it, and anything which was dragged through the soil was dragged by a horse; the horse was, indeed, made to turn its feet to almost anything, and when harnessed to a contraption rather like a giant capstan it supplied, through the horse-gin, cumbersome but reasonably reliable rotary power for driving machinery as diverse as spinning jennies, portable threshing machines, pumps, flour mills, and colliery[2] hoists. Though there was something to be said for this form of industrial power, since it was neither so fickle as wind nor so localised and unsteady as water, I do not propose to say it, since it had to all intents and purposes been technologically superceded by cheaper and more efficient stationary engines—whether water- or steam-powered—before the Victorian period. I am concerned, rather, with the locomotive power of horses. Why should I be concerned?

[1] Gasoline.
[2] A coal mine.

It is a question which can be approached on many levels. One at least, . . . the most fundamental, . . . is the level which leads straight to the nature and purpose of history. For, history being the study of the past, past horses are as fit a subject for that study as past politics, past ideas, or past buildings, though it may not have been widely recognised hitherto that they are of similar moment. That being the case, there is no difference in principle between the answer to the question: Why study Victorian horses? and the answers to the question: Why study history at all? which might be proferred by any historian who turned his interest to anything in particular which has exercised significant influence on human society in the past. . . .

. . . Horses and carriages were so much a part of ordinary life until the death of Queen Victoria[3]—and indeed until 1914—that as with other every-day objects they tended to be taken for granted, exciting little contemporary comment apart from attention to the technical side of their management and construction—much as today there is an abundant supply of manuals on the driving, maintenance, and production of motor vehicles, so the Victorian literature made ample provision for those whose business it was to look after horses or to build carriages. The disappearance of horses, from the streets in the 1920s and from the farms in the 1940s, is still so comparatively recent that it has only lately begun to strike some historians that there is something interesting to be said about the period of their ascendancy. . . .

It is the role of the horse and carriage in Victorian society and in the Victorian economy which lends the subject some importance, an importance which has not so much been denied by other historians, as somewhat over-looked. It has been overlooked for the very good reason that the historian's eye tends to be caught by what is dramatic, and what is dramatic is usually what is new. If we think of the Victorian age in transport terms at all, we think of railways and steamships; if we think of its social structure, we think of a developing class system, based perhaps on differences of wealth, of source of income, of religion, of education, of place of residence, or on some blend of all of these; if we think of its economy, we think of steam, iron, steel and electricity, the mechanisation of the processes of production and the application of power; if we think of the consequences of all this, we think of massive urbanisation, slums, and urban poverty, and possibly also of large Victorian mansions now converted into flats, with the large households of domestic servants which used to inhabit them. What I wish to suggest is that for all its bustle, smoke, and modernity, this was still at heart a horse-drawn society, and to argue that the degree of its dependence on the horse set some of the more important limits to its social and economic development. The horse is often regarded as the most noble of animals; and when serving as the vehicle of pleasure, sport, and entertainment it may well be so. It is integral to the argument, however, that as a practical and commercial means of locomotion the horse is expensive and inefficient. The corollary is that if some dreadful fate, such as the non-invention of the railway, had thrust the

[3]Queen Victoria reigned from 1837 to 1901.

horse even more into the Victorian limelight than it actually was, the result would have been an extremely impoverished society....

The pervasiveness of the role of the motor car today gives us a clue to the possible role of its predecessor, the horse and carriage. Not only is car production at the very centre of the economy—which carriage-making never was—but... it is farmed out among a number of component manufacturers, stoppage in any one bringing the assembly plants to a halt. Car makers anxiously scrutinise the trends in their sales, trying to forecast their future market as the initial demand due to the expansion of car ownership threatens to reach its limits and replacement demand takes over as the major component, only to have their gloomiest predictions upset first by the appearance of the two-car and then of the three-car family. Builders and estate agents find first that houses without garages, and then that houses in select districts without double garages, are unsaleable, and building societies[4] decline mortgages on the unfashionable properties; but at a later stage the city streets become so blocked with traffic that a car in town is a nuisance and town houses without garages are once more a highly-prized article, the owners being affluent enough to keep the car out at their country place. Meanwhile the cars themselves, having passed through a phase in which multitudes of makes and shapes flowered in luxuriant abandon, have settled down to a handful of basic sizes each suited to particular functions and definite markets. The affairs of buying and selling cars, and driving them, have given rise to a whole branch of the law, with special motoring offences, special enforcement officers, and very special social attitudes towards offending motorists, who are sharply differentiated from other kinds of law-breakers. Above all perhaps we nowadays cannot avoid entertaining views about the social implications of cars—as status symbols, sex symbols, emulation objects, group definers, and community creators and destroyers—and about their social effects—as producers of congestion, noise, and pollution, potential destroyers alike of our cities and of the peace and solitude of our countryside, able contestants for the place of chief enemy of the environment, but still indispensable possessions for all those who possess them.

... If then we confine attention to the topical problem of pollution, the horse struck his blow at the quality of urban life long before the waste products of modern technology began to cause trouble. Contemporary experts of an experimental turn of mind differed somewhat in their results, but agreed in their measurements on a range of 6 to $7\frac{1}{2}$ tons as the amount of droppings which one horse on normal feeding and workload produced in a year. Individually modest, cumulatively the amount could be rather more than simply a messy embarrassment. In their proper place, and mixed with about equal quantities of straw litter, the droppings of course formed the best kind of farmyard manure; and with an annual output of 12 tons of finished manure the average farm-horse could manure all the land which

---

[4]Roughly equivalent to savings and loan associations in the United States.

was used to feed it about once in four years, a neat example of the re-cycling process which is now the fashionable answer to the problem of awkward effluents. The trouble was that many horses lived far away from farms. The best estimate I can make is that already by the 1830s English towns had to cope with something like 3 million tons of droppings every year, and that by 1900 they had more like 10 million tons on their hands. It is true that if this could be recovered it was valuable agriculturally, particularly for the market gardens and intensive hay farms which clustered round the larger towns. But since the town droppings were worth barely five shillings[5] a ton to the farmer they could only stand transport over a couple of miles or so by road and ten times as far by barge, if there happened to be a canal handy. The result was that a high proportion never was recovered, and many scraps of waste land in the poorer quarters of towns were turned into vast dung heaps, considerably aggravating the squalor, stench, and unhealthiness of such parts of the urban environment. It was in any case exceedingly difficult to keep the streets clean in the press of daytime traffic, and pick-up operations had to be left largely to night squads who could shovel away without causing traffic jams. In this situation the crucial role of the crossing-sweeper in keeping town life tolerable can be readily appreciated. And while there is no question that the streets did improve considerably in appearance during the Victorian period, especially with the introduction of hard, smooth surfaces of tarred wood blocks or of asphalt, and with the construction of kerbside gullies and drains, which reached the main streets in the last quarter of the nineteenth century, there can equally be no question that the motor vehicle has raised the quality of urban life by driving the smell and the squelch off the streets.

Consideration of the waste products of society, and their disposal, has never been a subject for the fastidious; and you will remember that the Victorians of both sexes, if they could possibly afford it, never ventured out into the streets unless wearing ankle-length outer garments or other enveloping protective clothing, which had very necessary anti-splash functions. To suppose, as some have done, that such fashions were dictated purely by modesty, or that their primary or sole purpose was to muffle sexual excitement, is to forget that no one could set foot in a Victorian street without encountering dozens and dozens of horses. Henry Mayhew,[6] in the course of his fascinating investigation of the conditions of *London Labour and the London Poor* in 1851, attempted a computation of the annual droppings of horses—and other livestock on their way to markets—in the London streets. . . . As it happens Mayhew's estimate is not very useful, since it is concerned only with the refuse problem facing the public authorities in the City and Westminster, and

---

[5] A former unit of British currency; one-twentieth of a pound.

[6] 1812–1887, author and magazine editor, best known for his pioneering social research on London's working classes of the 1850s.

for this purpose he assumed that the average City horse only spent 6 hours of each day out and about on the streets and the remaining three-quarters of its time in off-street stabling where its wastes became a purely private problem. Hence the difference between his figure of 52,000 tons a year and the Board of Health's estimate of 200,000 tons for the same date and same area....

Next to smell and dirt, noise is the most resented intruder in our time. It cannot be pretended that any number of horses could out-neigh a jet engine in any conceivable equine chorus. But for mere street noise hooves and iron-rimmed wheels clattering on cobbles, stone setts, or granite chippings did not do at all badly. Residents on main thoroughfares certainly complained about the incessant rattle and rumble of horse-drawn traffic and said that the noise drowned their dinner-time conversation. And it was to deaden horse-drawn noise that the streets were habitually covered with layers of straw in front of hospitals, and of private houses whenever anyone was ill in bed. No one had thought of decibels or of measuring them before horse-drawn traffic vanished, so it is impossible to make any statement about the comparative noise levels of town streets in 1900 and 1970; but the possibility that the motor car made our streets quieter as well as cleaner should not be ignored. As to congestion, it was horse traffic which seemed to be threatening to bring our cities to a standstill in the closing years of Victoria's reign, and which caused a major part of the problem investigated by the Royal Commission on London Traffic which reported in 1906.... [I]t has sometimes seemed laughable to suppose that London could ever have imagined it had a traffic problem at that time: there were barely 10,000 motor vehicles in the entire country, compared with over 10 million today. Quite true; but in the peak year of horse-drawn traffic, 1902, there were close on half a million private carriages on the roads, 133,000 public passenger vehicles and cabs, and a fleet of commercial vans, wagons, carts and drays which was completely uncounted but which must have amounted to not far short of another half million. What proportion of all these were driving about London is not known, but it was enough to overload the road system; the evidence for this was plain enough by 1906, in terms of a 25 per cent fall in the average speed of the traffic in the previous 30 years owing to the growing congestion, and in terms of an equally sharp decline in the normal working life of bus horses due to the mounting strain on them of a crescendo of stopping and starting.

The reasons why what appear to us rather puny numbers of vehicles created very genuine and nearly desperate traffic chaos are not too far to seek. In the first place, the behaviour of horse traffic is unpredictable, its control of direction erratic, and its road discipline poor, in comparison with motors; hence any given number of horse-drawn vehicles occupied a good deal more road space than the same number of motor vehicles simply because of the extra elbow room required. But of far greater importance was the highly unfavourable ratio between useful space and overall length of horse-drawn vehicles. It was normal for the tractive power source to be at least as long as the vehicle being drawn, and it was frequently longer. Any given horse-drawn payload was therefore likely to occupy two or three times the road space of its motorised successor, on this score alone. This issue of the overall length of vehicles and horse teams was, indeed, seen as crucial to the traffic problem of the early 1900s and its solution. One witness to the London enquiry, a traction engine enthusiast, pointed out that one steam roadster with a train of trailers could do in 72 feet the work of 18 horses and carts stretched out over 360 feet of road, which at once promised to cut congestion to one-fifth of its current proportions. Another saw salvation in electric trams, which would remove traffic jams by cutting the length of tramcar and horses in half. In the event, of course, the jams were removed by motorisation. Or rather they were removed for half a century. It is hardly my province to suggest the form of technological miniaturisation which might push back our own problems for another half century.

All this amounts to saying, in short, that horse-drawn transport had its drawbacks and limitations. But until a substitute became available—and the demonstration that motors were something more useful and reliable than mere playthings of the eccentric rich dates almost precisely from the year of Victoria's death—horse-drawn transport was quite indispensable. The mistake is sometimes made of supposing that the railways dealt it a mortal blow. This is because railway competition did indeed kill off long-distance road transport very rapidly, and by 1850 the mail-coaches and stage-coaches, with all the elaborate organisation of coaching inns and post-horse establishments which had supported them, had all but vanished....

...Without carriages and carts the railways would have been like stranded whales, giants unable to use their strength, for these were the only means of getting people and goods right to the doors, of houses, warehouses, markets, and factories, where they wanted to be. All the railway companies kept their own establishments of horses and assorted wagons and vans for goods collection and delivery, and it is in railway records that one may find the best series of prices of van-horses and horse-fodder covering the whole Victorian age. In addition to the company fleets there was plenty of scope for independent operators in these feeder services. A firm like Pickfords, which had grown up as canal carriers of inter-city through traffic, soon adapted itself to the new railway situation and flourished as never before, as a distributor from railheads; the 4,000 horses which this firm had maintained in the 1820s to run its canal fly-boats between London and Birmingham were before long insufficient to cope with the new local town traffic generated by the London and Birmingham Railway. No wonder that a big railway terminus came to require about as much space for stabling as it did for locomotive sheds. As one elderly commission stablekeeper remarked in the 1870s, when his annual turnover had grown to 1,200 horses, 'We thought when the railways first came in that we should have nothing to do, but it has not turned out so...for every new railway [that is built] you want fresh horses...because there is the work to be done to and fro.' To and fro may be very commonplace, but there was a lot of it. The railway age was in fact the greatest age of the horse, albeit in terms of its total contribution to the economy rather than in terms of any heroic qualities in its unaided achievements. The threat of redundancy because of technological change, in other words, turned out to be as unreal for horses as it has so often been for men, and given adaptation to new or modified tasks the new technology did not diminish, but substantially increased, the demand for horse-labour. Taking all the varied forms of horse-drawn and horseback activity together, British society required about one horse for every 10 people—men, women and children—in order to keep going in the late Victorian period. The USA, with vastly greater spaces and distances, needed about one horse to every four inhabitants at that time. As in parallel situations, the increased demand brought higher rewards for horse-labour; or to put it more normally, raised its cost. The price of van-horses and cart-horses went up by 25 to 30 per cent between 1850 and 1873; and though it subsequently fell, in the last quarter of the century, it did not fall by as much as the general price level.

Railway travel also stimulated the transport of passengers by road, most obviously in cabs to catch trains and in inter-station horse buses. In London, for instance, the number of cabs increased virtually tenfold between 1830 and 1900, while the fleet buses grew from 1,000 in 1850 to 4,000, rates of growth which greatly exceeded the simple increase of population so that a provision of one cab to 1,000 head of people at the start of Victoria's reign had improved to one cab to every 350 people at its end. Less obvious was the effect of railways in stimulating horseback riding, but Trollope[7] fans will remember how, in *The Way We Live Now,* it was the ease and speed of railway travel which made it obligatory for young men about town to keep a string of hunters in the country, which they would pop down to use for a day's mid-week hunting without seriously interrupting their course of dissipation in the London clubs. At this point, however, the impact of railways simply acted alongside the general influences of economic growth and increasing affluence, and it would be absurd to attempt to disentangle it from them. The cabs, the horse buses, and the horse trams which developed from the late 1860s, were after all very largely employed in carrying traffic which both originated and terminated within their city catchment areas, and which never at any point touched a train; the trams in particular were almost exclusively devoted to serving this urban-generated traffic, and never had more than a very minor role as railway auxiliaries. As to the increase in hunting, it was an admiral who offered the most profound analysis when he was asked to explain the great increase in the turnover of the London horse sales in the fifty years before 1873: 'I think it is the money, the enormous wealth of London,' he said; 'so many people keep hunters now, who never dreamt of keeping them before. I know that at Melton there are 500 people in a field, where formerly there would not be 100, and many of them have two or three horses each in the field.' In answer to the further question 'whether in former days

[7]Anthony Trollope, 1815–1882, English novelist.

would not those gentlemen have hunted in their own countries in preference to going to Melton?' he replied 'My idea is that it is owing to their means; that their riches have increased, and that the love of hunting has increased in proportion to their means of being able to indulge their fancy.' Hunting in fact increased three- or four-fold in the period, in terms of numbers of separate hunts and packs of hounds; what demands this made on horseflesh we do not know, but by 1900 it was thought that some 200,000 horses were kept exclusively for hunting, at an annual cost in upkeep of £8 million, to which should be added a couple of million for remounts. It may help put the annual expenditure on hunting into perspective to point out that it was about half as large as the total expenditure on tobacco by all the smokers in the United Kingdom.

The hunters were a form of consumer durable. Rather more durable, indeed, than most cars or television sets today, but somewhat less durable than the private carriages which performed for the Victorian age many of the functions which are currently associated with consumer durables, in particular the functions of conferring prestige and defining status. Everyone has heard of the 'carriage trade' and 'carriage folk' as concepts which defined the standing of desirable residential suburbs, epitomised the social aspirations of people on the climb, outlined the markets aimed at by the producers, sellers, and advertisers of quality goods, and summed up one of the critical lines of class division. Surprisingly few people have attempted to define what the carriage trade was, to estimate its extent, or to examine its development. Luckily the taxman was as interested in private carriages as he now is in private cars, and his attentions have left behind a trail which indicates the broad dimensions of carriage-ownership and the directions of change. As with all tax returns, the figures must be handled with caution: they record licenses issued, which may or may not be the same thing as carriages on the road. Evasion of carriage duty was probably not a serious problem, since possession was not easy to conceal. But the Revenue classification of carriages, and changes in the categories, make interpretation of the returns a complicated and specialised task. The old horsepower rating car licenses were simplicity itself beside the classes of carriages: 4-wheel carriages drawn by 2 or more horses of over 13 hands, 4-wheel carriages drawn by 2 or more ponies under 13 hands, or by oxen, 4-wheel carriages drawn by 1 horse over 13 hands, 2-wheel carriages drawn by 2 horses, 2-wheel carriages drawn by 1 horse; these are but a few of the taxation classes which were used to apply differential rates of duty with refined precision. The more fashionable, prudent, or plain accident-prone among carriage owners used sometimes to keep spare bodies in their coach-houses, which could be mounted on the chassis in case of change of mood or of outright disaster: these additional bodies, also, had their special niche in the taxation manual.

...In the early, pre-railway, decades of the nineteenth century carriage-ownership increased quite fast, but possession of this coveted form of personal transport was still largely confined to the 'upper ten thousand' who comprised the ruling class—the aristocracy, gentry, and very wealthy commercial men. There were 15,000 privately-owned large carriages in 1810 and about 30,000 in 1840; the smaller 2-wheeled runabouts, over 40,000 of them by 1840, were partly owned by the same people, and partly formed the necessary stock in trade of businessmen, doctors, and solicitors.[8] The wealthy frequently had several carriages, for different functions, different types of weather, or to be kept in different parts of the country; they were in fact subject to progressive taxation with a scale of duties running from £12 per carriage for a person keeping only one up to £18.3. per carriage for a person keeping nine or more. In this period something like 20 per cent of the large carriages seem to have been owned by two-carriage families. After 1840, however, the early railway age witnessed a remarkable social deepening of the carriage trade. By about 1870 the number of large carriages had increased four-fold, to some 120,000, owned by some 100,000 individuals; this proved to be saturation point, the numbers remaining fairly static until decline set in after 1902. The light 2-wheelers proliferated even more rapidly, growing more than six times between 1840 and 1870; these were the vehicles of the middle classes *par excellence,* and were very largely in the hands of one-carriage families. In contrast to the large carriages these light ones continued to grow in number after 1870, but at a very much slower rate so that the 250,000 of 1870 had only become 320,000 by 1902.

Figures of this order establish that it was in the Victorian age that carriage-ownership spread right through the middle class. The upper class left its mark on its carriages in the shape of the coats of arms with which 'the quality' emblazoned their doors; these, too, did not escape the tax net, and the number of armorial bearings painted on carriages remained throughout very stable in the range of 15,000 to 19,000, so that all the rest of the carriages, ultimately over 400,000 of them, may be presumed to have been solidly bourgeois. It is perhaps more significant that carriage ownership, having grown from 4 per 1,000 inhabitants in 1840 to 14 per 1,000 in 1870, thereafter subsided gently to a level of 12 per 1,000 in 1902. Of course all these proportions are chickenfeed beside present day levels of car ownership, which are running at the order of 206 per 1,000 inhabitants in this country; though it should be noted that it was not until 1926 that car ownership surpassed the 1870 peak rate. The very sharp check to the growth of the carriage trade after 1870, however, has a number of interesting implications, because it is not at all what we might have expected to accompany the increasing affluence, the rising per capita real incomes, and the growing appetite for luxury, of the late Victorian period. The check was due, I believe, not at all to any lack of potential demand for personal transport, but to physical constraints on the supply side, in short to problems of horsefeed and carriage space.

[8]British lawyers who prepare briefs but who do not present cases in court.

A private carriage is a labour-intensive object, requiring a coachman and a groom for its management. It is possible that the available slack in the labour force was all taken up in the years before 1870, and that in the late Victorian economy the labour force, with all the other competing demands upon it, simply could not expand fast enough to sustain the earlier rate of carriage growth. At any rate the number of domestic coachmen and grooms barely managed to increase at all between 1881 and 1901. Space to keep a carriage was probably a more important constraint. A horse and carriage simply could not be parked in the street like a car. Ancient City regulations, dating from the late seventeenth century, were very firm about off-street stabling, and provided penalties for drivers who so much as fed their horses in the streets 'except with oats out of a bag, or with so much hay as he shall hold in his hands'; while impounding by police was avoided by the economical custom of London that 'if a horse stands at an inn till he eats out his value, the innkeeper may take him as his own, upon reasonable appraisement of four of his neighbours.' Possession of a horse and carriage implied possession of a stable and coach-house, either within the private grounds of the larger mansions, or in a separate mews[9] block provided for a group of houses. My contention is that a number of influences converged about 1870 to reduce very sharply the rate of mews provision. One was the competition for urban land, which yielded higher returns if covered with houses; another was the realisation that mews quarters introduced unwelcome lower class elements into otherwise respectable and refined residential districts; a third, connected with this, was a certain middle-class feeling that outdoor servants living at a distance were not amenable to the discipline and moral supervision proper for domestics; and a fourth was the appreciation that the growing scale of cities had thrown up tolerably adequate public services in buses and cabs, so that suburban carriage-owning was no longer worth so much candle. It was for reasons like these that one comes across cases of radical revisions in speculative builders' plans in the 1860s and 1870s, schemes for building estates with mews quarters being abandoned as they went along in favour of pure housing estates....

While sections of the middle class adapted their style of living to the approach of carriage saturation point, and peopled the carriageless suburbs of late Victorian England, the upper classes also were not unaffected by the physical difficulties of the carriage world. The demand for horses threatened to outrun the supply, and one large dealer announced: 'If you told me you would give me £400 for a pair of carriage horses that you dare put your wife behind, a pair of nice good horses worth £200, and gave me a fortnight to get them, I would not guarantee to buy them.' Scarcity of good horses apart, many gentlemen found that it was ceasing to be worth while to run their own carriages in London, the traffic was getting so intolerable and the recruitment of staff so difficult; instead they hired carriages for the season

[9]A mews is an alley behind a residential street, containing stabling for horses.

from one of the great jobbing masters—the Hertz rent-a-car people of their time—who flourished with their thousand-horse stables in late Victorian London.

The horse-drawn society did not in the event grind to a halt. But its progress slowed down, and it slowed down because in the final analysis there loomed behind these physical limitations the horse himself and the question of his feed.... [E]very horse...got through the produce of four to five acres of farmland every year. It is perhaps doubtful whether enough land existed anywhere in the world to support very many more horses than did in fact exist.

...Counting horses was not a habit with the British, their curiosity being satisfied when they had totted up the farm-horses, a mere fragment of the total population, and even that was tardily done. To conduct a horse census was the mark of a military nation, anxious about its potential horse supply in case of war. Hence one of the earliest acts of Italy on the morrow of her unification,[10] eager as in so many other spheres to cut a correct figure as a fledgling great power, was to hold a solemn census of equine population and to pass a law of horse conscription providing an apparatus of draft tickets and mobilisation centres for the nether part of the cavalry: running true to form Italian style, the first was wildly inaccurate and the second hopelessly elaborate. Peace-loving, or naval, Britain did without such bureaucratic trimmings; though the figure-conscious Americans counted horses methodically, along with almost everything else susceptible of enumeration.

The upshot is that in the year of peak horse populations, 1902, there were something like $3\frac{1}{2}$ million in Britain, and about 30 million in the USA. Scattered over the world, some 15 million acres were set aside for the sustenance of the British herd; for by this date only part of the hard stuff in the horsefeed—the oats and corn—was grown at home, and much was imported. In America the farm-horses by themselves ate their way through the produce of 88 million acres each year, or one quarter of the entire crop area of the nation; when the consumption of American city horses and other non-farm horses is added, horse-feed is seen to have pre-empted more like a third of the crop area, and even then there were export crops destined for overseas horses on top of this. All this, it should be remembered, refers to a world served by highly developed railway systems in which coal had been substituted for oats as the fuel of the railway sector. It provides grounds for supposing that any appreciably greater numbers of horses would have been quite literally insupportable.

Hence the somewhat stunted growth of the late Victorian carriage trade to which I have referred may owe much to the impossibility of expanding the supply of horsefeed at any appreciably greater rate than was in fact achieved; or more strictly, to the impossibility of devoting a greater proportion of cultivated lands to horsefeed without doing great injury to other demands

---

[10]That is, in 1860.

for agricultural produce, principally those of humans. Behind this modest conclusion there lies a rather startling prospect for those who have sought to measure the impact of railways by asking themselves what things would have been like if there had been no railways. Perhaps so many extra horses would have been required that everyone else would have starved. . . .

Is God French?

EUGEN WEBER

Many European historians have turned from the study of theology and church politics to the sociology of religion. Examining parish registers, wills, sermons, visitation reports by clergy, diaries, letters, and tracts and pamphlets written for the populace, historians have attempted to describe both daily religious behavior and the thought of the masses. Eugen Weber here elucidates the meaning of religion to nineteenth-century French people.

France in the second half of the nineteenth century appeared to be a solidly Roman Catholic nation. In the census that Weber cites, over 98 percent of the French affirmed themselves Catholics, and there were certainly enough priests to minister to the spiritual needs of the populace. Yet today the major religion of the French is indifference. What developments (from the French Revolution on) does Weber discuss that reflect a decline of religiousness?

Did people reject supernatural religion altogether or did they just lose faith in the institutional Church? After all, it is not uncommon for sincerely religious people to stay away from churches. To what extent did Church attendance measure religious belief? What role did the Church play in the lives of people in nineteenth-century France? Weber describes a panoply of popular religious beliefs, including attitudes toward saints and miracles, for example. From the Middle Ages there has been perennial tension between the institutional view of religion and the popular attitude toward religious practice. How did the Church feel about the parishioners' veneration of saints and craving for the miraculous? What functions did miracles serve? The popularity of Lourdes is a marvelous example of the strength of popular devotion and the Church's desire to control its flock's religious expressions. On the other hand, how did the flock view the priest's functions? Could the priest be considered a magician? What Church rules and prohibitions did the French come to disregard?

Religion did not simply mean belief and practice; there was a commercial side to religion that Weber does not neglect. Thus the pilgrimage signified more than a possible cure for a crippling disease or improved chances for salvation. There was money to be made from pilgrims, and, for their part, the pilgrims could play tourist and enjoy their escape from a humdrum existence. Was the priest involved in the commercial aspects of religion?

Weber concludes this selection with a story that illustrates "the requiem of nineteenth-century religion." Perhaps Weber is a bit premature, for the 1890s unleashed a torrent of religious feeling in the virulent anti-Semitism that colored the notorious Dreyfus affair. But there is no doubt that the traditional faith of the peasantry had changed in dramatic ways and that the Church had lost its hold on the hearts and minds of many French people.

. . . In the mid-1870's 35,387,703 of the 36,000,000 people in France were listed in the official census as Catholics. The rest declared themselves Protestants (something under 600,000), Jews (50,000), or freethinkers (80,000). The secular clergy of the Catholic church alone included 55,369 priests, one for every 639 inhabitants. Roman Catholicism remained, as it had been in 1801, "the religion of the majority of Frenchmen."

Whatever else this meant, it meant that the Church was an integral part of life. It presided over all the major occasions in a person's life—birth, marriage, death—and over the welfare of the community and the conduct of its members. It helped the crops increase and the cattle prosper. It healed, taught, and preserved from harm. . . .

Religion provided spells and incantations, often written down and passed on preciously like amulets. These, like its ceremonies, were efficacious and protective. The peasant . . . was proud to recite his prayers. "He has prayers for thunder, for sickness, for going to bed at night. They are good, very good, these prayers, says he, though he doesn't understand them very well, since they are in French," or in Latin. The ritual lent solemnity to private and public occasions, as the term solemnization applied to ceremonies like marriage attests. This was particularly important in rites of passage. The first communion, the first time one received the Eucharist, was crucial—a "great matter for country children; many cannot find a job before they have done it." Marking admission into the world of workers and of earners—almost an adult world—the first communion and the preparation for it, the catechism, provided the basic initiation into the moral mysteries of life. "The children did not know how to read, so the priest was teaching them the catechism by heart [which was] full of extraordinary words and which they laughed at," recorded Charles Péguy.[1] They must have had a sense that obscure powers were properly invoked with obscure incantations. . . .

Was Christ's personal message communicated in many a village church? We cannot tell. Those sermons that one finds concern themselves with the proprieties and transgressions of everyday behavior. Policemen were less concerned with immanent justice than with infringements of petty human laws; and village priests seem to have taken a similar view. This was their civilizing function. Along with this, it was their duty to see that their flock observed all of the formal and routine religious rites. It is by the practice of such rites that adherence to religion is generally measured. When there is little participation, even on high holidays, or when it declines, religion is said to decay. Yet what did church attendance mean to churchgoers?

[1] Essayist and poet, 1873–1914, from a working-class background.

"Sunday, the peasants go to church . . . some moved by religious feeling, most by habit or by fear of what people say." One went to church because it was the thing to do on Sunday, because it was one of the few social occasions of the week, because it was an opportunity for talking business or meeting friends, acquaintances, relatives. It was—especially for the women, once men had grasped at the opportunities that fairs held out—the sole occasion to escape the isolation in which many lived, the major recreation or diversion in a restricted life. Observance, business, and pleasure were combined. One went to mass wearing one's Sunday best. . . . Public announcements were made by the village crier as the congregation left the service, public sales were often timed to fall after it, one could slip off later to call on the notary or the doctor, or drop in to the tavern, circle, or café. Even if a majority did not attend the service but went about their work as on any other day, "a multitude of peasants gathered in front of the church, discussed politics, made deals, filled the taverns."

In a world where entertainment was scarce, church provided a certain festive diversion. Those attending might well "love the high mass, the rich ornaments, seeing a great many statues of saints in their churches." Writing about his grandmother, Charles Péguy presented church attendance as a treat for the lonely child raised in a woodcutter's hut in Bourbonnais in the early 1800's: "When she was good, she was allowed to go on Sunday to mass in the village—she wore her sabots[2] because one doesn't go to church barefoot, and she was happy because that's where everybody met, where they exchanged news, where one heard about deaths, marriages, births, where gossip flowed about what was going on, where servants were hired."

. . . But the belief and behavior of the peasants never ceased to oscillate between observance and transgression. Until the Revolution church attendance was compulsory, and religious sanctions that could cause serious social embarrassment menaced those who skipped their Easter duties. The elimination of constraints broke this decreed unanimity. Those who had been quietly uncommitted (as in Aunis-Saintonge, where the forced conversion of Protestants had made lukewarm Catholics) were free to fall away. Political divisions and internal schism during the 1790's confused many more, and deprived parishes of pastors or cut sections of a community off from the only priest. For a decade or more, at least until the Concordat of 1801,[3] a good number of young people grew up without catechism, whole communities did not attend church, and others ceased to celebrate traditional festivals. The Décadi[4] created the habit of working on Sunday. The absence of priests left marriages to civil authorities and led to prolonged delays before baptism, if the ceremony was performed at all.

[2]Wooden clogs.

[3]Agreement between the pope and the French government re-establishing religious peace and recognizing Catholicism as the religion of the majority of the French.

[4]The ten-day week created during the French Revolution to replace the seven-day week.

Some communities came to rely on the services of laymen, who took over the functions of absent priests, performing baptisms, marriages, and burials.... Ad hoc arrangements of this sort could prove enduring....

Canon Fernand Boulard doubts that the Revolution really affected rural religious practice very profoundly, or that much changed in this realm until the last decade or two of the nineteenth century. He may be right. But there were discordances where there had been at least outward unity. Men who had acquired Church property and would not submit, men who had married in a civil marriage and would not seek absolution for their sin, became centers of local opposition. Not many cases of this kind of sturdy opposition developed in communities that remained cohesive, but it flourished in areas where, as in Burgundy, the memory of clerical harshness and exploitation survived, along with the fear of a reconstitution of their great domains. In Mâconnais... the devil appears as the hero in some local legends and triumphs over Christ, disgraced by the men who served him. The peasants had burned churches there in the Middle Ages and did so again in 1789, or stayed away thereafter. But even where the road had not been so prepared, hard times frayed clerical authority. Priests were forced to ask for help from their parishioners. Rival clergymen accused each other of the worst transgressions, diminishing still further the influence of the cloth. "People begin to separate religion from its ministers," asserted the *Statistique*[5] of Lot in 1831. But religion *was* its ministers, just as the state was bailiffs and gendarmes. And when, after 1830, liberal local mayors opposed the influence of priests loyal to the old order, they sought to sap their authority by encouraging the drift of men away from the sacraments.

We see that in the churches, as in the schools, non-attendance is a way of measuring ineffectiveness. The growing numbers of migrant workers going to the cities added to this trend. Urban workers worked Sundays and holidays, or did so very often. The more earnest the man, the more he worked. The less responsible were the more likely to get drunk during their free time. The Church did not see them either way. Like the Revolution, acquaintance with the city did not destroy religious sentiment. It simply made nonconformity possible or created another kind of conformity. Men who attended church at home because their peers did ceased to attend church where such attendance was exceptional. The city merely provided an opportunity for the collapse of practices "shallowly rooted in the personality." Returning migrants may well have lost whatever impulse to religious conformity they had left with. They did not necessarily bandy this about so long as the priest retained his influence in the community. But they were ready to welcome emancipation when it came.

At any rate, all observers seem to have sensed the shallowness of faith behind the slackness of observance. In Beauce respectable farmers, "preoccupied by the care to augment their fortune, work to this end even on

[5] *Statistics*, a publication.

Sunday during the services, so that the churches are deserted." Not that they lacked respect for religion, "but they consider that the time they would spend in church would be lost for their work and their fortune." Not challenge, but indifference and hardheadedness.... "The absence of religious sentiment [in the countryside, especially] is such that there are communes where scarcely one marriage in six is blessed in church."...

Whether unconverted or disaffected, people lost their respect for Church rules and Church prohibitions. The proportion of civil marriages grew, the delays between birth and baptism became longer. Once set at 24 hours of birth, the outside limit for baptism was extended to three days in 1830, to eight days in 1887, to "the soonest possible time" in the twentieth century. In one Sologne parish the average delay between birth and baptism, which was 2.73 days in 1854, had stretched to 15.12 days by 1901; in 1950 it ran well over three months. Less fear for the newborn's life, fewer epidemics, greater closeness between husband and wife, who was increasingly expected to play a part in the ceremony, but also indifference to what the sacrament of baptism meant and to the authority of the priest.... One could do without the priest if one wanted to get married when he could not, or would not, perform the ceremony.

From the Church's point of view, every innovation only made things worse. The bicycle was blamed for enabling young people to avoid mass. Tourists, visitors, and returning emigrants felt increasingly free to speak of their indifference to religious practice or even their scorn of it. Military service side by side with "pagan" urban workers made some peasants ashamed of a show of piety as a mark of their bumpkin backwardness. Finally, with war in 1914 there came a culmination of the pressures toward detachment....

Religion was an urban import, like education, and, just like education, it reflected the scholarship of the Counter-Reformation and the Enlightenment—the two at one, at least, in being alien to the countryside. Tridentine[6] and post-Tridentine missionaries, where they could, replaced familiar native rites and practices with new ones that were strange. These had no time to settle into tradition before the Revolution and the cascade of changes following it. Religious custom remained superficial, even though convention and the need for ritual kept it in being. In this respect, reputedly devout areas appear little better than incredulous ones. For the outwardly pious Solognot, religion was "an artificial system that he bore without understanding, lacking in efficacy and well above his preoccupations."...

Such comments may explain the frequent conjunction between indifference and some form of practice, as in Bourbonnais where peasants "have recourse to religion in all great circumstances, but following ancestral traditions rather than any real faith." Religion had didactic uses: "It fills the young with fear," and that was good and necessary, "but when we're dead we're

---

[6] From the Council of Trent (1545–1563), which clarified doctrines and reformed the Roman Catholic Church.

dead," and that was common sense. Even those peasants who eschewed religious practice wanted a resident priest, for one thing, because he would teach the children to respect their parents and authority, but above all "for rites needed in social life and to ensure good crops, for festivals often connected with a healing saint." In short, the ritual and the ceremonies that were the very core of popular religion were fundamentally utilitarian. Accordingly, we might expect such pragmatic formalism to decline when its utility no longer seemed apparent, or when rival authorities and formalities beckoned.

This of course is advanced as merest supposition. I know no way of telling the spiritual hold that the Church had on people. At the visible level, however, its influence was based on practical services and subject to its ability to keep these up: consecration (in an officially acceptable sense), healing, protection, making wishes come true, and not least providing a center for traditional practices. In all these things, official religion drew generously on the popular cult of saints, of healing agencies and other useful "superstitions." Superstitions have sometimes been described as religions that did not succeed. Perhaps, in our case at least, it is they that should be called successful, since so much official religion depended on them and survived largely by indulging practices endorsed by popular belief. The people of Balesta in Comminges, noted the village teacher in 1886, "are the more religious, the more superstitious they are." ...

We know about the widespread usage of the cross—about how the plowman signed himself before he drew the first furrow, and again before he sowed the first handful of grain; about how he would not cut a slice out of a loaf without first tracing a cross on it. But how far did this, or prayers, or kneeling in the fields when the Angelus[7] tolled, go beyond the propitiation of powers that were feared but little understood? ...

Much that was expected of the priest indeed fell in the category of magic—white, of course, as when the priest said masses to cure animals that were under a spell, or when, during the traditional processions that wound their way through communal territory on Rogation Sunday,[8] he threw stones plastered with a small wax cross (priest's dung in Franche-Comté) into the fields to keep the storms and hail away. We have already seen the power over natural phenomena attributed to priests, and the logical belief that some men of the cloth wielded more powers than others. . . . It seems quite natural that when, in the early 1890's, the bishop of Mende visited the village of Saint-Enimie (Lozère), his flock should find that his blessing of their valley made the almond harvest more abundant. . . . In Meuse several priests were held to sit on clouds, thus helping to disperse them; and the Abbé Chévin, of Bar-le-Duc, who died in 1900, was accused of having made a violent storm break over his own parish.

[7] A Roman Catholic prayer said three times daily upon the tolling of the Angelus bell.

[8] The Sunday before Ascension Day, which marked the supposed bodily ascent of Jesus to Heaven.

For those who connected Catholicism and sorcery, plainly, priests could be sinister figures, holding the powers of black magic as well. As a result of natural associations, the Limousins of the twentieth century still dreaded that "priests would usher death" into the homes they visited. The fear that stalked all the inhabitants of the countryside found in the church service not only appeasement but fuel. When sermons did not deal with public discipline, they frequently stoked the fires of brimstone and hell. That was the only way "to move such an almost savage populace," remarked a Breton. "A voice like thunder, dire threats, fists belaboring the pulpit, sweat running down his cheeks, the eloquent pastor fills his hearers with delicious terror."

Benoît Malon (another hostile witness) has denounced the obsessive effects this sort of thing could have on people, especially children, haunted throughout life by the dread of hell-fire, torments, retribution, and circum-ambient fiends. But priestly menaces were bound to be intimidating to the most sober when menace was the staff of everyday life. Living was marginal, disaster inexplicable and uncontrollable. . . . Where harm and ill-fortune were swiftly come by, nothing was easier than to claim that they were punishments of heaven. Long centuries of trying to mollify and coax the powerful conjured up a religion where fear almost excluded love, a faith bent to flatter and do honor to the heavenly lords in order to obtain their protection or avoid their ire. Power and irascibility were what impressed. The peasants would not work their cattle on the feasts of the nastiest saints, the ones most likely to resent and revenge any irreverence. . . .

God was far away. The saints were near. Both were anthropomorphic. Saints were intercessors. One did not address God directly, but prayed to saints to request his favors, rewarded them if the crop was good or the weather fair, even chastised them, as at Haudimont (Meuse), where Saint Urban, accused of permitting the vines to freeze on May 25, his own feastday, was dragged in effigy through the nettles around his church. The greatest saint of all, of course, was the Virgin, an unparalleled source of delivery from harm. The *gwerz* (ballad) made up when a new pilgrimage to her was launched in 1894 at Plounéour-Menez recited only recent and concrete miracles: saving men from falling, drowning, prison, and so on. These were the functions of a saint.

But the chief function of saints on earth was healing, and every malady was the province of a particular saint. The attribution could vary from region to region, with some local patron saint taking over duties another saint performed elsewhere; but it was a creation of popular design. The conjunction between saint and illness was determined by associations, some naively evident, others lost in the mists of time. Thus Saint Eutropius healed dropsy . . . ; Saint Cloud healed boils . . . ; Saint Diétrine dealt with herpes and scurf . . . ; Saint Aignan coped with ringworm and scurvy. . . . Berry had its own array of saints destined by alliteration or obscure fiat to heal. For the deaf there was Saint Ouen; for the gouty, Saint Genou; for crabbed and peevish women, Saint Acaire. . . . In Finistère Our Lady of Benodet healed aches, depressions, madness, or simplemindedness—disorders associated with the head. Benodet literally means head of Odet, that is, the mouth of the Odet river....

Probably the most notorious saint born of popular whimsy and need was Saint Grelichon or Greluchon (from *grelicher*, which means to scratch or tickle). Saint Greluchon had started life as the funeral statue of a local lord of Bourbon-l'Archambault, Guillaume de Naillac, but we rediscover the figure in a recessed nook of that city's streets. Childless women came from afar to scratch a little dust from the statue's genital area and drink it in a glass of white wine. By 1880, when Sir Guillaume's lower parts had been scratched down to nullity, the dust was obtained from under the statue's chin. Finally, the statue—which had become a bust—was transferred to the museum for safekeeping.

... [M]iracle-working agents enlisted strong popular loyalties. So did the traditions that called for rites to be performed in scrupulous detail, or otherwise fail in their intent. At Maizey (Meuse) the relics of Saint Nicholas were carried in procession through the streets in May, and the following Sunday's services then had to be celebrated in a country chapel about a mile away. In 1889 the priest tried to avoid the chore and to say mass in his own church. This disturbed his flock, and most of the men in his congregation, dressed in their holiday clothes, marched to the designated chapel so that the rite would be carried out properly. On the other hand, it appears that the change of a patron saint was often treated with equanimity, as was a substitution of the supposedly sacred image itself. At Villeneuve-de-Berg (Ardèche) the blacksmiths had no statue of their patron, Saint Eloi, to parade on his feastday. They solved the problem routinely by borrowing Saint Vincent from the vintners' corporation, removing the statue's pruning knife, and replacing it with a little hammer. Similarly, in the Alps, at the feast of Saint Besse the saint's devotees brought medals "of him" bearing the legend "St.-Pancrace." When the discrepancy was pointed out to them, it bothered them not at all. The fact was, they said, the likeness was close, and the effects were the same. To the traditional mind the patron saint was secondary to the rite, and to the site as well.

We can see this in the cult of "good" [i.e. healing] fountains, a cult that was generally abetted by the clergy on the theory that the saints who protected the fountains would be given a share of the credit for their restorative powers. Yet popular customs connected with healing fountains were, as a student says, "often purely secular," and certain spas kept their appeal with or without the Church's blessing.... On Batz island, off the Breton coast, the old chapel dedicated to Saint Pol (de Léon) was shifted to the patronage of Saint Anne when, at the end of the nineteenth century, she was officially declared the patron saint of the peninsula. The pilgrimage continued as before. It was the place that mattered! ...

Alphonse Dupront has written that all pilgrimages are made to a source of healing. But we should add that the pilgrims as often seek protection and favors, too. In Bresse one went to pray to Saint Anthony that one's pigs should "gain" during the year. In Bourbonnais shepherdesses attended the annual pilgrimage to Saint Agatha's shrine at Saint-Désiré "in the first place to divert themselves and to secure a blessed hazel switch" with which to control their herds and be free of the fear of wolves.

Conditions obviously varied depending on the stand of the local priest; but priestly decisions were interpreted without illusions. At Carnac (Morbihan) the pilgrimage to the shrine of Saint Cornelius (Cornély), patron of horned beasts, was very profitable. Oxen and calves were offered to him; they were made to kneel in adoration of his statue, which stood above the portal of the church, then blessed by the priest and auctioned off under the saint's banner. Then, in 1906, the priests refused to bless the gathered beasts. "They haven't been paid enough," explained a hawker selling his toys at the local fair.... [P]riests too galled or too rigorous to keep up traditional devotions were in minority. As a general rule, they accepted current beliefs in healing fountains, stones, and megaliths. For one thing, as all observers hastened to point out, the gifts offered to their patron saints contributed to clerical revenues. Saint Anthony was offered pigs' feet, Saint Eloi horses' tails, and Saint Herbot cows' tails. More important, many saints were offered the beasts themselves, calves, lambs, chicken, and other gifts in kind. These would be sold by the verger after the ceremony, and the revenue could rise to as much as 1,500 or 2,000 francs—riches for men whose yearly income was only half as much.

For some priests the launching of a new pilgrimage spot meant big business, like the shrine in Picardy, complete with publicity, signposts, hostels, and eateries, which had to be suppressed in 1882 by the bishop of Beauvais. Others were satisfied with a modest but regular income gained from the sale of some small item, like the *saint vinage*[9] at Miremont in Combrailles, a mixture of 10 liters of water and one liter of wine that was blessed by the priest and sold by the sexton at very moderate prices, and that was said to cure all cattle ills....

That priests and their parishes profited from such religious undertakings does not make the undertakings any the less valid or the participants any the less sincere. Utility underlies most human enterprise, and in no way demeans it. The mother who trudged off carrying her child that it might be strengthened or healed was an admirable figure. The priest who sought funds to glorify the source from which such healing sprang—and perhaps its guardian as well—was human and perhaps even saintly.

But to return to pilgrimages: these were perhaps important above all as a form of access to the extraordinary.... The pilgrimage offered an excuse to leave the village, and with it, for a time at least, an inescapable fate. Pilgrimages were festive occasions involving food and drink, shopping and dancing. The most ancient pilgrimages coincided with great fairs; markets and sanctuaries went together.... Bakers and butchers, clothiers and peddlers, set up

[9]Reference to a process of making consecrated wine.

their stalls; people treated themselves to sweetmeats, wine, or lemonade, and purchased images, traditional cakes, and other ritual ex-votos[10] to deposit in the sanctuary or tie to the branch of a nearby tree. The healing statue of Saint Stephen at Lussac-les-Eglises (Haute-Vienne) was invoked, like a good many others, by binding a ribbon on the statue's arm. The ribbons were bought from cloth merchants or from the stalls local women set up in the village streets. So were the wax limbs carried in the procession of Saint Amateur at Lamballe (Côtes-du-Nord); the "saffron-flavored cakes shaped like hens,". sold to the devotees of Saint Symphorien at Vernègues (Bouches-du-Rhône); the yellow wax breasts offered by women to Saint Anthony's fountain near Brive (Corrèze); and the amulets or priapic figures, in cake or wax, sold from Normandy to Var at least since the seventeenth century. No wonder the peasants felt that priests were necessary because they made business go! And it is easy to dwell on the commercial aspects of religion. The point is that there was commerce because there were people, and people congregated because this was the only sort of festivity they knew.

"It's more a pleasure trip than a pious action," caviled an eastern teacher in 1888. What was wrong with its being both? At this unexalted level, the pilgrimage and traveling were one and the same thing.... Relations and friends met at pilgrimage places regularly every year, and such predictable gatherings were convenient in times when communications were rare and difficult. They also afforded welcome breaks, especially to women. The pilgrimage was chiefly a feminine activity—perhaps because it was the woman's only socially sanctioned means of escape from home and its daily routine. Men had opportunities to visit fairs or to travel to farther places. Their lives were far more varied than those of womenfolk. These found their opportunity in pilgrimages, which they often undertook alone over great distances....

But let us hazard further. Even quite humble trips, for secular or devotional ends, took a person out of his element and opened up unfamiliar spheres. The extraordinary began much closer to home then than it would do today, and a trip of any kind was an understandable aspiration for those whose ordinary lives offered so little change.

What could be more extraordinary than the miraculous? Perhaps this was what humble people welcomed in the news of the great miracles of the time. Miracles promise deliverance from the routine unfolding of predictable destinies; and they create a sense of expectancy and excitement the more potent for being the more vague. Millenarianism, which embodies all this in its most extreme form, is commonly attributed to bafflement—a sense of privation and restraint with no conceivable relief in sight. The promise carried by evidence of supernatural forces heals bafflement and frustration, and reinforces hope. It also holds out an opportunity to escape from the

---

[10] An ex-voto is an offering made in pursuance of a vow, in gratitude, for example, for recovery from sickness.

commonplace into the realm of the prodigious, to wonder over marvels and possibilities beyond familiar ken. . . .

Whatever the explanation, the rural world was eager for miracles. . . . Most of the time rumors of local miracles did not go beyond a limited radius. In 1840 the Holy Virgin seems to have manifested herself in several places in Vendée. But this was treated as local superstition. In the early 1860's the Ursuline nuns of Charroux in Poitou discovered what they claimed to be the Sacred Prepuce, removed from the Infant Jesus at the circumcision and, in the words of Monsignor Pie, bishop of Poitiers, "the only part of Christ's body left behind when he ascended into heaven." The name Charroux was associated with *chair rouge* (the red meat of the cut-off prepuce!), and an elaborate festival in 1862 brought the fortunate convent into the public eye. . . .

At about the same time, in the fall of 1862, the sixteen-year-old daughter of a rural postman of Saint-Marcel-d'Ardèche began to preach, predict the future and promise miracles. The people came en masse from all surrounding communes until, in a few days, the furor died down.

In other cases the feverish excitement did not pass so quickly. When, in September 1846, two shepherd children guarding their herds on the deserted mountainside of La Salette saw an unnatural light and a tearful lady announcing the wrath of Christ in their own patois,[11] curious pilgrims hastened there at once. The veracity of the children was contested, especially by the Church authorities, but the enthusiasm was too great to stifle. The evidence makes clear that miracles were validated and imposed by popular opinion, which the authorities—civil and clerical—accepted only unwillingly and under pressure. In a notorious trial of 1857, concerned with the reality of the miracle of La Salette, the lawyers continually referred to the supernatural needs of the lower classes (explained presumably by their ignorance). It was wholly understandable, they said, that the common people should believe in such things, but they expressed some surprise at finding members of the upper classes sharing these views.

This same division and the same pressure of popular need appear in the earliest stages of the first and perhaps the greatest modern pilgrimage site—Lourdes. In February 1858, eleven-year-old Bernadette Soubirous encountered a "Beautiful Lady" beside a stream. The local nuns, priests, and civil authorities, afraid of complications, refused to believe Bernadette's story. The local gendarme sought to tell "the people . . . that it is not in the nineteenth century that one lets oneself be carried away by such a belief." Yet belief was stronger than skepticism. It spread like wildfire. Within a few days large crowds, mostly women and children, began to gather at the grotto of Masabielle. By the beginning of March they numbered 20,000 (the population of Lourdes was less than a quarter of that). "Disorder caused in the name of God is none the less intolerable disorder," warned the gendarme.

---

[11] Local dialect.

All his superiors clearly thought the same. The records are full of it: "disorder," "regrettable agitation," "preserve order," "undeceive the population," "regrettable facts." But the population did not want to be undeceived. For it, disorder was hope and holiday. "The population...wants to believe. When there are no miracles, it invents them; it insists on baring heads, kneeling, etc."

There were few priests, sometimes no priests, in the assembled crowds. The clergy, as the imperial prosecutor reported, "maintained an excessive reserve." But the ritual pilgrimages developed without their intervention and despite that of the civil authorities. It was several years before the bishop of Tarbes confirmed the miracles in 1862, proclaiming the authenticity of the Virgin's appearance and the healing virtues of the grotto's spring. But clearly the voice of the people preceded the voice of God. In 1867 a railway line became available. By 1871 the pilgrimage had become international, and in 1876 the great basilica was consecrated before 100,000 pilgrims—a new tide in the affairs of men, flowing in the wake of the railroads....

What does all this tell us about religion? Conclusions do not come easily. That it was local and specific. That a peasant who did not believe in the Church, its foolishness or its saints, to quote a country priest, could share in local reverence and worship Saint Eutropius. That men who would not go to mass would undertake long pilgrimages to be healed or to have their beasts healed. And that, in one way or another, religious practices were interwoven with every part of life, but hardly in a manner that one would call specifically Christian. Leaving aside the entertainment that these practices offered, divinity was associated with vast unknown areas. God and saints—like fairies—possessed knowledge that was forbidden to men. They had to be propitiated and persuaded to perform tasks that men accomplish only imperfectly (like healing) or not at all (like controlling the weather). The more men came to master such tasks, plumb the unknown, shake the tree of knowledge, the less they needed intercessors.

The sales of the *saint vinage* at Miremont declined, to the despair of the sexton. In Sologne good Saint Viâtre, who had done so much to heal the local fevers (malaria), was badly hurt by the spreading use of quinine and by the drainage and sanitation projects beginning to show results in the 1880's. At Hévillers (Meuse) the priest read the Lord's Passion every day from May to September "to bring heaven's blessing on the goods of the earth"; then, before Christmas, the church treasurer went from door to door to collect grain in payment for this service. In the 1850's the treasurer got 800 lbs and more. By 1888...he garnered only 330. Things were worse still in Périgord, where the popularity of Saint John the Baptist, whose accompanying lamb had made him the patron of the local sheepruns, declined with the century....

...The observance of Rogation week declined—even in Brittany. The turn of the century saw fewer processions across the village fields with cross, banners, and bells to drive off evil spirits and to bless the crops. In the Limousin, where in 1876 many peasants still reckoned their age according to ostensions—great septennial processions with scores of villages in their entirety parading behind relics, drums, and banners—the emotional content gradually seeped away, and the penitents in their colorful costumes disappeared; and new religious groups that borrowed nothing from the old traditions meant little to the popular public. . . .

Local pilgrimages of the popular sort leveled off or declined. Some were domesticated into the Marian cult. Others were suppressed because they gave rise to scandalous practices, as when Morvan women seeking a cure for barrenness too often found it in adjacent woods; or because they always brought disorders, like the wrestlers' *pardon* of Saint Cadou at Gouesnac'h (Finistère) that never failed to end in fights and brawls. The mercantile activities that had grown around traditional devotions killed them, like trees stifled by ivy. Easter Sunday processions had to be given up in some places because the streets and squares were too crowded with stalls and carrousels. Tourists and sightseers helped to keep observances alive as pure pageantry, but finally, "when everyone wants to watch the procession, there is no one left to take part in it." Between the wars, automobiles denied the roads to those pilgrimages traditionally made on horseback, and the enclosure of fields discouraged them. In 1939 the *Courier du Finistère*[12] noted that the traditional procession stopped at the wires barring access to the ancient chapel of Saint-Roch at Landeleau. "What is the use in destroying the grass of a field to enter a building in ruins and without a roof?" No such reasoning could have been accepted half a century earlier.

Yet phosphates, chemical fertilizers, and schooling had spelled the beginning of the end. In 1893, a drought year in Bourbonnais when many men were having masses said for their emaciated cattle (which died anyway), the priest reproached Henry Norre, a self-taught man who farmed not far from Cérilly, for not attending church. "I haven't got the time," he answered. "And really, I haven't got much confidence in your remedies for the beasts. My remedies are better; you can check." Daniel Halévy[13] quotes another story about Norre. This time the farmer returned from the railway station with a cartful of fertilizer and met the priest. "What are you carting there?" "Chemicals." "But that is very bad; they burn the soil!" "Monsieur le curé,"[14] said Norre, "I've tried everything. I've had masses said and got no profit from them. I've bought chemicals and they worked. I'll stick to the better merchandise." It was the requiem of nineteenth-century religion.

[12] A newspaper.
[13] French historian.
[14] Chief parish priest.

Infanticide: A Historical Survey

WILLIAM L. LANGER

It has been suggested that one cause of the population increase in the late nineteenth century was a decline in the practice of infanticide. By now infanticide is rare enough in Western civilization to merit newspaper coverage, and it is difficult to imagine how pervasive infanticide was until recently. William Langer briefly traces the history of the murder of children, looking at methods of killing as well as cultural assumptions that justified the disposal of unwanted infants.

In some societies infanticide was an acceptable practice. Other societies condemned infanticide, but saw large portions of the population disobeying the ban. What socioeconomic conditions induced parents to get rid of infants? What intellectual arguments defended the practice of infanticide? Why were cultures more likely to eliminate female rather than male infants? (Here infanticide becomes a part of the history of women.) Langer's account is depressing reading for those of us accustomed to revere infants, but there were some historical developments that made infanticide unacceptable. Which societies forbade the practice? When infanticide was illegal, it became a gender-linked crime—why did European courts punish mothers and not fathers?

The nineteenth century saw important changes in the history of infanticide. What role did the Industrial Revolution play in this story? Why did foundling hospitals, intended to alleviate the problem of unwanted children, prove not to be an effective reform? The situation in Victorian England became a public scandal, and English society moved to abolish infanticide. Who killed Victorian babies, and why? What ended the widespread practice?

Infanticide is linked to the history of the family, and other changes in the family are related to the successful but not total abolition of infanticide. People married more often for love than had been the custom; affection bound children to parents as well as husbands to wives. These have been gradual, long-term processes that are among the most significant changes in Western civilization.

Infanticide, that is, the willful destruction of newborn babes through exposure, starvation, strangulation, smothering, poisoning, or through the use of some lethal weapon, has been viewed with abhorrence by Christians almost from the beginning of their era. Although often held up to schoolchildren as an abomination practiced by the Chinese or other Asians, its role in Western civilization, even in modern times, has rarely been suggested by historians, sociologists or even demographers.

Yet in these days of world population crisis there can hardly be a more important historical question than that of the chronically superfluous population growth and the methods by which humanity has dealt with it. Among non-Christian peoples (with the exception of the Jews) infanticide has from time immemorial been the accepted procedure for disposing not only of deformed or sickly infants, but of all such newborns as might strain the resources of the individual family or the larger community. At the present day it is still employed by so-called underdeveloped peoples in the effort to keep the population in reasonable adjustment to the available food supply. Among the Eskimos of Arctic Canada, for instance, many babies are set out on the ice to freeze if the father or elder of the tribe decides that they would be a continuing drain on the means of subsistence.

In ancient times, at least, infanticide was not a legal obligation. It was a practice freely discussed and generally condoned by those in authority and ordinarily left to the decision of the father as the responsible head of the family. Modern humanitarian sentiment makes it difficult to recapture the relatively detached attitude of the parents towards their offspring. Babies were looked upon as the unavoidable result of normal sex relations, often as an undesirable burden rather than as a blessing. More girls than boys were disposed of, presumably to keep down the number of potential mothers as well as in recognition of the fact that they would never contribute greatly to the family income. . . .

The attitude of the ancient Greeks in this matter is well reflected in the pronouncements of Plato and Aristotle. The former favored the careful regulation of all sex relations, so as to produce the most perfect type of human being, while Aristotle was more concerned with the problem of population pressure. With its limited resources, ancient Greece, according to a modern authority, "lived always under the shadow of the fear of too many mouths to feed." Neglect of this problem by many city-states was denounced by Aristotle as "a never-failing cause of poverty among the citizens, and poverty was the parent of revolution." He firmly contended that the size of the population should be limited by law and suggested that abortion might be preferable to exposure as a method of control.

In Hellenistic Greece, infanticide, chiefly in the form of exposure of female babies, was carried to such an extent that the average family was exceptionally small. Parents rarely reared more than one daughter, with the result that there was an altogether abnormal discrepancy in the numbers of the sexes.

The practice of the Hellenistic Greeks was continued under Roman rule and probably influenced Roman attitudes. After all, Rome itself was traditionally founded by the exposed youngsters, Romulus and Remus, who were saved from their certain fate by the nursing of a friendly wolf. Throughout the Republic and long after the authority of the father over his family had worn thin, unwanted children continued to be disposed of in the accepted way. It was thought altogether natural that proletarians, poverty-stricken and hopeless, should protect themselves from further responsibility. As among the Greeks, there was a marked disparity between the sexes, which suggests that many bastards and a substantial number of female infants were abandoned if not murdered by drowning. . . . Edward Gibbon, writing in the late eighteenth century on *The Decline and Fall of the Roman*

Empire, denounced this exposure of children as "the prevailing and stubborn vice of antiquity," and charged the Roman Empire with being "stained with the blood of infants." . . .

A decisive change of attitude came with Christianity. The Church fathers were undoubtedly, in this respect as in others, influenced by Judaic Law which, while it did not mention infanticide specifically in the discussion of murder, was always interpreted by Rabbinical Law as an equivalent. . . . Increasingly, Christian leaders thundered against infanticide as a pagan practice and insisted that all human life be held inviolable. Yet it was only with the triumph of Christianity that the Emperor Constantine in 318 A.D. declared the slaying of a son or daughter by a father to be a crime, and only at the end of the fourth century that the Emperors Valentinian, Valens, and Gratian made infanticide a crime punishable by death.

While the contribution of Christian theologians to the adoption of a more humane attitude is obvious, it should be remembered that the later Roman Empire apparently suffered from progressive depopulation, due to devastating epidemics, recurrent famines and general disorder. Under the circumstances there was clearly no need to limit population growth. On the contrary, increased fertility was desired. Hence the repetition of the exhortation of the Bible: "Be fruitful and multiply." Until the late eighteenth century at least, when the great upswing of the European population set in, large families were the fashion, being regarded as the blessing of a benevolent deity.

Yet there can be little doubt that child murder continued to be practiced, even in the most advanced countries of western Europe. Lecky,[1] in his *History of European Morals* (1869), speaks of the popular distinction in the early Middle Ages between infanticide and exposure, the latter offense not being punishable by law: "It was practiced on a gigantic scale with absolute impunity, noticed by writers with most frigid indifference and, at least in the case of destitute parents, considered a very venial offence."

Until the sixteenth century, and in some places until much later, the unenviable task of dealing with the problem was left to the Church authorities. In the hope of reducing the exposure and almost certain death of newborn children (especially girls), foundling hospitals were opened in the eighth century in Milan, Florence, Rome, and other cities. But these institutions proved to be ineffectual, since most of the children had to be sent to the country to be nursed, and the majority soon succumbed either through neglect or more positive action on the part of the wet-nurses.

Infanticide by out-and-out violence of various kinds was probably always exceptional. Throughout European history the authorities were baffled and frustrated primarily by the many cases of reputed suffocation, the "overlaying" or "overlying" of an infant in bed by its allegedly drunken parents. This could and surely did occur accidentally, but the suspicion,

---

[1]William E. H. Lecky, Irish historian and philosopher, 1838–1903.

always present and usually warranted, was that of intentional riddance of an unwanted child. Since it was impossible to prove premeditated crime, the authorities contented themselves with the imposition of penance in the case of married women, who were condemned to live for at least a year on bread and water. The unwed mothers and the presumed witches, however, were to bear the brunt as examples and admonitions. A girl known to have committed infanticide in any form might be absolved by pleading insanity, but was otherwise condemned to suffer the death penalty, usually in the most diabolical imaginable manner. Medieval sources tell of women being tied in a sack, along with a dog, a cock, or some other uncongenial companion and thrown into the river for a supreme struggle for life. This method was probably never in general use, and in any case seems to have been abandoned by the end of the Middle Ages. A detailed analysis of the court and prison records of Nürnberg from 1513 to 1777 lists by name eighty-seven women executed for infanticide, all but four of them unmarried girls who had committed violent murder. Prior to 1500 the penalty in Nürnberg as in most of Germany was burial alive, often with gruesome refinements. During the sixteenth century the usual method was drowning, and after 1580 decapitation. Hangings were quite exceptional. It was hardly worse, however, than being buried alive, being drowned or decapitated, penalties which continued to be practiced, though less and less frequently, until the nineteenth century.

In any case, overlaying continued to be a vexing problem until modern times. In 1500, the Bishop of Fiesole set fines and penalties for parents who kept babies in bed with them. In the eighteenth century, a Florentine craftsman designed a basket frame...which would protect the child from smothering. An Austrian decree of 1784 forbade having children under the age of five in bed with parents, and Prussian legislation of 1794 reduced the age of the infants to two.

Government authorities were apparently no more successful than the clergy in checking the practice of overlaying, at least among married couples. One may safely assume that in the eighteenth and nineteenth centuries the poor, hardly able to support the family they already had, evaded responsibility by disposing of further additions. But by the eighteenth century another form of infanticide became so prevalent that governments were at their wits' end in their efforts to combat it. For reasons too complex and still too obscure, there was a marked increase in sexual immorality, in seduction, and in illegitimacy. The evidence suggests that in all European countries, from Britain to Russia, the upper classes felt perfectly free to exploit sexually girls who were at their mercy. As late as 1871, Mr. Cooper, the Secretary of the Society for the Rescue of Young Women and Children, testified before a Parliamentary Committee that at least nine out of ten of the girls in trouble were domestic servants: "in many instances the fathers of their children are their masters, or their masters' sons, or their masters' relatives, or their masters' visitors." To be sure, lords of the manor often recognized the offspring as their own and raised them as members of the family. But in the new factory towns foremen favored amenable girls for employment. Young aristocrats, too, were much to blame. When traveling they expected to find relaxation with the chamber maids of the inn. It seems to have been taken for granted that the upper classes were entitled to the favors of pretty girls of the lower classes and that fornication was looked upon as an inevitable aspect of lower class life.

Yet if a girl became pregnant, she was left to shift for herself. She at once became an object of obloquy and might well be whipped out of the village by the more fortunate members of her sex. Many sought anonymity and aid in the cities, where professional midwives would, for a pittance, not only perform an abortion or deliver the child, but would also undertake to nurse and care for it, it being fully understood that the mother would not need to worry further about it. Starvation or a dose of opiates would settle the child's fate in a matter of days.

Naturally all girls in trouble were not willing to resort to so drastic a solution. There was always the possibility, admittedly slim, that if the unwanted baby were left on the steps of a church or mansion, it might stir the sympathies of a stranger and be adopted by him, as was Tom Jones by Squire Allworthy.[2] Many young mothers therefore bundled up their offspring, and left them at churches or other public places. In the late seventeenth century, St. Vincent de Paul[3] was so appalled by the number of babies to be seen daily on the steps of Notre Dame that he appealed to ladies of the court to finance an asylum for foundlings. His efforts soon inspired others to similar action, and before long most large towns in Catholic Europe had established similar institutions. In England a retired sea captain, Thomas Coram, was so depressed by the daily sight of infant corpses thrown on the dust heaps of London that he devoted seventeen years in soliciting support for a foundling hospital. Eventually a group of his supporters petitioned the King to charter a Foundling Hospital so as "to prevent the frequent murders of poor, miserable infants at their birth," and "to suppress the inhuman custom of exposing new-born infants to perish in the streets."

The story of the foundling hospitals is too long and complicated to be more than sketched here. For a time they were the favorite charity of the wealthy and huge sums were expended in lavish construction and equipment. Although the London and Paris hospitals were the best known, the establishment at St. Petersburg, actively patronized by the imperial court, was undoubtedly the most amazing.... It was housed in the former palaces of Counts Razumovski and Bobrinski and occupied a huge tract in the very center of St. Petersburg. By the mid-1830s, it had 25,000 children on its rolls and was admitting 5000 newcomers annually. Since no questions were asked and the place was attractive, almost half of the newborn babies were

---

[2]In *Tom Jones* (1749), a novel by Henry Fielding (1707–1754).

[3]French priest (1580–1660) famous for his charitable activity.

deposited there by their parents. A dozen doctors and 600 wet-nurses were in attendance to care for the children during the first six weeks, after which they were sent to peasant nurses in the country. At the age of six (if they survived to that age) they were returned to St. Petersburg for systematic education. The program was excellent, but its aims were impossible to achieve. Despite all excellent management and professional efforts, thirty to forty percent of the children died during the first six weeks and hardly a third reached the age of six.

The chronicle of the hospitals everywhere was one of devoted effort but unrelieved tragedy. The assignment was simply impossible to carry out. Everywhere they were besieged by mostly unwed mothers eager to dispose of their babies without personally or directly committing infanticide. Even so, actual child murder appears to have continued to an alarming extent, due to the fear of many girls of being identified at the hospital. Napoleon therefore decreed (January 18, 1811) that there should be hospitals in every departement of France, and that each should be equipped with a turntable (*tour*), so that the mother or her agent could place the child on one side, ring a bell, and have a nurse take the child by turning the table, the mother remaining unseen and unquestioned.

Although it is agreed that Napoleon's provision of *tours* helped to diminish the number of outright child murders, it meant that the hospitals were swamped with babies. It was impossible to find enough wet-nurses for even a short period, and most of the infants had to be shipped off to the country at once. Relatively few survived the long journey over rough roads in crude carts, and those happy few generally succumbed before long due to the ignorant treatment or the intentional or unintentional neglect of their foster parents. Small wonder that Malthus[4] referred to the asylums as "these horrible receptacles," while others spoke freely of "legalized infanticide." In the years 1817–1820, the number of foundlings in charge of the Paris hospital, many of them brought in from the provinces, and, interestingly, about a third of them children of married couples, was about equal to a third of all babies born in Paris in that period. Of 4779 infants admitted in 1818, 2370 died in the first three months. It would be unjust, no doubt, to put the entire blame for this situation on the foundling hospitals. Many of the infants were diseased or half dead when they arrived, and we may well believe that prior to the nineteenth century many newborn babies would in any event have succumbed to the methods of clothing and feeding then still in vogue.

By 1830, the situation in France had become desperate. In 1833 the number of babies left with the foundling hospitals reached the fantastic figure of 164,319. Authorities were all but unanimous in the opinion that the introduction of the *tours* had been disastrous, that they had, in fact, put a premium on immorality. Thereupon the *tours* were gradually abolished until by 1862 only five were left. Instead, the government embarked upon

---

[4]Thomas Malthus (1766–1834), English economist.

a program of outside aid to unwed mothers. Presumably the growing practice of birth control and the advances made in pediatrics also contributed to the reduction in infant mortality.

The story of the foundlings in England was no less tragic than that of France. The London Foundling Hospital (opened in 1741) was intended for the reception of London children only, but the pressure for admissions soon became so great as to give rise "to the disgraceful scene of women scrambling and fighting to get to the door, that they might be of the fortunate few to reap the benefit of the Asylum." Under the circumstances Parliament in 1756 provided a modest grant on condition that the hospital be open to all comers, but that at the same time asylums for exposed or deserted young children be opened in all counties, ridings, and divisions of the kingdom. Parish officers promptly took advantage of the act to empty their workhouses of infant poor and dump them on the new hospices, while others had them shipped to London. By 1760, the London Hospital was deluged with 4229 newcomers, making a total of 14,934 admissions in the preceding four years. It was impossible to cope with the situation, and "instead of being a protection to the living, the institution became, as it were, a charnel-house for the dead." In 1760, Parliament reversed itself by putting an end to indiscriminate admissions and returned the care of the provincial foundlings to the parishes. The London Hospital soon became more of an orphanage than a foundling asylum. By 1850, it had only 460 children and admitted only 77 annually.

The parish officers were helpless in the face of the problem. A law of 1803 specified that charges of infanticide must be tried according to the same rules of evidence as applied to murder, while yet another law required that "it must be proved that the entire body of the child has actually been born into the world in a living state, and the fact of its having breathed is not conclusive proof thereof. There must be independent circulation in the child before it can be accounted alive." In other words, to kill a child by crushing its head with a hairbrush or hammer, or cutting its throat was technically not a crime, so long as its lower extremities were still in the body of the mother. Since the required evidence was all but impossible to obtain, infanticide could be committed almost with impunity. In any case, juries refused, even in the most flagrant cases, to convict the offender, holding that capital punishment was far too harsh a penalty to pay when the real culprit was usually the girl's seducer. So infanticide flourished in England. . . . Dr. Lankester, one of the coroners for Middlesex, charged that even the police seemed to think no more of finding a dead child than of finding a dead dog or cat. There were, he asserted, hundreds, nay thousands of women living in London who were guilty of having at one time or another destroyed their offspring, without having been discovered.

By the mid-century the matter had become one of public scandal. One doctor in 1846 commented on "the great indifference displayed by parents and others in the lower ranks of life with regard to infant life." Women employed in the factories and fields had no choice but to leave their babies in the care of professional nurses, sometimes called "killer nurses," who made short shrift of their charges by generous doses of opiates.

Worse yet was the revelation that some women enrolled their infants in Burial Clubs, paying a trifling premium until, after a decent interval, the child died of starvation, ill-usage, or poisoning. They then collected £3 to £5 by way of benefit. Cases were reported of women who had membership for their babies in ten or more clubs, reaping a rich return at the proper time.

The institution of "killer nurses" or "angel-makers" eventually became known as "baby-farming." By 1860, it had become the subject of lively agitation, both in lay and in professional circles. In 1856, Dr. William B. Ryan was awarded a gold medal by the London Medical Society for his essay on "Infanticide in its Medical-Legal Relations." He followed this two years later by an address on "Child Murder in its Sanitary and Social Bearings," delivered before the Liverpool Association for the Promotion of Social Science....

A survey of the British press in the 1860s reveals the frequent findings of dead infants under bridges, in parks, in culverts and ditches, and even in cesspools. The *Standard* in 1862 denounced "this execrable system of wholesale murder," while the *Morning Star* in 1863 asserted that "this crime is positively becoming a national institution." In Parliament an outraged member declared that the country seemed to be reveling in "a carnival of infant slaughter, to hold every year a massacre of the Innocents."

In February, 1867, Dr. Curgeven, Dr. Ryan, and a formidable delegation of medical men from the elite Harveian Society called upon the Home Secretary with a lengthy list of specific recommendations for checking the increase in infanticide, with emphasis on the need for the registration of all child nurses and for annual reports on all "baby farms." The government acted with no more than its habitual alacrity, and it was only in 1870 that it was further pressed by the Infant Protection Society founded by Dr. Curgeven and when the country was shocked by the news that in Brixton and Peckham two women were discovered to have left no fewer than sixteen infant corpses in various fairly obvious places. The women were tried for murder and one of them was convicted and executed. Parliament at long last set up a committee to study the best means "of preventing the destruction of the lives of infants put out to nurse for hire by their parents." It can hardly have come as a surprise to the members that babies commonly died through being given improper or insufficient food, opiates, drugs, etc. In many baby-farms they were in crowded rooms, with bad air, and suffered from want of cleanliness and willful neglect, resulting in diarrhea, convulsions, and wasting away. The evidence was more than enough to induce Parliament to pass in 1872 the first Infant Life Protection Act providing for compulsory registration of all houses in which more than one child under the age of one were in charge for more than twenty-four hours. Each such house was required to have a license issued by a justice of the peace, and all deaths, including still-births, which had not previously been recorded, were to be reported at once. The penalty for violation of the law was to be a fine of £5 or imprisonment for six months.

Less was heard or written about infanticide in the last quarter of the nineteenth and in the twentieth century. This was certainly a reflection of the beneficial results of the abolition of the *tours* in France, Belgium, and other countries, and of the increasingly stringent regulations in Britain. But credit must also be given to the growing public interest in maternity and child care, and to the progress in pediatrics which contributed to the reduction of the high infant mortality rate. Finally, consideration must also be given to the adoption and spread of contraceptive practices, even among the lower classes. Nonetheless, infanticide continued and still persists, albeit on a much lower scale. The ignorance and recklessness of many young people, and initially the expense and inconvenience of contraceptive devices made the unwed mother and the illegitimate child a continuing social problem. Only since the Second World War has the contraceptive pill, the intrauterine devices, and the legalization of abortion removed all valid excuses for unwanted pregnancy or infanticide. To the extent that these problems still exist, at least in western society, they are due primarily to carelessness, ignorance, or indifference.

Crime and Punishment in the Russian Village: Rural Concepts of Criminality at the End of the Nineteenth Century

CATHY FRIERSON

One hallmark of the modern state is a national system of justice, whereby a centralized organization of courts and a national legislated or common body of law substituted for the previous local courts and laws. In the 1860s Russia implemented a thorough judicial reform establishing a system of justice modeled on western European systems. For the peasantry there were special courts that dealt exclusively with cases between peasants. The peasants did make use of these courts, but they often chose to ignore them in order to mete out their own rough justice. Why did the peasants sometimes bypass the formal judicial system and take matters into their own hands? How did they understand crime and punishment?

In the worldview of the peasants, what was the link between morality and legality? That is, to what extent did they believe immoral behavior to be illegal or illegal actions to be immoral? Did they believe they were acting in legal fashion when beating, mutilating, and killing suspected criminals? How did personal harm, the notion of sin, premeditation, and community affect the definition of a crime or the punishment of an offender? Often, the peasantry did not accept the Russian state's definition of what characterized a crime. Which state crimes appeared to the peasantry to be blameless? How did the peasants determine the seriousness of a crime? Did a person's social standing or religion affect his or her guilt? What role in dispensing justice did God have, according to the peasants?

This article shows implicitly if not explicitly that whereas the French government was able to turn French peasants into Frenchmen in the nineteenth century, the Russian state did not turn Russian peasants into Russians. The Russian peasants' view of the world was still extremely localized—they regarded even peasants from a neighboring village as aliens, to say nothing of the Westernized upper classes or of different minority groups, such as Jews. In short, the peasants lacked a national identity, which the czarist government failed to inculcate in the overwhelming majority of subjects in imperial Russia. This failure to instill nationalism (that is, patriotism) may help to explain the rapid collapse of the government during the Russian Revolution.

Frierson provides a means to understand the Russian peasants' legal consciousness and worldview. The peasants could be brutal, but they were flexible, had clearly defined norms of justice, and were extremely religious. They took into account the reasons for a crime as well as the personal situation of the accused. Do you find their justice superior or inferior to that of a more inflexible state system that operated according to written legal codes?

On 23 April 1873, the peasant Kuz'ma Rudchenko was found near the village of Brusovka. His head was completely crushed, his hands had been chopped off, and the plank that had been used to beat him had been thrust through his anus, piercing the full length of his body and extruding from his gaping mouth. In 1881, in the village of Mukhovitsie, Kiev province, peasants apprehended a thief and sliced the tendons in his right leg and left hand. In the same year and province, in the village of Iazvinkie, the peasants carved a special toothed stake, so that it resembled a series of arrowheads on one shaft. They then shoved it up the rectum of a suspected thief, with the arrows positioned so that he could not remove it.

These episodes were particularly brutal instances of *samosud*, the rural practice through which peasants took matters into their own hands and settled with a suspected offender through physical punishment, shaming, or exacting compensation. *Samosud*—literally, judging by oneself—was one example of the peculiarities of rural justice in Russia at the end of the nineteenth century. At a time when central authorities, local officials, and legal specialists actively debated the possibility and means of developing a respect for formal legality among the peasant population, the persistence of *samosud* in the village was an eloquent reminder that crime and punishment had specific and well-established meaning in rural culture.

Violent acts of *samosud* were only the most spectacular manifestations of rural, traditional legal consciousness, a subject of considerable interest and public debate for the last thirty years of the nineteenth century in Russia. Local observers reported various practices that combined to form the peasant's approach to misconduct in the village, to set his criteria for deciding the seriousness of the deed and the harshness of its punishment. This essay explores rural attitudes toward criminality and the elements of the peasant's world view that identified acts as criminal offenses, rather than as civil offenses or as sins. . . .

In the question of rural concepts of criminality, as in other questions about the Russian village, the issue of regional variation must be considered. Much was made at the end of the century of the localism of customary law, of the absence of any consistent norms from one village to the next on how to resolve conflict or to right wrongs. The sources for this study allow comparison from region to region on attitudes toward crime, sin, and wrongdoing. There was less variation than one might expect, a fact that suggests that customs and beliefs in this area of peasant life were not as subject to geographic, climatic, and economic regional differences as were responses to disputes involving contracts, property exchange, and other civil matters. . . .

Just as it is important to address the question of regional variation, so it is critical to keep the entire canvas of village existence in mind when discussing criminality. Rural concepts of criminality clearly were interwoven into the intricate fabric of rural life. Often, peasant attitudes toward what constituted crime bore the marks of other currents in village culture. Three such themes that resonate throughout the discussion of wrongdoing are the strong link between morality and legality in the village, the importance of family and community as the peasant's immediate universe, and the function of labor in defining concepts of property, damage, and injury. Beyond the conceptual framework of rural life also existed the world of the formal legality of the Russian Empire, the *zakonnost'*, which was increasingly penetrating the peasant's world toward the end of the century. The channel for that penetration was the reformed *volost'* court[1] under the supervision of the land captain. . . . By 1903 many local observers reported that the civil code had become so much the authority for the *volost'* court that the latter had virtually ceased to represent local customary law. As an example of dualism not only between the village and the educated world, but also within the village itself, peasants showed a growing willingness to take petty civil disputes to the *volost'* court at the same time that they continued to handle serious wrongdoing on their own terms outside the formal system. This dualism suggests that rural concepts of criminality held firm at the end of the century and continued to inform peasants' actions in dealing with misdeeds in their community.

---

[1]A *volost'* is a rural district. The *volost'* courts were established in the 1860s to deal with civil offenses among the peasantry.

This dualism also meant that the peasant's attitude toward law and order seemed divided, or "schizophrenic" as one observer described it, and did not offer much promise for the development of legal consciousness among the rural population, a goal held dear by *obshchestvo*.[2] Legal consciousness could mean either side of the peasant's concept of legality, however. As it was usually understood, it meant respect for the formal legal system of the Russian state and, thus, a recognition of law as a system of norms to be applied across the empire. Or, it could mean the set of concepts governing the resolution of conflict in the village and the approach to serious wrongdoing in the community. One can say that the peasants lacked formal legal consciousness but not that they lacked any legal consciousness at all. As the following discussion will show, there did exist in the villages across Russia a set of concepts, one can say norms, that, however they may have differed from the laws of the empire, functioned as a form of legality in the execution of justice in the village.

... [P]easants defined crime primarily in terms of four criteria: personal harm, sin, premeditation, and membership of the offender or victim in the community. The combination of these criteria for assessing acts within the peasant's world had the effect of particularizing both the offense and the judgment. It also had the effect of separating the world of peasant justice from that of the rest of the Russian population. While these criteria and the tenets or principles of the formal legal code were not necessarily mutually exclusive, the practice of customary law for criminal offenses was quite distinct from official legality in that innocence or guilt was assigned in terms of local criteria, according to the specific details of the given case, with no reference to, and often in defiance of, formal criminal procedure.

The offense of wood poaching highlights the criteria for deciding criminality in the village. When wood poaching consisted of peasants' theft of wood from the forest of the landlord or the state, peasants either did not consider it an offense at all or viewed it as so minor an infraction that it called for very light punishment. Rather than viewing the gathering of wood from another man's forest as theft—that is, perceiving the act first in the context of a broader system of criminality that identified seizure of another's property as stealing—the peasant appraised the nature of the act both in terms of the offender and the victim. In other words, no prescriptive norm in the rural consciousness identified theft as an offense that of its very nature called for an established reprisal. Instead, the peasants judged the act according to its effect and its motivation.

Because the peasant consistently personalized events in his world, his first question in the case of wood poaching was who took wood from whose land and who suffered as a result? When the forest belonged to the state, the peasant saw no issue of theft whatsoever, because the state was not a person who could suffer any harm from the loss of a few cords of wood.

[2]Educated society.

If the forest belonged to the peasants' former landlord, who had received it after the Emancipation,[3] the peasants also dismissed the issue of theft. Here, the village community simply rejected the notion that the landlord had the right to charge them for wood that they had gathered freely under serfdom. In the peasants' eyes, the individual landowner who had acres of forestland at his disposal had more wood than he could possibly need so no personal harm had resulted from the seizure of the wood. Furthermore, the concept of possession through labor came into play. If anyone had a claim on the wood from the forest, it was the man who labored to gather it. Thus, the peasant who chopped and hauled the lumber had the preeminent claim. Neither the state nor the landlord qualified as victims of loss or harm in the peasant's perceptions, because, "God grew the forest for everyone."

Within the peasant community, however, when one peasant took wood from another peasant's forest, the peasants were willing to recognize the act of theft as an offense. But the very act of stealing did not elicit a set response. The intent of the thief determined the form of punishment. If a peasant chopped wood in another man's forest, fully aware that he was on another man's property, he had to deliver all of the wood to the rightful owner. If, however, he could convince the community that he had trespassed unwittingly, he still had to return the wood to the rightful owner, who, in turn, had to pay him for his labor. The fluidity of sentences indicated that the aim was not so much to punish the offender for breaking a community code as it was to erase the harm of the deed. Even within the village, itself, then, wood poaching was not a criminal act once the offender repaid the victim. . . .

This example also illustrates that beyond personal harm, premeditation and personal need on the part of the offender contributed to the level of criminality of the deed. For the peasant, justice was not and should not be blind, but subjective. Justice should not follow some abstract system of law simply because it carried the tsar's authority but should consider the character of the individuals involved, the circumstances of the case, the effect of the deed, and the effect on the community of any punishment.

Although peasants were likely to deny their liability before the imperial legal system, they did recognize a higher court: the judgment of God Almighty. One of the most consistent observations from across central Russia was that in rural belief God was a ubiquitous, omniscient, and wrathful judge and that acts against God or his church would receive his punishment without fail, in this life or the next. This perception of God as both the ever-present witness and the ultimate judge was part of the conflation—contemporaries would term it confusion—of morality and legality in the rural consciousness. When faced with wrongdoing in the community, peasants seemed to assign the label of crime simultaneously with the label of sin. Sin as a concept affecting the execution of justice involved more than an infraction against

---

[3]The freeing of the Russian serfs in 1861.

God's law. For, sin had two separate meanings in the peasant's world view. The first included acts that violated the religious order. Through this definition, peasants identified and punished as crimes some offenses that did not concern the state. The most common of these involved working on holy days.

The other meaning of sin incorporated, again, the critical element of identifiable personal injury or loss, and the element of selfish premeditation. Those acts that were most harmful were most sinful and, thus, through this logic, most criminal. The relative position of the offender and the victim again came into play. To steal from the rich, for example, was not criminal, while to steal from the poor was. Similarly, to commit an act against someone who had caused harm to the perpetrator was significantly less serious than to act against a friend or someone who had once assisted the actor. One effect of this view of crime through the prism of sin was that it dismissed many offenses that the state identified as crimes. The example of wood poaching illustrates this attitude. Similar offenses included pasturing livestock on another man's land; gathering mushrooms, berries, or apples from a wealthy neighbor; fishing from a pond on another's property. Such acts the peasants made no effort to conceal from each other, although they did conceal them from the formal authorities. They recognized that these acts broke the formal law, but they felt no obligation to punish or report them. The proverb "God punishes sins, and the state punishes guilt" expressed the peasants' division of offenses that came under God's and the state's purview. Their level of participation in rural justice was largely limited to those deeds that they viewed as sins; they remained indifferent to offenses that called for the state's punishment as long as they were personally unaffected by the crime.

The evil of the crime, and the likelihood that the peasants would take action to punish it, increased under either of two circumstances: if it were clear to the community that the guilty party had planned and committed a harmful act solely to increase his own wealth or to serve his own material interests or if the crime had caused harm to a member of the immediate community. That peasants assessed the seriousness of crime according to the participation of, or effect on, the members of the community reflected strong division in their legal consciousness between laws for insiders and laws for outsiders.

Premeditation and personal gain as elements that increased the seriousness of a crime were particularly striking in cases of theft and murder. The time when the crime took place served as one indication of premeditation. . . . [C]rimes committed at night were considered more serious than those committed in the daytime, because they revealed previous planning and because evil attitudes motivated them. "At the basis of such crimes, there often lie bad sentiments—hatred, greed, envy," the peasants of the Cherepovetskii district in Novgorod explained. Those . . . who stated that, on the contrary, crimes committed during the day were more serious in the peasants' view also pointed to premeditation and added shamelessness as another factor. Peasants in Novgorod explained that thefts committed during the day showed of the criminal that "he has lost not only fear of God, but of man also.... He has lost his sense of shame." In a less obvious way, the offender's position in the community also contributed to the degree of premeditation his neighbors would assign to his wrongdoing. Again from the Cherepovetskii district came the report that peasants judged the offender more harshly if he were educated or well situated in the village, because the former quality should have prevented him from taking unjust actions and the latter protected him from want. Clearheadedness, education, and relative prosperity put a peasant above the need to commit serious offenses in the pursuit of personal gain.

The inverse was also true. Crimes of passion or as the result of drunkenness were less serious because passion and alcohol blurred man's reason and the possibility of premeditation. These crimes the peasants were likely to excuse from earthly punishment, while believing that they may indeed have been sins. Such misfortunes did not call for man's judgment, however, and the community left the matter to God. To illustrate this, N. Kuznetsov[4] reported from the Smolensk region that in his area the villagers had taken no action to report or punish a woman who had murdered her husband's lover upon discovering them in flagrante delicto. They admitted that she had sinned but refrained from punishing her themselves or from delivering her to the government for trial by the formal code. The importance of premeditation as a sign of criminality was evident in two other patterns. The first was that an attempted or threatened act often received the same punishment as it would if it had been carried out. Second, in the event of a crime that resulted from conspiracy among several people, the community also often assigned equal or greater guilt to those who organized or ordered the act than to those who actually committed it.

Misdeeds that occurred during a ritual of customary belief were also unlikely to fall into the category of crime. Outsiders used the term *superstition* to identify this factor that could ameliorate the criminality of even the most serious of actions. P. N. Obninskii[5] described such an incident in which a husband and wife killed his mother in the process of trying to exorcise the devil from her body. Neither they nor the crowd of bystanders from the village considered them guilty of a crime. Solov'ev[6] also found that this was true in the Volga region where the murder of a suspected sorcerer or witch was not considered a crime.

When great personal harm was combined with pure self-interest, the crime was indeed serious and inexcusable. Thus, a murder that occurred in connection with a theft was perhaps the most serious of village crimes,

[4]A respondent to a questionnaire about the peasants of central Russia sent out in 1897, 1898, and 1900. The responses to this questionnaire constitute the major historical source for this article.

[5]A respondent to the late nineteenth-century questionnaire about peasant life.

[6]A respondent to the late nineteenth-century questionnaire about peasant life.

because one person took another's life simply to get hold of the victim's belongings. Solov'ev ranked the crimes of personal harm and premeditation according to their seriousness and described their usual punishments as follows:

1. For murder during a robbery: murder of the criminal, often through dismemberment.
2. Adultery, stealing another man's wife, or rape: merciless beating, sometimes with the consent of the authorities. Also, the injured husband in adultery or abandonment may himself have killed the unfaithful wife.
3. Horse theft or other major theft: torture, hanging, shooting, mortal beating, or flogging and exile from the village.

... [I]n Tambov, ... also, murder for gain topped the list, followed by murder that took place during a heated argument, and murder connected with revenge for adultery.

These measures of criminality yielded however, to another, broader indicator, that of the proximity of the crime to the members of the community. Personal harm, premeditation, and personal gain were important factors only when the victims of the crimes were peasants within the village itself. As soon as an outsider was the victim, the peasants dismissed or played down the criminality of the deed. Thus, theft from another community or deception in trade with merchants, gentry, or peasants from elsewhere were not crimes, but achievements to be lauded. Again, the examples of wood poaching, gathering fruit, and pasturing livestock on another man's land illustrate this concept. Acts of self-defense or defense of a member of one's family were also exempt from definition as criminal. Here the peasants protected anyone who was protecting "his own" in the narrowest sense from any reprisal from within the community or from the formal authorities. Even within the boundaries of the community, there could be discrimination between *own* and *other*. ... [T]he concept of community applied to the Russian Orthodox inhabitants of the area, while crimes, even murder, against non-Orthodox local dwellers, were less serious than those against the Orthodox.

Horse stealing was an extreme and illuminating example of the peasant's definition of crime in terms of insiders and outsiders. The peasant who farmed was so dependent on his horse or horses that to lose one could very well mean ruin. In the empire as a whole, there were 35,473 reported horse thefts in 1889; 13,489 of these horses were found and returned to their masters. In fact, horse stealing had become a form of cottage industry in some areas, practiced through community artels[7] of horse thieves. Herein lay the contradiction. In terms of personal harm, horse stealing ranked near the top of rural crimes. Yet, the very existence of artels of horse thieves indicated

---

[7] A Russian cooperative enterprise, usually of peasant craftsmen.

that the peasants did not punish the crime itself, but only the harm it caused for those near and dear. Thus, members of a given village were likely to harbor and protect thieves (horse thieves and others) as long as they stole from residents of other communities. Thieves who had the misfortune to fall into the hands of the community whose horses they stole were frequently the victims of the most violent and infamous forms of *samosud*. Reports of *samosud* appeared in local papers throughout the post-Emancipation period, usually in connection with horse theft. The custom gained notoriety through a sketch by Gleb Uspenskii[8] that appeared as part of his series, *From a Village Diary*. In the sixth sketch of the series, a peasant narrated the events surrounding the murder of Fedia, the horse thief. The facts of the incident were that several peasants were guarding the livestock one night when they apprehended two horse thieves as they were stealing some of the village's horses. They bound both thieves, brought them back to the village and turned to the village elder for a decision on how to deal with them.

"Beat them!" he shouted. Well, there already—already everything had gone dark before us. . . . What happened! Most sacred Ruler! Mother of God! We beat them with stones, with sticks, with reins, with shafts, one even with the axle from a cart. . . . Each one tried to give a blow, without any mercy, with whatever came to hand! . . . The crowd carried them with their own force, then dropped them—then lifted them, drove them ahead and all the while, beat them, all the while beat them: one aimed from the back, another from the front, a third came from the side—with whatever fell into his hands. . . . The beating was brutal, truly bloody. I ran for the clerk (it occurred to me that maybe something should be done according to the law). I ran back with the clerk; I saw that the people were crowding around the storehouse in the middle of the street and I heard them saying, "Look, the little one's staring!" I broke through the people—I saw— exactly, the poor guys were sitting on the ground: one older than the other, one with his back leaning against the granary, and it was as though his eyes had stopped, were motionless, only his chest was moving, like a millstone. . . . And the other, Fediushka, was groaning, was grabbing his heart. The clerk turned to the older one with the question, "Who are you? Where are you from?" That one looked, stared, and didn't say anything. . . . Oh, God, how brutal. And it was impossible for him to answer. That one fell on his face and didn't breathe. "He's died!" they said; . . . Yes—the dead one (in fact, you see, the older one had died) on his back somehow, with anything that fell. . . . "He's passing! He's passing! And the other one is passing!" they cried . . . and it was so . . . Fediushka's eyes were growing dim also. I was seized by zeal . . . "Fedia! I say, do you want to taste a little milk, and maybe you'll pull out of it." And what did he answer me to these words? "A little h-honey would . . . " he whispered barely audibly, and his spirit passed. . . .

And horror seized all of us. No one thought he was beating them to death, each one beat them for himself, for his own suffering, didn't consider that the others were also beating them. And as soon as we saw that the two were dead,

---

[8]Russian writer of novels about peasant life, c.1840–1902.

everyone was dumbfounded and seized with fear. We scattered in all directions. "Not I, not I, not I. . . . " Everyone became terrified. "Nothing will happen," Ivan Vasil'ev (the elder) said, and he ordered that a hole be dug, that grass and ice be put in it, and that the corpses be put on the ice, and fresh grass heaped on again.

In this scene, Uspenskii captured several of the elements that other observers would describe. The first was the swiftness of the execution of justice. The second was that the beating had a momentum of its own, becoming more brutal as it continued. The third was that each peasant did not necessarily aim to kill but beat in revenge for his "own suffering." Finally, the elder was confident that there would be no further repercussions from the incident. Each of these details would reappear in later portraits of *samosud*.

Twenty years after the publication of this description, . . . *samosud* continued to be a very visible aspect of justice in the village. *Samosud* represented the peasants' reaction to wrongdoing that demanded response outside of the formal legal system and could range from a simple settling of accounts for property damage to violent and spectacular reprisal. Just as they had a set of criteria to decide the criminality of a deed, so they had a set of punishments to assign according to the seriousness of the crime. . . .

Beatings and more violent acts of *samosud* were the response for the most harmful criminal offenses, primarily for horse theft. Horse thieves apparently met their unpleasant fate most often on market days when they either arrived on the stolen animals as their means of transportation or tried to sell them at the market. Typically, the horse's proper owner would recognize the horse and cry out that the suspect was a horse thief. Then the victim's fellow villagers would chase the suspect and beat him mercilessly once they caught him. The violence of the beating would escalate, often encouraged by the peasants' drunkenness. If the thief were lucky enough to survive, he was likely to be maimed as a result of the beating. Death was the surest guarantee against future trouble from the thief, as the proverb, "Ni chem vora ne uimesh', kol' do smerti ne ub'esh'"[9] proclaimed. When the peasants caught a horse thief red-handed, they usually beat him to death on the spot. One respondent[10] described such a murder in which the villagers stoned the thief to death in the forest where they apprehended him. Another described how peasants working in the field spied a thief making off with a horse from their village; they chased him down and promptly hacked him to death with their sickles. Other forms of punishment included hammering nails into the thief's head or wooden pins under the finger and toenails, hanging or mutilation, even beating the victim until he was barely conscious and then throwing him under the hooves of a frightened, charging horse. . . . [P]easants in Belorussia were careful to kill horse thieves without leaving evidence of

[9]"The only way to stop a thief is to beat him to death."
[10]To the questionnaire about the peasants of central Russia.

the murder. One such method was to crush the thief's internal organs after tying a pillow around his chest so that no external marks would be visible. Arson, another crime distinguished by the harm, even ruin, it brought the victim, could also elicit violent punishment. . . . [I]n Kaluga, if the peasants caught an arsonist in the act of setting the fire, they were likely to throw him into the blaze to burn alive. Alternatively, the arsonist could meet his maker through drowning, as was reported from the Rovenskii district of Kiev.

These forms of *samosud* were spontaneous acts of summary justice. Another pattern was more orderly and resembled posses or lynching parties. In these incidences the community gathered at an assembly and decided on the punishment. Anyone who was interested could then take part in the execution of justice, including children. While the peasants often attempted to make the punishment look like an act of individual revenge on the part of the injured party, *samosud* was almost always carried out with the full consent of the community. Such was the murder of a peasant in the Cherepovetskii district of Novgorod who had survived as a habitual petty thief, but who was murdered one evening on the village street by members of the community after he stole and resold a neighbor's horse. A similar fate met a widow in Vologda province, where she had lived on the profits of her two sons' thieving. The neighbors long had suspected them of committing the unpardonable sin of stealing within the community but did not act until they caught one son with their tea and sugar. The stolen goods themselves were not so much the issue as was committing a crime against insiders. A group of neighbors murdered the widow when she met their accusations with curses and scorn.

Iakushkin's[11] collection includes reports of organized parties from one or more villages moving against artels of horse thieves. Perhaps the most remarkable was one posse of up to a thousand peasants in Volynia who gathered together and began to travel around the region punishing suspected horse thieves, usually beating them to death. This activity continued for almost a week before the authorities intervened.

Community sentences for less serious crimes could take the forms of shaming or compensation with vodka. Petty thieves and adulterers were the usual objects of shaming. Marching through the village carrying or wearing the stolen goods before a procession of taunting neighbors was the form of shaming for thieves. . . . [I]n the Griazovetskii district of Vologda . . . a habitual thief marched through the village wearing a wheel he had stolen, accompanied by his captors who cried out repeatedly, "Thief! Thief!" Horse thieves who escaped more brutal punishment could also be shamed by being tied to the stolen horse's tail and paraded around the community.

Vodka played a frequent role in community sentencing. The guilty party often had to buy liquor for the whole village after returning any stolen goods

---

[11] E. Iakushkin's four-volume *Customary Law* contained hundreds of newspaper reports of *samosud* between 1860 and 1889.

and enduring a group beating or shaming. The Bolkhovskii district, Orel province, was the setting for an incident of *samosud* in the summer of 1898 that combined all three punishments of beating, shaming, and demanding vodka. In the village of Padimlo, a posse of peasants broke into the house of a suspected thief and found the stolen goods in his storehouse. The thief fell to his knees and begged mercy of the crowd. They agreed to forgive him in exchange for two bottles of vodka. He produced the vodka, which they proceeded to drink. Suddenly an old man began to heckle and rebuke the thief for bringing shame to their village, which would now have the reputation of being a place where neighbors stole from each other. This caught the attention of the other men who began to beat him. The thief managed to break free and run away, leaving the posse in drunken, staggering pursuit. When they realized that they had lost him, they drank up the rest of the vodka before heading back to his house. There they surrounded the dwelling, some even crawled up on the roof, and called him out to meet them. When he did so, they tied a sack of wheat around his neck and paraded him through the village. The community then demanded more vodka, threatening to turn him in to the land captain if he refused. His son ran to the tavern for another bottle. The thief finally earned release by swearing never to steal from his neighbors again and by eating earth to seal the oath.

Despite elements of the ridiculous in this scene, this incident of *samosud* illustrates several of the concepts and the reality of crime and punishment we have been discussing. The community decided to act as a group against the thief because he had stolen From his neighbors, from his own. The aim in their action was twofold: first, they wanted to neutralize the harm of the deed by finding the stolen property and returning it to its owner; second, they wanted to make the thief pay for his crime of stealing within the community. Compensation with vodka was adequate for this purpose. As they drank, however, the members of the party became inebriated and the violence escalated, with the thief escaping a brutal beating only by virtue of his swift feet. The incident then became a rather confused affair, with no real goals related to the question of wrongdoing but simply the golden opportunity for demanding more liquor. The threat to report to the land captain and the victim's speedy response indicated that this possibility was a serious, fear-inducing move that any peasant was likely to avoid at all costs, thus ensuring that the community's sentence against him would go unchallenged.

It seems that the victims of *samosud* who survived rarely reported their punishment to the formal authorities for two reasons. The first was that they did not want to have any formal court record. The second was that they anticipated a second sentence from the court for the act they had committed. This unwillingness to report *samosud* to the formal authorities ensured that its agents would themselves go unpunished and that the rural community would continue to practice summary justice for acts that they either considered unacceptably harmful or suspected were less serious in the eyes of the state than in the code of the village.

The holdings of the Tenishev Archive[12] and the published materials on village *byt* at the end of the century enable us to delineate the major features of the village's code on crime and punishment. In the most general terms, crime could take two forms: crime against an individual and crime against property. The peasants' view of crime was a rather demanding, one may say narrow, one in that a wrongful act had to satisfy several criteria before it fell into the category of criminality requiring punishment. For an act against a person to constitute a crime, the victim had to be a member of the community and had to suffer clear harm from the deed. Furthermore, the offender had to have acted with premeditation and, for the most serious deeds, to have somehow sought personal gain from his action. Similarly, for an act against property to qualify as criminal, the owner of the property had to be a member of the community who had suffered serious harm through damage to or loss of his property. In the rural world, this primarily meant that acts that appropriated or handicapped a peasant's means of subsistence were the most serious crimes. For this reason arson; horse theft; theft of food, clothing, or grain; or theft of farm implements were the acts most likely to be considered crimes harmful enough to require *samosud*.

Punishment through *samosud*, that is, through the action of the community without reference to the "other" culture of formal legality, also followed an identifiable code. The aims were to compensate for harm or loss and to prevent the repetition of the crime. The forced return of stolen goods, the replacement of damaged property, and the exaction of payment with vodka constituted the usual forms of compensation for harm or loss in cases of less serious crimes against property. For the more serious crimes, such as horse theft and arson, the primary aim was to prevent repetition, and, here, death of the offender was the surest deterrent, with a crippling beating following as a close second. Deterrence was also the motivation behind shaming that advertised to the community that such acts as petty theft and adultery were not acceptable in its moral code. Beatings, mutilation, and death as community sentences against murderers, rapists, and adulterers reveal the element of straightforward revenge, "an eye for an eye," as well as of deterrence. In these instances, passion and a harsh morality combined to determine what form justice would take in the village.

Much of the moral and legal code of the village was not unlike that of the world of formal law in Russia. There we also find that the degree of harm, premeditation, and personal gain as a motive influenced the degree of criminality and the severity of the punishment. Of the four criteria peasants used in assessing crime and assigning punishment—personal harm, premeditation, sin, and membership of the offender or victim in the community—it was the final one that most distinguished rural legal consciousness and hindered the development of respect for the formal imperial legal system. As long as peasants believed that the setting of the deed, rather than its substance or

---

[12]That is, the responses to the late nineteenth-century questionnaire about peasant life.

content, determined its criminality, they would remain indifferent to any code that defined crime and meted out punishment according to precise categories of actions with the aim of uniform application.

A Woman's World: Department Stores and the Evolution of Women's Employment, 1870–1920

THERESA M. McBRIDE

So much a fixture of Western society today, the department store is actually a quite recent innovation. It first appeared in mid-nineteenth-century Paris, revolutionizing the retail trade. How did department stores differ from traditional retail businesses? What new merchandising principles did the new stores espouse? What did the French novelist Émile Zola mean in claiming that the department store helped bring about a "new religion"? How did department stores change attitudes to and patterns of consumption?

Theresa M. McBride depicts the department store as the "world of women," of female customers and employees. The work and lives of the female clerks especially interest McBride. Who were the female clerks? Why did they choose to find employment in department stores, where the hours were long, the pace often frantic, the rules stifling, fines and dismissal constant threats, and the supervision intense? What could they hope for in their careers? It would be difficult to imagine female employees now tolerating being locked up in dining halls, forced to live in company apartments, and having their sexual lives the subject of department store concern. But the department store owners mixed capitalism with old-fashioned paternalism, combining the pursuit of profit with the enforcement of morality. The owners believed it a necessity to concern themselves with the behavior of female clerks after work.

What were the lifestyles of the female clerks? How did they spend their lives in the evenings and on Sundays? Did other women of the same social background envy their jobs and status? How did the clerks form part of the new urban leisure culture? What major changes occurred by World War I that affected women's employment in department stores?

In the 1840s Aristide Boucicaut[1] took over a small retail shop for dry goods and clothing in Paris. This shop became the "Bon Marché," the world's first department store, and soon the idea was emulated by other commercial entrepreneurs throughout the world. The department store helped to create

---

[1]Merchant and philanthropist, 1810–1877.

a "new religion," as Emile Zola[2] described the passion for consumption nurtured by the department stores' retailing revolution. As churches were being deserted, Zola argued, the stores were filling with crowds of women seeking to fill their empty hours and to find meaning for empty lives. The cult of the soul was replaced by a cult of the body—of beauty, of fashion. The department store was preeminently the "world of women," where women were encouraged to find their life's meaning in conspicuous consumption and where they increasingly found a role in selling. Thus, the department store played a highly significant role in the evolution both of contemporary society and of woman's place in that society.

The department stores came to dominate retail trade by introducing novel merchandising principles. Most obviously, they were much larger than traditional retail establishments and united a wide variety of goods under one roof; specialization was retained only in the *rayons* or departments into which the stores were divided. Department store entrepreneurs throughout the world evolved the techniques of retailing between the 1840s and 1860s, which included the important innovation of fixed pricing, and eliminated bargaining from a sale. Fixed pricing was a revolutionary concept because it altered the customary buyer-seller relationship, reducing the buyer to the role of passive consumer, whose only choice was to accept or reject the goods as offered at the set price. Even the buyer's desire for certain items was created through the tactics of large-scale retailing: publicity, display of goods, and low prices of items. The salesperson became a simple cog in the giant commercial mechanism; instead of representing the owner, the salesclerk became a facilitator, helping to create an atmosphere of attention and service while the merchandise "sold itself."

The low mark-up of the large stores allowed lower prices (hence the name—Bon Marché)[3] and helped to attract crowds of customers from throughout the city. The department stores could not simply depend upon the traditional bourgeois clientele of smaller shops (the upper classes ordered goods from their own suppliers) and had to attract customers from among the petite bourgeoisie. By catering to the budgets and the "passion for spending" of the petite bourgeoisie, the department stores brought increasing numbers of people into contact with modern consumer society.

A significant part of the department stores' merchandising revolution was the presentation. Exhibits in the spacious galleries of the stores, large display windows, publicity through catalogs and newspaper advertising shaped illusions and stimulated the public's desires for the items offered. The salesperson was herself part of that presentation, helping to create an atmosphere of service and contributing to the seductiveness of the merchandise.

In order to attract customers and facilitate a heavy volume of sales, the department stores needed a new kind of staff. Whereas the shopkeeper could

[2]Novelist, 1840–1902.
[3]Cheap.

rely upon family members and a loyal assistant or two, the department store became an employer on the scale of modern industrial enterprises. In the 1880s the Bon Marché employed twenty-five hundred clerks; the Grands Magasins du Louvre ... by 1900 had a staff of thirty-five hundred to four thousand, depending on the season. Smaller provincial stores typically employed several hundred people. The Nouvelles Galeries in Bordeaux, for example, had 554 employees in 1912, divided into sales (283), office staff (60), and stock control (211). In 1906, by comparison, more than half of all commercial enterprises in France employed no more than five people (54 per cent), and two-thirds had ten or fewer employees. The average number of employees was 2.8. With such a large number of clerks, the entrepreneur could not expect to treat them like family members nor to encourage their ... hope that they might some day take over control of the store.

Beyond simple size, the department stores were innovators in the ways in which they recruited, trained, and treated their employees. The fixed price system and the practice of allowing customers to browse freely meant that a large percentage of the work force were simply unskilled assistants, who brought the items to the customers and took their payments to the cashiers. Costs were minimized by paying very low base salaries. But loyalty and diligence were assured by a highly graduated hierarchy in which the top ranks were achieved only through intense competition. Entrepreneurs like Boucicaut realized that in order to create the proper atmosphere in their stores they would have to reward top salespeople by the payment of commissions on sales and by allowing them to enjoy a high level of status and responsibility. The department stores formalized the system of recruitment, promotion, and rewards to create a group of employees who would espouse the interests of the firm as their own or be quickly weeded out.

Women were a crucial element in this system. In fact, although women did not form the majority of the stores' work force until after 1914, women dominated certain departments and came to symbolize the "world of women," as the department store was described. Women were both the clerks and the customers in this market place, for the mainstays of the new stores were fashions and dry goods. Women were scarcely new to commerce, but their role was expanding and changing in the late nineteenth century. A parliamentary investigation into the Parisian food and clothing industries found women clerks throughout those industries, and the report's conclusions insisted upon the importance of the unsalaried work of women who were *patronnes*[4] or who shared that responsibility with their husbands. Typically, several members of the family worked in family-run businesses, so that daughters also received some early work experience. Most shops could not have survived without the contributions of female family members. For the women themselves, this kind of work was both an extension of their domestic role and an important experience in the world of business. While

---

[4]Employers.

the department stores involved women in commercial activity in a very different way, traditional commercial roles continued to be exercised by the wives and daughters of shopkeepers well into the twentieth century.

One of the best descriptions of the new store clerks emerges from the investigations of Emile Zola for his novel, *Au bonheur des dames*,[5] in which the young heroine secures employment with a large department store closely modelled after the Bon Marché and the Grands Magasins du Louvre. Zola's heroine Denise is the carefully sketched model of the female clerk: young, single, and an immigrant to Paris from a provincial store.

Denise was hired at the store after the management assured itself of her experience and her attractiveness. In the first few days, she learned to adjust to the pace of work, the supervision of older saleswomen, and to the competitiveness of the older clerks who tried to monopolize the sales. Most beginners like Denise spent much of their time arranging displays of merchandise and delivering items to customers. During peak seasons, many clerks started as temporary help "with the hope that they would eventually be permanently hired," but only a small proportion of them survived this period of "training." During the first year, beginners received little more than room and board. But if the debutante could withstand the low salaries, long hours, and often heavy-handed surveillance of other salesclerks, she had a chance to enter the ranks of the relatively well-paid saleswomen.

At the highest level of the sales hierarchy were the department heads, *chefs de rayons*, and their assistants, whose responsibilities included not only sales but also the ordering of merchandise for their own divisions and the hiring and supervision of salespersonnel. Salespeople provided information about merchandise, and once items were sold, took them to be wrapped, and delivered the payment to the cashier. Saleswomen and men were generally divided into different departments: men sold male clothing, household furnishings, and even women's gloves and stockings, while women handled baby clothing and women's dresses, reflecting the pattern in the industry as a whole. Significantly, men made up the majority of department heads and assistants, though a few women managed to win out against the intense competition to head departments.

Department stores employed many women who were not sales clerks. There were office staffs of women who carried on the ordering, advertising, and the mail-order business. In addition, the largest stores employed hundreds of seamstresses, who were clearly distinguished from the sales force by the designation *ouvrière*[6] (rather than "employee"). The seamstresses received none of the benefits of the employees, such as free lodging or medical care, and the market provided by the department stores for the handwork of the domestic garment-making workers kept the institution of "sweated" labor alive well into the twentieth century.

---

[5] *The Paradise of Women.*
[6] Worker.

The proportion of women employed in the department stores steadily increased after a large strike by clerks in 1869. In part, employers recruited women because they represented a tractable labor force. Department stores gradually replaced some male clerks with female clerks who were more "docile" and "lacking in tradition" and who, consequently, would be less eager to strike. But there were other reasons for recruiting women clerks. Women were cheaper to hire than men and readily available because of the narrowing of other employment options for women. The spread of public education for women provided a pool of workers who were reluctant to work as seamstresses or domestics. And women workers impressed employers with their personal qualities of "politeness," "sobriety," and even a "talent for calculation."

Considering both the obvious advantages of a female work force and the important traditional role of women in commerce, it seems inevitable that women should have been hired as clerks in the new department stores. But women salesclerks were recruited from different sources than other female workers and remained a distinctive group through the period of the First World War. Why women clerks replaced men when the occupational opportunities expanded in commerce is, then, not so simple a question.

Department store clerks were very different from the largest group of women workers in the late nineteenth century—domestic servants. The young women who came to work in the Parisian *grands magasins*[7] were recruited from the cities and towns of France, while the domestic servants came from the countryside. Over half (53 per cent) of the female clerks who lived in the Parisian suburbs in 1911 and worked in Parisian stores had been born in Paris. Zola noted that one-third of the Bon Marché's saleswomen were native Parisians and that this was a larger percentage than among the male clerks. Salesmen were undoubtedly more mobile both geographically and socially. Both male and female employees who were not native Parisians had generally moved there from some provincial city where they had completed the essential apprenticeship in another store.

Department store clerks, like other commercial employees, often came from the ranks of urban shopkeepers and artisans. Children of shopkeepers frequently worked for a time in the large stores to learn commercial skills before returning to work in the family business. Over half of the shopgirls living with parents were from employee or shopkeeping families.... The occupational backgrounds of French clerks were primarily the urban, skilled occupations. A few even came from possible middle-class backgrounds, having parents who were teachers or *commerçants*,[8] but these were rare. In general, a clerk was not a working-class girl working her way out of poverty but more typically a lower-middle-class girl whose father was himself commercially employed, if not a shopkeeper.

[7]Department stores.
[8]Tradespeople.

Department store clerks were young. But unlike other women workers, who might begin their working lives at eleven or twelve, store clerks were rarely under seventeen years old. The Parisian *grands magasins* selected women only after a period of training, and thus the majority of the work force were in their early twenties. . . . Domestic servants and seamstresses included a wider range of ages because women could be employed at much younger ages in those occupations and could go back to work in small shops or as charwomen or seamstresses after their families were grown.

The career of the sales clerk, however, could be very short. Apart from the attrition due to marriage, the occupation simply wore some women out. Stores rarely hired anyone over 30, and the unlucky woman who lost her job after that age might be permanently retired. Younger women were more attractive, stronger, and cheaper to employ than older, more experienced women.

The life of the department store clerk was monopolized by the store. About half of the unmarried women were housed by the stores. The Bon Marché had small rooms under the roof of the store, while the Louvre housed its employees in buildings nearby. The rooms provided by the Bon Marché for their female employees were small with low ceilings; each contained a simple bed, table, and chair. But though these rooms were unadorned and sometimes overcrowded, they were often better than the rented room a young clerk could expect to find on her own. The lodgings at the Bon Marché included social rooms, where the management provided pianos for the women and billiard tables for the men. Visitors of the opposite sex were not allowed there, not even other employees. A concièrge kept track of the employees, and her permission had to be requested in order to go out at night. Such permission was nearly always granted as long as the eleven o'clock curfew was respected. Although department store entrepreneurs were innovators in retailing practices, their attitudes toward employees retained the strong flavor of paternalism that was typical of small-scale retailing. In small shops, the woman employee was almost a domestic, living in and working with other members of the family in the shop. Store managers of the department stores acted "in loco parentis"[9] at times, too, by exercising strong control over the lives of their saleswomen to preserve respectable behavior and to protect the public image of their firms.

The practice of housing female employees on the premises illustrates a variety of capitalistic and paternalistic motivations. There was considerable advantage to having salesclerks housed nearby, given the long hours they were expected to work. Employers also expressed . . . concern about the kind of . . . behavior, such as drinking, which could result from a lack of supervision. Women and young male clerks were both the victims and the beneficiaries of this system; adult men were allowed much greater freedom. The offer of housing and other benefits was combined with the opportunity

[9]In the place of the parents.

to more closely control the lives of salespeople. Because of the economic advantages of insuring a well-disciplined work force, department store owners prolonged the paternalism of shopkeepers long after the size of the new enterprises had destroyed most aspects of the traditional relationship.

Department store clerks were surrounded by their work. Not only housed in or near the store but also fed their meals there, the women were never allowed out of the store until after closing. The large dining halls where employees took their midday meal were an important features of the first department stores, and one contemporary described them as follows: "At each end of the immense dining halls were the department heads and inspectors; the simple male employees were seated in the center at long tables. Only the opening out of newspapers and the low hum of voices broke the silence, and everyone was completely absorbed in eating, for all were required to finish [in an hour]...." Female clerks ate in a different room, separately from the men. There were three sittings to accommodate the large number of employees, the first one beginning at 9:30 A.M. The break was closely supervised, and each employee had less than an hour, calculated from the time she left her post until she returned there. Although employees only rarely complained about the food they were served, much criticism was levelled at the conditions under which employees were forced to eat. Despite protests, women employees were never allowed to leave the store nor to return to their rooms during their breaks. At the Galeries Lafayette, they were locked into their dining hall during the meal. This kind of control indicates more strongly the "severity" than the "paternal indulgence" which managerial policy espoused.

Work rules throughout the store were very strict. Employees were dressed distinctively as a way of identifying them and making them conscious of their relationship to the store. Until after 1900, male employees were required to arrive at work wearing a derby or "melon," and the women were uniformly dressed in black silk. Surveillance by inspectors and supervisors assured that employee behavior was as uniform as their dress. Employees were expected to begin work at 8 A.M., and penalties were imposed on the tardy. At the Magasins Dufayel, a clerk was fined 25 centimes for being five minutes late; if she were two hours late, she could lose an entire day's wage. The average workday lasted twelve to thirteen hours, for the department stores did not close until 8 P.M. in the winter and 9 P.M. in the summer. During special sales or while preparing displays for the new season, clerks frequently had to work overtime without any special compensation. Although clerks in small shops often worked even longer hours, work in the department stores was judged more tiring by two parliamentary investigators in 1900, who argued that the large crowds attracted to the new stores quickened the pace of work.

By 1900 the workday for most female clerks had been reduced in accordance with an 1892 law setting a ten-hour maximum for women. The length of the clerk's workday had aroused much concern about the women's health, but their situation was still...better than that of the thousands of seamstresses who worked in sweatshop conditions in Parisian attics for little pay. Even before the reform, the workday of the salesgirl had been the envy of domestic servants, whose freedom was much more limited and whose employers did not allow the few hours of leisure which shopgirls enjoyed.

Characteristic of the way in which reforms were effected was the campaign for Sunday closing. In the 1890s . . . the large department stores began to adopt the practice of remaining closed on Sundays, giving most of their work force a day off. Although some employees were still needed to mount special expositions, prepare for sales, or unload deliveries, Sunday closing assured virtually all the women clerks a day off per week. The campaign for Sunday closing . . . inspired the most significant level of employee organization seen in this period. Concerted pressure was exerted by the predominantly male unions who occasionally solicited the support of women clerks and at times took up issues which were specifically female ones, such as the practice of locking up the women in their dining hall. As with other reforms, the chief opponents of reform were those who were concerned about the autonomy and survival of small shops that remained open longest in order to compete with the department stores. Overall, the challenge to the department store owners' authority was slight.

The authority of the employer, evident in the rigid work rules . . . was . . . obvious in the firing policies. The threat of termination was an excellent tool for shaping docile, hard-working employees, and employers did not use it sparingly. At the Bon Marché, the new recruits were quickly sized up in terms of their suitability as Bon Marché employees; among the four hundred new employees who were hired in 1873, 37 per cent were fired in the first five years. Most firings came without warning or compensation. Commonly, employers were not required to provide their employees with advance notice of termination, and employees lived with the sense of insecurity.

In the "severe yet beneficent" approach, however, there were also sweeter inducements to employee loyalty. Entrepreneurs like Boucicaut of the Bon Marché or Cognacq[10] of the Samaritaine knew that the success of their ventures depended in large part upon the formation of loyal employees. The department stores offered numerous incentives of various kinds. Compensation was high compared to other female salaries. Though young clerks received little more than their room and board, the average salary of a top saleswoman was three hundred to four hundred francs per month around 1900. Even a single woman could live very comfortably in Paris on a salary of that level. By contrast, the average wage of a woman employed in industry in 1902 was two francs per day, and the best industrial salaries scarcely exceeded three francs. Thus, a working woman rarely achieved an income of 75 francs per month, compared to the average saleswoman's income of 75 francs per week.

[10]T. E. Cognacq, 1839–1928.

Clearly the averages conceal an enormous range of salaries, since the greater part of the total was earned in commissions. All of the stores gave 1 or 2 per cent commissions on sales, . . . and, in addition, employees received discounts on merchandise purchased at the store. These incentives inspired many employees to associate their own interests with those of the firm but also to go into debt over their purchases of clothing and household items.

Long-term employees received the greatest advantages, such as the benefits from the provident fund begun by the Boucicaut family. After five years' service the store invested an annual sum on behalf of each employee. After 1886 a woman with 15 years of service could begin to draw benefits after the age of forty-five. The benefits averaged six hundred to fifteen hundred francs per year, depending on the individual's salary and length of service. . . . The fund paid death benefits to employees' families, and women clerks could draw a small sum from it when leaving the store to be married. At the Grands Magasins du Louvre, the store contributed two hundred francs per year to a similar fund. The Louvre also sponsored employee savings plans and invested in vacation homes for employees. In addition, Cognacq of the Samaritaine subsidized the building of inexpensive apartments on the outskirts of Paris, and the Boucicaut family built a hospital.

As a result, . . . department store owners earned a . . . reputation for philanthropy. . . . A parliamentary committee in 1914 reluctantly concluded that the department stores treated their employees better than family-run shops, even though the report . . . was generally hostile to large-scale retailing.

Critics of the department stores emphasized the destruction of the familial relationship between employer and employee in large-scale commerce, but store owners were scarcely indifferent to the quality of employees' family lives. Women employees received paid maternity leaves (up to six weeks at the Louvre)—an important innovation. Employers also promoted larger families by awarding gifts of two hundred francs for the birth of each child. The Samaritaine . . . ran a day nursery for the children of employees in 1890s.

Employers took an interest in the employee's welfare to prevent harm to the public image of the firm. Disreputable or disruptive behavior by employees was punished by disciplinary action, including firing. Informal liaisons among employees were strongly discouraged, and upon discovery employees were forced to "regularize" their relationship or face immediate dismissal. Relationships among employees of the same store were not encouraged for fear that they would disrupt the work atmosphere. . . . In spite of such disapproval, marriages among employees were probably common. Once formalized, the relationship between two employees received the blessings of the management in the form of a monetary gift (generally one hundred francs). Whether employers induced women to retire after marriage is impossible to determine, but the percentage of married women in their work force was low.

Employer investment in employee productivity produced plans for paid sick leave, health care, and annual vacations. Most stores assured their employees of several sick days per year, and the Bon Marché employees could be admitted to the Boucicaut hospital for long-term illnesses. The Louvre sent several employees each year to a store-owned estate in the countryside for a "cure." Commercial employees were also among the first workers to receive annual paid vacations, although at first many of these so-called vacations were actually unpaid leaves during the dead seasons of January–February and August–September.... [P]aid holidays of several days to two weeks became common for department store employees in the early 1900s.

The combination of paternalistic motivations and publicity seeking also inspired the organized choral groups supported by the Bon Marché. The employee groups "le Choral" and "l'Harmonie" presented regular public concerts for employees, customers, and invited guests in the great galleries of the store. A winter concert could draw an audience of several thousand. Employees were also encouraged to participate in other uplifting types of leisure activities, such as the free language lessons offered in the evening hours.

In spite of these programs, employee life was scarcely ideal. What seemed like a life of ease and relative glamour often more closely resembled the hardships of other working-class women in the nineteenth century. Like domestic servants, shopgirls worked long hours and were heavily supervised. The lodgings in the "sixième étage"[11] of the department stores were... little better than that of the "chambres de bonnes."[12]

Commercial employees, like other Parisian working women, had levels of mortality which were strikingly high. Employees often suffered from tuberculosis and other respiratory diseases. The high level of mortality was not easy to explain, but no one disputed the fast pace of work and long hours, which could produce fatigue and reduce the employee's immunity to certain diseases. Thus, the first protective legislation dealt directly with the problem of fatigue, requiring that a seat be provided for every female employee in the store. The legislation could not assure, however, that the clerks would actually be allowed to rest during the day. Noted an investigator in 1910:

> Among other examples, last October I saw a new salesgirl who remained standing from 8 A.M. to 7 P.M. near a sales table full of school supplies in the midst of an indescribable jostling, in a stuffy atmosphere, without stopping, often serving several customers simultaneously, accompanying them to the cashier and hurrying to return to her station; she was constantly under the threat of a reprimand from her department head, and with all of that, she had to be always smiling, amiable, even when the excessive pace of work rendered that especially difficult.

[11] The sixth floor (the seventh floor, counting the ground floor).
[12] The maids' rooms.

Street sales represented the worst abuse of employees, since they required a similar regimen but completely out-of-doors, even in the winter. These sales ... were an important part of retailing, but the consequences for employees could be tragic. Several saleswomen wrote to *La Fronde*[13] in 1898: "One of our fellow workers died last winter from an illness contracted when she was required, as we ourselves are, to work outside exposed to all kinds of weather." Even once Sunday closing was secured, the long, unrelieved days of work contributed to tuberculosis, anemia, and a variety of nervous disorders. The pace of work and the crush of customers induced a level of stress which combined with the inadequate diet of most shopgirls gave rise to a variety of gastro-intestinal problems. The medical reports stress the obvious dangers in shop work of tuberculosis and other long-term disabilities, but they also asserted a connection between the physical environment and the morally degrading aspects of work for women.

Social observers in the nineteenth century often felt that female employment offered ... too many opportunities for the sexual abuse of women.... The low salaries of most women made it impossible for them to support themselves without male companionship, which a girl acquired "at the price of her honor and her dignity." Some salesgirls could be seduced by wealthy customers or lecherous supervisors.... [T]he shopgirl was the victim of the role she had to play—an attractive amiable "doll," who was forced "to maintain an eternal smile." Whether or not she was sexually promiscuous, the salesgirl's role inspired moralists to imagine her debauchery.

A typical salesclerk was probably planning to marry a young employee or shopkeeper, and thus the suggestion of a sexual relationship might simply be a prelude to marriage. Salesgirls often came to the department stores with the hope of finding better suitors there. The inescapable fact that most salesclerks were young and single meant that their culture was that of young, urban, single people, whose attitudes and behavior were different from their middle-class employers.

The single state was almost a condition of employment, as it was with domestic service. Employees complained that the practice of providing housing inhibited their freedom to marry. About two-thirds of the female employees of the Louvre in 1895 were unmarried. In 1911, in the suburbs of Paris, only 14 per cent of the saleswomen were married. But the clerks hoped that work "was only a temporary occupation for them" and that they would ultimately retire from the occupation upon marriage....

The young single employee ... helped to create a new urban leisure culture in the years before the First World War. This culture included the attendance at concerts and sporting events. Employees took up bicycling, which itself allowed for freer sociability and a new style of courting. Employees also frequented cafés and certain restaurants. Musical groups and

[13]The first newspaper run entirely by women.

organized activities at the department stores were clearly intended to lure employees away from such public entertainments, but they did not succeed. Employees continued to use more of their leisure time in their own ways.

Women employees could expect to have the use of their Sundays and a few evening hours...between closing and curfew time. Department store clerks generally purchased their own evening meal at a restaurant, and thus they developed the habit of public dining. Whole chains of inexpensive restaurants...were established to supply inexpensive meals to a new class of consumers—clerks and office employees. Cheap but respectable, such establishments catered to the limited budgets of employees and office clerks and were located near the banks and stores. Shop girls could also dine inexpensively in the Latin Quarter, where, "needless to say, a woman alone is the commonest of sights and you will not hesitate to enter any of these establishments," according to the author of *A Woman's Guide to Paris.* Unlike the working classes, who frequented cafés mainly at mid-day, employees, especially the male clerks, were highly visible in the evenings in the cafés and restaurants of central Paris.

Leisure for the female clerk also included Sunday strolls in the parks, mixing with young soldiers, servant girls, and bourgeois families. Shopgirls were said to "shine" in their leather boots and stylish hats, which set them apart from the other working girls. The salesgirl's dress expressed the ambiguity of her position. On the street, employees' appearances showed a preoccupation with their public image; most of the women tried to dress attractively in spite of the cost. "The employees seem the queens of the urban proletariat. When one encounters them in the street, it is difficult to distinguish them from ambitious petit bourgeois: they wear hats, gloves, and fine boots. This is a necessity, it seems, in their occupation, but it costs them dearly." The stylish clothes of the shopgirl suggest two things about the experience of store clerks before 1914. The salesclerk herself was affected by the retailing revolution of the department stores and seduced by the attractiveness of current fashions. But the salesclerk's behavior was also the result of her ambiguous social position, a status which was complicated by the enormous range of salaries and benefits within the sales hierarchy. Zola suggested that the department store clerk was "neither a worker nor a lady...[but] a woman outside." Monsieur Honoré of the Louvre suggested that young clerks were recruited from the working classes because they were attracted by the idea of escaping a life of manual labor. But the reality is more complex than the desire of a working-class girl to become a bourgeoise. The department stores did offer their employees an important chance for mobility—the owners of the four major department stores had started their careers as simple employees. But for most clerks, and especially for a woman, the possibility of becoming a shop owner was distant. Instead, one could hope to be promoted in the store's hierarchy, although even this kind of promotion was more difficult for women to achieve than for men.

The reality of mobility is impossible to assess precisely, but one can gain an impression of what a female salesclerk may have achieved by her experience in a department store. Most salesclerks came from the petite bourgeoisie and in particular from employee families. Moreover, the young women who found suitors most often married other employees. During the 1880s, when the city of Paris gathered data on marriages, the percentage of female clerks who married male employees was between 45 and 50 per cent. The intermarriage of clerks was the result of their associations at work and also of their desire for a respectable life. Rather than raising them into the middle class, their endogamy helped to form an independent lower middle class culture. Through marriage, employees tied their lives and their fortunes together, forming a group whose experiences and aspirations were significantly different from those above and below them.

The transition from shopkeeping to modern merchandising did not represent an easy process for employees. It was the male department store clerks who organized the first union and mounted the largest and earliest strikes of employees. Again in 1919 and 1936, department store clerks, by this time predominantly female, contributed heavily to the labor struggles of those crisis years. Employer paternalism, which had characterized the first generation of department stores, earned the employers a reputation for philanthropy, but it ... enclosed the salesclerk in an interlocking structure of life and work that was difficult to escape.

Inevitably, fashions in clothing and in retailing changed, and the First World War accelerated the pace of those changes. The era of live-in clerks ended. Women came to predominate in the ranks of department store employees. Declining salaries and benefits during the war years were only partially restored by the wave of strikes in 1919. Female clerks gained a forty-eight hour week in 1917 but never recovered their élite status among working women.

As department store work evolved, so did the work experience of most women. By 1920 clerical work in offices as well as shops was much more common for women. Whereas in 1906 only one woman in ten worked as an employee, by 1936 one in every three was employed as a clerk. From the feminization of clerical work resulted the "deprofessionalization" of the clerk: lower salaries, the influx of unskilled labor, and declining benefits. The evolution of department store work since the 1840s has thus been an example of broader social changes. This "paradise of women," as Zola described the department store in the 1880s, became truly feminized only after the First World War, but the experience of female salesclerks in the first generation of department stores suggests much about the changing character of work and the place of women in that transformation.

III

THE TWENTIETH CENTURY

One might argue that the twentieth century has been the worst of centuries in the history of Western civilization. Mass murder and widespread torture, easier owing to new technologies, have made prior epochs seem remarkably humane. Totalitarianism and genocide are two of this century's contributions to humankind, while nuclear catastrophe, now apparently a permanent specter looming ominously offstage, may be the third. Few are the regions of Europe that have not experienced the sequence of recent horrors that include World War I, fascist and Communist brutalities; World War II and the Holocaust, and the terrorism that currently punctuates the rhythm of modern life.

These developments have markedly influenced the social history of contemporary Europe, for the lives of millions have been altered dramatically in short periods of time. (The significance of the long duration becomes less noticeable in the contemporary era.) Warfare in the twentieth century has become total, involving entire populations, soldiers and civilians alike. Because Europe in the twentieth century has become more closely knit through economic ties, travel, and communications systems, occurrences in one country create ripples throughout the Continent. Local isolation and agricultural self-sufficiency are things of the past, changes in the economy very quickly affect everyone, and consumers share a common culture. One of the ideals of modern citizenship is keeping abreast of the news, made readily available by the mass media, because we have come to realize that individuals and societies can no longer go their own way with impunity; we are all, in every aspect of our lives, at the mercy of changes that take place far from us. The peasant in an isolated village, eking out an existence in total ignorance of the outside world, is fast becoming extinct.

The Price of Glory: Verdun 1916

ALISTAIR HORNE

If war is Hell, then the Battle of Verdun, from February to December 1916, was the deepest circle. The French and Germans sustained approximately one million casualties. The horrors of the battle can scarcely be imagined, but Alistair Horne does manage to immerse us in the sights, smells, and feelings that this, the most destructive battle in history, evoked. Historians of warfare have begun to move from descriptions of military maneuvers and biographies of generals and heroes to reconstructions of war from the perspective of the ordinary soldier. This is what Horne does in this powerful, moving essay.

How did the battlefield appear? What was the approach march like? Horne frequently refers to colors, something that historians of warfare tend to ignore, save when discussing uniforms or flags. The odors of Verdun were overwhelming; the living mixed promiscuously with the dead. Indeed, Verdun was an open cemetery, with ghastly and mutilated corpses of both men and animals prominent everywhere. Filth and disease contributed to the enormous suffering. Above all this was the nearly constant artillery bombardment raining death on those who could do little to protect themselves from indiscriminate shells. What does Horne mean by the statement that "Verdun was the epitome of a 'soldier's battle'"? What was the fate of the wounded? Did the French support services do a commendable job in treating the wounded or in feeding and aiding the soldiers in the front lines?

Why does Horne consider the runners, ration parties, and stretcher-bearers to have been the greatest heroes of Verdun? How did the high probability of death or mutilation and the constant, seemingly unendurable suffering affect the soldiers physically and mentally? Did the saying that "there are no atheists in a foxhole" ring true at Verdun? Do you think, after reading this selection, that the suffering and deaths of the soldiers were meaningless, mere sacrifices on the altar of nationalism?

... Although from March to the end of May the main German effort took place on the Left Bank of the Meuse, this did not mean that the Right Bank had become a 'quiet sector'. Far from it! Frequent vicious little attacks undertaken by both sides to make a minor tactical gain here and there regularly supplemented the long casualty lists caused by the relentless pounding of the rival artilleries. Within the first month of the battle the effect of this non-stop bombardment, by so mighty an assemblage of cannon, their fire concentrated within an area little larger than Richmond Park,[1] had already established an environment common to both sides of the Meuse that characterized the whole battle of Verdun. The horrors of trench warfare and of the slaughter without limits of the First War are by now so familiar

[1] In London.

to the modern reader that further recounting merely benumbs the mind. The Battle of Verdun, however, through its very intensity—and, later, its length—added a new dimension of horror. Even this would not in itself warrant lengthy description were it not for the fact that Verdun's peculiarly sinister environment came to leave an imprint on men's memories that stood apart from other battles of the First War; and predominantly so in France where the nightmares it inspired lingered perniciously long years after the Armistice.[2]

To a French aviator, flying sublimely over it all, the Verdun front after a rainfall resembled disgustingly the 'humid skin of a monstrous toad'. Another flyer, James McConnell, (an American . . .) noted after passing over 'red-roofed Verdun'—which had 'spots in it where no red shows and you know what has happened there'—that abruptly

> there is only that sinister brown belt, a strip of murdered nature. It seems to belong to another world. Every sign of humanity has been swept away. The woods and roads have vanished like chalk wiped from a blackboard; of the villages nothing remains but grey smears. . . . During heavy bombardments and attacks I have seen shells falling like rain. Countless towers of smoke remind one of Gustave Doré's[3] picture of the fiery tombs of the arch-heretics in Dante's 'Hell'. . . . Now and then monster projectiles hurtling through the air close by leave one's plane rocking violently in their wake. Aeroplanes have been cut in two by them.

. . . The first sounds heard by ground troops approaching Verdun reminded them of 'a gigantic forge that ceased neither day nor night'. At once they noted, and were acutely depressed by, the sombre monotones of the battle area. To some it was 'yellow and flayed, without a patch of green'; to others a compound of brown, grey, and black, where the only forms were shell holes. On the few stumps that remained of Verdun's noble forests on the Right Bank, the bark either hung down in strips, or else had long since been consumed by half-starved pack-horses. As spring came, with the supreme optimism of Nature, the shattered trees pushed out a new leaf here and there, but soon these too dropped sick and wilting in the poisonous atmosphere. At night, the Verdun sky resembled a 'stupendous *Aurora Borealis*', but by day the only splashes of colour that one French soldier-artist could find were the rose tints displayed by the frightful wounds of the horses lying scattered about the approach routes, lips pulled back over jaws in the hideousness of death. Heightening this achromatic gloom was the pall of smoke over Verdun most of the time, which turned the light filtering through it to an ashy grey. A French general, several times in the line at Verdun, recalled to the author

[2]Of 11 November 1918, ending hostilities on the Western Front.

[3]French illustrator and painter (1832–1883), famous for his illustrations of books, including Dante's *Divine Comedy*.

that while marching through the devastated zone his soldiers never sang; 'and you know French soldiers sing a lot'. When they came out of it they often grew crazily rapturous simply at returning to 'a world of colour, meadows and flowers and woods...where rain on the roofs sounds like a harmonic music'.

A mile or two from the front line, troops entered the first communication trenches; though to call them this was generally both an exaggeration and an anachronism. Parapets gradually grew lower and lower until the trench became little deeper than a roadside ditch. Shells now began to fall with increasing regularity among closely packed men. In the darkness (for obvious reasons, approach marches were usually made at night) the columns trampled over the howling wounded that lay underfoot. Suddenly the trench became 'nothing more than a track hardly traced out amid the shell holes'. In the mud, which the shelling had now turned to a consistency of sticky butter, troops stumbled and fell repeatedly; cursing in low undertones, as if fearful of being overheard by the enemy who relentlessly pursued them with his shells at every step. Sometimes there were duckboards around the lips of the huge shell craters. But more often there were not, and heavily laden men falling into the water-filled holes remained there until they drowned, unable to crawl up the greasy sides. If a comrade paused to lend a hand, it often meant that two would drown instead of one. In the chaos of the battlefield, where all reference points had long since been obliterated, relieving detachments often got lost and wandered hopelessly all night; only to be massacred by an enemy machine-gunner as dawn betrayed them. It was not unusual for reliefs to reach the front with only half the numbers that set out, nor for this nightmare approach march to last ten hours or longer.

One of the first things that struck troops fresh to the Verdun battlefield was the fearful stench of putrefaction; 'so disgusting that it almost gives a certain charm to the odour of gas shells'. The British never thought their Allies were as tidy about burying their dead as they might be, but under the non-stop shelling at Verdun an attempt at burial not infrequently resulted in two more corpses to dispose of. It was safer to wrap the dead up in a canvas and simply roll them over the parapet into the largest shell-hole in the vicinity. There were few of these in which did not float some ghastly, stinking fragment of humanity. On the Right Bank several gullies were dubbed, with good cause, '*La Ravine de la Mort*'[4] by the French. Such a one, though most of it in French hands, was enfiladed by a German machine gun at each end, which exacted a steady toll. Day after day the German heavies pounded the corpses in this gully, until they were quartered, and re-quartered; to one eye-witness it seemed as if it were filled with dismembered limbs that no one could or would bury. Even when buried,

> shells disinter the bodies, then reinter them, chop them to pieces, play with them as a cat plays with a mouse.

[4] "The Ravine of Death."

As the weather grew warmer and the numbers of dead multiplied, the horror reached new peaks. The compressed area of the battlefield became an open cemetery in which every square foot contained some decomposed piece of flesh:

> You found the dead embedded in the walls of the trenches, heads, legs, and half-bodies, just as they had been shovelled out of the way by the picks and shovels of the working party.

Once up in the front line, troops found that life had been reduced, in the words of a Beaux Arts[5] professor serving with the Territorials,[6] 'to a struggle between the artillerymen and the navvy, between the cannon and the mound of earth'. All day long the enemy guns worked at levelling the holes laboriously scraped out the previous night. At night, no question of sleep for the men worn out by the day's shelling (it was not unknown for men in the line to go without sleep for eleven days). As soon as darkness fell, an officer would lay out a white tape over the shell ground, and the 'navvies' began to dig; feverishly, exposed, hoping not to be picked up by enemy flares and machine guns. By dawn the trench would probably be little more than eighteen inches deep, but it had to be occupied all day, while the enemy gunners resumed their work of levelling. No question of latrines under these conditions; men relieved themselves where they lay, as best they could. Dysentery became regarded as a norm of life at Verdun. Lice, made much of by combatants on other fronts, receive little mention. With luck, by the second morning the trench might have reached a depth of barely three feet.

Over and again eye-witnesses at Verdun testify to the curious sensation of having been in the line twice, three times, without ever having seen an enemy infantryman. On going into the line for the first time, one second-lieutenant who was later killed at Verdun, twenty-six-year-old Raymond Jubert, recalled his Colonel giving the regiment instructions that must have been repeated a thousand time at Verdun:

> You have a mission of sacrifice; here is a post of honour where they want to attack. Every day you will have casualties, because they will disturb your work. On the day they want to, they will massacre you to the last man, and it is your duty to fall.

Battalion after battalion decimated solely by the bombardment would be replaced in the line by others, until these too had all effectiveness as a

---

[5]From the École Nationale Supérieur des Beaux-Arts in Paris.

[6]The French Territorial Army was composed of veterans and older citizens. They usually took secondary jobs, thus freeing front-line troops for combat.

fighting unit crushed out of them by the murderous shelling.[7] After nights of being drenched by icy rain in a shell-hole under non-stop shelling, a twenty-year-old French corporal wrote:

> Oh, the people who were sleeping in a bed and who tomorrow, reading their newspaper, would say joyously—'they are still holding!' Could they imagine what that simple word 'hold' meant?

The sensation provoked by being under prolonged bombardment by heavy guns is something essentially personal and subjective; first-hand accounts cover a wide range of experience. To Paul Dubrulle, a thirty-four-year-old French Jesuit serving as an infantry sergeant at Verdun, whose journals are outstanding for their un-embellished realism, it seemed as follows:

> When one heard the whistle in the distance, one's whole body contracted to resist the too excessively potent vibrations of the explosion, and at each repetition it was a new attack, a new fatigue, a new suffering. Under this régime, the most solid nerves cannot resist for long; the moment arrives where the blood mounts to the head; where fever burns the body and where the nerves, exhausted, become incapable of reacting. Perhaps the best comparison is that of seasickness... finally one abandons one's self to it, one has no longer even the strength to cover oneself with one's pack as protection against splinters, and one scarcely still has left the strength to pray to God.... To die from a bullet seems to be nothing; parts of our being remain intact; but to be dismembered, torn to pieces, reduced to pulp, this is a fear that flesh cannot support and which is fundamentally the great suffering of the bombardment....

...More than anything else, it was the apparently infinite duration of the Verdun bombardments that reduced even the strongest nerves. Sergeant-Major César Méléra, a tough adventurer, who had sailed around the world in peacetime and who appeared little affected by the horrors of war, describes his experience of Verdun shell-fire initially with an unemotional economy of words: 'Filthy night, shells'. Three days later he was confiding to his diary that the night bombardment made him 'think of that nightmare room of Edgar Allan Poe, in which the walls closed in one after the other'. The following day: 'Oh how I envy those who can charge with a bayonet instead of waiting to be buried by a shell', and, finally, the admission:

---

[7]To us this kind of futile sacrifice symbolizes the First War mentality. Yet one must always remember the dilemma facing the French at Verdun.... By 1916 both sides had already experimented successfully with 'thinning out' the forward areas to reduce shell-fire casualties. But in the cramped space at Verdun where the loss of a hundred yards might lead to the loss of the city the risk of any such thinning out could not be taken by the French. Similarly the Germans, always attacking, could not avoid a permanent concentration of men in the forward lines. (Author's note.)

Verdun is terrible... because man is fighting against material, with the sensation of striking out at empty air....

...With the steadily increasing power of the French artillery, experiences of the infantryman on both sides became more and more similar. In June a soldier of the German 50th Division before Fort Vaux declared that 'the torture of having to lie powerless and defenceless in the middle of an artillery battle' was 'something for which there is nothing comparable on earth'. Through this common denominator of suffering, a curious mutual compassion began to develop between the opposing infantries, with hatred reserved for the artillery in general. To Captain Cochin on the Mort Homme,[8] it seemed as if the two artilleries were playing some idiotic game with each other, to see which could cause the most damage to the two unhappy lines of infantrymen.

What the P.B.I. felt about their own gunners may be gauged from a French estimate that out of ten shells falling on a Verdun trench, 'on an average two were provided by the friendly artillery'. Sergeant Élie Tardivel tells how in June seven men from a neighbouring platoon had just been killed by a single French 155 shell:

I met the company commander; I told him I had brought up some grenades and barbed-wire; I asked where I was to put them. He replied: 'Wherever you wish. For two hours our own guns have been bombarding us, and if it goes on I shall take my company and bombard the gunner with these grenades!'

Emotions between the infantry and gunners resembled those sometimes held towards the heavy-bomber crews of World War II, whom the ground troops viewed as sumptuously quartered well away from the enemy, making brief sorties to spray their bombs indiscriminately over both lines. A French company commander, Charles Delvert, describes passing two naval batteries en route for Verdun:

Not a single man on foot. Everybody in motors. The officers had a comfortable little car to themselves.... I looked at my poor troopers. They straggled lamentably along the road, bent in two by the weight of their packs, streaming with water, and all this to go and become mashed to pulp in muddy trenches.

Other infantrymen were irked by the impersonal casualness with which the heavy gunners crews emerged from their comfortable shelters to fire at targets they could not see, 'appearing to be much less concerned than about the soup or the bucket of wine which had just been brought'.

This picture is to some extent endorsed by the artillery themselves. Staff-Sergeant Fonsagrive, serving with a 105 mm. battery wrote in his journal

[8]The "Dead Man," a hill between the town of Verdun and the front line that was the scene of ferocious combat.

during the peak of the March battle on the Right Bank; 'the fine weather continues, the days lengthen; it is a pleasure to get up in the morning....' Watching the planes dog-fighting overhead, there was plenty of leisure time for day-dreaming about wives and families. Later, Fonsagrive notes with some vexation:

> One day when, quietly sitting underneath an apple tree, I was writing a letter, a 130 mm. shell landed forty metres behind me, causing me a disagreeable surprise.

...Not all French gunners, however, were as fortunate as Sergeant Fonsagrive. When death came from the long-range German counter-battery guns, it came with frightening suddenness. A gunner sipping his soup astraddle his cannon, a group of N.C.O.s playing cards would be expunged by an unheralded salvo. In action, the field artillery particularly had even less cover than the infantry; often reduced still further by officers of the old school of that notably proud French arm, *'La Reine des Batailles'*, [9] who believed (and there were still many like them) that to take cover under fire was almost cowardice. Casualties among some batteries were in fact often at least as high as among the infantry. Captain Humbert, a St Cyrien[10] of the 97th Infantry Regiment, testifies to the effect of the German artillery's systematic sweeping of the back areas, knowing that the French field batteries must all be there:

> Nobody escapes; if the guns were spared today, they will catch it tomorrow.... Whole batteries lie here demolished....

Lieutenant Gaston Pastre, though also a heavy gunner, provides a very different picture to Fonsagrive. Arriving at Verdun in May, he found the unit he was relieving had lost forty per cent of its effectives; 'If you stay here a month, which is normal,' they warned him, 'you will lose half of yours too'. The reverse slopes up to Fort St Michel on the Right Bank, where Pastre's battery was sited, were crammed with every calibre of gun; it was 'nothing more than one immense battery, there are perhaps 500 pieces there'. A wonderful target for German saturation fire—anything that falls between Fort Michel and the road is good'. There were generally only two periods of calm in the day; between 4 and 6 a.m. and between 4 and 7 p.m. when, like subhuman troglodytes, the French gunners emerged from the ground to repair the damage. For the rest of the time, to move from one shelter to another—a distance of about twenty yards—required considerable courage. By night the solitary road from Verdun came under constant fire from the German gunners, certain that French munition columns must be coming up it nose to tail. It presented 'a spectacle worthy of Hell', in which men not killed outright were often hurled off their gun carriages by shell blast, to be run over and crushed by their own caissons in the dark.

[9] "The Queen of Battles."
[10] St. Cyr was the principal French Military academy.

Next to the incessant bombardment, the stink of putrefaction, and the utter desolation of the battlefield, Verdun combatants testify again and again to the terrifying isolation, seldom experienced to the same degree in other sectors. Verdun was the epitome of a 'soldier's battle'. Within an hour or less of the launching of each organized attack or counter-attack, leadership over the lower echelons ceased to play any significant role. Company commanders would lose all but the most spasmodic and tenuous contact with their platoons, often for days at a time. The situation where one French machine-gun section found itself holding a hole in the front two hundred yards wide with its two machine guns for several days in complete detachment from the rest of the army, was by no means unique. To add to this demoralizing sense of isolation, the tenacious curtain of smoke from the bombardment meant that the front line frequently could not see the supporting troops behind; nor, worse still, could their rockets of supplication asking for the artillery to bring down a barrage, or cease shelling their own positions, be seen at the rear. Countless were the true heroes of Verdun, fighting small Thermopylaes[11] in the shellholes, who remained unsung and undecorated because no one witnessed their deeds.

> After twenty months of fighting, where twenty times I should have died [Raymond Jubert admitted] I have not yet seen war as I imagined it. No; none of those grand tragic tableaux, with sweeping strokes and vivid colours, where death would be a stroke, but these small painful scenes, in obscure corners, of small compass where one cannot possibly distinguish if the mud were flesh or the flesh were mud.

Of all the participants qualifying for the title of hero at Verdun, probably none deserved it more than three of the most humble categories: the runners, the ration parties, and the stretcher-bearers. As a regular lieutenant in charge of the divisional runners at Souville stated, simply: 'The bravery of the man isolated in the midst of danger is the true form of courage.' With telephone lines no sooner laid than torn up by shellfire, and the runner become the sole means of communication at Verdun, the most frequently heard order at any H.Q. was 'send two runners'. From the relative protection of their holes, the infantry watched in silent admiration at the blue caps of the runners bobbing and dodging among the plumes of exploding T.N.T. It was an almost suicidal occupation. Few paths were not sign-posted by their crumpled remains, and on the Mort Homme one regiment lost twenty-one runners in three hours.

Perhaps demanding even more courage, though, was the role of the *cuistot*,[12] *ravitailleur*,[13] or *homme-soupe*,[14] as the ration parties were variously called, in that it was played out in the solitariness of night.

---

[11]Thermopylae was a small mountain pass in Greece where the Persians in 480 B.C. annihilated a Spartan army to the last man.

[12]Cook.

[13]Carrier of supplies.

[14]Soup man.

Under danger, in the dark, one feels a kind of particular horror at finding oneself alone. Courage requires to be seen [noted Jubert]. To be alone, to have nothing to think about except oneself ... to have nothing more to do than to die without a supreme approbation! The soul abdicates quickly and the flesh abandons itself to shudders.

On account of the shelling, motor transport could approach no closer than a cross-roads nicknamed 'Le Tourniquet'[15] at the end of the *Voie Sacrée*.[16] The massacre of the horses, unable to take cover upon the warning whistle of a shell, had become prohibitive. Thus all rations for the men at the front had to come up on the backs of other men. The *cuistots*, three or four to a company, were generally selected from among the elderly, the poor shots, and the poor soldiers. One of the most moving pictures printed in *L 'Illustration*[17] during the war was of one of these unhappy *cuistots* crawling on his stomach to the front at Verdun, with flasks of wine lashed to his belt. Each carried a dozen of the heavy flasks, and a score of loaves of bread strung together by string, worn like a bandolier. They often made a round trip of twelve miles every night; even though, bent under their loads, at times they could barely crawl, let alone walk, in the glutinous mud. They arrived, collapsing from fatigue, only to be cursed by comrades, desperate from hunger and thirst, on finding that the flasks of precious *pinard*[18] had been punctured by shell fragments, the bread caked with filth. Frequently they never arrived. Fixed enemy guns fired a shell every two or three minutes on each of the few well-known routes with the accuracy of long practice....

For all the gallantry and self-sacrifice of the *cuistots*, hunger and thirst became regular features at Verdun, adding to the sum of misery to be endured there. Twenty-two-year-old Second-Lieutenant Campana notes how he dispatched a ration party of eight men one night in March. The following morning five came back—without rations. That night another eight set out. None returned. The next night some hundred men from all companies set forth, but were literally massacred by violent gunfire. After three days without food, Campana's men were reduced to scavenging any remnants they could find upon the bodies lying near their position. Many had been decomposing for several weeks. The experience was more the rule than the exception; so too, as winter sufferings gave way to a torrid summer, was this spectacle:

I saw a man drinking avidly from a green scum-covered marsh, where lay, his black face downward in the water, a dead man lying on his stomach and swollen as if he had not stopped filling himself with water for days ...

[15] The turnstile.
[16] The "Sacred Way," the road that took the French soldiers to Verdun.
[17] A French newspaper.
[18] Wine.

Worst of all was the lot of the stretcher-bearers, which usually fell—until the supply was used up—to the regimental musicians. The two-wheeled carts that comprised the principal means of transporting the wounded on other French sectors proved quite useless over the pock-ridden terrain at Verdun; the dogs used to sniff out the wounded went rabid under the shelling. Unlike the runners or the *cuistots*, when carrying a wounded man the unhappy *musiciens-brancardiers*[19] could not fling themselves to the ground each time a shell screamed overhead. Often the demands simply exceeded what human flesh could obey. Response to pleas for volunteers to carry the wounded was usually poor, and the troops at Verdun came to recognize that their chances of being picked up, let alone brought to medical succour, were extremely slim.

During the Second World War, there were cases when the morale of even veteran British Guardsmen suffered if, in the course of an action, they were aware that surgical attention might not be forthcoming for at least five hours. On most Western battlefields, it was normally a matter of an hour or two. Surgical teams and nursing sisters, copiously provided with blood plasma, sulfa-drugs, and penicillin, worked well forward in the battle area, so that a badly wounded man could be given emergency treatment without having to be removed along a bumpy road to hospital. For the more serious cases, there was air transport direct to base hospital, possibly hundreds of miles to the rear. In contrast, at Verdun a casualty—even once picked up—could reckon himself highly fortunate if he received any treatment within twenty-four hours. During the desperate days of July, the wounded lingered in the foul, dark, excrement-ridden vaults of Fort Souville for over six days before they could be evacuated.

Poorly organized as were the French medical services, demand far outstripped supply almost throughout the war, but several times at Verdun the system threatened to break down altogether. There were never enough surgeons, never enough ambulances, of course no 'wonder drugs', and often no chloroform with which to perform the endless amputations of smashed limbs. If a casualty reached the clearing station, his ordeals were by no means over. Georges Duhamel, a doctor at Verdun..., vividly describes the chaos in one of these primitive charnel houses in '*La Vie des Martyrs*'.[20] Arriving during the early stages of the battle, he noted in despair, 'there is work here for a month'. The station was overflowing with badly wounded who had already been waiting for treatment for several days. In tears they beseeched to be evacuated; their one terror to be labelled 'untransportable.' These, not merely the hopelessly wounded, but those whose wounds were just too complicated for the frantic surgeons to waste time probing, or who looked as if they would be little use to the army again, were laid outside in the bitter cold. It was not long before German shells landed among this helpless pile,

[19]Musician–stretcher-bearers.
[20]*The Life of the Martyrs*.

but at least this reduced the doctors' work. Inside, the surgeons, surrounded by dustbins filled with lopped-off limbs, did the best they could to patch up the ghastly wounds caused by the huge shell splinters.

Later Duhamel and his team were visited by an immaculate Inspector-General who told them they really ought to plant a few flowers around the gloomy station. As he left, Duhamel noticed that someone had traced *'Vache'*[21] in the dust on the brass-hat's car.

At the clearing stations the backlog of even the partially repaired mounted alarmingly as, with the constant demand of the *Voie Sacrée* supply route, all too few vehicles could be spared for use as ambulances. British Red Cross sections appeared on the front . . . and later American volunteers. Though the crews drove twenty-four hours at a stretch, unable to wear gasmasks because they fogged up, still there seemed to be more wounded than the ambulances could hold. Meanwhile in the overcrowded, squalid base hospitals, those who had survived so far were dying like flies, their beds immediately refilled. Clyde Balsley, an American very badly wounded with the 'Lafayette Squadron', noted in contrast that

> the miracles of science after the forced butchery at Verdun . . . made a whole year and a half at the American Hospital pass more quickly than six weeks in the [French] hospital at Verdun.

The wounded in these hospitals lived in terror of the periodical decoration parades; because it had become a recognized custom to reward a man about to die with the *Croix de Guerre*.[22] Of slight compensation were the visits of the 'professional' visitors, such as the patriotic, exquisite, 'Lady in Green', described by Duhamel, who spoke inspiredly to the *grands mutilés*[23] of

> the enthusiastic ardour of combat! The superb anguish of bounding ahead, bayonet glittering in the sun. . . .

Equipment in these hospitals was hopelessly inadequate, but at Verdun the situation was exacerbated still further by the poisonous environment, virulently contaminated by the thousands of putrefying corpses. Even the medically more advanced Germans noted the frequency of quite minor wounds becoming fatal. Gas gangrene, for which an effective cure was not discovered till a few weeks before the Armistice, claimed an ever-increasing toll; during the April fighting on the Right Bank, one French regiment had thirty-two officers wounded of whom no fewer than nineteen died subsequently, mostly from gas gangrene. In an attempt to reduce infection of

[21]Swine.
[22]Military Cross.
[23]Badly disabled.

head wounds, Joffre[24] issued an order banning beards; the *poilus*[25] complained bitterly, and still the wounded died. After the war, it was estimated that, between 21 February and the end of June, 23,000 French alone had died in hospitals as a result of wounds received at Verdun. How many more died before ever reaching hospital can only be conjectured.

So much for the physical; and what of the spiritual effects of this piling of horror upon horror at Verdun? Many were affected like the young German student, highly religious and torn with doubts about the morality of war, who wrote home shortly before being killed at Verdun on 1 June:

> Here we have war, war in its most appalling form, and in our distress we realize the nearness of God.

As in every war men confronted with death who had forgotten, or never knew how, began to pray fervidly. Sergeant Dubrulle, the Jesuit priest, was revolted above all by the hideous indignities he had seen T.N.T. perpetrate upon the bodies God had created. After one terrible shelling early in the battle when human entrails were to be seen dangling in the branches of a tree and a 'torso, without head, without arms, without legs, stuck to the trunk of a tree, flattened and opened', Dubrulle recalls 'how I implored God to put an end to these indignities. Never have I prayed with so much heart'. But, as day after day, month after month, such entreaties remained unanswered, a growing agnosticism appears in the letters from the men at Verdun. Later, on the Somme, even Dubrulle is found expressing singularly non-Catholic sentiments:

> Having despaired of living amid such horror, we begged God not to have us killed—the transition is too atrocious—but just to let us be dead. We had but one desire; the end!

At least this part of Dubrulle's prayer was answered the following year.

For every soldier whose mind dwelt on exalted thoughts, possibly three agreed with Sergeant Marc Boasson, a Jewish convert to Catholicism, killed in 1918, who noted that at Verdun 'the atrocious environment corrupts the spirits, obsesses it, dissolves it'.

Corruption revealed itself in the guise of brutalization. . . .

It was indeed not very exalting to watch wounded comrades-in-arms die where they lay because they could not be removed. One Divisional Chaplain, Abbé Thellier de Poncheville, recalls the spectacle of a horse, still harnessed to its wagon, struggling in the mud of a huge crater. 'He had been there for two nights, sinking deeper and deeper', but the troops, obsessed by their

---

[24]Joseph Joffre (1852–1931), French commander in chief, 1911–1916.

[25]French soldiers.

own suffering, passed by without so much as casting a glance at the wretched beast. The fact was that the daily inoculation of horror had begun to make men immune to sensation. Duhamel explains:

> A short time ago death was the cruel stranger, the visitor with the flannel footsteps... today, it is the mad dog in the house.... One eats, one drinks beside the dead, one sleeps in the midst of the dying, one laughs and one sings in the company of corpses.... The frequentation of death which makes life so precious also finishes, sometimes, by giving one a distaste for it, and more often, lassitude.

A period of conditioning on the Verdun battlefield manufactured a callousness towards one's own wounded, and an apathetic, morbid acceptance of mutilation that seem to us—in our comfy isolation—almost bestial. Captain Delvert, one of the more honest and unpretentious of the French war-writers, describes his shock on approaching the Verdun front for the first time, when his company filed past a man lying with his leg shattered by a shell:

> Nobody came to his assistance. One felt that men had become brutalized by the preoccupation of not leaving their company and also not delaying in a place where death was raining down.

In sharp contrast to the revolted and tortured Dubrulle, young Second-Lieutenant Campana recounts how, at the end of his third spell in the line at Verdun, he cold-bloodedly photographed the body of one of his men killed by a shell that hit his own dugout,

> laid open from the shoulders to the haunches like a quartered carcass of meat in a butcher's window.

He sent a copy of the photograph to a friend as a token of what a lucky escape he had had.

Returning from the Mort Homme, Raymond Jubert introspectively posed himself three questions:

> What sublime emotion inspires you at the moment of assault?
> I thought of nothing other than dragging my feet out of the mud encasing them.
> What did you feel after surviving the attack?
> I grumbled because I would have to remain several days more without *Pinard*.
> Is not one's first act to kneel down and thank God?
> No. One relieves oneself.

This kind of moral torpor was perhaps the commonest effect of a spell at Verdun, with even the more sensitive—like Jubert—who resisted the brutalizing tendency admitting to a congelation of all normal reactions. Jubert also recalls the man in his regiment who, returning from the front, was overjoyed to find his house on the outskirts of Verdun still intact; but, on discovering that all its contents had been methodically plundered, he simply burst into laughter.

To troops who had not yet been through the mill at Verdun, passing men whom they were about to relieve was an unnerving experience; they seemed like beings from another world. Lieutenant Georges Gaudy described watching his own regiment return from the May fighting near Douaumont:

> First came the skeletons of companies occasionally led by a wounded officer, leaning on a stick. All marched, or rather advanced in small steps, zigzagging as if intoxicated.... It was hard to tell the colour of their faces from that of their tunics. Mud had covered everything, dried off, and then another layer had been re-applied.... They said nothing. They had even lost the strength to complain.... It seemed as if these mute faces were crying something terrible, the unbelievable horror of their martyrdom. Some Territorials who were standing near me became pensive. They had that air of sadness that comes over one when a funeral passes by, and I overheard one say: 'It's no longer an army! These are corpses!' Two of the Territorials wept in silence, like women.

Most of the above accounts come from the French sources. For, compressed in their hemmed-in salient and hammered by an artillery that was always superior, maintained and succoured by organization that was always inferior, things were almost invariably just that much worse for the French. But, as time went on, the gap between the suffering of the opposing armies became narrower and narrower, until it was barely perceptible. By mid April German soldiers were complaining in letters home of the high casualties suffered by their ration parties; 'many would rather endure hunger than make these dangerous expeditions for food'. General von Zwehl, whose corps was to stay at Verdun, without relief, during the whole ten months the battle lasted, speaks of a special 'kind of psychosis' that infected his men there. Lastly, even the blustering von Brandis, the acclaimed conqueror of Douaumont[26] for whom war previously seems to have held nothing but raptures, is to be found eventually expressing a note of horror; nowhere, he declares, not even on the Somme, was there anything to be found worse than the 'death ravines of Verdun'.

[26]The major fortress at Verdun.

Inflation in Weimar Germany

ALEX de JONGE

The most celebrated instance of prices spiraling out of control is the hyperinflation in Weimar Germany in 1923. At the outbreak of World War I, the dollar was worth four marks; by November 1923, a person would need four trillion marks to purchase one dollar. To put this unprecedented devaluation of Germany's currency into perspective, consider the Price Revolution of the sixteenth century. This great period of inflation began in Spain and prices rose highest there, approximately 400 percent over the course of the century. Contemporaries had difficulty understanding the causes, not to mention the effects of that increase—significant to be sure, but small compared to the hyperinflation of 1923.

The German inflation was much more rapid and, obviously, intense. What were the reasons behind the hyperinflation? The Nazis found it easy and comfortable to blame the allied powers of the First World War and the Treaty of Versailles. Why? Many Germans came to believe the Nazi interpretation. Why would they not? After all, a man who should have known better, the director of the Reichsbank, implemented a solution for inflation that would have been laughable had it not been ridiculous: the use of printing presses to churn out more and more currency.

Hyperinflation had profound effects upon the German social fabric. How did the hyperinflation cause social chaos? What were its effects on morality, on the Germans' sexual behavior? Was it a coincidence that virulent anti-Semitism appeared at this time? Alex de Jonge offers dramatic and often pitiable stories of the wreckage of lives that resulted from the economic disequilibrium. Yet some benefited from hyperinflation. Which groups suffered and which prospered? What ended the period of hyperinflation?

The year 1923 has a special and dreadful connotation in German history, for it was the year of the great inflation. If defeat, abdication and revolution had begun to undermine the traditional values of German culture, then the inflation finished the process so completely that in the end there were no such values left. By November 1918 there were 184.8 marks to the pound. By late November 1923 there were 18,000,000,000,000. Although the mark was eventually "restored," and the period of inflation succeeded by a time of relative prosperity for many people, life for anyone who had lived through the lunatic year of 1923 could never be the same again.

Such a cataclysmic loss of a currency's value can never be ascribed to a single cause. Once confidence goes, the process of decline is a self-feeding one. By late 1923 no one would hold German money one moment longer than it was really necessary. It was essential to convert it into something, some object, within minutes of receiving it, if one were not to see it lose all value in a world in which prices were being marked up by 20 percent every day.

If we go back beyond the immediate cause of hyperinflation—beyond a total lack of confidence in a currency that would consequently never "find its floor," however undervalued it might appear—we find that passive resistance in the Ruhr[1] was a major factor. Effective loss of the entire Ruhr output weakened the mark disastrously, encouraging dealers to speculate against it, since the balance of payments was bound to show a vast deficit. Confidence in the currency could only begin to be restored when resistance ended late in 1923.

It has been the "patriotic" view that reparations were also a significant factor. Certainly they constituted a steady drain upon the nation's resources, a drain for which it got no return. But reparations alone would not have brought about hyperinflation. There were still other causes. Sefton Delmer[2] believes that the true explanation lay in Germany's financing of the war. She had done so very largely on credit, and was thereafter obliged to run a gigantic deficit. There were other more immediate causes, such as a total incomprehension of the situation on the part of Havenstein, director of the Reichsbank. Failing to understand why the currency was falling, he was content to blame it upon forces beyond his control—reparations—and attempted to deal with the situation by stepping up the money supply! . . .

By October 1923 it cost more to print a note than the note was worth. Nevertheless Havenstein mobilized all the printing resources that he could. Some of the presses of the Ullstein newspaper and publishing group were even commandeered by the mint and turned to the printing of money. Havenstein made regular announcements to the Reichstag to the effect that all was well since print capacity was increasing. By August 1923 he was able to print in a day a sum equivalent to two-thirds of the money in circulation. Needless to say, as an anti-inflationary policy, his measures failed.

. . . Certainly [inflation] had its beneficiaries as well as its victims. Anyone living on a pension or on fixed-interest investments—the small and cautious investor—was wiped out. Savings disappeared overnight. Pensions, annuities, government stocks, debentures, the usual investments of a careful middle class, lost all value. In the meantime big business, and export business in particular, prospered. It was so easy to get a bank loan, use it to acquire assets, and repay the loan a few months later for a tiny proportion of the original. Factory owners and agriculturalists who had issued loan stock or raised gold mortgages on their properties saw themselves released from those obligations in the same way, paying them off with worthless currency on the principle that "mark equals mark." It would be rash to suggest . . . that the occupation of the Ruhr was planned by industrialists to create an inflation which could only be to their benefit. Yet we should remember that Stinnes,[3]

---

[1] Belgian and French troops occupied the Ruhr Valley early in 1923 because the Germans had not delivered coal as the reparations agreement stipulated.

[2] A German newspaper reporter.

[3] Hugo Stinnes, speculator.

the multi-millionaire, had both predicted that occupation and ended up the owner of more than 1,500 enterprises. It should also be remembered that some businessmen had a distinctly strange view of the shareholder. He was regarded by many as a burdensome nuisance, a drag upon their enterprise. He was the enemy and they were quite happy to see him wiped out to their benefit. Inflation was their chance to smash him. Witness the behavior of a banker at a shareholders' meeting at which it was suggested he should make a greater distribution of profit: "Why should I throw away my good money for the benefit of people whom I do not know?"

The ingenious businessman had many ways of turning inflation to good account. Thus employees had to pay income tax weekly. Employers paid their tax yearly upon profits which were almost impossible to assess. They would exploit the situation of a smaller businessman, obliged to offer six to eight weeks of credit to keep his customers, by insisting on payment in cash. The delay between paying for the goods and reselling them eroded any profit the small man might make, while the big supplier prospered.

Whether or not the industrialists actually caused inflation, their visible prosperity made them detested by an otherwise impoverished nation. Hugo Stinnes became an almost legendary embodiment of speculation and evil. Alec Swan[4] remembers how hungry Germans would stare at prosperous fellow countrymen in fur coats, sullenly muttering *"Fabrikbesitzer"* (factory owner) at them. The term had become an insult and an expression of envy at one and the same time.

Hyperinflation created social chaos on an extraordinary scale. As soon as one was paid, one rushed off to the shops and bought absolutely anything in exchange for paper about to become worthless. If a woman had the misfortune to have a husband working away from home and sending money through the post, the money was virtually without value by the time it arrived. Workers were paid once, then twice, then five times a week with an ever-depreciating currency. By November 1923 real wages were down 25 percent compared with 1913, and envelopes were not big enough to accommodate all the stamps needed to mail them; the excess stamps were stuck to separate sheets affixed to the letter. Normal commercial transactions became virtually impossible. One luckless author received a sizable advance on a work only to find that within a week it was just enough to pay the postage on the manuscript. By late 1923 it was not unusual to find 100,000 mark notes in the gutter, tossed there by contemptuous beggars at a time when $50 could buy a row of houses in Berlin's smartest street.

A Berlin couple who were about to celebrate their golden wedding received an official letter advising them that the mayor, in accordance with Prussian custom, would call and present them with a donation of money.

[4]An Englishman who lived in Germany during the 1920s.

Next morning the mayor, accompanied by several aldermen in picturesque robes, arrived at the aged couple's house, and solemnly handed over in the name of the Prussian State 1,000,000,000,000 marks or one half-penny.

The banks were flourishing, however. They found it necessary to build annexes and would regularly advertise for more staff, especially bookkeepers "good with zeros." Alec Swan knew a girl who worked in a bank in Bonn. She told him that it eventually became impossible to count out the enormous numbers of notes required for a "modest" withdrawal, and the banks had to reconcile themselves to issuing banknotes by their weight.

By the autumn of 1923 the currency had virtually broken down. Cities and even individual businesses would print their own notes, secured by food stocks, or even the objects the money was printed on. Notes were issued on leather, porcelain, even lace, with the idea that the object itself was guarantee of the value of the "coin." It was a view of the relationship between monetary and real value that took one back five hundred years. Germany had become a barter society; the Middle Ages had returned. Shoe factories would pay their workers in bonds for shoes, which were negotiable. Theaters carried signs advertising the cheapest seats for two eggs, the most expensive for a few ounces of butter which was the most negotiable of all commodities. It was so precious that the very rich, such as Stinnes, used to take a traveling butter dish with them when they put up at Berlin's smartest hotel. A pound of butter attained "fantastic value." It could purchase a pair of boots, trousers made to measure, a portrait, a semester's schooling, or even love. A young girl stayed out late one night while her parents waited up anxiously. When she came in at four in the morning, her mother prevented her father from taking a strap to her by showing him the pound of butter that she had "earned." Boots were also highly negotiable: "The immense paper value of a pair of boots renders it hazardous for the traveler to leave them outside the door of his bedroom at his hotel."

Thieves grew more enterprising still in their search for a hedge against inflation.

Even the mailboxes are plundered for the sake of the stamps attached to the letters. Door handles and metal facings are torn from doors; telephone and telegraph wires are stolen wholesale and the lead removed from roofs.

In Berlin all metal statues were removed from public places because they constituted too great a temptation to an ever-increasing number of thieves. One of the consequences of the soaring crime rate was a shortage of prison accommodation. Criminals given short sentences were released and told to reapply for admission in due course.

It was always possible that one might discover an unexpected source of wealth. A Munich newspaperman was going through his attic when he came upon a set of partly gold dentures, once the property of his grandmother, long since dead. He was able to live royally upon the proceeds of the sale for several weeks.

The period threw up other anomalies. Rents on old houses were fixed by law, while those on new ones were exorbitantly high. As a result in many parts of Germany housing was literally rationed. If one were fortunate enough to live in old rented property, one lived virtually free. The landlord, however, suffered dreadfully: to repair a window might cost him the equivalent of a whole month's rent. Thus yet another of the traditional modes of safe investment, renting property, proved a disaster. Hitherto well-to-do middle-class families found it necessary to take in lodgers to make ends meet. The practice was so widespread that not to do so attracted unfavorable attention suggesting that one was a profiteer.... Real property lost its value like everything else.... More telling is a famous song of inflation:

> We are drinking away our grandma's
> Little capital
> And her first and second mortgage too.

As noted in the famous and highly intelligent paper the *Weltbühne*,[5] the song picked out the difference between the "old" generation of grandparents who had scraped and saved carefully in order to acquire the security of a house, and the "new generation" for whom there could be no security any more, who "raided capital" or what was left of it, and were prepared to go to any lengths to enjoy themselves. Where their parents' lives had been structured with certainties, the only certainty that they possessed was that saving was a form of madness.

Not all Germans suffered, of course. Late in 1923 Hugo Stinnes did what he could to alleviate the misery of his fellow countrymen by the magnanimous decision to double his tipping rate in view of the inflation. Along with rents, rail fares were also fixed and did not go up in proportion to inflation. Consequently, travel appeared absurdly cheap. Alec Swan recalls crossing Germany in the greatest style for a handful of copper coins. Yet even this was beyond the means of most Germans. A German train in 1923 would consist of several first-class carriages occupied entirely by comfortable foreigners, and a series of rundown third-class carriages crammed to bursting with impoverished and wretched Germans.

Although the shops were full of food, no one could afford it except foreigners. Germans often had to be content with food not normally thought of as fit for human consumption. In Hamburg there were riots when it was discovered that the local canning factory was using cats and rats for its preserved meats. Sausage factories also made much use of cat and horse meat. Moreover, ... some of the most famous mass murderers of the age used

---

[5]The *World Arena,* a left-wing journal.

to preserve and sell the meat of their victims in a combination of savagery and an almost sexual obsession with food that mythologizes much of the darkness and the violence that were latent in the mood of Weimar.

If 1923 was a bad year for the Germans it was an *annus mirabilis*[6] for foreigners. Inflation restored the sinking morale of the army of occupation; small wonder when every private found himself a rich man overnight. In Cologne an English girl took lessons from the *prima donna* of the opera for sixpence a lesson. When she insisted that in future she pay a shilling, the *prima donna* wept with delight. Shopping became a way of life: "All through that autumn and winter whenever we felt hipped we went out and bought something. It was a relaxation limited at home, unlimited in the Rhineland."

Germany was suddenly infested with foreigners. It has been suggested that the English actually sent their unemployed out and put them up in hotels because it was cheaper than paying out the dole. Alec Swan stayed with his family in a pension in Bonn. They had moved to Germany because life was so much cheaper there. . . .

To find oneself suddenly wealthy in the midst of tremendous hardship proved rather unsettling. Inflation corrupted foreigners almost as much as the Germans. The English in Cologne could think of nothing else.

> They talked with sparkling eyes and a heightened color, in the banks, the streets, the shops, the restaurants, any public place, with Germans standing around gazing at them.
> Scruples were on the whole overwhelmed by the sudden onslaught of wealth and purchasing power beyond one's dreams.

As Alec Swan put it:

> You felt yourself superior to the others, and at the same time you realized that it was not quite justified. When we went to Bellingshausen, which was a sort of wine place near Königswinter, we would start drinking in the afternoon. I would always order champagne and my Dutch friend would shake his head in disapproval. We'd have two ice buckets: he with some Rhine wine and me with German champagne. It was really rather ridiculous for a chap of my age to drink champagne on his own.
> Being as wealthy as that was an extraordinary feeling, although there were many things you couldn't get in Germany. It was impossible to buy a decent hat, for instance. But you could have any food you wanted if you could pay for it. I haven't eaten anything like as well as that in my life. I used to go to the Königshalle (that was the big café in Bonn) at eleven o'clock in the morning for a *Frühschoppen*[7] and a *Bergmann's Stückchen*, a large piece of toast with fresh shrimps and mayonnaise. For a German that would have been quite impossible.

---

[6]Extraordinary year.
[7]Lunchtime drinking.

I paid two million marks for a glass of beer. You changed as little money as you could every day. No, one did not feel guilty, one felt it was perfectly normal, a gift from the gods. Of course there was hatred in the air, and I dare say a lot of resentment against foreigners, but we never noticed it. They were still beaten, you see, a bit under and occupied.

My mother did buy meat for three or four German families. I remember I bought an air gun, and, when I grew tired of it, I gave it to my German teacher's son, with some pellets. Some time later the woman came to me in tears saying the boy had run out of pellets, and they could not afford to buy any more.

On another occasion Swan, all of twenty-two at the time, took the head of the Leipzig book fair out for a meal and looked on incredulously as the elderly and eminent bookseller cast dignity to the winds and started to eat as if he had not had a meal in months.

Stories of money changing and currency speculation are legion. *Bureaux de change*[8] were to be found in every shop, apartment block, hairdresser's, tobacconist's. An Englishman named Sandford Griffith remembers having to visit a number of cities in the Ruhr which had local currencies. He stopped at a dealer's to change some money, but when he produced a pound note the dealer was so overcome by such wealth that he simply waved a hand at his stock of currency and invited the astonished Englishman to help himself. Foreigners acquired antiques and *objets de valeur*[9] at rock-bottom prices. A favorite trick was to buy in the morning with a down payment, saying that one would fetch the rest of the money from the bank. By waiting until the new exchange rate had come out at noon before changing one's money into marks, an extra profit could be made on the amount that the mark had fallen since the day before.

The population responded to the foreign onslaught with a double pricing system. Shops would mark their prices up for foreigners. It would cost a tourist 200 marks to visit Potsdam, when it cost a German 25. Some shops simply declined to sell to foreigners at all. In Berlin a . . . tax on gluttony was appended to all meals taken in luxury restaurants.

Foreign embassies were also major beneficiaries of inflation, giving lavish banquets for virtually nothing. Indeed the *Weltbühne* noted with great resentment the presence of foreign legations of nations so insignificant that they would never hitherto have dreamed of being represented in Germany. The spectacle of foreigners of all nations, living grotesquely well and eating beyond their fill in the middle of an impoverished and starving Germany did not encourage the Germans to rally to the causes of pacificism and internationalism. The apparent reason for their inflation was there for all to see, occupying the Ruhr.

[8] Foreign exchange offices.
[9] Valuables.

The surface manifestations of inflation were unnerving enough, but its effect upon behavior, values and morals were to reach very deep indeed, persisting for years after the stabilization of the mark, right up to the moment when Hitler came to power. The middle class—civil servants, professional men, academics—which had stood for stability, social respectability, cultural continuity, and constituted a conservative and restraining influence was wiped out. A French author met a threadbare and dignified old couple in spotless but well-worn prewar clothes in a café. They ordered two clear soups and one beer, eating as if they were famished. He struck up a conversation with the man, who spoke excellent French and had known Paris before the war. "Monsieur," the man replied, when asked his profession, "I used to be a retired professor, but we are beggars now."

There was a general feeling that an old and decent society was being destroyed. If the year 1918 had removed that society's political traditions and its national pride, 1923 was disposing of its financial substructure. In response, people grew either listless or hysterical. A German woman told Pearl Buck[10] that a whole generation simply lost its taste for life—a taste that would only be restored to them by the Nazis. Family bonds melted away. A friend of Swan, a most respectable German whose father was a civil servant on the railways, simply left home and roamed the country with a band. It was a typical 1923 case history. Young men born between 1900 and 1905 who had grown up expecting to inherit a place in the sun from their well-to-do parents suddenly found they had nothing. From imperial officer to bank clerk became a "normal" progression. Such disinherited young men naturally gravitated toward the illegal right-wing organizations and other extremist groups. Inflation had destroyed savings, self-assurance, a belief in the value of hard work, morality and sheer human decency. Young people felt that they had no prospects and no hope. All around them they could see nothing but worried faces. "When they are crying even a gay laughter seems impossible . . . and all around it was the same . . . quite different from the days of revolution when we had hoped things would be better."

Traditional middle-class morality disappeared overnight. People of good family co-habited and had illegitimate children. The impossibility of making a marriage economically secure apparently led to a disappearance of marriage itself. Germany in 1923 was a hundred years away from those stable middle-class values that Thomas Mann[11] depicted in *The Magic Mountain*, set in a period scarcely ten years before. Pearl Buck wrote that "Love was old-fashioned, sex was modern. It was the Nazis who restored the 'right to love' in their propaganda."

Paradoxically, the inflation that destroyed traditional German values was also largely responsible for the creation of that new, decadent and dissolute generation that put Berlin on the cosmopolitan pleasure seeker's

[10] An American writer, 1892–1973.

[11] German author (1875–1955) and winner of the Nobel Prize in literature in 1929.

map, and has kept it or its image there ever since. It was no coincidence that 1923 was the year that the Hotel Adlon first hired gigolos, professional male dancers, to entertain lady clients at so much per dance. It was also a period when prostitution boomed. A Frenchman accustomed enough to the spectacle of Montmartre[12] was unable to believe his eyes when he beheld the open corruption of Berlin's Friedrichstrasse. Klaus Mann[13] remembers:

> Some of them looked like fierce Amazons strutting in high boots made of green glossy leather. One of them brandished a supple cane and leered at me as I passed by. "Good evening, madame" I said. She whispered in my ear: "Want to be my slave? Costs only six billion and a cigarette. A bargain. Come along, honey."
> ...Some of those who looked most handsome and elegant were actually boys in disguise. It seemed incredible considering the sovereign grace with which they displayed their saucy coats and hats. I wondered if they might be wearing little silks under their exquisite gowns; must look funny I thought... a boy's body with pink lace-trimmed skirt.

Commercial sex in Berlin was not well organized and was considered by connoisseurs to be inferior to that of Budapest, which had the best red-light district in Europe. But in Berlin there was no longer any clear-cut distinction between the red-light district and the rest of town, between professional and amateur. The booted Amazons were streetwalkers who jostled for business in competition with school children....

> Along the entire Kurfürstendamm powdered and rouged young men sauntered, and they were not all professionals; every schoolboy wanted to earn some money, and in the dimly lit bars one might see government officials and men of the world of finance tenderly courting drunken sailors without shame....
> At the pervert balls of Berlin, hundreds of men dressed as women, and hundreds of women as men danced under the benevolent eyes of the police.... Young girls bragged proudly of their perversion. To be sixteen and still under suspicion of virginity would have been considered a disgrace in any school in Berlin at the time.

Another visitor was struck by what he referred to as Berlin's "pathological" mood:

> Nowhere in Europe was the disease of sex so violent as in Germany. A sense of decency and hypocrisy made the rest of Europe suppress or hide its more uncommon manifestations. But the Germans, with their vitality and their lack of a sense of form, let their emotions run riot. Sex was one of the few pleasures left to them....

[12]District in Paris.
[13]German writer, 1906–1949.

In the East End of Berlin there was a large *Diele* (dancing café) in which from 9 P.M. to 1 A.M. you could watch shopkeepers, clerks and policemen of mature age dance together. They treated one another with an affectionate mateyness; the evening brought them their only recreation among congenial people. Politically most of them were conservative; with the exception of sex they subscribed to all the conventions of their caste. In fact, they almost represented the normal element of German sex life.

... There was a well-known *Diele* frequented almost entirely by foreigners of both sexes. The entertainment was provided by native boys between 14 and 18. Often a boy would depart with one of the guests and return alone a couple of hours later. Most of the boys looked undernourished. ... Many of them had to spend the rest of the night in a railway station, a public park, or under the arch of a bridge.

Inflation made Germany break with her past by wiping out the local equivalent of the Forsytes.[14] It also reinforced the postwar generation's appetite for invention, innovation and compulsive pleasure seeking, while making them bitterly aware of their own rootlessness. It is not surprising that cocaine was very much in vogue in those years. The drug was peddled openly in restaurants by the hat-check girls, and formed an integral part of the social life of Berlin.

Inflation was also taken as evidence that the old order was morally and practically bankrupt. Capitalism had failed to guarantee the security of its citizens. It had benefited speculators, hustlers, con men and factory owners. It had spawned Hugo Stinnes, but had done nothing for the common good. The need for an alternative system appeared universally self-evident, and until one came along the thing to do was to enjoy oneself, drink away grandma's capital, or exchange one's clothes for cocaine: a dinner jacket got you four grams, a morning coat eight.

Inflation and the despair that it created also acted as the catalyst of aggression. It was at this time that anti-Semitism began to appear in Berlin. An attractive German lady remembers walking through a prosperous suburb with a Jewish friend when someone called to her in the street, "Why do you go around with a Jew? Get yourself a good German man." In one sense she found it understandable. The ordinary German was very slow to adjust to the special situation of inflation, and in 1923 anyone who was not very quick on their feet soon went under. Jews were better at economic survival in such situations than were other Germans—so much so, she says, that by the end of inflation they had become terribly conspicuous. All the expensive restaurants, all the best theater seats, appeared to be filled by Jews who had survived or even improved their position.

One can imagine that Germans who had lost their own status might have resented the spectacle. One old conservative I spoke to added a

---

[14] A prosperous bourgeois family in novels by John Galsworthy (1867–1933).

second reason for the rise of anti-Semitism in a Prussian society which had traditionally been quite free of it. The arguments advanced are his own, and tell us something of his prejudices. He believes that the Weimar Republic was too liberal with regard to immigration from the East, admitting thousands of Jews from Galicia and the old Pale of settlement,[15] persons who, in his words, were "Asiatics, not Jews." They found themselves in a strange anonymous town, free of all the ethical restraints imposed by life in a small community where their families had lived for several generations. They tended therefore to abandon all morality as they stepped out of their own homes, morality being strictly a family affair. They would sail as close to the wind as the law would allow, for they had no good will, no neighborly esteem to lose. The gentleman in question is convinced that their mode of doing business during the inflation did a great deal to create or aggravate more generalized anti-Semitic feelings.

Yet precisely these immigrants were to prove a mainstay of the republic. An old Berlin Jew who had spent some time in prewar Auschwitz told me that it was just these Eastern Jews who offered the most active and effective resistance to National Socialism. They were activists where native Berliners, Jew and Gentile alike, were more inclined to remain on the sidelines.

Certainly the period saw a rise in pro-National Socialist feelings. The first Nazi that Professor Reiff[16] knew personally was a schoolboy in his last year. The young man's father, a small civil servant, had just lost everything through inflation, and as a result his son joined the party. Pearl Buck records the views of an antimonarchical businessman worried by inflation, who said of the Nazis: "They are still young men and act foolishly, but they will grow up. If they will only drop Ludendorff and his kind, maybe someday I'll give them a chance."

For many people, who felt that they had lost all zest for a life rendered colorless by war and poverty, who could see that they lived in a world in which *Schieber*[17] won and decent folk lost, a new ideology combining patriotism and socialist anticapitalism seemed to be the only viable alternative to a totally unacceptable state of financial chaos and capitalist *laissez-faire*. The shock of inflation had made people mistrustful of the past, immensely suspicious of the present, and pathetically ready to have hopes for the future. It was perfectly clear to them that new solutions were needed, equally clear that until such solutions should appear they could put their trust in nothing except the validity of their own sensations.

The mood of the inflationary period ... endured well beyond inflation itself to become the mood of the Weimar age, a blend of pleasure seeking, sexual and political extremism, and a yearning for strange gods.

[15]The Pale was an area where Jews were permitted to live in Russia.

[16]Professor of economics who lived in Berlin during the Weimar period.

[17]Profiteers.

It was an epoch of high ecstasy and ugly scheming, a singular mixture of unrest and fanaticism. Every extravagant idea that was not subject to regulation reaped a golden harvest: theosophy, occultism, yogism and Paracelcism.[18] Anything that gave hope of newer and greater thrills, anything in the way of narcotics, morphine, cocaine, heroin found a tremendous market; on the stage incest and parricide, in politics communism and fascism constituted the most favored themes.

It was indeed a time for the revaluation of all (devalued) values.

The mood of 1923 persisted long after inflation ended, which is why the manner of its ending is offered here as a postscript, for nothing was restored but the currency.

Restoration of confidence was only possible when passive resistance in the Ruhr ended in the autumn of 1923. At the same time, the Reichsbank appointed Hjalmar Schacht to deal with inflation. He was an extremely able man with a clear grasp of essentials. He realized that his main problem was to restore confidence both within and without Germany, and to try to prevent people from spending money as soon as it came into their hands. He established a new currency, based on the notional sum total of Germany's agricultural wealth, the *Roggen-Mark* (rye mark). This had the effect of restoring psychological confidence in the currency. He combined the move with a gigantic bear trap laid by the Reichsbank to catch the speculators who would regularly build up huge short positions in marks, in the almost certain expectation that the mark would continue to fall against the dollar: i.e., they sold marks they hadn't got, knowing that they could buy them for a fraction of their present value when the time came to meet the demand. When the mark stopped falling, thanks to the Reichsbank's engineering, they had to rush to close their positions, and were forced to buy marks which had actually begun to go up. Many speculators lost the entire fortunes which they had built up over the year.

Schacht's measures sufficed to stop the rot, but in the period between the ordnance declaring the new currency and the appearance of the first notes, there was an interim of pure chaos in which, as Lord d'Abernon noted, "four kinds of paper money and five kinds of stable value currency were in use. On November 20, 1923, 1 dollar = 4.2 gold marks = 4.2 trillion paper marks. But by December the currency was stable." The last November issue of the weekly *Berliner Illustrirter Zeitung*[19] cost a billion marks, the first December issue 20 pfennigs. Confidence seemed to have been restored overnight. Germany could breathe again. . . .

---

[18] Doctrines associated with the Swiss physician and alchemist Paracelsus (1493–1541).

[19] The *Berlin Illustrated Newspaper*.

The Nazi Camps

HENRY FRIEDLANDER

The Nazi death camps by themselves are sufficient to differentiate the twentieth century from all that had come before. The Germans murdered, with a callous equanimity that makes one shudder, approximately eleven million people. This figure does not include those killed in warfare, even the masses of civilians fallen victim to indiscriminate terrorist airplane bombardments or those civilians killed because of resistance to the Nazis. Historians use the term "Holocaust" to refer to the systematic extermination of the Jews, the primary target of Nazi barbarity. Of the eleven million killed in the German effort to "purify" Western civilization, six million were Jews and one million of those were children. What groups, besides the Jews, went to the Nazi camps? What was the difference between concentration camps and extermination camps?

Henry Friedlander explains that the camps before 1939, heinous though they were, did not match in numbers or brutality those after 1939, and especially those functioning after 1942. How exactly did World War II affect the development of the Nazi camps? Who ran the camps? How were they organized? What was life like at the camps for the prisoners who arrived there? What was the relationship between the camps and German industries? How did camps in western Europe differ from those in eastern Europe?

Why did the Nazis, after experimenting with various methods of exterminating masses of people, reach the conclusion that the killing centers provided the most effective means of attaining "the final solution"? What methods of murder did the Germans prefer at the death camps? How did Auschwitz, the best known of the camps, earn its infamous reputation?

The Nazis established camps for their political and ideological opponents as soon as they seized power in 1933, and they retained them as an integral part of the Third Reich until their defeat in 1945. During the 1930s, these concentration camps were at first intended for political enemies, but later also included professional criminals, social misfits, other undesirables, and Jews.

During World War II, the number of camps expanded greatly and the number of prisoners increased enormously. Opponents from all occupied countries entered the camps, and the camps were transformed into an empire for the exploitation of slave labor. Late in 1941 and early in 1942, the Nazis established extermination camps to kill the Jews, and also Russian POWs and Gypsies. These camps had only one function: the extermination of large numbers of human beings in specially designed gas chambers. The largest Nazi camp, Auschwitz-Birkenau, combined the functions of extermination and concentration camp; there, healthy Jews were selected for labor and, thus, temporarily saved from the gas chambers. In this way, small numbers of Jews survived in Auschwitz and other Eastern camps. In 1944–1945, as the need for labor increased, surviving Jews were introduced into all camps, including those located in Germany proper.

In the United States, the term "death camp" has frequently been used to describe both concentration and extermination camps. It has been applied to camps like Auschwitz and Treblinka—killing centers where human beings were exterminated on the assembly line. But it has also been applied without distinction to camps like Dachau and Belsen—concentration camps without gas chambers, where the prisoners were killed by abuse, starvation, and disease.

Six Nazi concentration camps existed on German soil before World War II: Dachau, near Munich; Sachsenhausen, in Oranienburg near Berlin; Buchenwald, on the Ettersberg overlooking Weimar; Flossenbürg, in northern Bavaria; Mauthausen, near Linz in Austria; and the women's camp Ravensbrück, north of Berlin. Other camps like Esterwegen, Oranienburg, or Columbia Haus had existed for a few years, but only the permanent six had survived; they had replaced all other camps. Dachau opened in 1933, Sachsenhausen in 1936, Buchenwald in 1937, Flossenbürg and Mauthausen in 1938, and Ravensbrück in 1939.

These camps, officially designated *Konzentrationslager* or KL, and popularly known as Kazet or KZ, were originally designed to hold actual or potential political opponents of the regime. A special decree had removed the constitutional prohibition against arbitrary arrest and detention, permitting the political police—the Gestapo—to impose "protective custody" (*Schutzhaft*) without trial or appeal. The protective custody prisoners—mostly Communists and Socialists, but sometimes also liberals and conservatives—were committed to the camps for an indefinite period. The camps, removed from the control of the regular prison authorities, were not run by the Gestapo; instead, they were administered and guarded by the Death Head Units of the black-shirted SS (*Schutzstaffel*),[1] a private Nazi party army fulfilling an official state function.

Reich Leader of the SS Heinrich Himmler appointed Theodor Eicke as Inspector of the Concentration Camps and Commander of the Death Head Units. Eicke had been Commandant of Dachau; he had built it into the "model camp." Eliminating unauthorized private murders and brutalities, he had systematized terror and inhumanity, training his SS staff and guards to be disciplined and without compassion. From the prisoners, Eicke demanded discipline, obedience, hard labor, and "manliness"; conversion to Nazi ideology was neither expected nor desired. Eicke issued rules that regulated every area of camp life and that imposed severe punishments for the least infraction. His petty rules were a perversion of the draconic training system of the Prussian army. This system accounted for the endless roll calls

[1] Elite guard.

(the *Appell*), the introduction of corporeal punishment (the *Pruegelstrafe*), and the long hours of enforced calisthenics. The SS added special refinements to this torture: suspending prisoners from trees, starving them in the camp prison (the *Bunker*), and shooting them while "trying to escape." In this system, labor was only another form of torture.

When Eicke became Inspector, he imposed the Dachau system on all concentration camps. Every camp had the same structure; every camp was divided into the following six departments:

1. The *Kommandantur*. This was the office of the commandant, a senior SS officer (usually a colonel or lieutenant-colonel and sometimes even a brigadier general) assisted by the office of the adjutant. He commanded the entire camp, including all staff, guards, and inmates.
2. The Administration. The administrative offices were charged with overseeing the camp's economic and bureaucratic affairs. Junior SS officers directed various subdepartments, such as those for supply, construction, or inmate properties.
3. The Camp Physician. This office was headed by the garrison physician and included SS medical officers and SS medical orderlies. The camp physician served the medical needs of the SS staff and guards; he also supervised medical treatment and sanitary conditions for the inmates.
4. The Political Department. This office was staffed by SS police officers (not members of the Death Head Units), who were assigned to the camps to compile the dossiers of the prisoners and to investigate escapes and conspiracies. They took their orders from both the commandant and the Gestapo.
5. The Guard Troops. These were the military units assigned to guard the camp. Quartered in barracks and trained for combat, they served under their own SS officers. They manned the watch towers and the outer camp perimeter. Officially, they had contact with the prisoners only when they accompanied labor brigades as guards.
6. The *Schutzhaftlager*. The protective custody camp was the actual camp for the prisoners; surrounded by electrified barbed wire, it occupied only a small fraction of the entire camp territory. It was headed by a junior SS officer (captain or major) as protective custody camp leader. He was assisted by the senior SS noncommissioned officer; this roll call leader (*Rapportführer*) supervised the day-by-day running of the camp. Under him, various SS men served as block leaders in charge of individual prisoner barracks and as commando leaders in charge of individual labor brigades.

The SS hierarchy of the protective custody camp was duplicated by appointed inmate functionaries. But while the SS were always called "leader" (*Führer*), the inmate functionaries were called "elders" (*Aeltester*). The chief inmate functionary, for example, was the camp elder, corresponding to the SS role call leader. The functionary corresponding to the block leader was the block elder, who was in charge of a single barrack. He was assisted by room orderlies, the so-called *Stubendienst*. The functionary corresponding to the commando leader was the *kapo* in charge of a single labor brigade. He was assisted by prisoner foremen, the *Vorarbeiter*. In large labor brigades with several *kapos*, the SS also appointed a supervising *kapo* (*Oberkapo*). (The unusual title *kapo*, or *capo*, meaning head, was probably introduced into Dachau by Italian workers employed in Bavaria for road construction during the 1930s. During World War II popular camp language, especially as spoken by non-German inmates, transformed *kapo* into a generic term for all inmate functionaries.) In addition, inmate clerks, known as *Schreiber*, performed a crucial task. The camp clerk assisted the roll call leader and supervised the preparation of all reports and orders. Clerks also served in labor brigades, the inmate infirmary, and various SS offices.

Until 1936–1937, the prisoners in the concentration camps were mostly political "protective custody prisoners" committed to the camps by the Gestapo. At that time, the category of "preventive arrest"...was added to that of "protective custody." The Criminal Police, the Kripo, and not the Gestapo, thereafter sent large numbers of "preventive arrest prisoners" to the camps. These included the so-called professional criminals....They were rounded up on the basis of lists previously prepared; later, the police simply transferred persons who had been convicted of serious crimes to the camps after they had served their regular prison terms. The Gestapo and Kripo also used preventive and protective arrest to incarcerate the so-called asocials, a group that included Gypsies, vagabonds, shirkers, prostitutes, and any person the police thought unfit for civilian society. Finally, the Gestapo sent to the camps those whose failure to conform posed a possible threat to national unity; this included homosexuals as well as Jehovah's Witnesses.

In the concentration camps, the inmates lost all individuality and were known only by their number. Shorn of their hair and dressed in prison stripes, they wore their number stitched to their outer garment (during the war in Auschwitz non-German prisoners usually had this number tattooed on their forearm). In addition, the arrest category of each prisoner was represented under his number by a color-coded triangle. The most common were: red for political prisoners, green for professional criminals, black for asocials, pink for homosexuals, and purple for Jehovah's Witnesses. Inmate functionaries wore armbands designating their office. The SS used mostly "greens" for the important offices, but during the war the "reds" often replaced them and in some camps even non-German inmates were appointed *kapos* and block elders.

Before 1938, Jews usually entered the camps only if they also belonged to one of the affected categories. In the aftermath of the *Kristallnacht*[2] in November, 1938, the police rounded up the first large wave of Jewish men. Approximately 35,000 Jews thus entered the camp system, but most were released when their families were able to produce valid immigration papers for them.

---

[2]"Night of the Broken Glass," Nazi anti-Jewish riots, 10 November 1938.

In 1938, after the roundups of criminals, asocials, Jews, and Jehovah's Witnesses, and after the waves of arrests in Austria and the Sudetenland, the camp population reached its highest point for the prewar years. But after the release of large numbers, it sank again to approximately 25,000 by the summer of 1939.

World War II brought substantial changes to the Nazi concentration camp system. Large numbers of prisoners flooded the camps from all occupied countries of Europe. Often entire groups were committed to the camps; for example, members of the Polish professional classes were rounded up as part of the "General Pacification Operation" and members of the resistance were rounded up throughout western Europe under the "Night and Fog Decree."[3] To accommodate these prisoners, new camps were established: in 1940, Auschwitz in Upper Silesia and Neuengamme in Hamburg; in 1941, Natzweiler in Alsace and Gross-Rosen in Lower Silesia; in 1942, Stutthof near Danzig; in 1943, Lublin-Maidanek in eastern Poland and Vught in Holland; in 1944, Dora-Mittelbau in Saxony and Bergen-Belsen near Hanover.

By 1942, the concentration camp system had begun to develop into a massive slave labor empire. Already in 1939, the SS had established its own industries in the concentration camps. These included the quarries at Mauthausen, the Gustloff armament works at Buchenwald, and a textile factory at Ravensbrück. During the war this trend continued; every camp had SS enterprises attached to it: forging money and testing shoes at Sachsenhausen, growing plants and breeding fish at Auschwitz, and producing fur coats at Maidanek. In addition, the SS rented out prisoners for use as slave labor by German industries. The prisoners were worked to death on meagre rations while the SS pocketed their wages: Both SS and industry profited. I. G. Farben established factories in Auschwitz for the production of synthetic oil and rubber; Dora-Mittelbau was established to serve the subterranean factories of central Germany. However, the largest expansion came with the creation of numerous subsidiary camps, the *Aussenkommandos.* For example, Dachau eventually had 168 and Buchenwald 133 subsidiary camps. Some of these—like Mauthausen's Gusen—became as infamous as their mother camp. The growing economic importance of the camps forced a reorganization. Early in 1942, the Inspectorate of the Concentration Camps, previously an independent SS agency, was absorbed by the agency directing the SS economic empire. It became Department D of the SS Central Office for Economy and Administration (*SS Wirtschafts-Verwaltungshauptamt,* or WVHA); chief of WVHA Oswald Pohl became the actual master of the camps.

After 1939, the concentration camps were no longer the only camps for the administrative incarceration of the enemies of the regime. They lost their exclusivity to a variety of new institutions: ghettos, transit camps, and different types of labor camps. In eastern Europe, the German administration resurrected the medieval ghetto, forcing the Jews to live

[3]Order issued 7 December 1941 to seize "persons endangering German security."

and work behind barbed wire in specially designated city districts. These ghettos served as temporary reservations for the exploitation of Jewish labor; eventually everyone was deported and most were immediately killed.

The Germans did not establish ghettos in central or western Europe, but a variety of camps existed in most occupied countries of the West. In France, camps appeared even before the German conquest. There the French government incarcerated Spanish Republican refugees and members of the International Brigade.[4] After the declaration of war, these camps received large numbers of other aliens: Jewish and non-Jewish anti-Nazi German and Austrian refugees; Polish and Russian Jews; Gypsies and "vagabonds." The largest of these camps was Gurs, in the foothills of the Pyrenees; others included Compiègne, Les Milles, Le Vernet, Pithiviers, Rivesaltes, and St. Cyprien. After the German conquest, these camps were maintained by the French and the inmates were eventually deported to Germany or Poland.

Most Jews from western Europe went through transit camps that served as staging areas for the deportations to the East: Drancy in France, Malines (Mechelen) in Belgium, and Westerbork in Holland. Theresienstadt, established in the Protectorate of Bohemia and Moravia, served the dual function of transit camp and "model" ghetto.

Captured Allied soldiers found their way into POW camps: the Oflags for officers and the Stalags for the ranks. Their treatment depended in part on the status of their nation in the Nazi racial scheme. Allied soldiers captured in the West, even Jews, were treated more or less as provided by the Geneva Convention. Allied soldiers captured in the East, however, did not receive any protection from international agreements. Camps for Red Army POWs were simply cages where millions died of malnutrition and exposure. Prisoners identified as supporters of the Soviet system—commissars, party members, intellectuals, and all Jews—were turned over by the *Wehrmacht*[5] to the SS Security Police, who either shot them or sent them to concentration camps.

Labor camps had appeared immediately after the start of the war. Hinzert in the Rhineland was opened for German workers and was later transformed into a Buchenwald subsidiary for former German members of the French Foreign Legion. Similar camps appeared in Germany for workers imported from the East (*Ostarbeiter*) and in most European countries for a variety of indentured workers, such as those for Jews in Hungary.

Most important were the Forced Labor Camps for Jews in the East. Hundreds of these camps, ranging from the very small to the very large, were established in Poland, the Baltic states, and the occupied territories of the Soviet Union. These forced labor camps were not part of the concentration camp system, and they were not supervised by WVHA. Instead, they were

---

[4]Foreigners who fought under the auspices of the Soviet Union for the Republicans during the Spanish Civil War.

[5]The German army.

operated by the local SS and Police Leaders, Himmler's representatives in the occupied territories. While executive authority rested with the SS Security Police, the camps could be run by any German national: police officers, military officers, or civilian foremen. Although the supervisors were always German, the guards were usually non-German troops. Some of these were racial Germans (*Volksdeutsche*), but most were Ukrainians, Latvians, and other eastern European nationals recruited as SS auxiliaries.

Conditions varied from labor camp to labor camp. Some were tolerable and others resembled the worst concentration camps. Like the Jews in the ghettos, those in the labor camps were eventually deported and killed; some labor camps, like Janowska in Lemberg, also served as places for mass executions. Only a few camps, economically valuable for the SS, remained in operation. In late 1943, WVHA seized them from the SS and Police Leaders and turned them into regular concentration camps: Plaszow near Cracow in Poland, Kovno in Lithuania, Riga-Kaiserwald in Latvia, Klooga and Vaivara in Estonia; other camps, like Radom, became subsidiaries of these or older concentration camps.

World War II also changed the function of the concentration camp system. On the one hand, it became a large empire of slave labor, but on the other, it became the arena for mass murder. During the war, persons sentenced to death without the benefit of judicial proceedings were taken to the nearest concentration camp and shot. Large numbers of inmates no longer able to work were killed through gas or lethal injections. Thousands of Russian POWs were killed in the concentration camps, while millions of Jews were systematically gassed in Auschwitz and Maidanek.

In 1943 and 1944, large numbers of Jews entered the concentration camp system. Many had been selected for labor upon arrival at Auschwitz; others had been prisoners in labor camps and ghettos that were transformed into concentration camps. These Jewish prisoners were retained only in the East. Germany itself was to remain free of Jews, and this included the camps located on German soil. But as the front lines advanced upon the Reich and the need for labor increased, Jewish prisoners were introduced into all camps, including those located in Germany proper. Eventually, Jews made up a large proportion of inmates in all concentration camps.

The end of the war brought the collapse of the concentration camp system. The approach of the Allied armies during the winter of 1944–1945 forced the evacuation of exposed camps. The SS transported all prisoners into the interior of the Reich, creating vast overcrowding. On January 15, 1945, the camp population exceeded 700,000. Unable to kill all the inmates, the SS evacuated them almost in sight of the advancing Allies. Inmates suffered and died during the long journeys in overcrowded cattle cars; without provisions and exposed to the cold, many arrived at their destination without the strength necessary to survive. Others were marched through the snow; those who collapsed were shot and left on the side of the road.

As the Russians approached from the East and the Anglo-Americans from the West, cattle cars and marching columns crisscrossed the shrinking territory of the Third Reich. The forced evacuations often became death marches; they took a terrible toll in human lives, killing perhaps one-third of all inmates before the end. Even camps like Bergen-Belsen, not intended for extermination, became a death trap for thousands of inmates. Thus, the Allies found mountains of corpses when they liberated the surviving inmates in April and May, 1945.

In 1941, Hitler decided to kill the European Jews and ordered the SS to implement this decision. After the invasion of Russia, special SS operational units, the *Einsatzgruppen*, killed Communist functionaries, Gypsies, and all Jews. These mobile killing units roamed through the countryside in the occupied territories of the Soviet Union, rounding up their victims, executing them, and burying them in mass graves. The units consisted of members of the Security Police and of the SS Security Service, recruited for this purpose by Reinhard Heydrich and his Central Office for Reich Security (*Reichsicherheitshauptamt*, or RSHA). They were supported by units of the German uniformed police and they used native troops whenever possible; local Lithuanian, Latvian, Estonian, and Ukrainian units participated in these massacres whenever possible. To increase efficiency, the Technical Department of RSHA developed a mobile gas van, which was used to kill Jewish women and children in Russia and Serbia. But the troops did not like these vans; they often broke down on muddy roads.

The *Einsatzgruppen* killings were too public. Soldiers and civilians watched the executions, took photographs, and often turned these massacres into public spectacles. The killings also demanded too much from the SS troops. They found the job of shooting thousands of men, women, and children too bloody. Some were brutalized; some had nervous breakdowns. To maintain secrecy and discipline, the SS leaders searched for a better way. They found the perfect solution in the extermination camps, where gas chambers were used to kill the victims. These killing centers were installations established for the sole purpose of mass murder; they were factories for the killing of human beings.

Murder by gas chamber was first introduced in the so-called Euthanasia program. Late in 1939, Hitler ordered the killing of the supposedly incurably ill. The program was administered by the Führer Chancellery, which established for this purpose the Utilitarian Foundation for Institutional Care, whose headquarters was located in Berlin at Tiergartenstrasse 4 and was known as T4. The victims (the mentally ill, the retarded, the deformed, the senile, and at times also those with diseases then considered incurable), chosen by boards of psychiatrists on the basis of questionnaires, were transferred to six institutions—Bernburg, Brandenburg, Grafeneck, Hadamar, Hartheim, and Sonnenstein—where specially constructed gas chambers were used to kill the patients. This radical ideological experiment in murder involved German nationals, and public protests forced the Nazi leadership to abort it in 1941. However, the program continued for adults and particularly for children on a smaller scale throughout the war, especially for the murder of ill concentration camp prisoners under the code designation 14f13.

Killing centers using gas chambers appeared late in 1941. In western Poland, the governor of the annexed area known as the Wartheland established a small but highly efficient killing center at Kulmhof (Chelmno) for the extermination of the Lodz Jews. A special SS commando, formerly occupied with killing mental patients in East Prussia, operated the installation. Using gas vans and burning the bodies, the commando killed at least 150,000 persons. In eastern Poland, the Lublin SS and Police Leader Odilo Globocnik headed the enterprise known as Operation Reinhard. Its object was to concentrate, pillage, deport, and kill the Jews of occupied Poland. He established three extermination camps: Belzec, Sobibor, and Treblinka. To operate these killing centers, he requested the services of the T4 operatives. A number of these, including the Kripo officer Christian Wirth, traveled to Lublin to apply their know-how to the murder of the Jews. Augmented by SS and police recruits with backgrounds similar to those of the T4 personnel, and aided by Ukrainian auxiliaries serving as guards, they staffed the extermination camps and, under the overall direction of Wirth, ran them with unbelievable efficiency.

Belzec opened in March, 1942, and closed in January, 1943. More than 600,000 persons were killed there. Sobibor opened in May, 1942, and closed one day after the rebellion of the inmates on October 14, 1943. At least 250,000 persons were killed there. Treblinka, the largest of the three killing centers, opened in July, 1942. A revolt of the inmates on August 2, 1943, destroyed most of the camp, and it finally closed in November, 1943. Between 700,000 and 900,000 persons were killed there. These three camps of Operation Reinhard served only the purpose of mass murder. Every man, woman, and child arriving there was killed. Most were Jews, but a few were Gypsies. A few young men and women were not immediately killed. Used to service the camp, they sorted the belongings of those murdered and burned the bodies in open air pits. Eventually they, too, were killed. Very few survived. Kulmhof and Belzec had only a handful of survivors. Sobibor and Treblinka, where the above-mentioned revolts permitted some to escape, had about thirty to forty survivors.

The method of murder was the same in all three camps (and similar in Kulmhof). The victims arrived in cattle wagons and the men were separated from the women and children. Forced to undress, they had to hand over all their valuables. Naked, they were driven towards the gas chambers, which were disguised as shower rooms and used carbon monoxide from a motor to kill the victims. The bodies were burned after their gold teeth had been extracted. The massive work of mass murder was accomplished by unusually small staffs. Figures differ (approximately 100 Germans and 500 Ukrainians in the three camps of Operation Reinhard), but all agreed that very few killed multitudes.

Thus, mass murder was first instituted in camps operated outside the concentration camp system by local SS leaders. But the concentration camps soon entered the field of mass murder, eventually surpassing all others in speed and size. The largest killing operation took place in Auschwitz, a regular concentration camp administered by WVHA. There Auschwitz Commandant Rudolf Hoess improved the method used by Christian Wirth,[6] substituting crystalized prussic acid—known by the trade name Zyklon B— for carbon monoxide. In September, 1941, an experimental gassing, killing about 250 ill prisoners and about 600 Russian POWs, proved the value of Zyklon B. In January, 1942, systematic killing operations, using Zyklon B, commenced with the arrival of Jewish transports from Upper Silesia. These were soon followed without interruption by transports of Jews from all occupied countries of Europe.

The Auschwitz killing center was the most modern of its kind. The SS built the camp at Birkenau, also known as Auschwitz II. There, they murdered their victims in newly constructed gas chambers, and burned their bodies in crematoria constructed for this purpose. A postwar court described the killing process:

> Prussic acid fumes developed as soon as Zyklon B pellets seeped through the opening into the gas chamber and came into contact with the air. Within a few minutes, these fumes agonizingly asphyxiated the human beings in the gas chamber. During these minutes horrible scenes took place. The people who now realized that they were to die an agonizing death screamed and raged and beat their fists against the locked doors and against the walls. Since the gas spread from the floor of the gas chamber upward, small and weakly people were the first to die. The others, in their death agony, climbed on top of the dead bodies on the floor, in order to get a little more air before they too painfully choked to death.

More than two million victims were killed in this fashion in Auschwitz-Birkenau. Most of them were Jews, but others also died in its gas chambers: Gypsies, Russian POWs, and ill prisoners of all nationalities.

Unlike the killing centers operated by Globocnik and Wirth, Auschwitz combined murder and slave labor. RSHA ran the deportations and ordered the killings; WVHA ran the killing installations and chose the workers. From the transports of arriving Jews, SS physicians "selected" those young and strong enough to be used for forced labor. They were temporarily saved.

Those chosen for forced labor were first quarantined in Birkenau and then sent to the I. G. Farben[7] complex Buna-Monowitz, also known as Auschwitz III, or to one of its many subsidiary camps. Periodically, those too

---

[6]SS Major (1885–1944) who carried out gassings on incurably insane Germans in 1939.
[7]The huge German chemical and dye trust.

weak to work were sent to Birkenau for gassing from every camp in the Auschwitz complex; they were simply replaced by new and stronger prisoners.

A similar system was applied in Lublin-Maidanek, another WVHA
concentration camp with a killing operation. But it closed much earlier
than Auschwitz; it was liberated by the Red Army in the summer of 1944.
Auschwitz continued to operate even after all other extermination camps
had ceased to function. But when the war appeared lost, Himmler ordered
the gassings stopped in November, 1944. Only a few hundred thousand
Jews survived as slave laborers in Auschwitz and other concentration camps.
Those who survived the evacuation marches of early 1945 were liberated by
the Allied armies.

Forbidden Death

PHILIPPE ARIÈS

*During the Romantic era of the late eighteenth and nineteenth centuries, death
represented a sudden rupture between the dying person and the immediate family.
The same development of sentiment and affection that saw people marrying for love
and parents adoring their children had a similarly profound effect on society's
attitude toward death. Family members seemed more anxious about the final
departure of spouses and offspring than about their own deaths; overburdened
with grief, they have left us evidence of their intense bereavement in literature,
diaries, and lachrymose funerary monuments.*

*Ariès argues that this Romantic view gave way in the twentieth century to a
death revolution, in which death became something shameful and forbidden. What
exactly does he mean? How has society interdicted death? What role has the hospital
played in the death revolution? What does Ariès say constitutes an acceptable
death? Customs have changed as well as attitudes. What innovations have appeared
in funeral rites and ceremonies?*

*What does it mean to say that death has replaced sex as a taboo and has become
the new pornography? What are the implications of this development? Is this taboo
more prevalent in the United States than in other Western countries? Ariès does
offer specific comments about American attitudes toward death. How does the
American way of death differ from the European?*

With his books, Western Attitudes toward Death: From the Middle Ages
to the Present *and* The Hour of Our Death, *Ariès opened up a new subject for
study, the history of attitudes toward death. Now, no one would deny the importance
of a society's collective feelings toward this event in life shared by all people. Why
do you suppose historians virtually ignored the history of death for so long? How
do Ariès's remarks about death help us understand the twentieth-century world and
the process of social change?*

During the long period...from the Early Middle Ages until the mid-nineteenth century, the attitude toward death changed, but so slowly that contemporaries did not even notice. In our day, in approximately a third of a century, we have witnessed a brutal revolution in traditional ideas and feelings, a revolution so brutal that social observers have not failed to be struck by it. It is really an absolutely unheard-of phenomenon. Death, so omnipresent in the past that it was familiar, would be effaced, would disappear. It would become shameful and forbidden.

...It...seems that this revolution began in the United States and spread to England, to the Netherlands, to industrialized Europe; and we can see it today, before our very eyes, reaching France and leaving oil smudges wherever the wave passes.

At its beginning doubtlessly lies a sentiment already expressed during the second half of the nineteenth century: those surrounding the dying person had a tendency to spare him and to hide from him the gravity of his condition. Yet they admitted that this dissimulation could not last too long, except in such extraordinary cases as those described by Mark Twain in 1902 in "Was it Heaven or Hell?" The dying person must one day know, but the relatives no longer had the cruel courage to tell the truth themselves.

In short, at this point the truth was beginning to be challenged.

The first motivation for the lie was the desire to spare the sick person, to assume the burden of his ordeal. But this sentiment, whose origin we know (the intolerance of another's death and the confidence shown by the dying person in those about him) very rapidly was covered over by a different sentiment, a new sentiment characteristic of modernity: one must avoid—no longer for the sake of the dying person, but for society's sake, for the sake of those close to the dying person—the disturbance and the overly strong and unbearable emotion caused by the ugliness of dying and by the very presence of death in the midst of a happy life, for it is henceforth given that life is always happy or should always seem to be so. Nothing had yet changed in the rituals of death, which were preserved at least in appearance, and no one had yet had the idea of changing them. But people had already begun to empty them of their dramatic impact; the procedure of hushing-up had begun....

Between 1930 and 1950 the evolution accelerated markedly. This was due to an important physical phenomenon: the displacement of the site of death. One no longer died at home in the bosom of one's family, but in the hospital, alone.

One dies in the hospital because the hospital has become the place to receive care which can no longer be given at home. Previously the hospital had been a shelter for the poor, for pilgrims; then it became a medical center where people were healed, where one struggled against death. It still has that curative function, but people are also beginning to consider a certain type of hospital as the designated spot for dying. One dies in the hospital because the doctor did not succeed in healing. One no longer goes to or will go to the hospital to be healed, but for the specific purpose of dying. American sociologists have observed that there are today two types of seriously ill persons to be found in hospitals. The most archaic are recent immigrants who are still attached to the traditions of death, who try to snatch the dying person from the hospital so he can die at home, *more majorum;*[1] the others are those more involved in modernity who come to die in the hospital because it has become inconvenient to die at home.

Death in the hospital is no longer the occasion of a ritual ceremony, over which the dying person presides amidst his assembled relatives and friends. Death is a technical phenomenon obtained by a cessation of care, a cessation determined in a more or less avowed way by a decision of the doctor and the hospital team. Indeed, in the majority of cases the dying person has already lost consciousness. Death has been dissected, cut to bits by a series of little steps, which finally makes it impossible to know which step was the real death, the one in which consciousness was lost, or the one in which breathing stopped. All these little silent deaths have replaced and erased the great dramatic act of death, and no one any longer has the strength or patience to wait over a period of weeks for a moment which has lost a part of its meaning.

From the end of the eighteenth century we had been impressed by a sentimental landslide which was causing the initiative to pass from the dying man himself to his family—a family in which henceforth he would have complete confidence. Today the initiative has passed from the family, as much an outsider as the dying person, to the doctor and the hospital team. They are the masters of death—of the moment as well as of the circumstances of death—and it has been observed that they try to obtain from their patient "an acceptable style of living while dying." The accent has been placed on "acceptable." An acceptable death is a death which can be accepted or tolerated by the survivors. It has its antithesis: "the embarrassingly graceless dying," which embarrasses the survivors because it causes too strong an emotion to burst forth; and emotions must be avoided both in the hospital and everywhere in society. One does not have the right to become emotional other than in private, that is to say, secretly. Here, then, is what has happened to the great death scene, which had changed so little over the centuries, if not the millennia.

The funeral rites have also been modified. Let us put aside for a moment the American case. In England and northwestern Europe, they are trying to reduce to a decent minimum the inevitable operations necessary to dispose of the body. It is above all essential that society—the neighbors, friends, colleagues, and children—notice to the least possible degree that death has occurred. If a few formalities are maintained, and if a ceremony still marks the departure, it must remain discreet and must avoid emotion. Thus the family reception line for receiving condolences at the end of the funeral

---

[1] According to the custom of the great ("social betters").

service has now been suppressed. The outward manifestations of mourning are repugned and are disappearing. Dark clothes are no longer worn; one no longer dresses differently than on any other day.

Too evident sorrow does not inspire pity but repugnance, it is the sign of mental instability or of bad manners: it is *morbid*. Within the family circle one also hesitates to let himself go for fear of upsetting the children. One only has the right to cry if no one else can see or hear. Solitary and shameful mourning is the only recourse, like a sort of masturbation....

In countries in which the death revolution has been radical, once the dead person has been evacuated, his tomb is no longer visited. In England for example, cremation has become the dominant manner of burial. When cremation occurs, sometimes with dispersal of the ashes, the cause is more than a desire to break with Christian tradition; it is a manifestation of enlightenment, of modernity. The deep motivation is that cremation is the most radical means of getting rid of the body and of forgetting it, of nullifying it, of being "too final." Despite the efforts of cemetery offices, people rarely visit the urns today, though they may still visit gravesides. Cremation excludes a pilgrimage.

We would be committing an error if we entirely attributed this flight from death to an indifference toward the dead person. In reality the contrary is true. In the old society, the panoply of mourning scarcely concealed a rapid resignation. How many widowers remarried a few short months after the death of their wives! On the contrary, today, where mourning is forbidden, it has been noted that the mortality rate of widows or widowers during the year following the spouse's death is much higher than that of the control group of the same age.

The point has even been reached at which... the choking back of sorrow, the forbidding of its public manifestation, the obligation to suffer alone and secretly, has aggravated the trauma stemming from the loss of a dear one. In a family in which sentiment is given an important place and in which premature death is becoming increasingly rare (save in the event of an automobile accident), the death of a near relative is always deeply felt, as it was in the Romantic era.[2]

A single person is missing for you, and the whole world is empty. But one no longer has the right to say so aloud.

The combination of phenomena which we have just analyzed is nothing other than the imposition of an interdict. What was once required is henceforth forbidden.

The merit of having been the first to define this unwritten law of our civilization goes to the English sociologist, Geoffrey Gorer. He has shown clearly how death has become a taboo and how in the twentieth century it has replaced sex as the principal forbidden subject. Formerly children were told that they were brought by the stork, but they were admitted to the great

---

[2]The late eighteenth and nineteenth centuries.

farewell scene about the bed of the dying person. Today they are initiated in their early years to the physiology of love; but when they no longer see their grandfather and express astonishment, they are told that he is resting in a beautiful garden among the flowers. Such is "The Pornography of Death"— the title of a pioneering article by Gorer, published in 1955—and the more society was liberated from the Victorian constraints concerning sex, the more it rejected things having to do with death. Along with the interdict appears the transgression: the mixture of eroticism and death so sought after from the sixteenth to the eighteenth century reappears in our sadistic literature and in violent death in our daily life.

This establishment of an interdict has profound meaning. It is already difficult to isolate the meaning of the interdict on sex which was precipitated by the Christian confusion between sin and sexuality (though, as in the nineteenth century, this interdict was never imposed). But the interdict on death suddenly follows upon the heels of a very long period—several centuries—in which death was a public spectacle from which no one would have thought of hiding and which was even sought after at times.

The cause of the interdict is at once apparent: the need for happiness—the moral duty and the social obligation to contribute to the collective happiness by avoiding any cause for sadness or boredom, by appearing to be always happy, even if in the depths of despair. By showing the least sign of sadness, one sins against happiness, threatens it, and society then risks losing its *raison d'être.* . . .

The idea of happiness brings us back to the United States, and it is now appropriate to attempt to understand the relationships between American civilization and the modern attitude toward death.

It seems that the modern attitude toward death, that is to say the interdiction of death in order to preserve happiness, was born in the United States around the beginning of the twentieth century. However, on its native soil the interdict was not carried to its ultimate extremes. In American society it encountered a braking influence which it did not encounter in Europe. Thus the American attitude toward death today appears as a strange compromise between trends which are pulling it in two nearly opposite directions. . . .

. . . In America, during the eighteenth and the first half of the nineteenth centuries, and even later, burials conformed to tradition, especially in the countryside: the carpenter made the coffin (the coffin, not yet the "casket"); the family and friends saw to its transport and to the procession itself; and the pastor and gravedigger carried out the service. In the early nineteenth century the grave was still sometimes dug on the family property—which is a modern act, copied from the Ancients, and which was unknown in Europe before the mid-eighteenth century and with few exceptions was rapidly abandoned. In villages and small towns the cemetery most frequently lay adjacent to the church. In the cities, once again paralleling Europe, the cemetery had in about 1830 been situated outside the city but was encompassed by urban growth and abandoned toward 1870 for a new site. It soon fell into ruin. . . .

The old cemeteries were church property, as they had been in Europe and still are in England. The new cemeteries belonged to private associations. ... In Europe cemeteries became municipal, that is to say public, property and were never left to private initiative.

In the growing cities of the nineteenth century, old carpenters or gravediggers, or owners of carts and horses, became "undertakers," and the manipulation of the dead became a profession. Here history is still completely comparable to that in Europe, at least in that part of Europe which remained faithful to the eighteenth-century canons of simplicity and which remained outside the pale of Romantic bombast.

Things seem to have changed during the period of the Civil War. Today's "morticians," whose letters-patent go back to that period, give as ancestor a quack doctor expelled from the school of medicine, Dr. Holmes, who had a passion for dissection and cadavers. He would offer his services to the victim's family and embalmed, it is said, 4,000 cadavers unaided in four years. ... Why such recourse to embalming? Had it been practiced previously? Is there an American tradition going back to the eighteenth century, a period in which throughout Europe there was a craze for embalming? Yet this technique was abandoned in nineteenth-century Europe, and the wars did not resurrect it. It is noteworthy that embalming became a career in the United States before the end of the century, even if it was not yet very widespread. ... We know that it has today become a very widespread method of preparing the dead, a practice almost unknown in Europe and characteristic of the American way of death.

One cannot help thinking that this long-accepted and avowed preference for embalming has a meaning, even if it is difficult to interpret.

This meaning could indeed be that of a certain refusal to accept death, either as a familiar end to which one is resigned, or as a dramatic sign in the Romantic manner. And this meaning became even more obvious when death became an object of commerce and of profit. It is not easy to sell something which has no value because it is too familiar and common, or something which is frightening, horrible, or painful. In order to sell death, it had to be made friendly. But we may assume that "funeral directors"—since 1885 a new name for undertakers—would not have met with success if public opinion had not cooperated. They presented themselves not as simple sellers of services, but as "doctors of grief" who have a mission, as do doctors and priests; and this mission, from the beginning of this century, consists in aiding the mourning survivors to return to normalcy. The new funeral director ("new" because he has replaced the simple undertaker) is a "doctor of grief," an "expert at returning abnormal minds to normal in the shortest possible time." They are "members of an exalted, almost sacred calling."

Thus mourning is no longer a necessary period imposed by society; it has become a *morbid state* which must be treated, shortened, erased by the "doctor of grief."

Through a series of little steps we can see the birth and development of the ideas which would end in the present-day interdict, built upon the ruins of Puritanism, in an urbanized culture which is dominated by rapid economic growth and by the search for happiness linked to the search for profit.

This process should normally result in the situation of England today . . . : the almost total suppression of everything reminding us of death.

But, and this is what is unique about the American attitude, American mores have not gone to such an extreme; they stopped along the way. Americans are very willing to transform death, to put make-up on it, to sublimate it, but they do not want to make it disappear. Obviously, this would also mark the end of profit, but the money earned by funeral merchants would not be tolerated if they did not meet a profound need. The wake, increasingly avoided in industrial Europe, persists in the United States: it exists as "viewing the remains," the "visitation." "They don't *view* bodies in England."

The visit to the cemetery and a certain veneration in regard to the tomb also persist. That is why public opinion—and funeral directors—finds cremation distasteful, for it gets rid of the remains too quickly and too radically.

Burials are not shameful and they are not hidden. With that very characteristic mixture of commerce and idealism, they are the object of showy publicity, like any other consumer's item, be it soap or religion. Seen for example in the buses of New York City in 1965 was the following ad, purchased by one of the city's leading morticians: "The dignity and integrity of a Gawler. Funeral costs no more. . . . Easy access, private parking for over 100 cars." Such publicity would be unthinkable in Europe, first of all because it would repel the customer rather than attract him.

Thus we must admit that a traditional resistance has kept alive certain rituals of death which had been abandoned or are being abandoned in industrialized Europe, especially among the middle classes.

Nevertheless, though these rituals have been continued, they have also been transformed. The American way of death is the synthesis of two tendencies: one traditional, the other euphoric.

Thus during the wakes or farewell "visitations" which have been pre-served, the visitors come without shame or repugnance. This is because in reality they are not visiting a dead person, as they traditionally have, but an almost-living one who, thanks to embalming, is still present, as if he were awaiting you to greet you or to take you off on a walk. The definitive nature of the rupture has been blurred. Sadness and mourning have been banished from this calming reunion.

Perhaps because American society has not totally accepted the interdict, it can more easily challenge it; but this interdict is spreading in the Old World, where the cult of the dead would seem more deeply rooted.

During the last ten years in American publications an increasing number of sociologists and psychologists have been studying the conditions of death in contemporary society and especially in hospitals.... [T]he authors have been struck by the manner of dying, by the inhumanity, the cruelty of solitary death in hospitals and in a society where death has lost the prominent place which custom had granted it over the millennia, a society where the interdiction of death paralyzes and inhibits the reactions of the medical staff and family involved. These publications are also preoccupied with the fact that death has become the object of a voluntary decision by the doctors and the family, a decision which today is made shamefacedly, clandestinely. And this para-medical literature, for which, as far as I know, there is no equivalent in Europe, is bringing death back into the dialogue from which it had been excluded. Death is once again becoming something one can talk about. Thus the interdict is threatened, but only in the place where it was born and where it encountered limitations. Elsewhere, in the other industrialized societies, it is maintaining or extending its empire....

Past and Present in a Greek Mountain Village

JULIET du BOULAY

The village of Ambéli, in Euboa in east-central Greece, could in the 1960s boast only 144 people and 35 houses. The village was poor and, because there was no effective transportation system, lacked any regular communication with the outside world. Yet this traditional village has experienced great social change since the 1940s.

More significant for Ambéli than the initial Nazi occupation of Greece were the two civil wars, from 1943 to 1945 (between resistance groups and the Nazis and among the partisan groups as well) and from 1947 to 1949 (between Communist guerillas and the royal government). These were dangerous and bitter times for the villagers. To what extent were they involved in the civil wars? One important consequence was the evacuation of the villagers to Katerini in 1949. How did the evacuation affect them? What had been the basic features of traditional village life? Was the village modernized? That is, did there appear new economic and social patterns that we associate with modernity? Did the inhabitants of Ambéli consider the new developments—in social relations and in values, for example—to have been important?

Juliet du Boulay points out that there have been successive waves of emigration from the village in the twentieth century but that the most recent emigration is of a different type. What has been the effect of this emigration, both on the emigrants and on the Greeks remaining in Ambéli? What future awaits the villagers?

... [T]he entry in the present century of the Greek nation into the world of industry and commerce, and its gradual transformation from a subsistence to a consumer society, have had repercussions which have penetrated into the remotest corner of Greek rural life, and which have affected very deeply this traditional world view. The effect of this movement has been to change not so much the central elements of the value system as the ways in which they are interpreted; but this does not mean that this change is superficial, for it amounts in many respects to the setting up of new values which are often, although they are not always recognized to be so, antithetical to the old.

Communications with the outside world, and contact with its values, have been achieved in two main ways—war and emigration. The participation of villagers in the Balkan Wars from 1912 to 1914, in the campaign in Asia Minor from 1920 to 1922,[1] in the Albanian campaign against the Italians in 1940, and later against the Germans in 1940–1, all tended to enlarge their horizons beyond that of traditional village culture. But it is emigration which has effected the deeper alteration to village thinking and incalculably changed the villagers' way of life.

The first significant instance of emigration was that to America at the beginning of this century. Many of the villagers of Ambéli were heavily in debt, others wanted to buy land, others to seek their fortunes permanently elsewhere—and several men left the village from 1905 to 1908, although most returned in 1912 at the outbreak of the Balkan Wars. Emigration also took place in the 1930s to America, but ended with the entry of Greece into World War II, and after that there was no further emigration from Ambéli until 1960 when there began the great exodus of young men to Canada, Germany, the United States, Australia, and Belgium, as well as recruitment of men for the Merchant Navy.

There was great difference, however, between they earlier types of emigration and the later, for whereas in the former cases the migration ideally involved return, in the latter it was, and was intended to be, permanent. In the earlier years the *émigré*[2] went abroad in order to send money home to his wife and children, to buy land, possibly a house, or houses, returning eventually himself to take up his old way of life on a stronger financial basis; and while some did leave the village for good, these were only people who could not be supported on the land and resources available. Anyone, therefore, who was already established in the village, went abroad to secure rather than to abandon his inheritance. In the post-1960 emigrants, however, the focus has been the reverse, and not one of these *émigrés* had—or has—any intention of ever returning to live in the village. They come back periodically, to see their parents and to have a holiday, but they have no thought at all of taking up permanent residence in the village; and those who are forced, as some are,

[1] Against the Turks.
[2] Emigrant.

to return and stay for some months because of difficulties with their visas or work permits, are discontented and oppressed by what they see as the narrowness and lack of culture (... meaning in this context the frequenting of cinemas, night-clubs, dance halls and restaurants), and resolute in their determination to get away for ever.

The men who emigrate as bachelors usually marry Greek girls whom they meet either abroad or on a trip back to their village, and many of these couples then settle permanently in their new country, and one by one organize the emigration also of their brothers, sisters, and cousins. Of those who emigrated after they had married and settled in Ambéli, some have managed to leave their children with relatives and take their wives with them to work, and all intend, on returning to Greece, to abandon the village and buy a building plot near some relatively urbanized centre in the plains. While these people are abroad they send money to their parents and thus in a sense support the village, but this money is not enough to provide for a real continuance of the traditional culture; nor is it enough to establish a house: it is to keep two unambitious and undemanding old people from destitution until they finally leave the village and go to live with a married son or daughter elsewhere. And although some men, though not all, send home money to help with their sisters' dowries, these dowries in fact also work against the continued existence of the village, for they enable the girls to marry 'well', into a different and, to however small an extent, more polished community. Thus while the tendency of the earlier types of emigration was in the long run to strengthen the village, the later type is destroying it.

... [W]hile the earlier emigrations, taking place from a firm basis in village culture and a belief in its value, were a confirmation of that culture, rather than a challenge to it, the post-1960 emigrations took place form a village that was already losing confidence in its own inherited way of life— that had looked beyond the confines of its own culture and found what it saw attractive. The situation therefore arose in which the village the *émigré*, into a total disillusion with his rural origin. And while this disillusion did not compromise the commitment of those who were kept in the village by lack of opportunity to leave, it was an image of the failure of these patterns in the most crucial sense to offer fulfillment to an entirely new generation. Thus it seems that at some time around 1950 there occurred the beginnings of a deeply hidden but very central collapse of village confidence—a collapse which even by 1966 had not affected the villagers' sense of the intrinsic validity of their inherited way of life, but which cast doubt on the viability of that way of life in terms of the future, and in terms, therefore, of that most important aspect of Greek life, the children.

As time goes on this particular balance is likely to change more and more. The *émigré* of 1960 was impelled by hope of better things outside, rather than by disillusion from within. The *émigré* of 1970 goes because, 'This isn't a life'.... And yet this paradox, whereby the village survives in its own village-centered terms even while it fails completely in terms of the outside world, is never likely to be finally resolved, for the degree of emigration has by now taken the situation too far. In many of the larger or less remote towns and villages of Greece, the recent pattern has been one of increasing modernization whereby the world moves in before the inhabitants move out. This has not proved possible in Ambéli, and it is not going to be the infiltration of the modern middle-class ethos which will eradicate the traditional patterns still remaining to it, but final depopulation.

Of the earlier emigrations and the contact of village men with war and invasion, two general effects on village life may be isolated. One has been to highlight in many ways the traditional polarity of male and female roles, among the older married couples, by deepening the discrepancy between the experience of the men and that of their wives. The other has been to provide a basis for the older generations from which they can understand and sympathize with the younger ones who want to leave the village and make a new life for themselves elsewhere. Experimentalism and ambition, in terms of the ability to adventure into completely new worlds, are characteristics not foreign to the people of Ambéli. The result of this is that the village as a whole helps its sons to emigrate, its daughters to marry out, and in the most practical terms understands, while it laments, the permanent departure of its children from the family hearth.

Apart from the emigration discussed above, the political events which has the greatest impact in recent times were the two outbreaks of civil war in 1944 and 1947, with the consequent evacuation of the whole village to Kateríni for one year, from November 1949 to November 1950.

The two great periods of civil war, when fighting was generalized throughout all Greece and extended even into the towns, were in 1943 until February 1945, and in 1947 to 1949. However, during the whole period from 1942 to 1950 there was a state of disturbance in various parts of Greece with guerrilla bands operating in the mountains. During the first period the fighting was relatively localized between rival Resistance bands all over the country, interspersed with actual Resistance activity. During the second period, however, the Communist guerrillas involved the villagers by both persuasion and terrorism and, especially after the American involvement in Greece in 1947, were themselves hunted by the National Army in the mountains.

The villagers' involvement in the civil war was, primarily, caused by the position of their village in the wooded mountains which were to become ideal refuges for the Communist guerrilla fighters or *andártes* ... as they came to be called. ... With the development of guerrilla movement ... the village split naturally into Left and Right, with those of the Left helping the Communists out of sympathy, those of the Right out of fear—neither however, at any rate in the beginning, aware of the real political movements in which they were so disastrously taking part. The villagers were, as always, the victims of the struggles of others rather than the active element of the struggle itself.

It was not surprising that the villagers were at first in ignorance of the real issues of the conflict, for this ignorance was a state shared initially also by the Greek Government in exile, and by the Allies. EAM/ELAS[3] was initially the Resistance group which provided most of the effective partisan opposition to the Germans, and as such was given aid by the Allies—money and arms. It came quite rapidly, however, under the control of the Greek Communist Party (KKE) and thus became involved in a struggle with EDES, a Resistance organization operating mainly in northwestern Greece, which, originally Republican, became increasingly Rightist under the control of General Napolean Zervas. Straightforward opposition to the invaders was thus confused with the struggle for power between these two rival groups, and the villages all over Greece were involved in this confusion.

There is no doubt that when Resistance groups all over the country were formed at the beginning of the occupation, they were formed in answer to an intense popular resolution to evict the Germans. However, from the way in which the villagers now remember those days, it seems that later events overwhelmed this initial fervour, and that EAM/ELAS came eventually to exercise a hold over village imaginations in the opportunity it offered for adventure and excitement, and as a catalyst for the villagers' own private passions or generalized political leanings, rather than as a revolutionary cause to which they were dedicated. During the civil war which followed the evacuation of Greece by the Germans, several of the villagers actively enlisted with the *andártes,* some because they were forced to, others as a means of implementing private grudges, others as a result of an ill-timed spirit of heroism or a general sympathy with the Left. It is said that one man joined the Communists with the express intention of killing a rival inheritor of his father's; there was a young boy who involved himself with the first outbreak of civil war and then found himself too deeply involved to draw back. There was a boy of thirteen who was taken from his home at night by the *andártes* and retrieved only at the last moment by his mother who pleaded with the leader that her son was too young to be of any use to them....

The nature of the movement first began to reveal itself in Ambéli when speakers for the Communist Party had come round the villages exhorting disbelief in the Church and proclaiming the joys of communal living. A fat woman speaker, who scratched her behind as she was talking, made a particular impression on the villagers, ever, as is their nature ready for a joke; and there was a man who appalled them by cutting tobacco on an icon in demonstration of the hallowness of faith. Still clearer to them were the political implications of the open fighting which broke out in the streets of Athens between ELAS and the liberating British troops in December 1944;

[3]EAM, the National Liberation Front, was the name of the political Resistance coalition which was set up at the beginning of the occupation, and is usually referred to in conjunction with ELAS..., the National Popular Liberation Army which refers to the guerrilla bands which first began operations in the mountains in the summer of 1942. (Author's note.)

but by that time those who had involved themselves with the *andártes* found it too late to withdraw.

The *andártes* only stationed themselves permanently in the village after it was evacuated in 1949, but before that they made periodic swoops for food, for conscription, or for revenge. It was a time of terror for all, both Left and Right, for betrayal was rife, and death was threatened from the *andártes* for opposition or refusal to help, while severe beatings were courted by villagers who came under suspicion of the Government troops. The slower-minded villager ran the risk of being beaten up by both parties for not being quick enough to evade accusation; the cunning one had a soft answer ready at all times. One old man told me how he used to watch his sheep on the mountain sides, and from time to time unidentifiable groups of men would approach him and ask roughly, 'What are you?' 'I'm a shepherd,' he would insist, feigning ignorance of the real implications of the question, 'I'm a shepherd'; while to me he said, 'How did I know what to say? You couldn't tell who they were, and if you said the wrong thing you might have got killed. That was how I escaped.' In the village at night the same thing would happen. A family sitting at its evening meal would be terrified by a thunderous knocking at the door. Trembling, the head of the house would open it, 'Welcome!' he would say. To me he explained, 'To the *andártes*, "You're welcome!" To the Government troops, "You're welcome!" What could we do? We wanted to live.' ...

In Ambéli there were six deaths during that time. Four of these were young men who had joined the *andártes* and were shot by the army at varying times; the other two were inhabitants of the village, Royalists, who were killed by the Communists. The first was, it is said, popular with nobody, for he was a bully and also—a thing insupportable in such a period and never at any time considered admirable—a betrayer of people in the village to those outside. The *andártes* came for him one night early in the civil war, bound his hands, took him, chalk-white and trembling, from the village, and later killed him on the mountain slopes. They took his wife a few nights later, but released her when, as they say, the entire village rushed after them begging for her life and for those of her four children whom they were thus making destitute. The second of these men, however, was universally popular, and nobody could believe that the man with whom they had laughed a moment before, as he made jokes with them outside the church, had been taken and shot where he stood. At the same time as this was happening, other *andártes* were at work setting fire to his widow's house and burning in it everything she possessed. People still remember how the oxen bellowed from within the conflagration, and how the widow and her five children, all under the age of eight, left the next day for Kateríni with nothing but the clothes they wore. It was in the autumn of 1949 that this occurred, and the barbarity of this act is explained by the villagers as being the result of long years of fighting and suffering, the increase of passion, and the deepening of bitterness.

Immediately following this event, the order went out that the entire village should be evacuated, and within a week this was done, carried out by the army with mules and men temporarily conscripted from the surrounding villages, and the villagers lodged in Kateríni in rooms commandeered form local families. It was a hard time, for although they had brought with them enough wheat to give them bread for that year and into the subsequent year to last them until the harvest, they were not able to bring down the straw which was then vital to the animals, and many of the villagers returned to Ambéli in November of 1950 with their flocks depleted by half. However, this year was noticeable in a positive sense for one thing, in that it 'woke up'—to use their own terminology—the villagers to an awareness of a standard of living and a range of ambitions of which they had until then been hardly aware. This new awareness coincided, after the return to the village, with a period of national economic expansion, and from the date is observable a noticeable degree of social change. In response to any question referring to the beginnings of new ways of thought and new customs in the village, the answer is almost invariably—'After we returned form Kateríni'.

In the old days, the people of Ambéli had been primarily shepherds, and 2,000 to 2,500 head of sheep and goats are reported to have grazed on their mountains before 1955.... Agriculture was practised intensively, with up to twelve or thirteen acres of wheat being sown per family ... and owing to the number of grazing animals and the fact that almost all the villagers owned at least a few animals and some as many as 200, the sowing had to be organized on a community basis in special areas set aside for certain crops....

The normal houses included, in the days before 1940, the joint family, which would split up either on the death of the father, or on the development of quarrels or the birth of more children than the house could adequately contain. A common size for such families is said to have been eight. Therefore to the high degree of integration created by the communal co-operation over the land was added the more particularized focus of smaller groups, integrated through kinship and common interest, and related outwards to the community by their various affinal links.

These large families provided the manpower to make complete exploitation of the properties possible, and consequently the land had a value immediately realizable in economic terms. Small children would herd the goats and sheep and watch the cows, one or two men would go to the forest, the remaining members of the family would go to the fields or do any other necessary tasks. There was therefore great competition over land, considerable variation of wealth within the village, and a hierarchy of prestige according to the pre-eminence of a few families....

The standard of living is said to have been the same for both rich and poor. All families would work equally hard, wear the same sort of clothes, eat the same sort of food. But the rich families had more prestige, more gold coins tucked away in their wooden chests, could afford to give their daughters good dowries, to pay workmen, have more animals, and perhaps more yards of material in the sleeves and skirts of the men's dress, and finer trimmings on the women's best clothes. . . . All the villagers slept in the same way, rolled up in rugs in rows upon the floor, and each family ate in the same way from one big dish set on a rug in front of the hearth, while the pig had to be driven away again and again, the cocks crowed from the beams above. . . .

The German conquest of mainland Greece in April 1941, the stoppage of imported wheat, and the appropriation of the existing stocks by the invaders, had by the winter time brought famine to much of Greece. In Athens there was a period when hundreds of people a day died of starvation, the bodies being collected by carts which went round scouring the streets, and all over the land the townspeople flocked to the country offering jewellery, clothes, anything they had, for bread. The people of Ambéli, though better off than those of other villages owning less land, found their bare subsistence livelihood threatened, and from February until the harvest in June 1942 they eked out their meagre stocks of wheat and maize with roasted roots, and ate wild greens till their stomachs revolted at them. . . .

The ten years from 1940 to 1950 marked a serious run-down of social and economic activity. Marriages were reduced to a minimum and the resin trade stopped totally until 1945, although the people of the villages were able after 1943 slowly to begin saving a little money here and there by trading locally and by intensive cultivation of their land. Otherwise their lives were concerned chiefly with the perils and tensions of the Italian and later the German occupying troops, and the *andártes.* These empty years formed a break between the old world and the new, and this period can be seen now as the turning-point from which the Greek community as a whole departed from a way of life which accorded coherently with itself and with the system of values it embodied and by which it was organized, to one which, in adjusting to new economic and social conditions, was forced into tension and paradox and the abdication from the totality of many of the former beliefs.

After 1950 everything was to change. The previous living standards had not been due to lack of money only, but also to lack of knowledge, and after personal experience in Kateríni of living in separate rooms, of sleeping in beds, of wearing shoes and socks regularly to work, the villagers decided that they would continue in this way. They began to partition their houses to keep the animals in one half and themselves in the other; to buy clothes and household implements that they had previously done without; they began to use paraffin lamps instead of oil wicks, and to have coffee, sugar, and tinned milk as everyday necessities instead of rare luxuries. At the same time as these household improvements were going on, farming methods were also changing. Tin cups for collecting the resin became more popular, and replaced the wasteful scrapes in the ground at the foot of the trees. Instead of the wooden ploughs tipped with iron, which frequently broke, iron ploughs began to be used, and instead of oxen, horses and mules began to be bought.... The advent of fertilizer revolutionized the wheat farming and by 1956 all the villagers were using fertilizer in both the autumn and the spring and had quadrupled their crop.

After 1950 the claims of the school for the attendance of the children became more stringent, and families found that they increasingly lost their children as goat-, sheep-, and cow-herds to the demands of education. There had, since the school was started at the turn of the century, been a law that all boys should attend, and in 1916 school was made compulsory for girls as well. But parents needed the children to guard the herds, the children did not enjoy school anyway, the community was poor, and the teachers sympathetic. During the troubled times from 1940 to 1950 the school functioned only sporadically.... But after 1950 the rule governing school attendance became more strict, and this was later matched by the parents' own wish that their children should, unlike so many of themselves, be literate.

The loss of the children to the school, of the growing daughters to the marriages which blossomed in the years of release after 1950, and after 1960, of the men to the ships and countries abroad, coincided with the easier farming conditions as a result of fertilizer and resulted in the gradual selling, chiefly from 1958 until 1963, of the flocks of sheep and goats, until only two flocks were left. Resin gathering, however, still continued, and in 1965 the stabilizing of the resin prices at 4 drs. a kilo by government subsidy ensured a regular cash income for all those who owned forests and were able, or willing, to work them.

As a consequence of all this, the standard of living within the village and expectations from the outside world began to change, and instead of extreme physical hardship and a high degree of self-sufficiency, people began to reduce their hours of toil in the fields, to live more comfortably in their homes, and to develop a way of life involving increasing dependence on more modernized communities and a gradual acquaintance with urban ways of life.

One of the most significant features to arise from this change was an altered form of self-interest, and a very radical shift in the balance of forces which kept the community together. Ironically, with the entry into village life of material improvements and wider ambitions, the whole structure of the community life began to disintegrate, and inroads began to be made into the traditional pattern which were to result eventually in emigration and depopulation.

Before the war the necessity for reciprocity over the fields and animals, and for a high degree of interdependence in the internal affairs of the village because of the lack of amenities, meant that the interests of the village as a whole forced upon its inhabitants a certain degree of mutual co-operation. Self-interest in a narrow sense had to give way to the good of the community, and within the joint family individualism had to be strictly suppressed for the group as a whole to be able to function....

Before 1950, joint families and a system of patronage linked the family groups to the outside community by relationships of marriage and obligation; the pre-eminence of the kindred, marriage into a hierarchy of prestige and wealth associated with possession of the land, the unquestioning acceptance of the agricultural and pastoral life and the related values of independence and honour, were all values which kept the community solidly rooted in itself and in its environment; and these factors resulted in a total system in which the interests of the various families and those of the community coincided to a very great degree. Today the reverse applied, and the increasing reliance on the outside world, the diversification of ambitions, the decreasing value of the land and the increasing dependence on cash, the fragmentation of the family group, the dispersal of the flocks and the incomplete exploitation of the farms, the rise of individualism and the weakening of traditional ties between the family, its kin, and its land, all involve the different families of the community in interests which basically diverge from those of their neighbours. The same force, that of self-interest in terms of the survival of the family, still persists; but the changed economic and social scene now provides an environment in which the impulses of generation and survival no longer act towards the exclusiveness and solidarity of the community, but flow outwards to cause village society to identify itself more and more with the nearby towns. Thus, along with a higher standard of living, a divergence of aims and a latitude for the individual are being brought into village life that act against a united social organization, and towards the breakdown of many of the traditional curbs on hostility and quarreling.

The villagers' unanimous verdict on the worsening of social relations in recent years has been referred to earlier, and expressed in the phrase, 'The community has fallen into a state of hatred'.... Two other phrases express the same idea. In the older days, the villagers say, 'People were on good terms with one another' ..., whereas now, 'Hatred exists'....

One cause for this change from, as the villagers put it, love to hatred, or, as it may otherwise be put, from social solidarity to fragmentation, lies in the altered form of self-interest already discussed. Another lies in the altered value now given to the concept of 'advancement' or 'progress', for because of the increasing attraction of the way of life presented by the outside world, the terms in which progress is defined now relate exclusively to that outside world. While in the old days progress could be realized within the terms of the village life, it can now be realized only by leaving that life for good. Thus the only really prestigious individual is one who has left the village....

.... Now that the whole traditional way of life has been devalued, envy continues to work and competition is as fierce as ever, but failing any outlet in a struggle for the effective attainment and retention of wealth and prestige, it is forced to express itself increasingly in words and actions which result in gossip and quarrels. At the same time there exists to a much lesser extent the traditional bar to unlimited quarreling which was in earlier times provided by the villagers' need of one another. It is partly as a result of this that the word used to describe relationships within the village in the present day is not 'love' but 'hatred'....

A further effect of the focusing of ambitions in terms realizable outside the village rather than within it, coupled with the inability of the villagers to exploit their properties fully and the levelling out of financial inequality in the crisis of 1940, is a radical change in the values attributed to the land. Land, it is frequently said, is immortal—it cannot die, it is always a secure investment; the man of property will live in the knowledge of the acres he has behind him, with their potential productivity and their possible monetary value should the wheel of fortune turn and Ambéli become accessible to timber merchants or building prospectors. Yet as he finds himself in the reality of the present economic moment the villager realizes that he is in possession of a commodity which he is not able to sell or fully to exploit, and which has no value as a dowry for his daughters or a legacy for his sons. Thus although people are still thought of as rich or poor in accordance with the property they own, this is an assessment gauged in unreal terms according to past standards of prestige which are not applicable to the present day....

The alteration in the value placed on land is not the only factor which has affected this change in prestige values, although it is an important one. The break-up of the family through emigration and marriage out of the village has resulted in prestige being centred not in the good name of the house but in the individual achievement, while the low esteem in which the village is held means that prestige through the marriage alliance is no longer achieved through the linking of the honour and wealth of two families, but by casting off for ever the bonds of village life. In this situation the part played by cash becomes increasingly important, for land can no longer be given in dowries.... At the same time, the cost of food, clothes, schoolbooks, and the extra expenses involved in higher education (which is becoming a necessity for girls as well as for boys and is another way in which the traditional dowry is being replaced) takes up a very large proportion of family incomes. Thus although the economic situation in Greece began to improve dramatically in the mid-1950s and has retained the same momentum until the present day, the expectations of the villagers are, as time passes, overreaching more and more their actual financial capabilities. In comparison with the past they are, materially speaking, infinitely better off. In comparison with the modern competitive world they are barely holding their own, and their self-respect suffers accordingly. If poverty may be judged by the discrepancy between what people have and what they want, the villagers of Ambéli today are probably poorer than they have ever been....

Packaging Pleasures: Club Méditerranée and French Consumer Culture, 1950–1968

ELLEN FURLOUGH

In the generation following World War II, Western societies, benefiting from improved technologies, increasing prosperity, and relative international peace, have given more attention, effort, importance, and money to leisure time than ever before. In a seemingly relentless pursuit of pleasure outside of work, people have flocked to new organizations and businesses that purport to convert spare time into happiness.

Ellen Furlough examines one such business that aimed to provide an "antidote to civilization" for French people. How did Club Med attempt to offer this antithesis to civilization? What paradoxes does the author see in Club Med's endeavor to furnish an escape from modern consumer society? What does she see as the social appeal of Club Med?

What was the Club Med "formula"? What were the living conditions and the atmosphere at the Club Med vacation spots? What was the "Club spirit"? How did the Polynesian and Tahitian themes affect the dress, the behavior, and the goals themselves of the vacationers? What were the roles of "congenial organizers," the GOs? Why did Club Med permit them to fraternize with the "congenial members," the GMs? What rituals did the villages perform and how did those rituals function to close the GMs off from the outside world? Do you think that the GMs discovered their natural selves? How did leisure time on a Club Med vacation differ from work time?

Club Med emphasized leisure social/behavioral roles that it believed to be antithetical to everyday French society. Can you give some examples of such role playing? There was a major emphasis on beautiful, naturally enhanced bodies, proudly adorned, and quintessentially erotic, and on exercise and hearty eating. Did the stress on comeliness and forthright sexuality represent successfully a reaction to French civilization?

What paradoxes does the author see in Club Med's strategies? Why does she not believe Club Med successfully escaped consumer society? What types of people took Club Med vacations? What social groups resisted the alluring appeal of Club Med's paradise vacations? Did the Club Med program bear a relationship to Western imperialism and colonization? Were the little Gardens of Eden the Club intended to establish doomed to be pale reflections of certain aspects of the dominant French culture? Do you think Ellen Furlough is sympathetic to Club Med claims and practices?

In the midst of the French revolution of May 1968, a crowd of student radicals targeted and shattered the glass windows of the Parisian head-quarters of Club Méditerranée. Club Med epitomized all they rejected about

French consumer society—huge meals, idle bronzed bodies, abundance in the midst of underdeveloped countries, and a commitment to narcissistic, apolitical hedonism. Club Med officials responded by offering some of the students free visits to Club Med vacation villages, insisting that the students would realize that Club Med was an "antidote to civilization," set apart from the values and experiences of French consumer culture.

The students' critique and Club Med's response raise the question that I will address in this article: to what extent was it possible for Club Med to be an "antidote to civilization" and to what extent was its representation in those terms the key to its consumer appeal? I will argue that Club Med was not an antithesis to "civilization"; rather, Club Med was central to and indeed helped to construct French consumer culture and consumer capitalism—the very "civilization" that it claimed to counteract. A second and related concern will be to explore the social bases for Club Med's appeal. Here I will argue that Club Med's "formula" expressed, and helped consolidate, the orienting practices, attitudes, and values of the "new" French middle class during what has been termed the "postwar regime of accumulation."

Gérard Blitz founded Club Med in the spring of 1950. Blitz had grown up in Belgium, where his father was a socialist Jewish diamond cutter with a passion for, what was called at the time, "physical culture." In 1945 the Belgian government offered Gérard Blitz, who was with the Belgian intelligence service during the war, the job of operating a center for the rehabilitation of concentration-camp survivors. Blitz spent the immediate postwar years thus engaged at a hotel in the Haute-Savoie region of France. Meanwhile, his sister Didy and his father operated a vacation club for people who shared a love of sports and a desire to break with wartime memories. As Didy later recalled, people "wanted to live/be alive after those dark times." While visiting this club, Blitz was struck by the similarities with his project in the Haute-Savoie and by the recuperative power of relaxation, play, and the sun. Unlike previous tourist enterprises which stressed moral self-improvement, education, public service, health and fitness, Blitz stressed self-indulgent physical pleasure and a break from habitual social relations. The goal was to remake the self, an especially appealing ethos for people who had lived through the sacrifices and bodily harms of the war.

On 27 April 1950, Blitz deposited the statutes for "Club Méditerranée" and placed a modest notice in the Paris metro showing the sun, the sea, and his telephone number. In the summer of 1950, some twenty-five hundred people spent two weeks at his first Club Med village, situated on the Bay of Alcudia on the Spanish island of Majorca. Socially, most in this first group were urban and middle class—primarily students and young cadres; others were secretaries, lawyers, and doctors. They hailed primarily from France and Belgium, but also from Holland, England, Switzerland, Norway, and Denmark. There was not a single building; people lived in U.S. Army surplus tents and slept on allied army cots. Blitz provided a small orchestra and sports equipment and presided with his wife Claudine, who had lived in Tahiti and regularly dressed in a Polynesian sarong. People swam, played sports, ate at tables for eight, and were entertained at night by flamenco dancers. Yet, after various troubles, including a hurricane, people demanded their money back. Blitz averted disaster by addressing the assembled guests as *gentils membres* (congenial members, hereafter GMs) and guaranteeing satisfaction or money back. Apparently, most were satisfied in the end. At regular reunions in Paris, GMs shared summer photos and danced in grass skirts and bathing suits until dawn. They also received copies of the Club's bulletin, the *Trident*, which contained news of the Club's off-season activities and of marriages and births of new GMs (children of members were, for a while in the 1950s given free memberships), and which served as a kind of "wish book" for the upcoming summer activities. Club Med villages proliferated.

What Club Med administrators, managers, employees (*gentils organisa-teurs* or congenial organizers, hereafter GOs), and the GMs would soon label the *esprit du Club*[1] was being created, and it was this "esprit" that served as the basis for the Club's self-representation as an "antidote to civilization." The crucial element of this "esprit" was that it was to be diametrically different from everyday life and provide "mental and physical detoxification." Villages were seen as "closed" spaces, isolated from their surroundings and from other tourists, places where people could "rediscover the needs that urban reality repressed." The indigenous society was portrayed as a per-turbation or perhaps a curiosity that one might visit later on an organized excursion. Inside, the village represented personalized and more intimate relations, intensity of life, liberty of choice, a place where people would be limited only by their capacities. Closure within the villages was not seen as a limit, but a condition of liberty. Within the villages was thus to be realized the utopian society of abundance and ease, and the operative logic inside the villages was to each his or her desires.

By the early 1950s the explicit model for this "counter-society" was a mythologized Polynesia, and this "Polynesian" theme informed the rhetoric and practices of the Club. There were poems in the *Trident* about how the GMs, or "Polynesians," dreamed of "the arch of the beach, the Polynesian huts under the palms, and dug-out canoes, men pushing their canoe into the foam of the surf, chasing young girls wearing flowers, and fishing all day." As the army surplus tents began wearing out, they were replaced by Polynesian huts, and the costume of choice at Club Med villages became the flowered Tahitian sarong. Worn by both women and men, the sarong signified the "liberated" body and nativism, and the *Trident* obligingly provided full-page illustrations on the various ways to tie one (using "Tahitian-looking" models). By 1953 Claudine Blitz arranged for groups of Tahitian students from Paris to introduce GMs at the village on Corfu to Tahitian music and

[1] The Club spirit.

dances. Then, in 1955, Club Med established a village on Tahiti and advertised it as a "pilgrimage to the source . . . an earthly paradise." Here Club Med constructed an alternative landscape for French people confronting the implications of military defeats along with an emerging technocratic order. Representations of the "Primitive" can offer "a model of alternative social organization in which psychological integrity is a birthright, rooted in one's body and sexuality, and in which a full range of ambivalences and doubts can be confronted and defused through the culture's rituals, customs, and play."

Because villages were to be distinct from everyday life, there evolved elaborate welcoming and leaving rituals so that people would both symbolically and physically enter and leave its "closed" world. For example, GOs in sarongs greeted new arrivals with a trumpet fanfare and placed flowers around their necks. Once inside the village, physical accommodations and social activities were calculated to remind GMs that they had entered a space devoted to a "total rupture with daily habits, a period of return to the forgotten rhythms of nature." The architecture, whether the tents of the early 1950s, "Polynesian" huts from the mid-50s, or the later buildings built in "local styles," emphasized its opposition to urbanism and materialism and its connection to "nature."

More important, however, was the stated objective of erasing social barriers and distinctions. This process entailed abolishing the most visible signs of social distinction, in essence peeling away social conventions to reveal people's "authentic" selves. It was the convention in all villages for people to address each other in the familiar "tu"[2] form and to call each other by their first names. All discussions about one's occupation within "civilization" were discouraged. One of the "rules of the game" most closely attended to was a different mode of dress. Spending several weeks wearing bikinis and sarongs was seen as a "rupture with daily life," and one of the most common phrases heard in a village was that "there are no social differences when everyone is in a bathing suit." Another strategy that Club executives argued muted external signs of status was the practice of replacing cash with colored beads. In order to have a drink at the bar, for example, people detached some of the colored beads that they wore around their necks or ankles. A journalist joked, "It's so hard to carry real money in sarongs." The *Trident* called this the "disappearance of money," a revealing formulation that acknowledges the way this practice rendered invisible the cash nexus of the enterprise.

Another area in which Club Med positioned itself as different from "civilization" was in its emphasis on play rather than work. Even the labor of the GOs was constructed so that they would not appear to be working. A Club Med village was instead said to be a "leisure society" wherein people

[2]"You."

would rediscover their natural selves, rhythms, and desires. Sports and ludic activities were uppermost in Club Med's definition of leisure. Every village had a wide range of available sports, and there were often lessons from Olympic champions. Opportunities for play in the villages were also to be found in the nightly "animations." A favorite prank was to have a male GM lie on the floor as a squalling baby. A woman GM would change his diapers and powder his fly. The ability to participate in such playful, one might say ridiculous, activities was to demonstrate not only one's willingness to change the rules, but the ability to refuse superiority, rediscover childhood playfulness, and demonstrate that seriousness was a convention of another time and place. Ridicule was cast as a form of relaxation.

Club Med vacations were also characterized by ease rather than effort. Unlike most forms of tourism, Club Med advertising assured people that everything would be taken care of. It emphasized the convenience of the single-price format, the ease of comfortable transport, and the generally well organized nature of villages run by "specialists." Although everything was foreseen, little within the village was programmed; people could choose whether or not to participate in the village's activities. Time was to become "indefinite." Club literature deployed a language of individual choice, insisting that "how you fill your time is your business."

The result of the village's closed and controlled environment and its available experiences was to be the physical and mental well-being of the individual body. Club Med was ultimately packaging the care of the self and its recuperation through play, relaxation, and pleasure. Physical health and physical beauty were central to this vision. Outward appearance was the mark of one's personality, discipline, and inner essence. These corporeal preoccupations were shot through all aspects of Club Med, and I will only mention four aspects here. First, the Club's press constantly created a discourse of bodily description, in essence creating images of ideal—and ultimately normative—physical shapes. Club literature routinely published pictures of the managers of villages and described their bodies. And, because most managers were male, this particular discourse constructed ideal masculine bodies. Here is one description: "André Baheux, 41 years old, . . . height 1 m77, weight 60kg, spread . . . 1 m80; biceps, thighs, and calves fully formed."

A second ongoing theme concerned the making of beautiful bodies. Club literature constantly emphasized that "thanks to the numerous physical activities that we offer, you will refind, at whatever age, your shapely figure." Exercise was the dominant issue here—there was no mention of dieting. Although there were some discussions of women's bodies and exercise, the creation of beautiful feminine bodies tended to be portrayed in terms of various means of adornment that were not unlike similar discussions within other aspects of French consumer culture. There were articles in the *Trident* on "How to be Beautiful in the Village" with advice about appropriate fashions and makeup. Club Med publications encouraged women to bring beauty products with them—suntan lotion, hand cream, deodorant, indelible eye makeup, and cream to protect the skin and brown it lightly while waiting for a tan. Women's "natural" beauty was to be enhanced with beauty products and proper clothing.

A third kind of discussion about the body was overtly narcissistic and self-congratulatory. A striking example of this was the poem "Creed" published in the *Trident* in 1952. The poem has four stanzas, and the first three begin: "I love my arms," "I love my legs," and "I love my torso." These are followed by paeans to the body part in question, for example within the "I love my arms" stanza: "rippling deltoids,... flesh furrowed with veins which swell forth during vigorous play." The final stanza reads:

> I love my body where so many forces rest in order to rise up at my command. / I love its colors and I love its shapes as eternal things. / I love the "gay science"[3] as I love healthy life. / I love to train as I love to study. / I love competitions as I love books. / I love races as I love my poems. / I love joy as one loves a friend. / I love struggle as one loves a woman. / I love all that which is Effort and Life. / I love my body as my soul. /

And a final theme, more muted in the printed literature but central to all the others, was that of the erotic/libidinal body. An erotically charged climate was central to the "pleasures" that Club Med promised. The sexuality valorized at Club Med was predominately heterosexual, casual, spontaneous, and blurred the edges of definitions of propriety. One could, in this sense, speak of Club Med as a site for performing an expanded repertoire of sexualities and playful (and perhaps even transgressive) desires. For women, this could at once defy ... the "highly rigid regulatory frame" of gender and sexuality and remind them of the risks involved in an era when both birth control and abortion were illegal in France.[4] Whether one chooses to interpret this erotically charged climate as "liberating" or not, it is certain that for people at the time, a Club Med vacation signified a loosening of the rules regarding sexuality. Club Med villages came to have a reputation as places with "an erotic morality" involving many "brief encounters," despite Blitz's insistence that there was "no more and no less libertinage than on any other kind of seaside holiday." Though unmarried GMs were housed in single-sex arrangements, Club conventions were that a towel folded over the outside door meant "do not disturb." A male GO boasted: "I knew the taste of all the suntan oil in the village." These four discussions were not distinct, but

---

[3]Ellen Furlough states that the subtext of the penis is obvious here and that the phrase "gay science," difficult to translate, probably refers to the German philosopher Friedrich Nietzsche's (1844–1900) *The Gay Science*.

[4]In 1967 the Neuwirth Law authorized the sale of contraceptives, and in 1974 the law forbidding abortions was repealed. (Author's note.)

formed a discursive web that placed the beautiful, healthy body at its center. As the village manager in Tahiti, which had the reputation of being the village with the most emphasis on physical beauty and "liberated" sexuality, asserted: "the Club was the revenge of the beautiful on the intelligent."

Despite the Club's self-representation as the "antidote to civilization," Club Med was squarely within, and constitutive of, French consumer culture and consumer capitalism. This is not to say, however, that Club Med's self-representation as the "antidote to civilization" was a kind of false advertising, but rather that the seeming contradiction between Club Med's self-representation and its realization were part of its essence and indeed crucial for its success.

Club Med's ethos as an isolated and recuperative Eden was as carefully packaged as any other consumer commodity. Club Med was, and is, a large, multinational corporation and an important player in the tourism and leisure industry. Like other institutions that construct sites for consumption, Club Med created integrated environments promising predictable pleasures. Although Club Med was originally founded in 1950 as a nonprofit association, in 1957 it was legally reconstituted as a commercial organization.... From the early 1960s, a significant proportion of Club Med was owned by the Rothschild bank, and its business decisions were within an economic logic that was not unlike any other consumer industry. By 1958 Club Med's business strategies were increasingly under the purview of Gilbert Trigano, a former communist who had become involved with Club Med through his family's camping supply business. After joining the Club in 1954 and moving rapidly up its hierarchy, Trigano decided that the Club needed to move into "mass" tourism, sharpen its business aspects, and attend to such issues as market segmentation. Plans for and decisions about villages were, like any other consumer commodity's design and execution, created in Parisian corporate offices and replicated in selected environments. By 1967 the club operated 31 villages in Europe and did about 20 million dollars worth of business. It had a rapidly expanding membership of over four hundred thousand, and there were around two thousand employees at the height of the summer tourist season. The Club was the largest civilian customer of the Italian State Railways and the largest short-haul charterer of Air France planes. Its expansion was further aided in 1968 by an agreement with American Express. This not only provided an important infusion of capital but guaranteed promotion of Club Med's programs throughout American Express's extensive network of travel agencies.

Like other aspects of consumer culture, and despite the Club's rhetoric, the villages were not utopian worlds without social hierarchies. In the 1950s and 1960s, Club Med was an experience constructed by and for white, economically advantaged Europeans, and later for Americans. There was no "class erosion" at work, although there may have been some mild shaking up of conventions. GMs were young (67 percent under 30 in 1961), and the largest group was drawn from middle-class salaried sectors. The largest proportions were teachers, secretaries (predominantly women), and technicians, but GMs also included cadres, people from the liberal professions (mainly doctors), and commerce, students, and a small group of workers (mostly from the relatively well-paid trades of metallurgy and printing).

The social composition of Club Med consumers drew heavily from the social group that Pierre Bourdieu[5] and others have termed the "new middle class," a group seen as a "new petit bourgeoisie"[6] of service people and technicians and the "new bourgeoisie" of cadres and "dynamic executives." It was the ethos of this new middle class that provided a template for the "esprit" of Club Med. Bourdieu argues that the "new" or renovated bourgeoisie and the "new" petit bourgeoisie "collaborated enthusiastically in imposing the new ethical norms (especially as regards consumption) and the corresponding needs." He points especially to new notions of pleasure and new perceptions of the body. In a passage strikingly similar to the ethos of Club Med, Bourdieu states that these new formulations of pleasure and the body

> make it a failure, a threat to self-esteem, not to "have fun," . . . pleasure is not only permitted but demanded. . . . The fear of not getting enough pleasure, the logical outcome of the effort to overcome the fear of pleasure, is combined with the search for self-expression and "bodily expression" and for communication with others (relating—*échange*), even immersion in others (considered not as a group but as subjectivities in search of their identity); and the old personal ethic is thus rejected for a cult of personal health and psychological therapy.

He adds that this group's conception of bodily exercise aimed "to substitute relaxation for tension, pleasure for effort, 'creativity' and 'freedom' for discipline, communication for solitude." It worked toward a "a body which has to be 'unknotted,' liberated, or more simply rediscovered and accepted." In Luc Boltanski's[7] analysis of the "cadres" (a group he argues typified the new middle class), he agrees that there was a strong link between the formation and consolidation of this new middle class and a new "lifestyle." Boltanski characterizes this lifestyle as an "easy-going American style simplicity, . . . a new, relaxed way of being bourgeois, a new way of life, . . . and a new system of values." Among those values was a "cult of the waistline and devotion to the physique." I am not arguing here that Club Med was reducible to a class phenomenon, but rather that it provided an ideal space to act out this new culture and thereby contributed to its formation. This was, in short, space for redrawing social and cultural boundaries and

---

[5] French social theorist (b. 1930).

[6] The lower middle-class.

[7] Author of *The Making of a Class: Cadres in French Society*.

hierarchies rather than abolishing them. Despite such stories as the one involving GMs who struck up a friendship only to discover later that one of them was a director and the other a nightwatchman at the same factory, Club Med instead offered and helped consolidate another kind of cultural capital to be traded as a shared experience among privileged vacationers.

Club Med also reinforced, and in some cases reinvented, social hierarchies and boundaries between people in the villages and in host countries. Club executives saw the geographical locations for Club Med villages as culinary resources and inspirational guides for ersatz architecture (that is, "Moorish bungalows in Morocco"), populated by people who were potentially objects for the excursions and the "tourist gaze." Club Med was, in this sense, a reconfigured colonialist adventure that could be purchased. In this period of French decolonization, Club Med vacationers could continue to partake of colonialist "exoticism" even if their country no longer controlled the region politically. One journalist who went to a Club Med village in Morocco in the mid-1960s observed an excursion to "the Club's own Moroccan village." He delineated the "modern" playful vacationers from the "natives" by describing the way the Club's beach property was carefully roped off; while the Club's vacationers were cavorting on the beach and working to tan their white bikini-clad bodies, Moroccans guarding the areas "spent most of their time inside straw beehives, in which they avoid the sun that the members have come so far to find." Like other aspects of consumer society, Club Med created and sustained hierarchies privileging those who were economically advantaged, physically vigorous, "attractive," and "modern."

Club Med's claim to be an "antidote to civilization," devoid of work, preoccupations with time, seriousness, or effort can also be seen as reinforcing the very issues from which it claimed to be separate. For example, for its employees, the villages were hardly leaving behind "work"; rather, their work environments were at the forefront of the growth and proliferation of consumer service industries where . . . "the social composition of . . . those who are serving in the front line, may be a part of what is in fact 'sold' to the customer." . . . Such services "require what can loosely be called 'emotional work' such as smiling and making people feel comfortable." This can be seen as a proliferation of "feminized" work, whether women do the majority of this labor or not, and it will tend to be low paid—a characteristic aspect of the salaries of GOs. The fantasy that Club Med was creating was one where workers did not really work and where "natives" were not really oppressed—a fantasy that masked and thus helped perpetuate power relationships. Further, to "experience" the loss of a mentality of time, seriousness, and effort means one must experience their ongoing realization "outside" the vacation experience. In other words, one kind of experience (vacations) depends on and helps perpetuate its supposed opposite (everyday life).

Another way that Club Med was constructing aspects of the "civilization" that it supposedly repudiated was that its "naturalness" always depended on certain material props. Consumers bought vacations at villages containing hair salons, sophisticated sports equipment, and stores on the premises. Not only was "materialism" never absent, but Club Med fostered a key element of tourist culture—that of the souvenir. Club Med villages regularly scheduled shopping expeditions to local markets. There one could buy souvenirs—material witnesses to the commercialized "experience" of a Club Med vacation. One's transformed body could also be seen as a souvenir—returning from vacation with a tan, for example, signified physical beauty, eroticism, and a "successful" vacation.

The materialism and the consumerist theme of abundance was especially evident regarding food, an element that figured prominently in the ambiance and imaginary of the Club. Food and wine in the villages were unlimited and included in the basic cost, and both were universally said to be excellent. Club Med also fostered materialist consumer culture in the realm of clothing. From 1959, it had its own mail-order catalogue uniquely for GMs who were registered for a village for the next summer. Tahitian sarongs figured prominently in the selection.

Finally, the Club was also involved in constructing a cultural pastiche that placed it squarely within, and helped to create, other aspects of consumer (and postmodernist) culture. Not only did Club Med evoke the "natural" in the midst of a carefully packaged environment, but cultural productions were carefully utilized to create an ambiance mixing elements of "high" and "mass" culture. For example, in 1963 Club Med introduced "The Forum" into its villages. These were cast as "occasions to follow a spectacle, to participate in it, to discuss, to understand the givens of new problems, . . . to make vacations not only a rest for the nerves and the body but also an enrichment of the spirit and of the imagination." Forum discussions included Hellenism, Italian geniuses of the Quattrocento,[8] heart surgery, and the mysteries of the universe. From the mid-1960s, there were taped concerts of classical music that included a commentary in French so "no one need wonder what to think of the music." (Here again we can see Club Med attending to cultural capital.) The Club's ambiance also incorporated aspects of popular culture. One account of a British woman's journey to Club Med noted that on the journey they "twisted into the early hours of the morning." At one village, a participant described lazing in the sun next to the bar, where "the hi-fi pipes out Jacques Brel[9] and Pete Seeger."[10] Like advertising, which is, of course, another constituent element of consumer culture, Club Med promoted a "pastiche or collage effect in which the breadth and depth of cultural values can be ransacked to achieve a desired effect."

In conclusion, Club Med emerged at a particularly promising historical moment. Culturally . . . even if the reality for French people of the 1960s

---

[8]The fifteenth century.

[9]Belgian singer and composer (1929–1978).

[10]American folk singer and composer (b. 1919).

was more nuanced, by the late 1960s "the imaginary had changed: consumer society was in people's heads." ... This consumer society had its symbols (the TV, the auto, the washing machine), its privileged moments (prime time, the weekend, vacations), and its recognized places (the salon, the supermarket, beach, or camping). It fostered values of abundance, comfort, and youth, and an ideology of individual choice. Club Med was all of these things, a symbol, a place, and a set of values, and its meanings were those of the larger consumer society of which it was a part.

A central tenet of Club Med was that it proclaimed the body as a vehicle for pleasure. Club Med celebrated, permitted, promoted, and commodified, the fitness, beauty, energy, and health of the libidinal "natural" body. Club Med participants were to pay, in all senses, attention to the self, and part of the grammar of pleasure that Club Med helped create was a heightened concern with the "care of the self." One's body, in essence, was one's text to be endowed with meaning. Crucial to this project was (and is) the endless longing and impossibility of attaining and retaining a youthful, healthy, playful, sexy body. One could, by definition, never be satisfied. What is particularly interesting about Club Med was the way this dynamic interplay between longing and lacking was initially played out within an inventive cultural landscape laced with the "primitive" Polynesian. Here we can read the longing for a culture where one could be at one with nature and find sexual pleasure along with mental and physical health, ... using the primitive within a "rhetoric of desire." And yet, Club Med fostered the notion that people could count on having easy access to a beauty parlor, mixed drinks, and piped music. Here again we see the ways in which Club Med's utilization of what might seem to be contradictory messages and strategies was indeed crucial for its success.

This raises questions about the relationship between the social management of pleasure for profit and the consumers themselves. Is this yet another instance of a Foucaultian[11] institution controlling and regulating a set of disciplines on the individual body? Or, do we need to analyze Club Med in terms of the ways in which people understood, enjoyed, created, and perhaps subverted those "experiences"? How can we understand and theorize the historical roles and experiences of pleasure as they adhere to consumption, and how do we differentiate ... between "real pleasure and mere diversion"? Although answering these questions is beyond the scope of this article, it is certain that the "care of the self" was closely aligned with consumer culture's message of individualist self-determination and expression. The language of the self and of individual pleasure was crucial for the cultural consolidation of a new middle class, and it obviated a language of class linked to an oppositional spirit or an ongoing political struggle. The notion of the "new middle class" was itself politically important in the 1950s and 1960s, a

---

[11]Referring to the philosopher-historian Michel Foucault (1926–1984) who saw institutions such as the prison and the asylum as modern developments whose functions were to discipline and punish.

time heralded by some as a new social order whose social center of gravity would be the middle class. This new middle class was portrayed as "a vast group of people leading comfortable lives, sharing similar values, and employed by large organizations—individualists governed by the competitive spirit and the drive to achieve."... [T]he new class would support the "end of ideology" and "alleviate class tensions" through a "more equitable distribution of consumer goods and education." Bourdieu offers another way to look at this group's "new ethic of liberation"—it could supply the economy with "the perfect consumers" who were "isolated...and therefore free (or forced) to confront in extended order the separate markets...of the new economic order...untrammelled by the constraints and brakes imposed by collective memories and expectations."

Club Med in particular, and tourism in general, were at the forefront of consumerism's culture of distraction, fantasy, and desire. Club Med accented, packaged, and marketed key components of an emergent consumer culture: a rhetoric of longing and desire, the elevation of the autonomous, healthy and pleasurable body, a (post) modern reliance on pastishe, and a belief in (and commodification of) the recuperative necessity of non-workplace touristic "experiences." Modern "mass" tourism has been a crucial engine— both culturally and economically—for modern consumer societies. While one could argue that both Club Med and French students of 1968 were questioning disciplinary boundaries and structures, it can also be argued that to accept and experience the values, definitions, and "pleasures" that Club Med offered was to believe that the system of consumer capitalism giving rise to Club Med worked.

The Rise and Fall
of the Swedish Model

KRISTINA ORFALI

Is post–World War II Sweden a paradise, a model worthy of emulation and envy? With the demise of the Soviet Union, which had provided a model society for eastern European states, for some individuals and political parties in the West, and certainly for Third World countries, Sweden may now provide the only viable alternative to the creeping Americanization of Europe.

Sweden has been at the forefront of progressive legislation. What aspects of life were the Swedes the first to regulate? What are the goals of Swedish legislation? What does Kristina Orfali mean by the "antisecrecy model"? How has the expanded role of government affected the family? To what extent has the family been "deprivatized"? Are children better off in the Swedish system? Are immigrants? Are women? What is the role of religion and the Lutheran Church?

Sweden has a reputation for being open sexually. Why? How have changing mores and laws affected marital relations, homosexual culture, prostitution, and the distribution of sexually explicit materials? What did the sexual revolution comprise in Sweden?

To what extent is Swedish society transparent? Where do Swedes find privacy? No one would argue that Swedish society is perfect, even if it is admired. What problems exist in spite of Swedish social engineering? How solvable are they?

Does Orfali believe that Swedes prefer their lifestyle and culture to other systems? What are the alternatives?

Sweden is a country that has long fascinated many parts of the world. In the 1960s a whole generation grew up on clichés of blondness and liberation, on fantasies of a sexual El Dorado filled with shapely Ekbergs[1] and sirenic Garbos[2]—but also with Bergman's[3] anguished heroines. Little by little, however, this fantasy-land metamorphosed into a dark country inhabited by bores, morbid minds, and would-be suicides, a nation of "disintegrated families," "disoriented sex," and "liberated lovers in search of love"—in short, a "paradise lost." The Swedish ideal, once the object of extravagant praise and extravagant denunciation, ultimately was converted into a hyperborean mirage. The idyll was gone. The welfare state, recast in the role of meddling nuisance, no longer was a country to be imitated. Yesterday's middle way (between communism and capitalism) had become a utopian dream. Today it is fashionable on the part of many people to denounce Sweden as a "benign dictatorship" or "kid-glove totalitarianism."

There is nothing fortuitous about either the initial enthusiasm or the subsequent disillusionment. The Swedish model—in part economic and political but primarily societal—did indeed exist (and to some extent still does). The very word *model* (not, it is worth noting, of Swedish coinage) is revealing. People are apt to speak of the "Americanization of a society," of the "American myth" (that "everyone can become rich"), or even of "American values," but when they speak of a Swedish model they conjure up the image of an exemplary society. Swedish society is endowed not just with material or political content but with philosophical or even moral significance, with "the good life." As long ago as 1950 Emmanuel Mounier[4] asked himself, "What is a happy man?" The Swedes, he answered, "were the first to have known the happy city."

More than may meet the eye the Swedish model is a model of social ethics. Insofar as Sweden is a nation above suspicion, a nation that aspires

[1]Anita Ekberg, Swedish film actress (b. 1931).

[2]Greta Garbo (1905–1990), Swedish film actress, noted for her beauty and her passion for privacy.

[3]Ingmar Bergman (b. 1918), Swedish film director, famous for his complex depiction of morality and faith.

[4]French philosopher (1905–1950).

to universality (in the form of pacifism, aid to the Third World, social solidarity, and respect for the rights of man), and a nation whose ideological underpinnings are consensus and transparency, it can perhaps be seen as the forerunner of a new social order. In this respect the distinction between public and private in Sweden is highly significant. Hostility to secrecy, deprivatization, public administration of the private sphere—in all these areas Sweden has shifted the boundary between public and private in noteworthy ways. But the ethos of absolute transparency in social relations and the ideal of perfect communication, both characteristic of Swedish society, are seen in many parts of today's world as violations of individual privacy. The antisecrecy model has come to be seen as an intolerable form of imperialism.

The antisecrecy model affects all areas of social life down to the most private. In Sweden, perhaps more than anywhere else, the private is exposed to public scrutiny. The communitarian, social-democratic ethos involves an obsession with achieving total transparency in all social relations and all aspects of social life.

In Sweden money is not a confidential matter. Just as in the United States, material success is highly valued and ostentatiously exhibited. Transparency does not end there. Tax returns are public documents. Anyone can consult the *taxering kalender,* a document published annually by the finance ministry that lists the name, address, date of birth, and declared annual income of each taxpayer. Turning in tax cheats is virtually an institutionalized practice. While the fiscal authorities state publicly (in the press, for example) that informing on cheats is morally reprehensible, they admit that such information is frequently used. Even in the ethical sphere the imperative of transparency takes precedence.

Another illustration of the imperative is the principle of "free access to official documents" (*Offentlighets Principen*). Under the free-access law, which derives in large part from a 1766 law on freedom of the press, every citizen has the right to examine official documents, including all documents received, drafted, or dispatched by any agency of local or national government. The law allows for examination of documents in government offices as well as for having copies made or ordering official copies from the agency in return for payment of a fee. Any person denied access to public information may immediately file a claim with the courts. In practice the right of access is limited by the provisions of the secrecy act, which excludes documents in certain sensitive areas such as national security, defense, and confidential economic information. Nevertheless, the rule is that "when in doubt, the general principle [of free access] should prevail over secrecy."

As a result of the free-access principle the Swedish bureaucracy has been exceptionally open. For a long time Sweden has been an "information society," one in which information circulates freely. Computerization has accentuated this characteristic by facilitating the exchange of large quantities of information, in particular between the private sector and government agencies. There are few other countries in which the computers of several insurance companies are closely linked to those of the vital records office. Private automobile dealers may be electronically linked to vehicle registration records; a state agency may make use of a private company's credit records. Since 1974 information stored in computers has been treated just like other public documents and thus made subject to free access.

Sweden was the first European country to establish a central Bureau of Statistics (in 1756). It was also the first to issue citizen identification numbers. Comparison of different databases has been facilitated by this assignment of a personal identification number to each citizen. The practice was begun in 1946, and the numbers were used by state agencies before being incorporated into electronic databases. They are now widely used in public and private records.

If computers make individuals transparent to the state, the machines themselves must be made transparent to individuals. The computer security act of 1973 (amended in 1982) was the first of its kind in the West. It established the office of Inspector General for Computing Machinery with the authority to grant authorization to establish a database, to monitor the use of databases, and to act on complaints relative to such use. While authorization to establish a database is usually a mere formality, it is much more difficult to obtain when the data to be gathered includes information considered to be "private." Encompassed under this head are medical and health records, records of official actions by social welfare agencies, criminal records, military records, and so on. Only government agencies required by law to acquire such information are authorized to maintain these sensitive files. Finally, any person on whom information is gathered has the right to obtain, once a year at any time, a transcript of all pertinent information.

Some view this computerization of society as a highly effective, not to say dangerous, instrument of social control. Many foreign observers have seen it as marking an evolution toward a police state in which all aspects of private life, from health to income to jobs, are subject to shadowy manipulation. Interestingly, computerization has aroused virtually no protest within Sweden. Everyone seems convinced that it will be used only for the citizen's benefit and never to his detriment. The consensus reveals a deepseated confidence in the government (or, rather, in the community as a whole, which is ultimately responsible for control of the information-gathering apparatus). To Swedes, the whole system—private individuals and government agencies alike—is governed by one collective morality.

We must guard against the simplistic notion that Swedish society is a kind of Orwellian[5] universe, a world of soulless statistics. Paradoxically, this society of numbered, catalogued, faceless individuals is also a society of individualized faces. Every daily newspaper in the country publishes a

[5]Referring to the totalitarian future described by the English writer George Orwell (1903–1950) in his novel *1984* (1948).

half-page of photos to mark readers' birthdays, anniversaries, and deaths. Society notes take up at least a full page, and the absence of social discrimination is striking. One obituary recounts the career of a Mr. Andersson, *Verkställande dirktör* (plant manager), while another is devoted to a Mr. Svensson, *Taxichaufför* (taxi driver). Every birthday—especially the fiftieth, to which great importance is attached—is commonly marked by several lines in the paper and by time off work. This mixture of a modern, computerized society with still vital ancient customs is a unique aspect of Swedish society.

Transparency is also the rule in collective decisionmaking. The ombudsman is one Swedish institution that is well-known abroad. The parliamentary ombudsman, oldest of all (dating back to 1809), handles disputes over the boundary between public and private and is especially responsible for protecting the individual's "right to secrecy." He hears complaints, takes action when the law is violated, and offers advice to government agencies. Less well known, perhaps, but just as important is the procedure of public investigation. Before any major law is enacted, an investigative committee is appointed to consider pertinent issues. The committee includes representatives of different political parties, important interest groups, and various experts such as economists and sociologists. After hearings, surveys, and perhaps on-the-spot investigation, the committee transmits its report to the legislative department of the relevant ministry, which then makes public recommendations. Any citizen may also submit advice to the ministry. Thus the most "private" subjects such as homosexuality, prostitution, violence, and the like become the focus of major public debates, on an equal footing with such "public" issues as price controls, the regulation of television, the Swedish book of psalms, or the country's energy policy.

This uniquely Swedish procedure plays an important role in the elaboration of policy decisions and in the achievement of consensus. Its existence demonstrates not only how the most apparently "private" subjects are dealt with by institutions but also how individuals can take part in the various phases of the decisionmaking process. Two key ethical imperatives are highlighted: transparency of the decision process and consensus concerning the results.

Many people are unaware that Lutheranism is the state religion of Sweden and that the Lutheran Church is the established church. (Contrast this with Italy, where Catholicism is no longer the established religion.) It was in 1523, at the beginning of the Reformation, that the Lutheran Church began to function as an integral part of the governmental apparatus. The church played an instrumental role in the political unification of Sweden, since participation in religious services was then considered to be a civic obligation. The strength of the bond between church and state is illustrated by the fact that until 1860 Swedes were not permitted to quit the church—and even then they were required to become members of another Christian community. This requirement was not eliminated until 1951. Any child born a citizen of Sweden automatically becomes a member of the Church of

Sweden if either its father or its mother is a member. Thus 95 percent of the Swedish population nominally belongs to the official church.

Sweden therefore remains one of the most officially Christian of states, but it is also one of the most secular. The church is controlled by the government, which appoints bishops and some clergymen, fixes their salary, collects religious taxes, and so on. (A citizen who does not belong to the Church of Sweden still must pay at least 30 percent of the religious tax because of the secular services performed by the church.) The church is responsible for recording vital statistics, managing cemeteries, and other public functions. Thus, every Swedish citizen is inscribed on the register of some parish. The pastor who performs religious marriages is also an official of the state, so a religious marriage also serves as a civil marriage.

The institutional character of the Church of Sweden is reflected in public participation in religious ceremonies. Roughly 65 percent of all couples choose to be married in church. More than 80 percent of children are baptized and confirmed in the Lutheran Church. Some members of the official state church also belong to one of the "free," or dissident, Protestant churches that derive from the Lutheran evangelical wing of the religious awakening movement *(Väckelse rörelser),* most active in the early nineteenth century. Taken together, the free churches claim a higher proportion of the religious population in Sweden than in other Scandinavian countries.

Nevertheless, this formal presence of ecclesiastical institutions cannot hide the widespread disaffection with religion among Swedes. Fewer than 20 percent claim to be active churchgoers. In contrast, a tenacious, almost metaphysical anxiety is a profound trait of the Swedish temperament. Swedes may not believe in hell, but they surely believe in the supernatural. To convince oneself of this one need only glance at the half-pagan, half-religious festivals that fill the Swedish calendar or recall the importance of trolls and the fantastic in Swedish literature, folklore, and films. Or consider a writer as profoundly Swedish as Nobel prize winner Pär Lagerkvist, author of *Barabbas* and *The Death of Ahasuerus,* whose work is one long, anguished religious interrogation. André Gide,[6] another tormented conscience, wrote of *Barabbas* that Lagerkvist had pulled off "the tour de force of walking the tightrope across the dark stretch between the real world and the world of faith."

The reconciliation of the real with the spiritual is thus more tenuous than it may first appear. The collective religious morality of the past has been transformed into a new morality, still collective but now secular, while literature and film continue to reflect the spiritual world, the metaphysical anguish and tenacious guilt that have left such a deep imprint on the Swedish imagination.

The degree to which the private sphere is open to the public is clearly visible in the evolution of family structure. There is nothing new about the

---

[6] French author (1869–1951) and winner of the Nobel Prize in literature in 1947.

fact that in a modern state "functions" once left to the family have been taken over by the government or community. In Sweden, however, this deprivatization of the family has taken on a rather specific aspect. The point is not merely to intervene in private life but to make the private sphere totally transparent, to eliminate all secrecy about what goes on there. If, for example, an unwed or divorced mother applies to the government for financial assistance, or if a child is born in circumstances where the paternity is dubious, a thorough investigation is made to identify the father. Any man who, according to the woman or her friends, has had relations with the mother can be summoned to testify. Putative fathers may be required to undergo blood tests. If necessary the courts will decide. Once paternity is established, the father is required to provide for the child's upkeep.

The justification for such a procedure is not so much economic as ethical: every child has a right to know its true father. Clearly, however, acting on such a principle may yield paradoxical results. A single woman who wants to have a child and then raise it alone forfeits her social assitance if she refuses to cooperate with the paternity investigation. Although the 1975 abortion law grants women the right to control their own bodies, they do not have the right "to give birth without providing the name of the father." The child's rights take precedence over all others; even if the mother refuses social assistance, all available means (including the courts) will be used to force her to reveal the father's identity, on the grounds that the question is fundamental and that the child will wish to know. In paternity, therefore, there is no secrecy. Kinship is supposed to be transparent and clearly determined. The notion of legitimacy thus sidesteps the family, and the institution of marriage rests on public information, which is guaranteed by law.

Recent Swedish legislation on artificial insemination is also based on the requirement of transparency. Göron Ewerlöf, judge and secretary of the Commission on Artificial Insemination, put it this way: "It is to be hoped that future artificial inseminations will be more candid and open than they have been until now. The objective should be to ensure that birth by insemination is not unthinkable and indeed no more unusual than adoption. In matters of adoption Sweden has long since abandoned secrecy and mystery. According to specialists in adoption, this has helped to make adoptive children happier." Sweden was the first country in the world to adopt a comprehensive law governing artificial insemination (March 1, 1985). Previously, artificial insemination involving a donor had been shrouded as far as possible in secrecy. All information concerning the donor was kept hidden (or destroyed). The chief innovation of the new law—and incidentally an excellent illustration of the antisecrecy model—was to eliminate anonymity for donors. Every child now has the right to know who his biological father is and may even examine all hospital data concerning the individual. (Not even adoptive parents have access to this information.) In the past attention was focused on preventing the child from learning how it was conceived. Today it is the opposite: the primary objective is to protect the child's interest, which means not blocking access to any available information about the identity of its biological father. The commission underscored the importance of a frank and open attitude toward the child on the part of the parents. In particular, it recommended (although the law does not prescribe) that at the appropriate moment parents tell the child how it was conceived. The interest of the child was again invoked to justify the decision not to authorize artificial insemination except for married couples or couples living together as though married. It is not authorized for single women or lesbian couples. Thus the image of the standard family—father, mother, and children—has been maintained, even though the number of single-parent families in Sweden has been on the rise. Various psychological and psychiatric studies were invoked in support of this decision. The primary goal is to ensure the child's optimal development. Adoption laws are even more restrictive, and adoption is limited in most cases to married couples.

The status of the child in Sweden tells us a great deal about Swedish culture and ethics. Children are regarded both as full citizens, and as defenseless individuals to be protected in almost the same manner as other minority groups such as Laplanders and immigrants. The changing status of children is the clearest sign of deprivatization of the family. Since 1973 Sweden has had a children's ombudsman, whose role is to act as a spokesperson for children and to educate the public about children's needs and rights. The ombudsman has no legal authority to intervene in particular cases. He can, however, apply pressure to government agencies and political representatives, suggest ways to improve the condition of children, instruct adults about their responsibilities toward children, and, thanks to a twenty-four-hour telephone hot-line, offer support to individual children in distress. Thus children in Sweden enjoy specific rights and an institution whose purpose is to defend them. The objective is, while respecting the individuality of children, to make sure that they will be integrated as harmoniously as possible into the society.

The same ethic prevails in regard to immigrant children, who are entitled to receive instruction in their native language. Since 1979 the state has allocated funds to provide language lessons for immigrant children of preschool age, and nursery schools increasingly group children by native tongue. Everything possible is done to make sure that immigrant children have the tools they need to learn their mother tongue and preserve their culture by maintaining bilingual competence. Results have not always kept pace with ambitions, however. Many children have a hard time adapting to one culture or the other and a hard time mastering one of the two languages. Integration is envisioned, but respect for the immigrant's native culture is considered imperative.

Immigrants in Sweden enjoy many rights: they can vote in municipal and cantonal elections and are eligible to hold office; they are not confined to ghettos but scattered throughout the society in order to encourage integration; they receive free instruction in Swedish; and they receive the same social benefits as natives. Nevertheless, Sweden has not really been able to achieve a fusion of cultures, a melting pot in the manner of the United States.

The autonomy of the child vis-à-vis familial and parental authority is reflected in the law prohibiting corporal punishment. Since July 1979 the law governing parent-child relations has prohibited all forms of corporal punishment, including spankings, as well as mental cruelty and oppressive treatment. Examples explicitly mentioned in the law include shutting a child in a closet, threatening or frightening, neglect, and overt ridicule. Admittedly, no specific penalties for violation of these provisions have been set, except in cases of physical injury. Nevertheless, any child who is struck may file a complaint, and the person responsible cannot protest that he believed he had the right to administer a spanking. This once private right, covert yet in a sense symbolic of parental authority, no longer exists.

In various ways the political sphere controls more and more of what used to be private space. The family no longer bears exclusive responsibility for the child. The child's rights are determined not by the family but by the entire national community in the form of legal and social protections. The child therefore spends more time outside the private realm and is increasingly socialized outside the family. Parent-child relations are no longer a strictly private matter; they are governed by the public. The society as a whole is responsible for *all* its children.

This way of thinking is illustrated by the so-called parental education reform of 1980. All prospective parents were invited to participate in voluntary discussion and training groups during gestation and the first year after birth. (Those who attended these groups during working hours were entitled to compensation under the parents' insurance program.) The goal of parental training was to "help improve the situation of children and families in the society": "The community and its institutions should not themselves assume responsibility for children but should try instead to give parents the means to do the job." Interestingly, this parental training, usually administered outside the home to groups of parents, was also a way of encouraging group experience, a way of fostering solidarity among individuals faced with similar problems. Individuals were drawn into group activities, and most who began with a prenatal group continued with a postnatal one. The social reforms helped to reinforce the highly communal nature of Swedish society by emphasizing all the ways in which the individual or family cell is integrated into the larger group or society.

Because the Swedish child is considered to be a full citizen, he or she may, at an appropriate age, take legal action to alter unsatisfactory conditions. This principle applies in particular to disputes arising out of divorce. The child may be a party to hearings to determine custody and visiting rights and is entitled to legal representation. Small children may even be represented by a proxy appointed by the court. In case of separation the child may choose which of its parents it wishes to stay with, even contesting the amicable settlement reached by the parents (although visiting rights are not subject to challenge). In short, the child's opinion may be expressed and defended in exactly the same manner as that of any other citizen.

If family life is largely open to public scrutiny, so is the life of the couple. Since 1965 sexual offenses such as marital rape have been subject to criminal prosecution. Since 1981 battered women have not been required to appear in person to accuse their husband or partner; a declaration by a third party is sufficient to initiate proceedings. Of course homosexuality is no longer a crime in Sweden; criminal penalties were abolished as long ago as 1944. In 1970, following a period in which a wave of sexual liberation spread over the country, homosexuals founded the National Organization for Equality of Sexual Rights, or RFSL (Riksförbundet för Sexuellt Likaberättigande).

In 1980 the government conducted a sweeping investigation into the possibility of reforming legislation concerning homosexuals so as to prevent discrimination. The investigative commission not only proposed a series of laws guaranteeing complete equality between heterosexuals and homosexuals but also advocated active support for homosexual culture and organizations. The possibility of institutionalized cohabitation of homosexual couples conferring the same benefits as marriage was also discussed. These proposals stemmed from an official investigative commission.

Paradoxically, the proposal encountered vigorous opposition on the part of certain lesbian groups, which contended that the new laws would have the effect of forcing lesbians to accept the outmoded institution of the family, which deserved no additional support from the government. They insisted that the law concern itself not with couples, whether homosexual or heterosexual, but with individuals, regardless of their relationship. The upshot was that homosexual marriage is still legally impossible in Sweden.

Well before the sexual revolution of the 1960s sexuality had lost something of its totally private character owing to the introduction of sex-education classes in the schools. In 1933 the National Association for Sexual Information, or RFSU (Riksförbundet för Sexuellt Upplysning) was founded. The goal of this nonprofit organization was to "promote a society without prejudice, tolerant and open to the problems of sexuality and to the life of the couple." At the time the chief concern was not so much to liberalize sexuality as to combat venereal disease and abortion. Nevertheless, the effort to make sexual information widely available gradually broke down a series of taboos. In 1938 a new law on contraception and abortion struck down the ban that had existed since 1910 on distributing information about or selling contraceptives. The rules governing abortion were also modified. Abortion was authorized for three reasons: physical disability; pregnancy resulting from rape; and the possibility of serious congenital defects.

In 1942 optional sex education was made available in the schools, and in 1955 it became compulsory. Such instruction initially was quite conservative; students were told that the sole purpose of sexual relations was procreation in marriage. Soon, however, students as young as seven were studying sexuality, or what *Le Monde*[7] in a December 1973 headline called *"la vie à deux."*[8] It was stressed that "the act of love should be based on reciprocal affection and mutual respect." Nevertheless, matters as intimate as "masturbation, frigidity, homosexuality, contraception, venereal disease, and even pleasure" were discussed. By 1946 the law required pharmacies to stock contraceptives, and in 1959 the sale of contraceptives outside pharmacies was authorized.

At last sexuality was out in the open, in a quite literal sense. Finally, in 1964, advertising for contraceptives (sponsored by the RFSU) began to appear in newspapers and magazines. This advertising was meant to be informative, even technical, but frequently it adopted a playful and engaging tone, because its purpose was not only to inform but also to sell. Before long, advertising went far beyond condoms and diaphragms to include all sorts of sex-related products.

The demystification of sexuality, which initially grew out of a concern to stamp out disease, misery, and ignorance, in the 1960s came to be associated with debate about censorship. In 1951 the Swedish film *Hon dansade en sommar* (*She Only Danced One Summer*) caused a scandal because in it Folke Sundquist and Ulla Jacobsson, both stripped to the waist, are shown embracing. The film helped establish Sweden's reputation as a sexually liberated country. In 1963 the Bureau of Censorship passed Ingmar Bergman's *The Silence* despite numerous provocative scenes; but it prohibited screening of Vilgot Sjöman's *"491"* (1966) until a scene in which youths force a woman to have sexual relations with a dog had been cut. This act of censorship gave rise to an impassioned debate, until ultimately the uncut version of the film was allowed to be shown. Homosexual scenes began to appear on the screen in 1965.

Finally, in 1967, another Sjöman film, *I am Curious: Blue*, eliminated the last cinematic taboos. It gave rise to a polemic that resulted in its being banned for viewing by children, but the film was not cut. At this point several commissions were appointed to recommend changes in laws that were clearly outmoded. Documentaries on various sexual subjects were issued, including *The Language of Love*, which dealt with female sexual pleasure, and later, in 1971, *More on the Language of Love*, which, among other things, dealt with male homosexuality and the sexuality of the handicapped. That same year censorship of films was permanently abolished (except for scenes of excessive violence).

Pornography was to the sexual revolution of the 1960s and 1970s what sex education was to the 1940s and 1950s. Pornography is perhaps the most immediate manifestation of sexuality since, unlike eroticism, it places no mediator between the spectator and the object of desire. Nothing is suggested or even unveiled; everthing is exhibited. It is interesting to note

[7]*The World*, France's leading newspaper.
[8]"Life for two" or "conjugal existence."

that the Swedish literary tradition contains virtually no erotic novel, no *Justine* [9] or *Histoire d'O*,[10] no equivalent to the works of Bataille,[11] the Marquis de Sade, or even Diderot[12] in *Les Bijoux indiscrets*. Sweden's only frivolous, libertine literature dates from the eighteenth century when the country was considered the "France of the North." Otherwise Swedish literature, particularly in works dealing with sex, is not much given to understatement, suggestion, or indirection. It is either overtly pornographic or resolutely didactic.

The sexual revolution seemed to sweep away the last taboos. Once the right to sexual information was established, the right to sexual pleasure was next to be proclaimed. No one was to be left out—equality for all: from homosexuality to voyeurism and zoophilia, all sexual practices were equally legitimate. The very notion of a "crime against nature" disappeared from the law and was replaced by that of "sexual offense" (*sedlighets brotten*).

A reaction was not long coming, however. Indeed, when examined closely, the sexual revolution of the 1960s and 1970s turns out to have been partly illusory. Formal taboos were eliminated, but traditional patterns remained largely untouched. At least that is the view of Swedish feminists, who vigorously attacked the portrayal of male-female relations in pornographic literature. One anecdote is worth recounting. The magazine *Expedition 66*, intended to be a female equivalent of *Playboy*, first appeared in 1964. It ceased publication fairly quickly, partly for lack of readers but even more for lack of models. (In a gesture typical of Swedish honesty, the magazine's editor, Nina Estin, refused to use photographs from the files of homosexual magazines.) Subsequently almost all pornography was directed toward men.

An excellent illustration of the reaction against sexual liberation, and in particular of the role played by institutions in that reaction, can be found in prostitution. Rather paradoxically, it was in the early 1970s—at a time when sex ostensibly had ceased to constitute a transgression—that prostitution in Sweden increased sharply. At the peak of this phenomenon (1970–1972) more than a hundred "massage parlors" and "photographic studios" were operating in the Stockholm area alone. At the same time various voices were raised in favor of greater freedom and openness for prostitutes. . . .

In 1976 a commission was appointed to study the prostitution question, and a plan for retraining prostitutes was developed in 1980. The commission's report was extremely detailed and analyzed all aspects of the trade: prostitute, client, and procurer. It gave rise to a polemic between those who favored repression (most notably feminist groups) and those who feared

---

[9] Pornographic novel (1791) by the Marquis de Sade (1740–1814), author of many licentious works.

[10] Pornographic novel (1954) by Pauline Réage (pseudonym).

[11] Henri Bataille (1872–1922), French poet and author of psychological dramas.

[12] *The Indiscreet Jewels* (1748) was a pornographic story by Denis Diderot (1713–1784), a leading thinker of the French Enlightenment.

that treating prostitutes as criminals would not eliminate the problem but would, by forcing it underground, render control impossible. The commission demonstrated in particular that prostitution in Sweden was closely associated with illicit drugs. Those who championed prostitution in the 1960s have therefore been forced to ask themselves whether it was truly "liberating." Finally, the commission noted that prostitution served exclusively as a means of satisfying male sexual needs. Here too the sexual revolution had not truly "liberated" women.

In the wake of this report, a series of restrictive measures was adopted. Although the new laws did not punish the client (except in cases involving sexual relations with a minor), they did provide for the prosecution of any person owning property used for the purpose of prostitution. Combined with an effective program for retraining prostitutes, the new laws have led to a marked decline in prostitution since 1980.

Laws were also passed against sexual activities involving violence, a common subject in pornographic publications. Peep shows were outlawed in 1982. The commission found that most of the patrons were older men, especially foreign businessmen, and concluded that "this was one part of the Swedish cultural heritage not really worth preserving." And so a specialty for which the country was internationally renowned came to an end. In fact, the whole flood of pornography that poured from the presses in the 1960s and 1970s has been, if not stopped, then at least channeled. Debate once focused on sex has been refocused on violence in all its forms, including sexual violence.

For all the transparency of Swedish society, certain opaque areas remain. Some things are prohibited, and because their number is small they are all the more fiercely protected. Violence, though uniformly condemned and prosecuted everywhere, is still present. Alcoholism is probably the area in which consensus is most tenuous and social control most vigorously challenged. Certain places are jealously guarded and kept strictly private: some exist in geographical space—the home, the boat, the island—while others exist only in poetry or the imagination.

The passions are soft-pedaled in Sweden. If violence is not significantly more prevalent than in other countries, when it does occur it is much more shocking. Accordingly it is sternly proscribed, even in private, as in the ban on spanking. Sometimes the obsession with preventing violence can seem rather silly. Since 1979, for example, Sweden has prohibited the sale of war toys. In 1978 an exposition on the theme "Violence Breeds Violence" lumped together allegedly violent comic books, estimates of the number of children killed annually in automobile accidents, and statistics on drug use.

The goal is not just to prohibit violence but to prevent it. The government considers open, public violence as the culmination of violence born in private, including at home and on the playing field. At a deeper level, violence, whether internal or external, private or public, constitutes a threat to order and consensus. It remains one of the last areas of Swedish life outside public control.

Another area yet to brought under control is alcoholism. To consume alcohol in Sweden is not an innocuous act. Feelings of guilt weigh on those who drink—not just the inveterate drunkards but the average Swedes who line up furtively at the *Systembolaget* (state liquor store) and sneak away with a few bottles carefully hidden away among their other parcels. Regulations governing the sale of alcohol are very strict. Temperance is officially praised, drunkenness publicly condemned. People rarely drink in public, not only because prices are high but even more because the community quietly but firmly disapproves. Drinking is permissible—and even valued—only on specific occasions, at holidays such as Midsummer's Night or the mid-August crayfish festival; at such times one drinks in order to get drunk. According to the official morality, it is just as inappropriate to drink at home in private and for no "social" reason—that is, without a justifying ritual of communication—as it is to drink in public. A daily apéritif or glass of wine can become a reprehensible secret act, something that can produce feelings of guilt.

Swedish laws on alcohol are extremely harsh. There are heavy penalties for drunk driving, which is defined as operating a motor vehicle with a blood level of more than 0.5 grams of alcohol. Alcohol cannot be purchased by anyone under the age of twenty-one, even though the age of legal majority is eighteen. This severity is hard to understand in terms of statistics alone. Alcohol consumption in Sweden in 1979 amounted to 7.1 liters per person, compared with 17 liters for France. Sweden ranks roughly twenty-fifth in the world in per-capita alcohol consumption.

The severity of the law can be understood only in terms of history. The manufacture and sale of alcoholic beverages were regulated long before the turn of the century, but it was around then that the temperance movement, having gained a powerful position in the Swedish Parliament, won adoption of a law unparalleled elsewhere in the world—the so-called Bratt System, under which anyone who wished to purchase alcohol had to present a ration book. Even today, no issue unleashes passions as strong as those connected with the alcohol problem, largely owing to members of temperance societies, whose influence in Parliament is out of proportion with their numbers in the population. Not so very long ago one deputy in three belonged to a temperance organization, and anti-alcohol societies have traditionally been a fertile breeding ground for politicians.

Nevertheless, alcohol seems to be one area in which breakdown of consensus is possible. Swedish unanimity in opposition to alcohol is more apparant than real, for in private Swedes readily violate the ban and boast, like people everywhere, of their ability to "hold their liquor."

There is a much more solid consensus in opposition to drugs. Since 1968 laws against narcotics abuse have become stricter. Serious infractions of the narcotics laws incur one of the stiffest penalties in Swedish law: ten years in prison. Furthermore, the law does not distinguish between "soft drugs" and "hard drugs." Compared with alcoholism, however, drug abuse is quantitatively a minor problem.

Violence, alcoholism, drugs: these are the principal forms of deviant behavior in Swedish society, the last areas not entirely controlled by the political sphere, the last transgressions in a society liberated from the taboos of the past.

In such a highly communitarian society, so tightly controlled by the "public," where can the individual find a private refuge? In his home, his rustic frame *sommarstuga*[13] lost in the forest or tucked away on some lake shore. The individual home is like an island, private space par excellence, cut off and personalized. In "Scandinavian Notes" Emmanuel Mounier remarked that "the most collectivist nations—Russia, Germany, Sweden—are those in which housing is most solitary."

The dream of every Swede is essentially an individualistic one, expressed through the appreciation of primitive solitude, of the vast reaches of unspoiled nature. Often built without running water and with the most rudimentary facilities, the *stuga* enables its owner to return to his rural roots and to commune intimately with nature. Virtually no Swede will travel abroad during that beautiful time in May and June when nature, at last emerged from the interminable sleep of winter, bursts forth with a dazzling and liberating light and Sweden once again becomes the land of 24,000 islands and 96,000 lakes! The small cabin lost in the country or forest thus remains, along with the island, the archipelago, and the sailboat (of which there are more than 70,000 in the Stockholm area alone), the last refuge of individualism in a highly communitarian society.

The themes of isolation, nature, and archipelago are omnipresent in Swedish literature and film. The novel entitled *The People of Hemsö* figures as a moment of illumination in Strindberg's otherwise somber oeuvre. The beautiful film *Summer Paradise* starring Gunnel Lindblom takes place entirely in the enchanting setting of a wonderful lakeside house. Though a genuine refuge, this private space can in certain situations become a tragic trap in which individuals seek desperately to recover some lost primitive state of communication, some original purity.

...Crimes of passion are rare in Sweden (when one does occur, it is headline news). People almost never raise their voices and rarely gesticulate; usually they keep silent. Curiously in this society, where all sorts of things are said out loud and with unaccustomed frankness, people have difficulty conversing. Although workplace relations are simple, direct, and devoid of hierarchy and everyone addresses everyone else familiarly, dinner invitations are stiffly formal and prissy, something that constantly surprises foreign visitors. It does not make conversation any easier. In Swedes, Mounier

---

[13]House in the woods.

saw "the diffuse mysticism and poetry of lonely men: the Swedish people remains, in a sense, incapable of expression." This truly private side of a self that manifests itself not so much in action as in imagination is a good starting point for exploring Swedish society and attempting to grasp its paradoxes and contradictions. How else can we understand the coexistence of such highly communitarian and public feeling with such intensely inward individualism? The solitude of that world of silence, the Great North, the intimate communion with nature—therein lies the source of Scandinavian individualism. Primitive solitude compensates for community in all its forms—organization, group study, celebration. Everything, from holidays to laws, is directed toward breaking down solitude, allowing each person a say, maintaining the traditional community intact as a necessary condition of physical survival in the harsh world of the past and of moral survival in the harsh world of the present. What else could account for the incredible popularity of the ancient pagan festivals, generally associated with rural life but now transformed into Christian holidays? Walpurgis Night celebrates spring, Saint Lucy's Night the winter solstice, Saint John's Night the middle of summer (*Midsommar*), to name only a few of the holidays that dot an unchanging calendar. For one night everyone forgets hierarchy, social class, differences, and enmities and, in togetherness and unanimity, recreates the perfectly egalitarian, perfectly consensual utopian community. During one unbridled *Midsommar* Miss Julie in Strindberg's[14] play talks, drinks, sleeps, and plans a future with her father's valet. Then morning comes and restores social difference, the impossibility of communication, and rebellion. A night's folly ends in death. How can one possibly understand the Swedish imagination if one sees this as nothing more than an insipid story of impossible love between a countess and a valet?

The Swedish model can be interpreted as a "total" or "totalizing" society. It depends on a perfectly consensual communitarian ethic, which in turn depends on absolute insistence on transparency in social relations (from the old ritual know as *nattfrieri* to the child's right to know the identity of his father today). Private life cannot escape the influence of the dominant ethos. The Swedish model combines yesterday's communitarian morality with the modern social-democratic ethos.

In the 1930s Marquis Childs[15] referred to "Sweden, the middle way," thus characterizing the country in a manner that would influence first his fellow Americans and, later, others. Sweden's material prosperity, which as early as 1928 included "a telephone in every hotel room, a plentiful supply of electricity, model hospitals, [and] broad, clean streets," along with an almost flawless social organization, lent credence in the 1930s to the notion of a Swedish model. European countries suddenly took a lively interest in the country, hoping to unearth the secret of its astonishing material success.

---

[14] August Strindberg (1849–1912), Swedish novelist, poet, and playwright.
[15] American newspaperman (1903–1990) and author of *Sweden: The Middle Way*.

Spared the ravages of the Second World War, Sweden maintained its productive apparatus intact. To much of postwar Europe it seemed utopia incarnate, and Swedes became "the Americans of Europe." In many respects Sweden was seen as a more attractive model of social organization than the United States because inequality in Sweden was less pronounced. As Queffélec[16] pointed out in 1948, the Swedes "question all this natural prosperity." Also, the country's "moral health" enabled it to "avoid the dreadful consequences of Americanization." Mounier delightedly recounted the comment of one Swedish observer who was quite appreciative of American civilization: "The Swede, however, is actually much more attached to the individual than is the American."

In the 1940s and 1950s some in the West saw the typical Swedish woman as one who was "beautiful, athletic, and healthy." While "the legendary freedom of Scandinavian morals" was taken for granted, "to the traveler these young people seem distant and not very emotional. Couples dance quite properly" (*Action*, September 1946). Louis-Charles Royer wrote in *Lumières du Nord* (*Northern Lights*, 1939): "It is extremely difficult to court women in this country, because they always treat you as a pal." In 1954 François-Régis Bastide in his book *Suède* (Sweden) asked: "What should you say to a young Swedish woman?" His answer: "Whatever you do, it is extremely dangerous to mention the well-known reputation that Swedish women have... That is certain to chill things off."

The Swedish woman's reputation was no doubt associated with the campaign to provide sexual information, which since 1933 had done so much to break down sexual taboos. Sweden had provided sex education in the schools since 1942, at a time no other country had gone to such lengths. The West had confused sexual information with sexual freedom, creating an image of Sweden as sexual paradise.

In 1964 French Prime Minister Georges Pompidou visited "this strange socialist monarchy" and in a famous phrase characterized his social and political ideal as "Sweden with a bit more sun." Thus attention was once again focused on the Swedish ideal, which would attain the peak of its glory in the 1970s. During this period Sweden was in vogue; whenever it was mentioned, it was held up as an example.

Everywhere Sweden was exalted and glorified. Some had dreamed the American dream; others had idealized the Soviet Union or China or Cuba. Now the "Swedish model," the image of a just compromise, seduced Europe. Sweden became a journalistic cliché. The sexual revolution of the 1960s reinforced the myth. A cover story on "Free Love" appeared in 1965, and one French magazine devoted a special issue to Sweden.... Sweden was the wave of the future: the press said it, television showed it, books explained it. The "Swedish case" was analyzed and dissected. People also began to ask questions.

---

[16] Henri Queffélec, French novelist, essayist, and poet (b. 1910).

By 1975 articles criticizing Sweden had begun to appear. Headlines such as "Women Not Totally Free" and "The Disintegrating Family" were read. Roland Huntford launched a vigorous attack on social-democratic Sweden in his book *The New Totalitarians* (1972). The defeat of the social democrats in 1976, after more than forty-four years in power, raised questions about the political stability of Sweden. . . . Sweden was portrayed in France as a perverse model, a highly coercive society. This "prodigiously permissive" society was said to have engendered its own destruction. "Sweden: Liberated Lovers in Search of Love," was trumpeted in 1980. That same year one could read: "The Swedish mirror, much admired abroad, is broken. Something is amiss in the world's most unusual system." One headline asked, "Sweden—paradise lost?"

The Swedish model had not lived up to its promise. Racism, xenophobia, suicide, and alcoholism all existed there too. The countermodel was now at its height, even if traces of the old paradise remained. In 1984 *Le Point*[17] asked students at France's leading institutions of higher education what country best corresponded to their idea of the good society. Switzerland led the list, followed by the United States; Sweden came in fifth, behind France.

If the Swedish model had lost its appeal, it was because the country had slipped badly. Claude Sarraute[18] wrote of "incessant investigations by the tax and welfare authorities, unreasonable, Orwellian interventions in people's lives. The government keeps tabs on incomes and individuals. The meddlesome welfare state sticks its nose everywhere, even into the way you bring up your children. It encourages children to turn in 'deviant' parents." Much of the West decided it wanted no part of this "revolution in private life." Though the Swedish model may still exist, the Swedish myth is dead as a doornail.

---

[17]The French weekly newsmagazine, *The Point.*
[18]Journalist at *Le Monde* and author of numerous books (b. 1927).

Deciphering Middle Eastern Women's History

NIKKI R. KEDDIE

In this analysis of the condition of women in the Middle East, Nikki R. Keddie underscores the variety of influences that have prevailed from the ancient world to the present. The history of women in the Middle East is complicated, for women's lives varied according to time, culture, geographical location (urban-rural, for example), social class, or under the influence of new forces, such as Islam, secularism, capitalism, and the West.

When did veiling and seclusion develop in the Middle East? Which women were affected? Why did (do) many women wish to be veiled? Why have men wanted to veil and seclude women?

In what ways has Islam affected women historically and in the Middle East today? Does Islamic scripture argue for equal treatment of women? What influence has the life of the prophet Muhammad had on the treatment of women? What features of Islamic customs regarding women actually predate Islam? How has Islamic law been interpreted to justify both equal and oppressive treatment of women? There are many variables at work, of course, but do you think that Islamic marriage and family life have treated women better than Christianity has?

The nineteenth and twentieth centuries have brought momentous changes to the Middle East through Westernization and the rise of nationalism. Recently, there have occurred reactions against Western influences. Why and where? What developments have strengthened these reactions? How has the fate of women been involved in the new opposition to Westernization? Which women tend to oppose both Westernization and modernization? How have gender relations, the veil, and women fallen victim to the Islamist response to Westernization?

Keddie astutely points out that we cannot measure women's lives simply by looking at laws and customs. Rather, women in the Middle East have carved out for themselves spheres of activities and power that are often hidden from outsiders. In what ways have women in the contemporary Middle East managed to circumvent law, religion, and patriarchal custom in order to wield power in society and, even, over men?

The position of women in the Middle East has aroused much interest, but serious scholarly work on Middle Eastern women's history has been limited, in comparison both with the study of women's history elsewhere and with the study of contemporary problems. Existing volumes of articles about women in the Middle East contain little that is historical....

The relative neglect of women's history has occurred mainly because historians, unlike social scientists, cannot construct their own research projects based on people who can be directly observed, interviewed, or given questionnaires. Most historical work relies chiefly on written sources, which are heavily male oriented, and a great mass of documents needs to be unearthed or restudied with women's questions in mind.

Discussions of Middle Eastern women's history are also often ideologically charged. Such discussions may be wrenching ones for scholars who wish to overcome widespread prejudices against Islam, but not ignore the problems of Muslim women. One group denies that Muslim women, who comprise the great majority of women in the Middle East, are any more oppressed than non-Muslim women or argues that in key respects they have been less oppressed. A second says that oppression is real but extrinsic to Islam; The Quran,[1] they say, intended gender equality, but this was undermined by Arabian patriarchy and foreign importations. An opposing group blames Islam for being irrevocably gender inegalitarian. There are also those who adopt intermediate positions, as well as those who tend to avoid these controversies by sticking to monographic or limited studies that do not confront such issues. Some scholars favor shifting emphases away from Islam to economic and social forces.

... Differences between Muslims and non-Muslims concerning gender status are usually attributed mainly to the Quran, to early Muslim tradition and holy law. There are also other, including pre-Islamic, roots of difference. Differences between the Middle East and other cultures regarding gender relations were in most ways smaller in the past than in modern times. Muslim resistance to Western-sanctioned change is tied to a centuries-old hostility between the Muslim Middle East and the West, which has increased in modern times. The home has become a last line of defense against a West that has won out in political and economic spheres. So-called fundamentalists, or Islamists, see Western practices toward and views on women as part of a Western Christian and Jewish cultural offensive, accompanying political and economic offensives, and turn to their own traditions as a cultural alternative.

The origin of gender inequalities in the ancient Near East is disputed but it is known that hunter-gatherers and other pre-plow peoples are more egalitarian between genders than are people who have experienced the neolithic and agricultural revolutions. Technological developments that made possible a surplus, states, and ruling classes were accompanied by a greater division of labor, including class hierarchies and slavery, and encouraged the limiting of many urban women to domestic occupations. Class differences developed among women as well as among men, with some being slaves who filled menial or sexual roles, others who performed both nondomestic and domestic labor, and upper-class women who did not have to venture outside the home. Veiling and seclusion developed in the pre-Islamic Near East and adjacent areas as markers for urban upper- and middle-class women, showing that they did not have to work and keeping them from strangers.

As women in ancient societies became more subordinate, often treated as property, many peoples developed myths about them as the source of evil and sexual temptation—dangerous and needing control. Once inheritance in the male line became important, female virginity and fidelity became central concerns. Males in most cultures were not required to be faithful, and male polygamy was often legal. Muslims note that female polygamy would raise doubts about fatherhood, which is unthinkable. Women had to be controlled largely to minimize their chances of contacts with outside men.

The guarding of women has been strong in Near Eastern and Mediterranean societies from ancient times. As many "Islamic" customs go back

---

[1]Or Koran, Islamic scripture believed to have been revealed to the Prophet Muhammad. The Quran is one of the two natural sources of Islamic law.

to the pre-Islamic Near East, something should be said about that before discussing Islam. In the first known reference to veiling, an Assyrian legal text of the thirteenth century B.C., it is restricted to respectable women and prohibited for prostitutes. From the first, veiling was a sign of status. Respectable Athenian women were often secluded, and veiling was known in the Greco-Roman world. Veiling and seclusion existed in pre-Islamic Iran and the Byzantine Empire, the two areas conquered by the first Muslims, though we do not know how widespread they were.

A husband who had the means to keep his wife veiled and secluded showed that she was protected from advances and did not have to work or shop outside. Full veiling has been both a class phenomenon and an urban one. Early Muslims adopted veiling from conquered peoples, and both non-Muslims in Muslim societies and Mediterranean women in Christian societies were subject to many of the same forms of control and isolation from men. Mediterranean societies, Muslim and Christian, also had the same idea of the centrality of a man's honor, which lay chiefly in the purity of the women of his natal family.

...Mediterranean peoples favor endogamy, which increases the tendency to control women in tightly interrelated lineages....[A]ncient Egyptians and Persians favored "incestuous" unions, whereas most Mediterranean peoples favor cousin marriage....[O]ne could say that tribal groups, who are numerous among the Muslims of the Middle East, have special reasons to want to control women and to favor cousin marriage, and that the interaction of tribes with urban groups practicing seclusion added segregation to control.

The term *tribe* has been so misused that many, especially Africanists, avoid it. Whereas those who study Africa may justly react to a word misused to characterize groups with millions of people, there is a role for the word *tribe* in the Middle East. It translates terms in the main Middle Eastern languages that refer to contiguous groups claiming descent from one ancestor. A tribe is a political-economic unit, and its leaders, generally chosen from one lineage, command more loyalty than the central government, though they may now have little real power. In recent times tribes tend to be strong when central governments are weak, and central governments usually try to weaken tribes.

Tribes are not a primitive form of social organization. Pastoral nomadic tribes, the most common in the Middle East, can evolve only after animals are domesticated and there is a settled population with whom to trade animal products for agricultural and urban ones. Cohesion requires group decisions, which are facilitated in groups tied by kin. This favors cousin marriage, as does the Islamic provision for female inheritance, which encourages strategies to keep property in the lineage....Muslim Arabs increased cousin marriage after the Quran required female inheritance. When women inherit according to Muslim law, there are clear advantages in cousin marriage. Certain familial controls may be tied to the prevalence of tribal structures. In other areas, however, many tribes have strong and quite liberated women, and veiling and seclusion are more urban than tribal phenomena. The interaction between tribal and urban controls on women was an important influence on Middle Eastern gender relations.

The Quran was written in a context of different levels of sexual inequality among Arab tribes and in adjacent non-Arab empires. How it affected the position of women is controversial. The classic Muslim view is that pre-Islamic Arabs lived in ignorance and barbarism and that the divinely revealed Quran provided a great step forward on all questions. Some scholars, however, have documented (especially in Arab poetry) conditions of matriliny, greater activity for women, even on the battlefield, and freer divorce. Such sources do indicate some matrilineal and matrilocal customs, as well as freer divorce for women in certain tribes, and a greater outspokenness and activity for many women than became common after the rise of Islam, but we do not know how widespread these patterns were.

The Quran did bring in some reforms, however, including the outlawing of infanticide and the payment of the male dower to the bride, not to her guardian. The Quran also prescribed female inheritance—half that of a male heir—and women's control over their property (which was known earlier, however, as seen in Muhammad's[2] first wife, the merchant Khadija). Unfavorable features were free divorce for men but not for women and polygamy for men (which already existed).

Although Islamic traditions say veiling and seclusion for all Muslim women are in the Quran, this is a tendentious reading. One verse tells women to veil their bosoms and hide their ornaments, later taken to mean all except the hands, feet, and perhaps the face. This interpretation makes no sense, because if everything was to be veiled, there would be no point in ordering bosoms to be veiled separately. Another verse tells women to draw their cloaks tightly around them so they may be recognized and not annoyed. These are the only words generally taken to refer to veiling.

Other verses suggest seclusion for Muhammad's wives, and these stricter rules for an elite later spread, encouraged by the example of the conquered Near East, to the urban middle and upper classes. Later veiling was not, however, simply in emulation of the Prophet's wives.... Muhammad's veiling of his wives reflected the growing prosperity of the Muslim ruling group, enabling them to have servants and to keep women from nondomestic work, and also the Muslims' growing contact with surrounding societies where women were veiled. As Muslim society became state centered and class divided like those of the surrounding and conquered peoples, many of their practices concerning women, appropriate to stratified social structures, and their reliance on family regulation to maintain social control were naturally also found appropriate by the Muslims.

The Quran gives men control of their wives, which extends to beatings for disobedience, and adulterers of both sexes are to be punished by lashing

[2]Founder of Islam, A.D. 570?–632.

when there is either confession or four eyewitnesses to the act. Islamic law and tradition changed this to the far more severe punishment of stoning to death, but in practice women were often killed by their brothers and many escaped punishment.

Islamic practices about women are often said to be resistant to change because of their Quranic sanction, believed to be the word of God. This has some truth, but there has been much breaking and bending of Quranic admonitions throughout Muslim history. The Quran has been interpreted, against the meaning of its text, as enjoining veiling, whereas Quranic rules on adultery are rarely followed. Quranic inheritance rules were hard to follow in rural and nomadic societies, as daughters married out of the family, with only a minority marrying paternal first cousins. Land or flocks inherited by an out-marrying woman reduced the property of the patrilineal line. Hence means were found, in most rural and a minority of urban areas, to evade women's inheritance rights. Also, the general inheritance rules of the Quran were interpreted in a more patriarchal way by Islamic law.

In all these cases, later practice was more patriarchal than the Quranic text warrants. In general, the Quran was followed when it was not too inconvenient to men or to the patriarchal family to do so, and not followed when it was. This gives some basis to modern feminists and reformers who want to return to, and reinterpret, the Quran, although their interpretation sometimes moves as far in a new direction as the old one did in the opposite one. Islamic law and Traditions tended to stress and rigidify gender distinctions, seen as crucial to an ordered world, and went to great lengths to avoid gender ambiguities....

Urban middle- and upper-class women, traditionally the most veiled and secluded, were also much more likely to inherit Quranically. This is a paradox only to a Westerner who reads back our concepts of women's rights into the past and thinks that "disadvantaged" veiled women should have fewer rights in other spheres. Urban residence in fact both made women's inheritance easier, by not involving flocks and fields, and encouraged veiling, because contact with unrelated strangers was more likely; also there were more middle- and upper-class women with more servants and slaves. Differences in class, place, and time meant that there was never one set of Muslim women operating under one set of rules.

A variety of historical and anthropological works contribute to the following overall picture of different female statuses: in general, rural and tribal women do not inherit as the Quran and Muslim law says they should, though "in return" they generally get permanent protection from their natal family, and in some cases their sons may get all or part of their share. Court records past and present suggest that urban women, however, usually do inherit and are willing and able to go to Islamic courts to protect their property rights, generally successfully. Sources also suggest that urban women have had more rights than agriculturalists, although the great freedoms and powers of tribal nomadic women are also noted. These differences are accentuated by a class-difference pattern, with ruling class and upper-class women in both tribes and towns often notable for their powers and independence whereas poorer women were more dependent. Hence modern differences in styles of living between town, tribe, and countryside and between classes in town originate in earlier times and in continuing functional differences.

This does not mean that the prescriptions of the Quran and Muslim law counted for little. The rules on polygamy, divorce, and child custody (to the father's family after a young age) were widely followed. If polygamy and divorce were less general than Westerners might imagine, they remained a threat to a wife. Divorce was generally common, but polygamy seems to have been a rare, mainly upper-class, custom.

The condition of most women seems to have been broadly comparable to that in the ancient Near East and the later Mediterranean and eastern and southern Asia.... Most women were valued mainly as producers of sons and were brought up to marry, produce children, and safeguard the family honor by not transgressing rules of sexual conduct and segregation. Most were married young in arranged marriages in which the husband's family had to pay a dower. This often included a delayed payment in case of divorce or death, which provided some protection for the wife when it was observed. Brides frequently lived in the husband's father's household, often with a menial position until the first son might be born. Young brides were often dominated by mothers-in-law more than by husbands, and they gained status mainly through their maturing sons. By the time the sons became adults their mother might be very powerful in the household, ready to dominate her sons' wives in turn.

This brief outline cannot suggest the variety and satisfactions that went along with the difficulties of women's lives. In the long preindustrial period when nuclear and extended families were the main productive units— in agriculture, herding, crafts, or trade—the organization of society around families and the superior power of dominant males and of male and female elders probably seemed natural to most people all over the world. It was only modern changes in economy, politics, and society that made these structures less functional and called them into question. Even before they were widely questioned, structures of male domination caused much suffering, however.

Dramatic differences between Muslims and non-Muslims came with nineteenth- and twentieth-century Muslim resistance to change, and with contemporary Islamic revivalism. Regarding gender relations, Islamism has no strict parallel in other civilizations, even though some practices in India and elsewhere indicate that the Muslim world is not the area of the worst atrocities toward women.

Whereas some scholars think the limitation of women's roles after the rise of Islam was due to borrowing from non-Muslims, others stress that this restriction began in Muhammad's time. The strongest women appeared at the beginning of Islam. Khadija, the merchant, who employed and married

Muhammad, fifteen years her junior, was his first convert and helped him in every way. Muhammad's young wife 'A'isha, whom he married when she was a child and whose heedlessness of opinion sometimes caused trouble, exercised much power. After Muhammad's death she joined the coalition against Muhammad's son-in-law 'Ali and participated in the crucial battle against him.

If these figures were unparalleled in later generations, neither internal nor external forces were exclusively responsible. As Islamic society became more like the societies around it in stratification and patriarchy, it was natural to adopt their ways. Families wealthy enough to have slaves or servants could afford seclusion. Women often acquiesced in veiling and seclusion when to be less covered and to work outside were marks of low status.

Muslim women's lives have varied greatly by class, mode of production, time, and place. What generalizations one can make in a brief essay are partly based on Islamic laws and practices, even though their observation varied. Islamic law developed in the first few centuries of Islam, and recent scholarship has shown how much it reflected regional Middle Eastern customs—hence that much of it was in fact followed more in the Middle East than elsewhere, though far from all, is not surprising. There were four orthodox law schools, plus Shi'i[3] schools, which differed on some points important to women. Regarding marriage, schools differed as to whether a virgin's consent was needed, or only that of her father or guardian. In all schools marriage is a contract, not a sacrament, and the man must provide materially for the wife and perform sexually. The wife must have sex whenever the husband wishes, but she has no material obligations. A man may divorce a wife by a thrice-pronounced declaration, whereas women can divorce only for specified causes, agreed to by a judge in court. Polygyny up to four wives was permitted, although the Quran says only if all are treated equally, which came to mean a norm of equal space and rotated sexual relations and overnight stays. Men were permitted concubines and female slaves, and their children's status was regulated. Another Shi'i practice goes back to pre-Islamic Arabia and seems to have been condoned by the Prophet, though it was outlawed for Sunnis[4] by the caliph 'Umar.[5] This is temporary marriage—a contract entered into for a definite period. As in all marriages there is a payment to the woman and children are legitimate. It flourishes especially in pilgrimage centers where men may come alone. It is wrong to consider it prostitution, and it has uses besides satisfying men's sexual desires. Women are supposed to obey their husbands, and the Quran authorizes beating if they do not. This is one of several verses that has been reinterpreted by modernists.

---

[3]Or Shiite, the smaller of the two branches of Islam. The division in Islam originated in a political dispute over who would be Muhammad's successor.

[4]Members of the larger branch of Islam.

[5]The father-in-law of Muhammad, caliph from 634–644.

Women could hold and manage any amount of property, although seclusion often made effective management difficult. Regarding the two-thirds or more inheritance that followed fixed rules, women were supposed to receive half the share of men. In Shi'i law daughters without brothers inherited everything, whereas in Sunni law they generally got no more than half. In spite of the presumption of female inheritance by all schools, it was common for women not to inherit, especially land. This kept land from passing outside the paternal family. Partial compensation in the form of gifts or sustenance in case of divorce or widowhood was sometimes given to a woman who renounced inheritance. In addition, the institution of *waqf*, inalienable endowment, was sometimes used to endow descendants in the male line, thus avoiding both property division and female inheritance. Some waqfs, however, benefited women particularly, both as recipients and as guardians....

Regarding the most effective form of birth control then known, coitus interruptus, most jurists and theologians allowed it, but some said it was licit only if the wife agreed, as she might want children or object to limiting her pleasure. Some say the authorization of birth control came mainly because powerful men had slaves and concubines by whom they might not want children....

As in many societies, particularly Mediterranean ones, the code of honor and shame has been central. A family's honor was seen as resting mainly on the purity of its girls and women, and shame lay in any aspersions cast on this. Purity meant not only virginity for girls and fidelity for wives, but also the impossibility that anyone should think or say these were in doubt. Neither girl nor wife should talk to an outside man. The ideal of segregation from gossip-provoking situations encouraged veiling and seclusion. Some wealthy families kept women from going out of the house except fully covered to see close relatives. In less wealthy families women might have to have some business interaction with men, but they were supposed to keep talk to a minimum and their eyes down. It seems that outdoor dress for the upper classes usually included a facial veil and loose covering for the body. Working, rural, and tribal women usually had no facial veil. Most women passed the greater part of their lives in homes, where they could wear and show off their more important clothing and ornaments. Fashion was important, and current reporters who are surprised that Arabian and Iranian women may wear jeans or miniskirts below their veils are really reporting nothing new, as Muslim women at home have long followed fashions, often ones from far away.

Honor and shame encouraged early marriage, as leaving a girl unmarried after puberty was seen as creating a situation in which she might be violated or impregnated. Mothers often played a greater role than fathers in finding a groom, and matchmakers were sometimes used. Paternal cousin marriage, which kept property in the patrilineal line, was favored. Despite this, only a minority of marriages were to paternal first cousins; even when this is claimed, investigation often shows a more distant relationship. This may have limited bad genetic effects from such marriages, although today many educated Muslims oppose cousin marriage for genetic reasons.

As in much of traditional Mediterranean Europe, that a girl and a man alone can be doing only one thing is widely assumed, and the girl is often punished. Traditional ideology assumes that a woman who behaves immodestly arouses uncontrollable urges in men. She is a cause of *fitna*, serious trouble, a word that also means revolt or civil war. Fathers, husbands, and brothers are given formal control over women and the family, as in many traditional societies, but observers often note the real power of women in the home and family.

In spite of formal and legal male dominance, Middle Eastern women followed a number of strategies to increase their sphere of power and freedom. Although men might control the quantity of sex, women had much control over its quality and the amount of pleasure the man had. Women controlled cooking, which many men found important, and they could keep the home neat or messy, noisy or tranquil, attractive or unattractive for the husband's visitors. Throughout Islamic history many rulers were ruled by their wives or mothers, and the same thing happened in many private homes. More equal husband-wife relations were also known. Women taught one another how to overcome formal inequalities, and the theoretical rules of Islamic law and the honor code were often not enforced.

Too little research has been done to provide a true history of how women fared over time in the Middle East. Here we can essay a few generalizations. There seem to be four periods that saw the greatest freedom of action for a significant number of Middle Eastern women: the earliest period of Islam; its first two centuries; the periods of nomadic and steppe-based rule (those of the Seljuks,[6] Mongols,[7] Mamluks,[8] early Safavids[9]); and the period of modern reform. In the first of these, the activities of Khadija and 'A'isha have been mentioned, and there were also many lesser powerful women, not to mention women who participated as aides in battle, or even fought (as they had in pre-Islamic times). The next period was more mixed . . . , but women continued to be more important and powerful as queens, traditionists, and in mystical and sectarian religious movements. At the same time, however, slavery and class divisions were spreading. The invasions of Turkic and other military groups and nomads from the eleventh century on, and their rule over much of the Middle East, brought in, at least for the ruling classes

---

[6]Turkic people who converted to Islam and conquered Iran, Syria, and much of present-day Turkey in the eleventh century.

[7]Central Asian people who created an enormous empire in the thirteenth century stretching form China to Russia.

[8]Or Mamelukes, people of slave origin who ruled Egypt from 1250 to 1517. The Mamluks continued to exercise much power in Egypt to the early nineteenth century.

[9]Rulers of Persia from 1501 to 1722.

and the nomads, more egalitarian treatment of women. Powerful women participated in rule in the Seljuk, Mongol, and Mamluk empires, where restrictions on women appear to have been lessened. . . .

Through the centuries nonorthodox religious spheres have provided a forum for female power. Shi'ism has women mullas,[10] and Sufi (mystic) orders include powerful and creative women leaders, and all had many women followers. . . .

Since the nineteenth century there have been modern, mainly legal and economic, reforms in the position of women, and the growth of reformist and feminist ideas. Although, as elsewhere, changes have been contradictory in their impact, the general trend thus far has been toward greater legal equality between the sexes and greater real equality among the urban Westernized middle and upper classes, although some in other classes have suffered.

Women's position, past and present, tended to become limited in times of economic contraction. At the very top, however, the role of women was determined most by court conditions. Where royal heirs were brought up within palace walls they might be subject to the influence of women or eunuchs. One example is the Ottoman Empire, where from the late sixteenth century potential heirs to the throne were kept from threatening the ruler by being immured in the harem. This greatly increased women's and eunuchs' influence on them, even after they came to rule. The negative phrase "harem rule" will probably have its revisionist historians, though it is probably true that sultans with experience of the outside world ruled better than those without. The influence of Ottoman queens and queen mothers, as with their lesser-known counterparts in Mamluk, Mongol, and Seljuk times, not to mention Safavid and Qajar Iran,[11] shows how possible it was for women to exercise great power, given the right circumstances.

The common Western view of the harem has little relation to reality. The Arabic word *harim* does not have sexy connotations, but means the part of the house forbidden to men who are not close relatives. For the non-elite it mostly was not polygamous and had no slaves or concubines. The harem was where the indoor work of the family was planned and carried on, usually under the supervision of the wife of the eldest male. In polygamous households and those with servants and slaves, the activities of the harem were more complex, but it was not the den of idleness and voluptuousness depicted from their imaginations by Western painters. (Westerners who saw photographs of harems were disappointed to find the clothing and furniture to be in keeping with Victorian propriety, bearing no resemblance to the paintings of Delacroix.[12]) The main work of household production, including its textiles and other crafts, and of reproduction, was done in the harem.

---

[10] A judge or someone trained in Islamic sacred law.

[11] The Qajar dynasty ruled from 1796 to 1925.

[12] Eugène Delacroix (1798–1865), French romantic painter who often depicted the exotic.

Partly owing to difficulties of documentation, little study has been done of pre-modern working women, rural or urban, or of slaves. Slavery in Islam was rarely characterized by heavy gang labor, but was overwhelmingly either household or male military slavery. Muslims could not be enslaved, and so slaves were either war captives or purchased from among non-Muslims. Slaves were often sexually subject to their masters. Unlike those in the medieval West, their children were free. Some slaves rose very high—slaves could be queens—and many were freed by their masters. Although slavery was less onerous than, say, in the New World, it still entailed a lack of freedom and a sexual subjugation that were more severe than those experienced by free women. Slaves were often trained to be singers and dancers—professions that were not quite respectable in the Islamic world or in many other traditional areas.

Although it was suggested above that many tribes are highly concerned about the purity of lineage, in most other respects treatment of women among tribal peoples tends to be more egalitarian than among urbanites. It may be something about the long-term confluence of nomadic and urban cultures that helps explain Middle Eastern patterns of gender relations and controls. The greater gender egalitarianism of tribal peoples shows up among pre-Islamic and early Islamic Arab women, and among the Seljuks and Mongols in Iran, with their powerful women in government. Early European accounts and indigenous painting suggest that tribal women did not veil. The Safavids in Iran (1501–1722), who made Shi'ism Iran's state religion, came in supported by the military backing of Turkic nomadic tribes, and early Safavid miniatures are full of unveiled women. Italian travelers to Iran in those years wrote that women were shockingly exposed! By late Safavid times, the influence of the religious classes had grown, and women were increasingly veiled and secluded.

In recent decades, as veiling and seclusion were rejected by many modernists and feminists, and as local nationalisms grew, those who opposed veiling ascribed it to a different nationality from their own. Many Arabs say veiling was imposed on them by the Ottoman Turks. In fact, Turks began to veil only when they became assimilated in Islam, and if many Ottomans in Arab lands veiled this was mainly because ruling classes veiled, not because Turks in particular did. There is abundant evidence that widespread Arab veiling preceded the Ottomans, although it appears that pre-Ottoman Mamluk Egypt was freer in this respect than Ottoman Egypt. Iranian modernists often blame veiling on Arabs, and Turks on Arabs or Persians. As noted, veiling and seclusion are ancient Near Eastern customs, long adopted by all major language groups in the Middle East.

Some writers, reacting to Western hostility to veiling, deny its significance. Although veiling and seclusion do not prevent women from living varied and significant lives, they are parts of a system where males are dominant and females are to be controlled. The system affects even non-secluded women, who are expected to be modest and circumspect and are subject to sanctions if they transgress the rules. It is true that the overall system is more important than veiling as such.

The degree to which women follow the rules should not be exaggerated, however. Outside observers may see only heavily veiled shapes and assume that these women's lives are completely controlled by their menfolk. When seen from the inside, however, the same woman may give quite a different impression. Thus two eighteenth-century Englishwomen wrote admiringly of the lives and freedom enjoyed by Ottoman ladies, whereas their Western male colleagues reported no such views. Various peoples have reported transgressions of the rules by Egyptian women.... Even in parts of the Middle East where Western influence is small, there have been recent reports of great independence on the part of women. These center on the Arabian peninsula and Berber[13]-influenced North Africa, both areas of tribal strength. In the latter, among several signs of a freer position for women is the institution of the free woman, who may take lovers after divorce or widowhood without loss of respect or of opportunities for remarriage. In Arabia, where women are veiled and secluded ... [there are] deviant and independent behavior and views by women in the United Arab Emirates and Oman.... [T]he relative success in organizing women to assert their rights in Marxist South Yemen owes much to the Arabian women's independence in views and action. From both Yemen and Iran come reports of women's theater games in which male arrogance and other male cultural qualities are mercilessly mocked, and such mockery must have existed in the past. Egyptian women have also been noted for their independence from pre-Islamic times to the present, indicating that local traditions and conditions can be as important as tribal background in variability. Differences not only by country but among city, tribe, and countryside and between classes in degrees of women's independence have already been noted, and further research will surely show more variation. Women's independent attitudes are also expressed in folktales, popular poetry, and women's religious ceremonies. Female religious leaders and ceremonies express women's initiative. It would be wrong, however, to ignore the widespread oppression and enforced subordination of women.

Changes in economy and society in the past two centuries, along with the Western cultural impact, brought about forces within Middle Eastern societies favoring changes in the conditions of women. At first this did not involve legal changes, but rather such things as women's education. Changes in Islamic law pertaining to women have met considerable resistance. Only the Catholics, of major religions, vie with the Muslims for tenacity regarding women's position and control of her body. Islamic conservatism as it affects family law comes partly from the prominence of laws on women in the Quran. Also, however, change concerning women was felt by Muslim men to be a final invasion in the last sphere they could control against aggressive

---

[13]People native to North Africa before the Muslim conquest of the seventeenth century. The Berbers today comprise much of the population of Morocco, Libya, and Algeria.

infidels, once sovereignty and much of the economy had been taken over by the West. The need to guard women from the stares of the traditional Christian enemy has been documented since the French came to Egypt with Napoleon,[14] and veiling increased as a reaction to their presence.

In the past two centuries those Muslims who became Westernized tended to be those in the middle and upper classes who had profitable contacts with Westerners. For larger if less visible groups, Westernization was generally unpopular. The petty bourgeoisie and bazaar traders tended to support traditional Islamic ways. Modernizing liberals generally belonged to the higher social classes, whereas those who defended traditional ways appealed to the traditional small bourgeoisie. The upper classes were in alliance with Westerners, but the small bourgeois classes competed with larger Western trade and tended to reject Western ways partly from a desire to defend their own position. Women were and are used in a game that is really more about politico-ideological questions, including relations with the West, than about women per se. The petty bourgeoisie in most Middle Eastern countries have stuck to essentially traditional positions on women. Some traditional bourgeois and lower-class women also prefer the old ways to being forced to obtain unpleasant and low-paying jobs.

Until recently battles for women's rights in Middle East resulted in broadening those rights. The first names associated with those struggles were male, but from the beginning women too were involved. Public and independent activity for women's rights became widespread in the twentieth century.... These movements are only one aspect of complex changes that include those in marriage..., the family..., the economic role of women ..., their social role..., their ability to be public figures..., and the like. Rural women have also undergone major transformations, often becoming more stratified and more secluded, but sometimes also more political.... Modernization has had contradictory results in the Middle East and elsewhere, and whereas some women's positions have changed for the better, some poorer women have suffered from modernization's economic effects, becoming more, rather than less, restricted; having to work in unhealthful and poorly paid positions; and often removed from the community security of rural life. Veiling and seclusion spread in the countryside among the status conscious as they declined among Westernized city dwellers, and women's roles were sometimes limited by the economic effects of Western contacts. These contradictions have been reflected in conflicting women's attitudes on modernization versus tradition.

Although the success of reform was tied to economic and social changes, its immediate problems were often ideological; mainly, what attitude to take toward the holy law. A few, notably the reforming Turkish ruler Ataturk,[15]

---

[14] Army commander and later emperor of the French, Napoleon (1769–1821) invaded Egypt in 1798.

[15] Kemal Ataturk (1881–1938), founder of modern Turkey and president from 1923–1938.

took a secular position, legislating substantial legal equality for women on the basis of European law. Far more widespread have been modernist interpretations of the Quran and Islamic law. Attachment to these is strong not only because they are sacred texts, but also for identity vis-à-vis the West. There is an impetus to ground arguments in Islam, even for many who are privately secularists.

Varied modernist arguments have some widespread features. One is that the Quran has several meanings, with its literal one for its own time, and later interpretations to be made by modernists. Some stress the "spirit of the Quran," which is said to be egalitarian (largely true), and argue that several passages show that rights and egalitarianism were intended for women. There has been much reinterpretation of key verses. Modernists hold that the Quran opposes polygamy, because it says the conditions for it cannot be met. Various passages are seen to mean male-female equality, as the Quran sees them as equal believers and often explicitly addresses both men and women.

Reformists usually refer to the earliest sources—the Quran and selected Traditions about Muhammad—and reject most later interpretation. Subsequent Islamic law is rightly seen as more patriarchal than the Quran. If the Quran is reinterpreted, law can be reshaped. Such new interpretations could end polygamy and improve women's rights.

Reformist arguments arose partly because of a rapidly changing economy and society that was undergoing the influence of the capitalist and imperialist West. As in the West, the rise of capitalism and of paid jobs created new positions in the labor market for women, who had worked chiefly in the household economy. In the Middle East early demand was for nurses, midwives, doctors for women, and teachers. Demand soon spread to low-paid factory and white-collar work. . . . As elsewhere, the development of capitalist relations had a contradictory impact on different women. Putting women in the paid labor force could change rules about sexual segregation, although not always. Some popular-class women became more restricted than before. . . . Wealthier families, in contact with Westerners, saw advantages in women's education and participation in the wider world. Women's education was favored by reformists to improve child rearing and to prepare some women for jobs. The first arguments said that women's education would improve the rearing of sons, but women and men soon argued for women's rights. Although steps toward women's education, jobs, and freedom met resistance, until recently change was in the direction of greater equality.

Women's schools and women's or mixed universities were built in almost every Muslim country; new jobs were opened; and laws were reformed almost everywhere. The most radical reforms were those of Ataturk in Turkey. He took the unique path of adopting Western codes that outlawed polygamy and created substantial legal equality for women. Women got the vote in Turkey earlier than in France and Italy. Turkey was able to move radically owing to long contact with the West; to its experience of long, gradual reform;

because Islamic leaders were discredited after World War I; and also due to Ataturk's huge popularity, as a leader who, uniquely in the Middle East, had taken territory back from Western powers.... The next most thorough reforms, outside Eastern Europe, were in Tunisia and Marxist South Yemen. In Tunisia, Habib Bourguiba's[16] Personal Status Code of 1956 outlawed polygamy on Muslim reformist grounds and created substantial legal equality for women, while retaining a few Islamic features and male privileges. In South Yemen polygamy is allowed in a very few circumstances, but family law is otherwise egalitarian, and as important, women's organizations were encouraged to carry out education and propaganda. Elsewhere legal reform is more limited, but significant. In spite of Islamist agitation there has until now been little retreat in reform except in Iran and, on a few matters, in Pakistan.

The main thrust of legal reform where it is in egalitarian is to place restrictions on divorce, polygamy, and age of marriage, often by means of Islamic precedents and often by making men justify divorce or polygamy to the courts. This is in line with a modern trend to put personal and family matters increasingly under state control and reduce the power of Islamic courts. Reforms are, however, called Islamic, and Islamic courts generally keep some power. Equally important, women's roles in education, politics, and most parts of the work force have continued to grow.

Since World War II, a number of trends have undermined liberal reformism and encouraged Islamic revival. Among these are: (1) the growing cultural gap between the Westernized elite and the majority; (2) the growth in the power of the West and of Israel; (3) socioeconomic dislocations resulting from rapid urbanization, oil-backed modernization, and growing income distribution gaps; and (4) disillusionment with the failures of Westernized rulers and theories in the Middle East. The gap between the elite and the masses has created two cultures in the Middle East. Elite cultures tend to be Western-oriented, with young people getting a Western-style education and having little contact with the traditional bourgeoisie or the masses. Sometimes the two speak different languages, as in North Africa. The popular classes identify much more with Islam than the elite does. Among students and migrants from rural or small-town Islamically oriented backgrounds who migrate to overcrowded cities, alienation and Islamic revival are strong. It is also strong among some urban groups who stress identity and anti-imperialism.

Western consumer goods and experts are more evident than ever. Most important to Islamism, Western cultural influence is pervasive—in consumption, the media, and all cultural forms. Although many of these are items of choice, the backlash of rejection of Western cultural dominance is not surprising. Also, Israel is widely seen as a Western bastion of neocolonialism, bringing further reactions against pro-Western leaders and ways.

---

[16]President of Tunisia (1957–1987).

Socioeconomic dislocations, reinforced by fluctuations in oil income, include rapid urbanization, with the rich but rarely the poor getting richer; the problems of migrants; and the breakdown of accustomed family and rural ways. Islamism provides a social cement that appears familiar in the face of new problems.

Disillusionment with postcolonial governments that had nationalist and Westernizing, not Islamic, ideologies has focused on the Pahlavis[17] in Iran, Anwar Sadat[18] in Egypt, the National Liberation Front[19] in Algeria, and Bourguiba in Tunisia. Nationalist and Western ideologies were discredited among many attracted instead by new visions of Islam, with major implications for women. Islam had the advantage of familiarity and of not having ruled recently, which could have discredited it.

Modern Islamic revivalism has roots in the Egyptian Muslim Brethren[20] founded in 1928 and in the work of Abu al-A'la Maududi[21] for Islamic government in Muslim India. Islamism grew after World War II, and especially after the 1967 Arab defeat by Israel and the 1973 oil price rise, with its resultant economic and social dislocations. In advocating state enforcement of Islamic law Islamism is innovating, as traditional Muslim states since the development of Islamic law have not applied it as states or in a centralized, codified way. What is demanded is novel, a modern centralized theocracy, using many modern economic and technical means, sometimes renamed.

Islamist movements are populist in appeal, stressing the rights of the oppressed and the socially egalitarian nature of the Quran. They are far from egalitarian about women, however, and take what they see as the Islamization of women's role as a touchstone of Islam. This is partly because matters affecting women make up much of the legislation in the Quran, and also because a return to Quranic injunctions on dress, polygamy, and so forth is a highly visible way to show one is a good Muslim. Dress is a symbol of Islamist beliefs, and the dress adopted by Islamist women is almost as important as a badge of ideology as it is a means to modesty or seclusion. In fact, Islamist women are not secluded from the world, but are found heavily among students, young working women, and the like, and are also engaged in political activity. The dress of most Islamist women also is not traditional, but newly fashioned.

There is separation of the sexes among Islamists. This is part of an ideology that can be stated, in terms familiar to the American past, as one of

[17]Ruling dynasty in Iran (1925–1979), toppled by an Islamic revolution.

[18]President of Egypt (1970–1981).

[19]Insurgent group that fought for Algeria's independence from France in the 1950s and early 1960s.

[20]Society of the Muslim Brothers, an orthodox Islamic group that has worked for the overthrow of secularism and the creation of an Islamic state.

[21]Theologian, Muslim reformer, and political organizer (1903–1979); one of the leading interpreters of Islam in the twentieth century. He called for a truly Islamic state with an Islamic government, banking, and economic institutions.

"separate but equal." Islamists often say that men and women are equal, but have different capacities according to their different roles. They stress the importance of homemaking and child rearing, and are divided on whether women can work provided it does not interfere with child rearing. Practices in Islam that are unequal are justified as based on men's and women's different natures and needs. Polygamy is seen as better than the West's prostitution and mistresses, and early marriage as better than Western-style promiscuity. (Many Western ways shock strict Muslims just as many Muslim ways shock Westerners.) As in the former U.S. Supreme Court separate but equal doctrine for blacks, however, separation, in fact, means inferior rights—whether in education, work, or the family. The real strains of recent decades encourage nostalgia for an idealized past, including its sexual roles.

Though in most countries the leading Islamists tend to have partly Westernized educations, this was not true of Khomeini's[22] clerical group in Iran, who took a hard line on reversing reforms concerning women. Other governments with Islamic claims, like those of Sudan, Saudi Arabia, Pakistan, and Libya, have been less absolute in their approach to women. And in Algeria, Pakistan, and Egypt threats of Islamist legislation have been a catalyst to mobilize women against this. Iran today is becoming less strict about women, but other countries are becoming more restrictive.

Islamist movements have had an appeal for some women, especially among students in some faculties and among the traditional classes. In Iran more women demonstrated for Khomeini than against him. Elsewhere Islamist women are also active and organized. Islamists encourage women's participation in many spheres. Many women have chosen to wear Islamic dress, and one of the reasons they give is that it keeps men from bothering them in street or social contacts. Islamic dress is again a badge—here saying that this is a serious respectable woman who should not be touched or annoyed.

Other aspects of Islamism that appeal to many women include their frequent women's circles and organizations, where women discuss important matters in all-woman surroundings that are not intimidating. They are also encouraged to undertake propaganda activities. Girls and women whose parents or husbands do not normally let them out allow them to go to mosque meetings, and some even reject proposed marriage partners on the grounds that they are not good Muslims.

Many Islamist women experience protection and respect. The legal reforms in Muslim countries affected chiefly the elite, so that for many women Islamism may not seem a step backward and may even restore recently lost protections. Those who had experienced benefits, however, often suffer under Islamist rule or pressures. Hence there are radically

[22] Ayatollah Ruhollah Khomeini (c.1900–1989), leader of the 1979 Islamic revolution in Iran and ruler until his death in 1989.

different views about Islamism, often and understandably voiced and acted on with vehemence.

Feminists disagree about whether they should continue trying to interpret Islam in reformist ways or rather should stand foursquare for secularization, saying that Islam should be a matter for private belief and worship only. This is one of the key problems for Middle Eastern feminists today, extending from Pakistan's influential Women's Action Forum to the arguments among Middle Eastern women in many journals. . . . Those who stress the reinterpretation of Islam hope to meet some of the cultural needs of ordinary women, including Islamists, but their opponents say they are prolonging the repressive life and practices of political Islam.

A few modernists in a sense combine the two positions, presenting an Islam that does not require following Quranic practices regarding women. One Egyptian scholar claimed that the legal parts of Quran were intended only for the lifetime of the Prophet. And a small group of Sudanese say that only the Meccan suras[23] of the Quran (which have religious rather than legal content) and not the legalistic Medinan ones are valid after the Prophet. Such views are rejected by most Muslims today, but they could fare better in the future.

Islamist trends will not necessarily continue strong far into the future. Khomeini was able to appeal to various kinds of discontented people, but once in power he aroused discontent. Even where Islamists do well in elections, many elements of a protest vote are involved. The Islamist phase of the 1970s and 1980s may continue, but it seems unlikely in radical form to outlive widespread experience with so-called Islamic governments. Only Iran in the Middle East to date has repealed major legislation favorable to women, although women's groups in Egypt and Pakistan have had to struggle to forestall major changes, which could still occur there or elsewhere.

Economic realities bring women in the Middle East more and more into the labor force and the public sphere, and this continues, despite Islamist trends. Yet women's legal struggles today are mostly defensive. Both the feminists who are convinced that Islamic theory must be reinterpreted in their cause and those who say that this approach will only play into the hands of the anti-feminists are trying to find the most promising way to bring back a situation in which women's rights may be actively furthered. It may be that both the Islamic reformist and the secularist path can contribute to this, especially if they concentrate more on the needs and desires of popular-class women. And although the study of history is not simply a pragmatic exercise, understanding the reasons for the positions of women in the near and distant past can also help to formulate how those positions might be changed.

[23]Chapters of the Quran.

Acknowledgments (*continued from p. iv*)

"The Commercialization of Fashion." Neil McKendrick, reader in Social and Economic History and Director of Studies. University of Cambridge, England. From *The Birth of a Consumer Society: The Commercialization of Eighteenth-Century England*. Neil McKendrick, John Brewer, and J. H. Plumb, eds. (Bloomington: Indiana University Press, 1982), pp. 34–47, 49–56, 98.

"The Devils of Toulon: Demonic Possession and Religious Politics in Eighteenth-Century Provence," B. Robert Kreiser. Richard M. Golden, ed., *Church, State and Society Under the Bourbon Kings of France* (Lawrence, Kansas: Coronado Press, 1982), pp. 173–200. Copyright © Richard M. Golden. Reprinted with permission.

"Death's Arbitrary Empire." John McManners. *Death and the Enlightenment*, 1981, pp. 5–23. Edited selection reprinted by permission of Oxford University Press.

"The Sans-Culottes." Albert Soboul. From *The Sans-Culottes*. Copyright © 1965 by Editions du Seuil. Translation copyright © 1972 by Doubleday. Reprinted by permission of Georges Borchardt, Inc.

"Factory Discipline in the Industrial Revolution." Sidney Pollard. From *Economic History Review* (16) December 1963, pp. 254–271. Reprinted by permission of the author.

"The Industrial Bourgeoisie." J. F. Bergier, *The Fontana Economic History of Europe*, volume 3, ed. Carlo M. Copolla, 1973. Reprinted by permission of the author.

"The Potato in Ireland." K. H. Connell. The Past and Present Society. This article is here reprinted in abridged form, with the permission of the Society and Mrs. H. Connell, from *Past and Present: A Journal of Historical Studies*, no. 23 (November 1962) pp. 57–71.

"Victorian England: The Horse-Drawn Society." F. M. L. Thompson. From a lecture given at Bedford College, University of London, on October 22, 1970. Copyright © 1970, 1991, 1996 by F. M. L. Thompson. Reprinted by permission of the author.

"Is God French?" Adapted from "Dieu Est-Il Francais?" in *Peasants into Frenchmen: The Modernization of Rural France, 1870–1914* by Eugen Weber, with the permission of the publishers, Stanford University Press. Copyright © 1976 by the Board of Trustees of the Leland Stanford Junior University.

"Infanticide: A Historical Survey." William L. Langer, *History of Childhood Quarterly*, vol. 1, No. 3 (Winter 1974) pp. 353–362. Reprinted with permission of the publisher.

"Crime and Punishment in the Russian Village: Rural Concepts of Criminality at the End of the Nineteenth Century." Cathy Frierson. From *Slavic Review*, 46 (Spring 1987). Copyright © 1987 by the American Association for the Advancement of Slavic Studies. Reprinted by permission.

"A Woman's World: Department Stores and the Evolution of Women's Employment 1870–1920" by Theresa M. McBride. *French Historical Studies*, X (Fall 1978) pp. 664–683. Copyright Society for French Historical Studies, 1978. Reprinted with permission.

"The Price of Glory: Verdun 1916." Alistair Horne. Pages 185–210, *The Price of Glory: Verdun 1916.* Macmillan Publishers Ltd (1978). Reprinted by permission of the Peter Fraser & Dunlop Group Ltd.

"Inflation in Weimar Germany." Alex de Jonge, *The Weimar Chronicle, Prelude to Hitler,* New American Library, pp. 93–105. Copyright © 1978 Alex de Jonge. Reprinted with permission of the author.

"The Nazi Camps." Henry Friedlander. Reprinted from *Genocide: Critical Issues of the Holocaust,* eds. Alex Grobman and David Landes. (Los Angeles: Simon Wiesenthal Center, 1983) pp. 222–232. Copyright © 1983 by the Simon Wiesenthal Center, Los Angeles, California. Courtesy of the Simon Wiesenthal Center.

"Forbidden Death." From Philippe Ariès, *Western Attitudes toward Death: From the Middle Ages to the Present.* The Johns Hopkins University Press, 1974, pp. 85–103. Reprinted by permission of The Johns Hopkins University Press.

"Past and Present in a Greek Mountain Village," from *Portrait of a Greek Mountain Village* by Juliet du Boulay, pp. 232–252. First published in 1974; reprinted 1979. Second edition 1994, Denise Harvey, Publisher, 34005 Limni, Greece. Copyright © 1994 by Juliet du Boulay. All rights reserved. Edited selection reprinted by permission of the author.

"Packaging Pleasures: Club Méditerranée and French Consumer Culture, 1950–1968," from *French Historical Studies,* vol. 18, No. 1 (Spring 1993) pp. 65–81. Copyright Society for French Historical Studies, 1993. Reprinted with permission.

"The Rise and Fall of the Swedish Model," from *A History of Private Life,* vol. V, edited by Philippe Ariès and Georges Duby, translated by Arthur Goldhammer. Copyright © 1991 by the President and Fellows of Harvard College. Reprinted by permission of the Belknap Press of Harvard University Press. Originally published in *Histoires de La Vie Privée,* Vol. 5, De La Première Guerre mondiale a nos jours, © Editions du Seuil, 1987.

"Deciphering Middle Eastern Women's History," from *Women in Middle Eastern History: Shifting Boundaries in Sex and Gender,* edited by Nikki R. Keddie & Beth Baron. Yale University Press (1991) pp. 1–19. Reprinted by permission of Yale University Press.